MW01031616

MUSIC IN AMERICAN LIFE

Books in the series:

Joe Scott

JOE SCOTT
The Woodsman-Songmaker

Edward D. Ives

UNIVERSITY OF ILLINOIS PRESS
Urbana   Chicago   London

For permission to reprint copyrighted material, the author is
indebted to the following:

Alfred A. Knopf, Inc., for the passage from Wallace Stevens's
"The Idea of Order at Key West," from *The Collected Poems of
Wallace Stevens*.

Bowling Green University Popular Press, for portions of my
essay "A Man and His Song: Joe Scott and 'The Plain Golden
Band,'" from Henry Glassie, Edward D. Ives, and John F.
Szwed, *Folksongs and Their Makers*.

Houghton Mifflin Company, for the extract from James Agee
and Walker Evans, *Let Us Now Praise Famous Men*.

M. B. Yeats, Miss Anne Yeats, and the Macmillan Co. of London & Basingstoke, and Macmillan Publishing Co., Inc., for
the passage from William Butler Yeats's "Ego Dominus Tuus,"
from *The Collected Poems of W. B. Yeats*. Copyright 1918 by
Macmillan Publishing Co., Inc., renewed 1946 by Bertha
Georgie Yeats.

Library of Congress Cataloging in Publication Data

Ives, Edward D.
Joe Scott, the woodsman-songmaker.

(Music in American life)
Bibliography: p.
Includes index.
1. Scott, Joseph William, 1867–1918.   2. Composers—
Maine—Biography.   3. Lumbermen—Maine—Biography.
4. Lumbermen—Songs and music.   I. Title.

ML410.S4364I9   784'.092'4 [B]   78-8149
ISBN 0-252-00683-6

This book is for

HERBY RICE

There was always a certain class of those old lumber-jacks that would be here today and gone tomorrow. Every winter that you went into the woods they'd probably appear to the particular camp that you might be at. They'd be there sometime during the winter. They were good men while they worked, but they just wouldn't stay a great while in one place. Used to be one fellow—he always would stay if he came at some camp; unless something was drastically wrong with it, why, he'd put in the winter there. But I always have remembered him. His name was Herb Rice. And he was a—well, he was an expert lumberjack, that's what. He could do any job they put him at. . . . He was a teamster or a chopper or a cant dog man, anything. . . . He had been in the lumber-woods all over Maine, New Hampshire, and Vermont, and he'd been in the Pacific Northwest in the woods, and he'd been in Michigan and worked in the woods. But he was actually a Maine native. He always drifted back here.

BEN COLE, Glenburn, Maine (NA 720.079–080)

Contents

All that each person is, and experiences, and shall never experience, in body and in mind, all these things are differing expressions of himself and of one root, and are identical: and not one of these things nor one of these persons is ever quite to be duplicated, nor replaced, nor has it ever quite had precedent: but each is a new and incommunicably tender life, wounded in every breath, and almost as hardly killed as easily wounded: sustaining, for a while, without defense, the enormous assaults of the universe.

JAMES AGEE AND WALKER EVANS,
Let Us Now Praise Famous Men

Preface

Joseph William Scott was born in Lower Woodstock, New Brunswick, "on the banks of the Saint John," in 1867. Temperamentally unsuited to farming, he left home as a young man for the lumberwoods of Maine, arriving just as the burgeoning pulp and paper industry was creating a boom in the woods that would equal anything ever seen when lumber was king. He settled in Rumford Falls, a raw paper-mill town and woods depot that had been carved out of the wilderness only a few years before he arrived, and he worked up and down the Androscoggin River, where he became known as a crack woodsman and river-driver and a great guy, a man among men—and among women. In 1894 he was jilted by a beautiful girl, and it marked him. Except for a few side excursions, he kept to the woods until that notoriously roaring life caught up with him, and in 1916 he wound up in the Augusta State Hospital, where it took him almost two years to die of what his death certificate called "general paralysis of the cerebral type."

It was not a happy life, or on the surface of it a very distinguished one. Except insofar as any man's story is worth telling simply because he *was* a man and *did* sustain those enormous assaults for a while, Joe Scott's story wouldn't concern us—were it not that he was a maker of ballads, an artist working in a tradition where we have had so little opportunity to observe artists working that for a long time we even denied their existence. Then, when we came to acknowledge that, we denied them their art, claiming they counted for nothing, "the tradition" being what mattered. That's nonsense, of course, but it is also ancient history. No responsible contemporary folklorist that

Preface

I know of doubts for a minute that the ballad is a work of art created by an individual artist working within an artistic tradition. The problem has been that we haven't really had any well-documented studies of the ballad artist at work. And that is what this book is all about.

First, I have re-created Joe's life as completely as possible, not only for its own sake but also as the matrix out of which his songs grew. Then I have taken each of his songs and tried to show first of all how he went about creating it and then what happened to it in its sixty or more years in oral tradition. Finally, I have described the nature of that tradition itself. The material for the study has come from hundreds of hours of interviews with people who knew Scott or his songs, a careful search of all relevant public records, and the usual dusty search through archives, libraries, old newspapers, and the like. I have been at it off and on for eighteen years, which in the sum of things means absolutely nothing except that the more I think about it the more remarkable it seems.

My two previous books have many similarities to the present one, which in a very real way grew directly out of them. *Larry Gorman* was a study of a songmaker working within a tradition that up to then had hardly even been acknowledged to be a tradition at all: local satire and invective.[1] It got things going nicely, hopelessly hooking me on the problems involved in writing non-elitist biography and studying events that not only never made headlines but seldom even got in the paper. Almost at the beginning of my research on Gorman, I ran across Joe Scott and his songs (the Prologue tells of my very first introduction to him), and while I continued to gather material on him, I didn't really get into high gear until after *Larry Gorman* had been published.[2]

High gear or no high gear, after several years' work on Scott I found I was spinning my wheels. I had a good swatch already written and I knew pretty well what I wanted to do from there, but I had bogged down. Rescue came, as it so often has, through the purest serendipity. I had gathered some material on a Lawrence Doyle, a gentler and less single-minded poet than Gorman, whose songs—commentaries on local affairs—had flourished in the tradition of a few townships of eastern Prince Edward Island but never spread beyond. Not only was I fascinated by Doyle and his songs, I also saw in this material a chance to do on a smaller scale what I wanted to do for Joe Scott and see how it worked. It worked fine, and *Lawrence*

Doyle was in every way both a model for the present work and an inspiration to me to get back at it.

Most of this book is devoted to Joe Scott's songs, but the fact that I preface them with his biography and follow them with a study of lumbercamp tradition will show my two main emphases. First, I want to show what the songs meant to Joe, which means seeing them in the context of his life. It has been impossible for me to do that without frequently moving beyond what I know for sure into what I think is probable. In other words, I have done a lot of interpreting. Some of this interpretation comes out as free-wheeling psychologizing, some as a penchant for creating imagined scenes. All such speculations are clearly labeled for what they are, and I offer them without any further apology.

Second, I want to show what these songs have meant to the men and women who sang them, which means seeing them in the context of the tradition that carried them on. Part of this information has been developed through direct questioning of the singers, but I have also reached some conclusions through analysis of what happened to the songs as they passed on. If material was omitted, favored, or otherwise altered by a significant number of singers, I assume there was a reason for it, and wherever possible I have tried to reach some conclusions about what that reason might have been. Once again, clear labels and no apologies.

There is a third aspect of this book, though, that while it may be less scholarly, less scientific, is at the same time more concrete and perhaps the only aspect on which I can comment without speculation of any sort. I would like to show what the whole thing has meant to me, which means seeing it in the context of *my* life. This I do for two reasons. First, since such material fascinates me when I find it in other folklorists' writings—and I often feel cheated when I don't find it—I assume they will be similarly pleasured to find it in mine. Second, it gives the reader a chance to see how I went about my work or how a particular idea or cluster of facts developed for me, and that should put him in a better position to form his own judgments about the validity of the book as a whole. In sum, I hope it makes the book not only more readable but also more accurate.

Since so much of my documentation comes from oral interviews, I have maintained certain distinctions consistently. Quotations preceded by an asterisk are taken verbatim from tape recordings; false starts, "uh's," and the like are the only things that have been elimi-

Preface

nated without my indicating the omission with standard ellipsis marks. Within these verbatim passages, material in brackets indicates that the speaker's words were not absolutely clear but this is my best guess as to what he was saying. In some places I have added words of my own to clarify a passage or to include a "stage direction." All such additions are italicized and bracketed. Oral material that I have not marked with an asterisk is taken as accurately as possible from field notes, but I cannot guarantee its word-for-word accuracy. Occasionally, I have given in to my lamentable tendency to invent a quotation, to present what I think someone might have said or (worse yet!) *should* have said under certain circumstances. All such conjectures are given entirely in italics, unbracketed.

Most of the tapes and their accompanying transcripts used in this book are on file in the Northeast Archives of Folklore and Oral History, South Stevens Hall, University of Maine, Orono, Maine. Tape numbers (e.g., NA 423) are given wherever possible, and if a complete and final transcript is available the page numbers are also given (e.g., NA 423.157–159). Materials taken from other archives are so indicated, with specific references following that archive's system. However, in order to avoid a plethora—a swamp, even—of notes, I have not annotated every oral quotation; instead I have included a general reference under the name of the informant in the Appendix, indicating exactly where the tapes or transcripts of interviews with that person can be found. My system of citing and annotating versions of the ballads will be found in chapter 8, and a complete list of abbreviations and catchwords used will be found at the beginning of the Appendix.

It remains for me to make the usual acknowledgments of people and organizations who have helped me in one way or another. To begin with organizations, let me first thank the John Simon Guggenheim Memorial Foundation for their awarding me a fellowship in 1965. That allowed me to put full time into the work, but it did more than that: it almost made me respectable. Colleagues who before had been polite but only too obviously unconvinced that what I was doing was for real suddenly became, if not convinced, at least a little less sure of themselves now that their amused tolerance had to include the Guggenheim Foundation. My thanks for that laying-on-of-hands. It has helped, and it's been fun.

xvi

Preface

Yet if I get in a dig at a few colleagues, I don't want to leave the impression that I have been persecuted or neglected here at the University of Maine. That would be a pretty cheap pose for me to assume in light of the facts. Every time I have asked the Faculty Research Funds Committee for support they have given me what I wanted, including two generous Summer Research Grants, with no questions asked. My department chairman, Richard Emerick, has done everything he can to support my folklore activities and to help me arrange a schedule that has allowed me time for writing and research. But then again, I *have* been neglected, thank God! No one, that is, has appointed me a vice-president, a dean, or even chairman of the educational policies committee; nor (up to this year) have I even been asked to serve on any of the major and time-consuming college or university committees. In short, for many years now I have been let alone and told to go do whatever it is I do. Not that everything's been perfect or that I couldn't find things to bitch about, but considering some of the academic horror stories I've heard in my time, I don't think I've had it half bad.

Special thanks should also go to Carolyn Jakeman and the staff at the Houghton Library at Harvard University; Rae Korson and Joseph Hickerson at the Archive of Folk Song, Library of Congress; Carmen Roy and her staff in what was then the Human History Branch of the National Museum of Canada, Ottawa; the staff of the *Family Herald* in Montreal, particularly Sheila Bûcher; and to the staffs of the old Bonar Law Bennett Library at the University of New Brunswick and the Fogler Library at the University of Maine, Orono. I spent many hours working in all of these places, and I wish I could do it all again.

So many people have helped me in so many ways in the writing of this book that I almost hesitate to begin listing names because I am sure I will leave some out. Any such list, however, will have to begin with Lisa Feldman, who gave the entire manuscript an extremely careful and critical reading. We have spent so much time talking about parts of this book that some of the ideas expressed are probably as much hers as they are mine. For the kind of help she has offered there is no adequate reward; all I can do is say thanks. Thanks, too, to Ellen Stekert, who made many excellent suggestions, and to Dick Wentworth and (especially) Judy McCulloh and the others at the University of Illinois Press who saw my work into print. Norman

xvii

Cazden autographed the tunes from my original transcriptions; while doing so he suggested a number of changes in detail that would make for easier reading, almost all of which I accepted. The maps are the work of my colleague Claude Z. Westfall of the College of Engineering. Then there are a lot of students who have worked in my office and who had a direct part in producing this book, typing manuscript, transcribing tapes, collating versions of ballads, and so forth. Some of the names that come to mind are Joyce (Benson) Paton, Sharon (Sperl) Berry, Joan Brooks, George Chappell, Jayne Lello, Jo Walker, Sandy Wells, and (especially) Flo Ireland. The pay was low, their loyalty constant, their friendship honest, and my gratitude is deep. In my mind they will always be young.

Helen Creighton made a lot of her collectanea available to me and answered numerous and pesty questions on details. The late Helen Hartness Flanders granted me permission to make whatever use I needed of the material in the Flanders Ballad Collection in the library at Middlebury College, Middlebury, Vermont. And, of course, Louise Manny. My debt to her will be obvious not only from the number of references to the Beaverbrook Collection and the Miramichi folksong festivals, but also from the number of singers I have met through her (not the least of them being Wilmot Mac-Donald). She also offered me hospitality; her home was my home when I was on the Miramichi, and in this connection thanks are also due to Clara MacLean, Louise's housekeeper. Others who have been equally hospitable: Burt and Jane deFrees of North Rumford, Maine, and Fred and Pat Cogswell, of Fredericton, New Brunswick. To them, thanks.

Thanks are also due to several people who have gone well out of their way to help me track down official records. Mrs. M. Robertson, assistant archivist at the New Brunswick Museum, Saint John, New Brunswick, made a very careful check of census records and other materials in their archive, which saved me at least one trip and a whole lot of trouble. Bill Perkins, city clerk of Rumford, Maine, simply couldn't have been nicer, and the same goes for Robert Rich, clerk of the superior court, Lancaster, New Hampshire. Nor do I want to forget to mention Rosa Jutras and Mary Morgan of the city clerk's office in Berlin, New Hampshire. The kind of work I was doing depended on easy access to the kinds of records they kept. All of them made my work easier—and pleasanter.

Preface

Several of my colleagues around the country have helped me in different ways, through direct support, through letters and conversations on this or that idea, or both. To wit: Norman Cazden, William Doerflinger, Richard Dorson, Henry Glassie, John Hankins, MacEdward Leach, Peter McKenna, Neil Rosenberg, Francis Utley, D. K. Wilgus, and Howard Woodward. Notes will, I hope, honor some of the other very specific debts I owe, but the people I have named represent general accounts that can't really be paid that way.

There are even more general accounts than these, so general they can't be said to have contributed to the content of this book, but in my mind they were so important that they were there all the time by being there when they were needed. For example, Osprey and Molly B., my two golden retrievers, who walked the mile to the river with me thousands of times while I thought or didn't think or whatever. For example, Manuel Velazquez, who made me a magnificent guitar, and Robert Paul Sullivan, who has helped me learn to play it. For example, Addie Weed, with whom my family and I have shared a house for many years and who turned over her spare room to me for a study, allowing me thus to be at home and not at home all at once.

And then there's my wife, Bobby. In the preface to *Larry Gorman*, I offered her "the highest tribute I can manage: the final paragraph all to herself." In *Lawrence Doyle* I repeated most of that paragraph, but added a separate one: "This time she gets two paragraphs." She thinks that three paragraphs would be a bit much, and maybe she's right.

This time I'd like to include mention of my three children: Steve, Nat, and Sarah. It's a pretty great outfit they've been. But come to think of it, Bobby's wrong. Three paragraphs isn't a bit much; it isn't enough.

Not by a long chalk.

NOTES

1. Herbert Halpert's "Vitality of Tradition and Local Songs" is a notable exception. (Full citations for materials cited in the notes may be found in the Bibliography.)
2. I did publish one article on Scott before *Larry Gorman* appeared. See " 'Ben Deane' and Joe Scott: A Ballad and Its Probable Author."

Prologue

The letter was from the Welfare Department, City of Bangor. Now what the deuce, I wondered.[1] Somebody need a recommendation, or what? But then why to home and not to the office? I tore the envelope open at one end.

Dear Mr. Ives:

I am writing you in connection with the death of Mr. Herbert Rice, since it has come to my attention that you knew him. We are most anxious to contact some survivor or relative, and while we have heard something about his having a son, we have been unable to get any further information. We will be grateful for any help you can give us.

Herby Rice. Sure, I remembered him all right, but it all seemed like such a long time ago. . . .

. . . EASTERN EATING HOUSE, the big letters painted on the front windows proclaimed, and the small letters along the bottom edge said "Cocktails," "Booths," and (in the corner) "Ladies Invited." This was the place all right—about as far down on Bangor's lower Exchange Street as you could get. I pushed the door open, went up to the bar, and ordered a beer.

"Can you tell me where I can find a man by the name of Herbert Rice?" I asked the bartender. "He lives here, doesn't he?"

"Yeah, he lives here all right," he said, looking me over, "but he went out just a little while ago. Why?"

"Well," I said, "I just wanted to talk to him about a guy he knew in the woods years ago—fella by the name of Gorman, Larry Gorman.

Ever hear of him?" I was talking loudly enough to make myself heard to the half-dozen or so woods types that were nursing beers in some of the booths, wondering if the old poet's name would spark any recognition. It didn't.

"Gorman, Gorman," he mused. "Gorman, you said?"

I nodded.

"No, I don't think I ever knew him. But if Herby knew him of course it might have been before my time. What was he? Some relation of yours?"

"No," I said. "He made up songs. They used to call him 'the man who made the songs' in the woods, and I'm thinking maybe I'll write a book about him, so I want to talk to anyone who might have known him. And your cleaning woman called me the other day. She'd seen me on TV Sunday asking people to get in touch with me if they knew anything about this Gorman. She said she asked Mr. Rice if he'd ever known him and he said he had. And she asked would he talk to me and he said sure. So that's why I'm looking for him."

"Well, it wouldn't surprise me none that Herby did know the guy, 'cause he's been around the woods a hell of a long time now," the bartender said, obviously interested. "And he *was* here not so long ago. Had some supper and sat around for a while. Then he went out, not more'n ten, fifteen minutes ago. He probably ain't far off, but—hey, Frank," he called to a man in a booth near the door, "did Herby say where he was going?"

"No," said Frank, "but if I was lookin' for him I'd start in the Northern Hotel. He sits there in the lobby a lot."

"Where's that at?" I asked.

"Come on," said Frank, getting up, "I'll help you find him. He'll be glad to talk to you, if he's still sober."

We went out into the cold November night and started up Exchange Street along the sidewalk, past the gated pawnshops, bars, and cheap clothing stores, through the loose crowd of men that is always on Exchange Street (and on Exchange Streets everywhere): gray men in frayed overcoats and work rubbers, young men in checked shirts or jackets, hunting caps cocked over their old eyes. But mostly the old men, hands in pockets, shoulders hunched, smoking, walking to the gutter to spit, waiting.

The Northern Hotel was just like the Eastern Eating House from the outside, but darker and narrower, the whole thing being about the width of a small store front. The lobby was just a shallow partitioned-off section at the front; to the left was the desk and a dark stairway, and to the right three or four battered chairs and a table with a torn copy of *Argosy* on it.

"There's Herby," said my guide, pointing to a small man in a windbreaker sitting in one of the chairs. "Hey, Herby! This guy wants to talk to you about—what was that guy's name?"

"Larry Gorman," I said.

"Oh yeah, Larry Gorman. Know him?"

Herby looked up at me from under the brim of his stained felt hat. There was a scrape on his cheek and a heavy scab on the bridge of his nose. "You the fella that's writing the book?"

"Yes. You knew him, didn't you?"

He laughed. "I'll say I did. Come on, let's have a drink."

We found an empty booth in the crowded barroom, in which it soon became clear that I was the only stranger. The waitress brought our beers, and I tried to pay.

"No," said Herby. "I'll buy my own."

"Herby, this ain't your boy, is it?" said the waitress as she took our money.

"I don't have a boy. You know that," said Herby curtly. "This fella's up at the university. He's writing a book."

She looked at me squarely. "A book? On Herby? You oughta write a book on me! I thought you was his son. Herby, I thought you—"

"He's writing a book," said Herby.

She went off.

We talked for a couple of hours, beginning with Larry Gorman and from there going on to Herby's life as a woodsman. He'd driven logs for old VanDyke on the Connecticut; he'd worked for the Henrys in New Hampshire, for the great John Ross (and later for Fred Gilbert) on the Penobscot, for Glaziers on the Saint John. His friends had become legends: Dan Bossy, "cattiest man on logs that ever was, excepting maybe little Ike Butler. You couldn't shoot Ike Butler off a log!" Jigger Johnson, bald Archie Stackhouse, Kelly the Swede, Paul King, Jack Mann—he'd known them all. Into the woods in the fall to stay the route: days of cutting the tall spruce, swamping roads, hauling to the yards and to the landings; beans "twenty-one times a week"; evenings along the deacon seat as the oil lamps burned in the heavy air to light the talk of tired men; nights under the long spread (twenty or more men to a blanket) "and sometimes you could see the stars through the holes in the roof." In the spring down to Bangor with a winter's pay for a few blazing hours: Barney Kelly's Saloon, the Devil's Half Acre, Hancock Street, Aunt Hat's up in Veazie; then Pope McKinnon would stand you for room and board until you went back upriver on the drive "and he'd always give me a bottle of whiskey to take me through to Greenville." Any number of men in that barroom could have told the same story, but I was listening to Herby. Occasionally someone would drop by the table, some friend of his, curious about me. They'd talk to Herby a few minutes; then they'd turn to say something to me, but Herby would head them off. "Come on now, he don't work like us. He's from the university. He's writing a book." It was a friendly place.

We were on our fourth or fifth bottle of beer. "Lookit," he said, "you've been asking me a lot of questions. Let me ask you one. Why are you writing a book on Larry Gorman?"

"Well," I said, "from all I've been told, Larry Gorman was just about the best woods poet there was. At least I never heard of anybody who was as good at making up songs as he was."

Herby looked amused. "There were guys in the woods who were better poets than Larry Gorman ever thought of being. Much better."

"Oh?" I said doubtfully. "Who, for instance?"

Herby was in no hurry to answer. "Who for instance?" he said. He looked out into the room. "For instance there was Joe Scott. Joe was a better poet than Larry by far."

"Did you know this Scott, too?" I asked.

"Hell yes, I knew him, knew him well. We worked in the same camp over there in Lincoln, New Hampshire, for Henrys one winter for one place, and there were other times, too. Joe Scott came originally from Grand Falls, New Brunswick, and he was around the woods for years."

"Well, I'm damned," I said. "That's interesting, because this is the first I've heard of him. Tell me about him. What songs did he make up?"

"Let's see now. Well, he made up 'Benjamin Deane.' That was about a man who shot his wife over in Berlin, New Hampshire. It begins like this:

> My name it is Benjamin Deane
> My age is forty-one.

Then came something about 'the Bay of Fundy where the seagulls fall and raise,' but I can't remember now. That was a good song, though, 'Benjamin Deane.' That was one he made up. Another one was—oh what was that man's name? Damn it. Anyway, it was about this guy who got syphilis and hung himself in his room in Rumford Falls:

> The agony I'm undergoing I can't long endure
> I'll tie this cord onto a hinge on the door—

something about 'beneath it and the floor.' What in hell was that fella's name? Howard—Howard something. Howard Carey! 'Howard Carey' was the name of that song. It was syphilis."

Herby emptied his glass and poured out the rest of his bottle. I did the same. "How about that!" I said. "I never even heard of those songs."

Herby laughed. "Do you know how to make whiskey with a teakettle and a tin plate?" he asked.

"No," I said, "but I know we need some more beer."

He caught the waitress's eye. He still wouldn't let me pay for his drink. "I got money," he said, showing me a rather astonishing roll of bills.

"Was this Scott fella ever here in Bangor?" I asked.

"Sure he was, plenty of times. He used to stay at the Central House, and he'd be around town with the rest of us. I've seen him right here in this room."

"Was he a heavy drinker?" I asked.

"We were *all* heavy drinkers, mister," Herby shot back.

I let the matter drop at that. "Did he make up any other songs?"

"He was always making up songs. I suppose he made up hundreds of them. I think he made up 'Jack Haggerty.' You know that one, do you? Well, he made that, I'm sure. And then there was 'The Plain Golden Band.' That was about his own life, that one. This girl he'd given the plain golden band to, she left him, and he made up this song about it. It was a nice song, too, but I can't remember it. He made up some great songs, but that 'Plain Golden Band' was about his own life."

Herby stopped for a moment and turned and looked right at me. His eyes were bright. "You know," he said, "come to think about it, Joe Scott was an awful lot like you."

"Like me?" I said, surprised. "You mean he looked like me?"

"No, no, he didn't look like you at all. He was a sort of red-headed man and smaller than you all the way around. I don't mean that way, but just the same Joe was like you. I mean he—well, Joe always wanted to write a book."

"A book? I said. "What kind of a book?"

"I don't know that," said Herby, "but that's what he said. He wanted to write a book."

"I wonder if he ever did?" I said.

Herby shrugged. "If he did I never knew it."

We finished our beers. "Maybe instead of Joe writing a book I'll write one about him," I said.

He grinned and settled back in the booth. "That was a long time ago," he said. . . .

. . . I remembered him all right, although I didn't know anything that would help the Bangor Welfare Department, I was sure. But I called anyway, more for curiosity than for any help I could be to them, and asked for the caseworker who had signed the letter.

"He died about a week ago," she said. "The funeral was Tuesday. As so often happens, there being no one else, the city buried him out on Strangers Row."

"Poor old Herby," I said. "What happened to him anyhow?"

"The usual story," she said. "Drank himself into a stupor. They found him in his room and couldn't bring him around. Took him to the hospital and he died there without ever regaining consciousness. There was no one. I was the only one at his funeral."

"I'd have come," I said, "but I didn't even know."

"How did you know him?" she asked me.

I told her the circumstances. "But how the devil did you get my name?" I asked.

"When we went through his effects," she said, "we found a card that said, 'Thanks for your help. See you again,' with your name on it. Do you remember it?"

Prologue

"Yes, yes, of course," I said, "a Christmas card. I always send cards to people who've helped me, just as a way of saying thanks. But that was two years ago, and I find it hard to—"

"That card," she interrupted, "was the only coherent piece of paper the man possessed."

There was nothing more to be said. I hung up softly. As I sat at the kitchen table I shut my eyes to see a small lone figure in a windbreaker walking forever up an empty Exchange Street sidewalk under the dim and separate streetlights. Bits of old newspaper blew about his feet.

I went over to the icebox to see if there was any beer. There wasn't.

NOTES

1. While cast in the form of a short story, this account is factual. I cannot claim verbatim accuracy for every speech, but nothing essential has been added or changed.

Part

I

The Man

1

"On the Banks of the Saint John": The Early Years

The Saint John River starts out as a small wilderness stream not far north of Moosehead Lake in Maine. It flows north by east until it becomes the quite respectable river that forms the Maine border with New Brunswick from Saint Francis to Grand Falls. Then it becomes entirely a New Brunswick river and flows generally southward through a splendid wooded valley that becomes wider and more pastoral the further south it goes. Below Woodstock it swings to the east toward Fredericton and Grand Lake before beginning its final southward run to the Bay of Fundy, and it is the landscape of this long, leisurely bend below Woodstock that is the setting for both the beginning and the end of Joe Scott's story. And for me, once I had started on his trail, the end was very much the beginning.

In my mind's eye I always see this part of the valley as I saw it the first time from the hill back of Meductic after driving out of thirty miles of woods. The river, wide and sparkling in the distance, came down from the north between the long, low slopes of the wooded hills on either side. I drove across the narrow bridge that spanned Eel River. I was now in Lower Woodstock, and about a mile from the bridge I found the home of the man I was looking for, Angus Scott, Joe's nephew. He lived on the old Scott property just across the highway from the house where Joe was born. We talked for some time, and while he was too young to remember Uncle Joe, he told me what he knew and recommended several other people I ought to see. We had tea and some lunch; then I left, but not before I had asked one question more: did he know where Joe was buried? "It's just about a mile from here," he said, and gave me full directions.

It was getting late when I parked my car by the gate of a field that

3

sloped toward the river that I knew was about half a mile down there beyond the trees. The sun had set and the dew was just beginning to gather, as I started along the road that was really no more than a depression in the tall grass. Once it reached the woods the road gave out altogether, and I had to pick my darkling way through brush and burrs before I climbed the fence and came out on the railroad. A fox that had been sitting on some piled ties fled in startled haste down the track and into the woods.

I crossed the tracks, and there was the cemetery, a score or so of headstones sticking up in random rows through the encroaching weeds. Briars caught at my ankles as I searched, bending down occasionally to rub some lichen from a name or get a better view in the fading light. Perhaps there had been no headstone, I thought. Then I found it, a sunken grave with the stone almost ready to topple over, but the lettering was clear:

> In loving memory of
> JOSEPH W. SCOTT
> died
> June 22, 1918
> Aged 50 yrs.
> Though lost to sight
> To memory dear

Over all this was a shining-star emblem and the words LEAD KINDLY LIGHT.

It was very quiet. I could hear a tiny stream bubbling down over the steep bank to the Saint John, which I could still see a few rods below me through the trees and gathering dark. It was impossible not to think of the last stanza of Joe's best-known song:

> In a cool shady forest so far far away
> Where the deer loves to roam and the fawn loves to play
> Where all nature is bright and the scene wild but grand
> There the author you'll find of "The Plain Golden Band."

So much, then, for the end. I started back up the hill to the road and the many years of work that would lead me back full circle to the beginning. I didn't see the fox again when I crossed the tracks.

We don't have to go very far back. Almost all the first permanent settlers of this area were United Empire Loyalists (we Americans call

4

them Tories) from Connecticut and other nearby states who arrived shortly after the Revolution. The grants were about two hundred acres apiece, each having approximately a thousand feet of river frontage and extending back up and over the sides of the valley for about three miles. This arrangement of long, narrow plots made it possible for the houses to be fairly close together, keeping the families in touch, while at the same time it gave each settler a good-sized farm to work. These early arrivals were mostly of English stock, and later immigration did nothing to change this pattern. The town that grew up at the mouth of Eel River at first took the river's name for its own, but sometime before the turn of the present century that part of the settlement south of the river took the name Meductic. The area just north of it, though officially named Lower Woodstock, was sometimes called Riceville or Hay Settlement, and it was often spoken of informally as if it were part of Meductic. Woodstock itself, Carleton County's shire town, is more than eight miles upriver, and the city of Fredericton is sixty miles downriver. Although a stage line was operating from Woodstock to Fredericton in the mid-1830s, the land around the mouth of Eel River was still quite an isolated section when the first Scott, whose name was also Joseph, arrived.

The census of 1861 lists old Joseph (b. ca. 1802) as "Novascotian," his wife, Esther, as "Native"; the census of 1871 repeats this information, adding that he was "Scotch," she "English." That may mean either that he was born in Scotland or that his parents were, but it is clear that his grandson and namesake thought of himself as Scottish. "He'd always introduce himself by saying, 'I'm Joe Scott, descended from the great Sir Walter,'" William Bryant told me, and Joe's hospital records in Augusta show that he claimed his "paternal grandfather came from Scotland." Whichever way it was, old Joseph was in New Brunswick by 1853, when John William, the oldest of his six children, was born.

Our first "official" record of old Joseph shows that on November 25, 1843, he purchased from John and Rhoda Porter "all that certain piece or parcel of land situate lying and being in the Eel River Settlement (so called) in the Parish of Woodstock aforesaid known and distinguished as Lot Number Fifty one in the first tier of lots from the River Saint John granted to one Henry Charleton."[1] What he got was "two hundred acres more or less" and it cost him exactly £100. A year later he bought another hundred-acre plot about a mile upriver, but he had to let that go before long at a considerable loss. He took out two mortgages in the next four years, probably to buy stock and to build, but ultimately he paid them both off. Then on August 6, 1869, when he was seventy-one, he and Esther made over the property to their son John, who is described as "his heir and assign," for the price of $500, which is just about what Joseph had paid for it in the first place. He went on living on the property, though. His house was on the uphill side of the road, the side away from the river; John's house was down from the road on the river side. Old Joseph lived on there until his death in 1882.

Taking title to the land in 1869 was, of course, only a legal formality, because John was already well established and had probably been doing the active farming for some time. He was thirty-four years old, and eight of his nine children had already been born. He couldn't have been more than eighteen or nineteen when he married Sarah Teeling, the daughter of an Englishman who lived nearby. *"My Aunt Sarah was the hardest working person I ever saw in my life, for a woman," recalled Emma Merrithew. "She could do three women's work. . . . And her butter was the sale of the country. Anything she laid her hand to! He was just the opposite. . . . Sometimes I thought he was dreaming or sleeping when he was walking," she said, continuing the comparison, "but she was the head. She was the head! . . . She knew what she was doing. She could handle that farm. She was the head team. She'd put on a man's pair of pants and go right out and work with the men when she was young. A great worker—and quite nice looking." But as for her husband, *"I've heard them all say, my mother and all of them, he was come-day-go-day. . . . I don't think he'd sweat over it whether it was good or bad."

"Come-day-go-day" does not do John Scott justice, but that is how he might have appeared. Rather, he seems to have had great plans, but either his luck or his abilities as farmer and man of affairs did not allow him to carry them through. He wanted more land, for instance, and in 1871, two years after he took title to his father's two hundred acres, he bought an adjoining hundred acres, but he had to take out a mortgage for $360 of the $480 cost. This mortgage he paid off in a year by taking out a new mortgage, this time for $560, and in 1894 he took out a second mortgage for an additional $200. He was unable to discharge these debts until 1900, and then only after he had sold his land to his sons. Meanwhile, in 1887 he bought the next farm but one downriver for $725, $600 of which he had to mortgage. His plan was probably to try to buy the hundred-acre farm in the middle, too, and thus have an estate of six hundred acres that he and his five sons would farm. But Wallace went off to college, Maurice died, and Joe had just plain disappeared. At any rate, John sold this second farm in 1894 for $800, which must have represented a rather serious loss for him.

If he was not a rousing success as a farmer, he had plenty of other activities to keep him occupied. In politics he was a Liberal, and in the hotly contested election of 1878 he supported the local MacKenzie man, Stephen B. Appleby. Appleby lost, and we hear no more of John Scott and politics. For many years he had the mail route from Woodstock to Eel River. Like many others along this river, he set salmon nets in season, but he was also the "Fishing Warden for the district lying between Woodstock and Eel River." He was a pillar of the local Baptist church (although word has it that before he got religion he brewed a potent whiskey), and during the eighties and nineties he was several times superintendent of the Sabbath school. In 1886 he was one of the organizers of "a new division of the good old order of the Sons of Temperance," which took the name of Dufferin Division. He was its first Worthy Patriarch, and he remained an officer for many years. Then too, he was a good fiddler, a tolerable singer, and by all accounts an extremely pleasant and sociable person, who remained active in local affairs until his health began to fail him. In 1900, he divided his farm in thirds and sold a hundred acres each to three of his sons: Ensley, Hazen, and Joe. He died March 5, 1905, just three months short of his allotted three-score and ten.

Altogether, John and Sarah had five sons and four daughters. Of the sons, John Ensley (everyone knew him as Ensley) was the oldest, and for all practical purposes he was the one who took over the farming when his father died. Like many men around the area, he spent a number of winters working in the Maine lumberwoods, and he even made a couple of trips to the West, notably to Oregon and California, each time staying for more than a year. He was a hard worker—*"He didn't know a thing but work!" said Emma Merrithew approvingly—and most people agree that he was by far the steadiest of the Scott boys. Maurice (pronounced "Morris") was a

7

huge man with a reputation not so much as a fighter or brawler as of a quiet man who simply could not be beaten once he was roused to anger. The story goes that he died of a heart attack following an epic two-hour sawmill fight; others say it was "hasty consumption" that did him in. But whatever it was, he was dead by age twenty-seven (1892).

Hazen (b. 1869) was almost as musical as Joe and much in demand at local entertainments, for which he sometimes made up his own songs. But there was a shadow over the last part of his life: a mental disorder for which he was twice committed, the second time at his own request (so I was told) because he knew what was coming and did not want to hurt anyone (we will hear that story again in regard to Joe himself). He died in the hospital. "He was a talented singer and writer," his obituary reads, "and his death has cast a gloom over the community."

Ensley, Maurice, and Hazen stayed in Lower Woodstock all their lives, farming and working out. All of them were active, public-spirited men, frequently involved in local politics or holding town office, members of this-or-that organization such as the Sons of Temperance or the Young Men's Literary and Athletic Association, and to a man they were solid supporters of the local Baptist church. Even Wallace, the baby of the family (b. 1871), fitted this pattern while he was around. He, too, was a poet, and several of his efforts were published in the local newspapers.[2] Then in 1889 he went away to Acadia College in Wolfeville, Nova Scotia, where he stayed for two years taking what was called "a ministerial course." He spent a few years around Lower Woodstock, where he evidently did some preaching, but much of his life was spent elsewhere—in Montreal, Halifax, and Toronto, for example—and finally he headed for the Klondike in 1897. The last anyone ever knew, he was in British Columbia. When he died, his body was not shipped home.

Of the four daughters, Bertha, the oldest child (b. 1855), married Charles Taylor and lived across the river in Millville. She died at age forty, leaving her husband and three daughters. Clarienda Maud, mercifully known as Carrie or (after her marriage to Thomas Porter) "Mrs. Carrie Tom," spent most of her life in Lower Woodstock, although she and her husband lived at times upriver in Ed-mundston. Even when there she often spent winters with her mother in Lower Woodstock while her husband was in the woods. *"That Carrie," said Emma Merrithew, "you couldn't beat her. She could lead it. She could lead Sunday school. She could sing a solo. You never heard anything better. And she could teach a Sunday school class." She was also the one, I am told, who was most interested in "family" and the closest one to Joe. *"She was the only one would miss him," said Emma Merrithew. "She was the only one would care about him. . . . And I think it worked on her quite a lot to know what had become of him. . . . She was his favorite. He'd go to her if he had anything to go for." This much is certain: she wrote constantly to the hospital during Joe's last years to ask how he was and was there anything she could do. Sadie (Sarah Jane), Maurice's twin, was an active "division" and Sabbath school worker; she married a local man by the name of Dow. Annie Laura, the fourth child, died at the age of two: "A flower too fair to bloom on Earth is gone to bloom in Heaven."

There they are, the Scott family of Hay Settlement near Meductic, standing as if for a daguerreotype: old John Scott with his full beard, Sarah standing just behind him to the right (her hand on the back of his chair), the children grouped around them. The neighbors saw them as a clever and imaginative lot who loved to act and perform, and we can see the justice in that judgment. They were a musical family, too; they sang in the church choir, and at home the old organ in the front parlor (it is still there) got a lot of use. They were farm people, all of them, to whom church, home, and family meant a great deal; yet we can see an energy there that had to reach out for other things, too. *"They were quite high-minded people, wanted to be. You know," said Emma Merrithew. "They were all proud." But that pride was not all in the Scott line, she felt; the Teelings had their own. *"We thought we took that from my grandfather. . . . He was mighty high-minded. He was so proud he wouldn't let his children play with any other children. And we always thought we got a little bit of that loftiness from our old grandfather." Old daguerreotypes have a way of making everyone look severe, but perhaps no photographer had to tell the Scott family to lift their chins up just a little bit—and hold it.

There is one person who is missing from the picture, and that is Joe. Joe was the seventh child, and he wouldn't hold still.

Joseph William Scott was born February 5, 1867, and before he was twenty he was across the line and into the woods. With the exception of his name appearing once in the newspaper, there are no written records to tell us anything about Joe's early life. Some few stories have come down through the family, but they tell us very little. We are dependent on eyewitness accounts, then, and during the sixties when I was doing most of my research, I knew that anyone who could remember much to the point about those early years in Lower Woodstock wouldn't be much less than ninety at the very least. Even such a person's memory of Joe would be apt to be limited to an anecdote or two, unless he or she were quite close to him. Needless to say, the chance of finding a good informant for those early years was small. But I was lucky.

The notation on the card I was carrying said, "Emma Merrithew, first cousin to JS. May know something," but I had no great hopes on that hot August day in 1964 in Woodstock as I stepped into the phone booth to call her. Did she remember anything about a cousin of hers by the name of Joe Scott, I asked. Her answer was unequivocal: "Oh boy, do I!" She lived in a second-floor apartment in a house behind the Catholic church, and I was there in about five minutes.

Mrs. Merrithew was ninety-one. Joe's mother had been her Aunt Sarah, and as a child she had often visited the Scotts, sometimes staying on for several weeks at a time. She had plenty of opportunity to watch Joe—after all, he was only six or seven years older than she was—and it became obvious as I talked to her that she not only *had* watched him but had also listened to what her elders said about him in after years. I already knew a good deal about Joe Scott's later years; the boy she described was so clearly the child who fathered the man that I have no hesitation in presenting him here almost entirely through her eyes. They are good, clear, friendly eyes—and they are the only eyes we have.

*"He was just a natural boy," she said. "I wouldn't say one thing unnatural, only I do really think he was lazy about settling down with them to work. He didn't seem to be at home on the farm, and they wanted him to be at home on the farm and help out." But was he different, I wondered. *"No, I wouldn't say Joe was so much different than any other boy in the world. I've seen boys just like him. But he was different from *that* family," she said:

*[He was] just a little different from the rest of them. They would hay all day in the fields. All the boys would go out and help their dad on the hay [with] the raking machine. We'd all go out, just thought it was fun—and I'd go, too. But Joe never was raking hay much. If he would go at

noon he would probably be away by three o'clock and they wouldn't know where he was. . . . For instance, I can tell you we'd go blueberrying. We'd all pile in [with] a double team of horses [and] some hay in the bottom of a hayrack. But he never was with us. . . . I can remember he swarmed bees. He'd go out with the swarm, you know. He'd help his uncle get a swarm of bees or something like that. But he never, I don't think he ever—he *might* have hayed some or worked on the farm some when I didn't know it, but. . . .

People remember Joe as musical, even in this musical family. Mrs. Merrithew recalled him singing *"coming through the fallow there, the trees there where they were cutting down their new piece of ground, you know. He'd be coming through there singing to beat the band—one of the old songs, you know." But when it came to singing with the others Joe kept his distance. *"They was great to sing in the choir, but he didn't want to sing in no choir, but he could sing," she said. "When we'd get around the organ playing and practicing for church service or anything, he'd probably stick his head in the door and say, 'That's fine!,' you know, and at other times he'd make another remark, but he'd never come in to join us." Nor did the church itself interest him. *"They didn't say anything too much about it, but I think they'd like to have had him went to church. Oh, he did go to church and Sunday school, but he didn't take no important part."

Joe had his little ways, and they fascinated his younger cousin. *"He was jolly," she said:

*Never saw him cross. He was always playing little pranks. For instance, he brought home two white mice, and he had them named and he tried to make them caper in the cage in the corner of the house. And it amused me very much to see them because I had never saw white mice, you know, and I played with them along with him. I'd give anything if I could just remember the names he gave them. . . .

I'll tell you another thing Joe would do. The steamboats were running and . . . the steamboat landing was just this side of the Baptist church where it goes down to the river. And we'd hear it whistle. And Joe would always take the [row] boat and just as soon as [the steamboat] went by he'd always ride the waves. . . . One day he got me and I went too. There was three or four of us and I never was so scared in my life. I was about ten years old. . . .

Not everyone shared her fascination, she felt. *"I've seen him black his face and come through the woods and crouch all over and walk funny, just to take a rise out of people and make them—you know—amused. But they didn't take him [*that way*]. They took him more that he wasn't like the rest, see?"

If they felt Joe "wasn't like the rest," there'd be nothing like a little sleepwalking to reinforce that feeling—and Joe obliged. Mrs. Merrithew recalled the following incident:

*Well, I remember he walked in his sleep and he would stroll out every—well, he wouldn't every night. No, maybe once a week. But he'd always go somewhere. [*This one time I was staying there*] his older sister Sarah (we called her Sadie) said, "Let's sleep over the ell tonight." Her and I used to have a room over the living room but [*Aunt Sarah*] she'd let us sleep over the ell. They were pretty well-to-do people at the time. And we watched him.

And my Uncle John Scott fished salmon, and he always had a salmon net out. So [*Sadie*] she said, "Don't put your night dress on tonight, and we'll follow Joe." So it was quite dark then. They was no electric lights, believe me, and it was dark. . . . And we followed him. We didn't want him to see us, you know, 'cause she said to me, "Don't say a word, because if we wake him he'll fall or something."

So we followed him to the bank of the river, and [*hid*] in a little cluster of bushes where you could sort of hide from him. He went to the beach. . . . He untied that boat just as nice as if he was wide awake, and he went out and fished that net. . . . Well, we didn't dare say a word, so we crouched in those bushes so when he came back he wouldn't know we were there, because we didn't want to wake him until he got home. . . . He put that net back just as nice as Uncle John could have did in the daylight. . . . We went up the path again right behind him so close. He goes in and took off his pants and went to bed and went to sleep.

And he wouldn't believe us when we told him. No, he wouldn't believe us that he did it, fished the net. He said we was just making one up on him now.

All that she had told me made me wonder whether she felt Joe was happy at home. *"We never could tell," she said. "You couldn't tell. . . . He wasn't the kind you could judge feelings. I'd often wondered if he wasn't discontented. I don't know why. I think he had a roving disposition, didn't want to stay on the farm. You wouldn't see him anything else but pleasant," she added. "I never saw even a scowl on him. I never saw him even ugly to his folks. But he wasn't with them a great deal. He kept his distance."

How long did Joe stay around? There is no way to be sure. The only time his name ever appeared in the paper in these early years was when he was elected the charter Outside Sentinel in the local Sons of Temperance in January, 1886, and it must have been shortly after that that he disappeared, not to return again even for a visit for fourteen years. *"He went out the path by the spring . . . ," Mrs. Merrithew recalled. "There was a spring behind the house and he went to the path to the spring. He often went out, and that was the road to Meductic. That was the way they cut short to go to Meductic. And they never see him [after]."

There is no reason to believe that Joe's disappearance would have been looked on as anything unusual at first, since it was so much the custom for young men to go into the woods. I am sure, too, that his older brothers had already put in winters in the lumbercamps by this time, but they always came home in the spring. Joe was probably the first of the Scott family really to leave home, and as that winter went into spring and months turned into years, those at home must have wondered about him. They'd get reports of him from time to time, but not much more. Mrs. Merrithew remembers one time hearing her mother and Mrs. Scott talking about him and wondering where he was. "Oh," said Mrs. Scott, "he'll come back some day." That sounds casual enough, but surely she kept all these things and pondered them in her heart.

*"I can see him just as plain as day," said Mrs. Merrithew, as she pictured Joe walking out to the spring. "The grass was high on the side of the path there and he'd be switching that with his hands. . . . Isn't memory a funny thing?" Her memory was certainly remarkable, but no less remarkable was her final summing-up. We will have reason to come back to her judgment time and time again as Joe's story unfolds:

*Sometimes when you'd think about him, I think he was planning for something that he didn't quite have or didn't, couldn't get. He was planning to do things maybe that he couldn't ever attain to the heights that he wanted to. And I think if someone had been behind him that understood him as they do in these days, you never know what he would have made. But no one understood that gay—in those days there was nothing, nothing to take your mind much off the church, you know. . . . And I think Joe wanted to push some way in the right direction. . . . And probably if the right person had got ahold of him like they can in these days. . . . Well, say for instance supposing that there'd been anything like television. Joe would have been a good hand. He could've made every-body laugh. He'd 've been a good comedian. There'd've been something for him in that that was what he wanted. And it wasn't to be gotten! He couldn't get it. It seemed to be something he was reaching for. I always thought he was reaching for something he couldn't get.

[*You*] wanted to make of him and be so nice with him, you know, and he just had the laugh and smile and the pat on the back, and you never could get near him like to sit down and talk to him because he had something else on his mind. Now, how do we know that if he'd had somebody that had understood all of what he wanted he might've made a great man? . . . He wouldn't work heavy. He seemed like he might've made something else.

NOTES

1. This and all similar material in this chapter is taken from deeds, mortgages, etc., on file in the Carleton County Records Office, Woodstock, N.B.
2. See the *Carleton Sentinel* for Sept. 28, 1889; Sept. 9, 15, 29, Nov. 3, 17, 1894; Mar. 30, 1895.

2

"Arriving in the State of Maine": Matters Historical

Not only are we not sure just when Joe left home, we can't be sure just where he started his life in Maine. As I said at the end of the last chapter, 1886 is the last date we have for him at home, and it is likely that he came to Maine shortly thereafter. Though I doubt it, there is a possibility that he worked along Wassataquoik Stream, a tributary of the East Branch of the Penobscot, while Tracy and Love were conducting operations there in the late eighties (more about that later on). But the first place where we begin to get any real informa- tion on Joe is over in the Androscoggin valley. Wherever he went, he worked in the woods, and it just so happened that he hit the Maine woods right at the beginning of its second great boom. Since this boom created some circumstances that will bear on both Joe's story and the story of his songs, this is a good point to pause for a little history.

The great pine era was over in the woods of the Northeast, and the depression following the panic of 1873 lingered on well into the eighties in Maine. Maine woodsmen and river-drivers were being attracted further west by offers of better wages, creating a labor vacuum in the lumberwoods, into which rushed thousands upon thousands of young men from the Provinces. To be sure, plenty of them had come over earlier, but now they came in a steady stream. "In 1881," David Smith points out, "handbills were printed and scattered throughout the Maritimes in hope of raising the one thousand men needed on Maine rivers."[1] The call was successful, and the Provincemen kept coming. Of course, there was much adverse comment about these bluenoses, herringchokers, P.I.'s—

call them what you will—but they were good workers and they'd work for what was being paid. "The hiring of the Provincemen was a regular business," says Smith. "Bangor boarding houses recruited them, housed and fed them, and then contracted them out to Penobscot operators."[2] He gives as an example "the proprietor of a Washington Street hotel who had sent 286 men in from his hotel, 250 of them from P.E.I." They began coming in the lean years and kept coming as times improved. And the times did improve; in fact, there came a boom as impressive as anything seen in the great pine era as the nascent pulp and paper industry began to make its demands felt.

To be sure, the history of paper manufacture goes back well beyond the mid-century even in Maine, but until the industry developed efficient methods of mass production from wood pulp it was an interesting but unspectacular star on the edge of the state's long economic night. Those methods *were* developed, and the light from that star brought new day to the lumberwoods of the whole Northeast. Big sawmills like the Eastern Corporation in South Brewer set up pulp mills to utilize their waste wood, but it wasn't long before the parent sawmill was simply an insignificant if noisy adjunct of the great smoking and smelly digesters in whose shadow it now lived. Things were not moving fast enough, however, and just before the turn of the century, the Northern Development Company (soon to become the Great Northern Paper Company) bought up the wilderness around the old Fowler Farm and began building the present city of Millinocket, not to mention a tremendous paper mill. Naturally the lumber barons did not like it much, and they waged a long fight that was as game as it was useless. The great paper corporations were taking control of the woods all over the state, not just along the Penobscot, and since Joe Scott spent a large part of his life in the upper Androscoggin valley in the western part of the state, let's take a look at what was happening there.

The Androscoggin River takes its rise in Umbagog Lake, right on the Maine–New Hampshire border. After making a loop through New Hampshire's Coos County, where it flows south through Errol, Milan, Berlin, and Gorham, it reenters the state of Maine at Gilead. From there it flows generally eastward through Bethel and Rumford to Livermore Falls, where it turns southward to Lewiston and Brunswick, ending its 160-mile journey when it joins the Kennebec at Merrymeeting Bay. The river falls about fifteen hundred feet in its

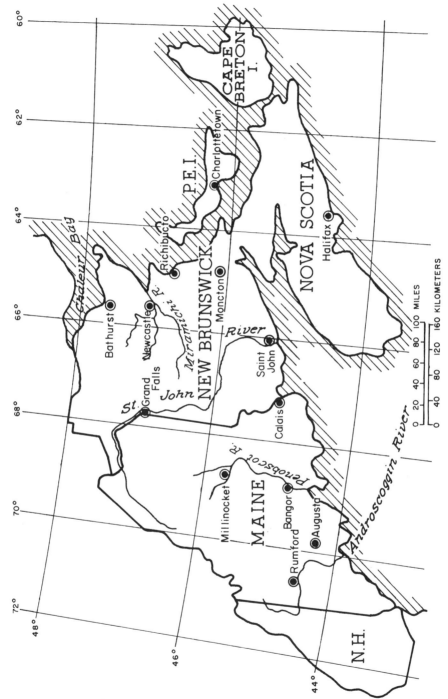

Maine and the Maritime Provinces

17

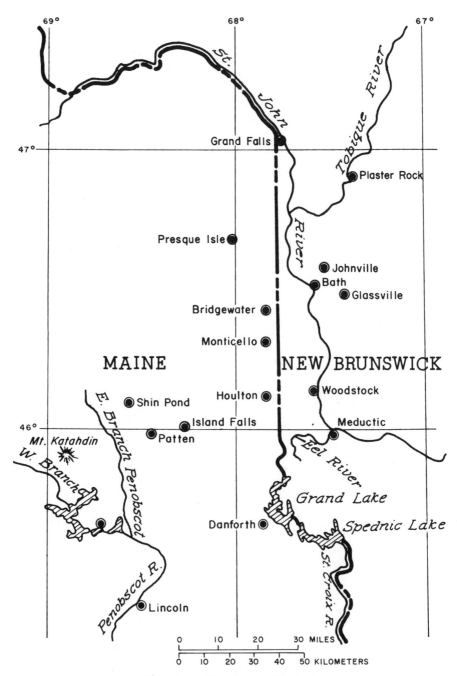

The Maine–New Brunswick Border

18

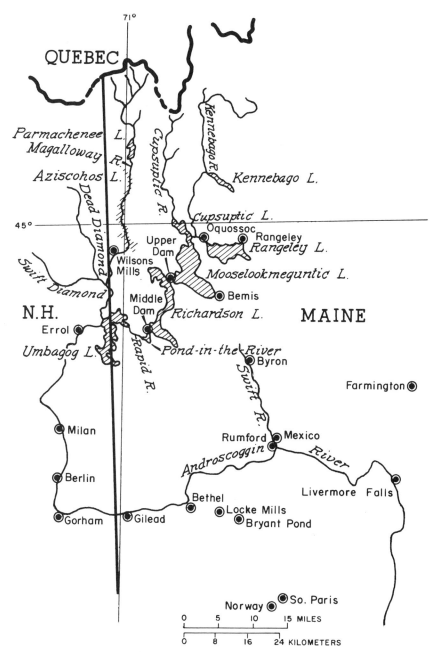

The Upper Androscoggin Valley

19

course, with major falls at Berlin, Rumford, and Lewiston, and others at Livermore Falls and Brunswick. In the history of lumbering in Maine, it is second in importance only to the Penobscot, although its production was often so close to that of the Kennebec that it is a bit fussy to talk about which was larger.

During our period, say from 1885 to 1915, most of the big lumbering was done in the country above Umbagog Lake on the three river-and-lake systems that make up the Androscoggin's headwaters: the Magalloway, the Cupsuptic, and the Kennebago. The largest branch, the Magalloway, takes its rise within a mile of the Canadian border and flows directly south through Parmachenee Lake to Wilsons Mills, crossing the New Hampshire border just above Wentworth Location and emptying into the Androscoggin just below Umbagog Lake (now, of course, Aziscohos Dam, a few miles above Wilsons Mills, has flowed the Magalloway back some twelve miles, but it wasn't built until 1913). A good deal of New Hampshire water enters the Magalloway just as it crosses the line, where it is joined by the combined waters of the Swift Diamond and the Dead Diamond.

A few miles to the east, the Cupsuptic River flows south from the Canadian border into Cupsuptic Lake, and still further to the east it is paralleled by Kennebago River. The waters of these last two streams become part of the great lake system that makes up the main reservoir for the Androscoggin. Rangeley and Cupsuptic lakes lead into Mooselookmeguntic, which joins with Upper and then Lower Richardson lakes; and finally, by way of Rapid River, the whole system flows into Umbagog Lake. All in all, it makes for a pretty impressive watershed. As one authority saw it in 1902, "the Androscoggin is one of the best controlled rivers in the country. There are eighty-seven lakes connected with its sources, aggregating about 230 square miles of surface, and many of these lakes are capable of being utilized for storage purposes by means of dams. The Rangeley lakes are now controlled by a series of magnificent stone dams. The lakes can be drawn down thirteen feet if necessary."[3]

Although lumbering operations had been carried on for some time in this country, these woods had never felt the fantastic pressures the Penobscot had. In fact, it wasn't until after the mid-century mark that the Grand Trunk Railroad was extended to Berlin, New Hampshire, which then began to develop as a sawmill town. Even then, most of the cut was on the New Hampshire side, leaving the woods around and above the Rangeley lakes relatively untouched. Some of the drives from that country used to take as long as two years, logs having to be boomed in the lakes over the winter. As Defebaugh, writing as late as 1907, put it, "although operations there have been going on for thirty-five years, the growth is still heavy and in some sections, as about Cupsuptic and Kennebago lakes, the length and difficulty of the drives have prevented any considerable inroads into the spruce, which today remains practically as good a stand as it was fifty years ago."[4]

But of course even as Defebaugh was writing, the burgeoning pulp and paper industry was making itself felt in this country, too. It was the old story: what started as an ancillary to the sawmills soon all but shut them down. The Berlin Mills Company, for example, had had a lucrative lumber business almost all to itself in this area since its formation shortly after mid-century, and when the pulp mills came to Berlin in the eighties the Berlin Mills Company ultimately bought one out and established what was to become the present-day colossus of this country, the Brown Company. What these pulp mills meant to Berlin can best be seen in the Selectman's Report for 1887:

The rapid and unprecedented growth of Berlin, which in the space of little more than half a dozen years has increased from a scattered community of a few hundred to a chain of villages numbering nearly four thousand men, women, and children, brings us face to face with problems and responsibilities worthy of serious consideration, whether socially, morally, economically or politically. This phenomenal and sudden growth has sprung upon us many of the conditions belonging to large towns and cities alone, and finds us in a degree without the advantages of that experience which they, in their slower and steadier advancement, had benefit of. The doubling of our population in little more than a year has forced the demand for additional accommodations far beyond what was anticipated or imagined, and has compelled extraordinary effort and outlay to meet it. A hundred tenements, many of them built among the crags of our rough and inaccessible places, have been put up, and the means of communication with them supplied, though at considerable cost.

Obviously, Berlin was having trouble just taking care of its own. Imagine, then, what it must have been like when the drives came down in the spring, turning loose hundreds of river-hogs with both

21

Fig. 1. Congress Street, Rumford Falls, as it appeared in 1892, when construction was just getting started. (Courtesy of the Rumford Historical Society. NA photo 494.2.)

Fig. 2. Congress Street, Rumford Falls, about 1895. (Courtesy of Peter McKenna and the Rumford Historical Society. NA photo 494.1.)

Fig. 3. "The Island," or downtown section, of Rumford Falls as it appeared about 1895. To the left is the Androscoggin River; to the right the canal, with Canal Street facing it. Congress Street runs down the center of the island. In the background are the paper mills. (Courtesy of Peter McKenna and the Rumford Historical Society. NA photo 498.2.)

fists full of money and with emphatic and colorful plans for spending it. Berlin was a boom town with all the vigor and optimism that implies, and all the hangovers.

But if Berlin was a small town with ferocious growing pains, Rumford Falls went it one better. Berlin at least began from something; Rumford Falls began from nothing, the way Millinocket was to do ten years later. Back in 1882 Hugh Chisolm and Waldo Pettengill began buying up land around the falls, and by 1890 they had begun a power company and dam, platted a town, and laid out its streets. By 1892 they had brought in the railroad, and the next year the Rumford Falls Paper Company (sold to the International Paper Company in 1897) was in operation. "Rumford Falls took on all the character of a boom town," says David Smith. "Buildings were being erected every day and rents skyrocketed. . . . Electric lights lit the main streets and most homes, two miles of water main and one-half mile of sewers had been laid, three bridges built, and schoolhouses and churches were in operation."[5] In that same year, 1894, the Rumford Falls and Rangeley Lakes Railroad was organized to bring the logs directly down from the lakes rather than waiting for them to come by the drive; by 1900 this amazing little line had pushed its curving way some twenty-seven miles up over the height-of-land (there were several miles of continuous 2 percent grade!) to Bemis. That was the year the Oxford Paper Company began building its plant at the falls, too.

By 1902, there were six thousand people living in Rumford, where twelve years before there had been fewer than nine hundred people scattered in many small farming communities over the whole township—and as late as 1891 there had been no one at all living at the falls! And here the drives came in, and here the woodsmen came after their winter's work. What Bangor had been for generations to the Penobscot, Rumford Falls became overnight for the Androscoggin: a place where money could be interestingly spent in a hurry. "In these years Rumford was supposed to be a dry town," a recent history tells us. "However, police raids kept turning up seemingly endless supplies of beer, wine, and whiskey. One night in August, 1907, police raided sixteen saloons which was a rather large number of such emporiums for a dry town with a population of 6,500."[6]

Mike Noonan of Saint Stephen, New Brunswick, remembered Rumford the way he saw it shortly after 1900. *"It was more of a river town," he said. "It was rough. Plank sidewalks, and I don't think there was any street paved. And of course the business was practically all woods work or lumbermen who moved through there. . . . The people coming in and out were mostly all woodsmen and river-drivers. And I know you'd think nothing in the world to see a couple of men coming down the sidewalk drunk and singing, but nobody'd pay any attention to them. Plenty of rumshops or barrooms, of course, and liquor was sold openly. And some of the boardinghouses, too, had a bar, sold liquor." There were plenty of women to be had, too, but of course, he added, he was too young at the time. *"But the stories the men would tell!"

Thus in the late eighties and all through the nineties there was plenty of work in this part of the world, and as might be expected a disproportionately large number of the newcomers were from New Brunswick, Nova Scotia, and Prince Edward Island. Many came directly to work in the mills, many others came to work in the woods and on the drives and then stayed on to work in the mills, while still others put in their winters and went back home. At any rate, the valley was alive with Provincemen coming, going, and staying. How often have I borne greetings from families on "the Island" ("Prince Edward Island! What other island is there?") to other members of the family in Rumford, or had someone like Leland Nile of Rangeley tell me to say hello to old Will Bryant for him next time I was on P.E.I. (I had just told Leland I'd seen Will the week before) and remind him how they'd worked together up Cupsuptic sixty cold winters ago! There was good money to be made here, and they crossed the line, these Rorys and Auguses, in thousands to make it.

The country was booming and great changes were taking place, but once a man got back into the woods the life was pretty much what it had been for almost a century. True, the handwriting was on the wall, but there was no Daniel to tell the men of the passing of the all-winter camp, the ax, and even the two-man saw—or of the coming of four-foot wood, the chain saw, and (God save the mark!) the mechanical tree harvester. For the woodsmen, the boys who did the work "up there in out back of beyond," it was still a wearisome life,

> Sleeping in the shanty so bleak and so cold
> While the cold winter winds they blow,

"Arriving in the State of Maine"

And as soon as the morning stars do appear
To the wild woods we must go.

Hard work it may have been, but it was no harder than work back home on the farm; in fact, some men have told me it was a good deal easier than farming both in hours and in effort—and it paid real hard money, something they seldom saw back on the farm. Whatever their reasons may have been, the Provincemen kept coming.

PARENTHESIS

What that life was like can best be seen, perhaps, if we take a typical, if composite, example. We'll call him Harry McNeill, and he's from Lot Seven in West Prince County, Prince Edward Island. He's had about all he can take of the farm from predawn chores to all day grubbing potatoes to barn chores once again—all for nothing of his own. Linus Murphy from down the road was in to help with the haying, and they talked about going into the woods this winter. Linus has an Uncle Mike who's been taking charge in the woods for the Berlin Mills Company for some years now, and the last time he wrote he said there was plenty of work and if any of the boys came over they should look him up. Harry and Linus agree to go together after the potatoes are dug.

They make preparations. As the old song has it,

> *A new suit of clothes is prepared for the journey*
> *A new pair of boots made by Sherlock or Clark*
> *A fine kennebecker well stuffed with good homespun*
> *And then this young Island boy he does embark.*

Then one cold November morning they catch the train at Howlan station. They cross the Strait on the ferry and then continue their train trip to Portland, Maine. Here they change trains for Rumford. Uncle Mike's careful directions tell them where to get outfitted, because however sturdy homespun may be, they can't expect to put in a winter in their traveling clothes. They go into Charlie Israelson's and buy larrigans (high-top laceless moccasin boots), mackinaws, mitts, and other things they may need in the long winter, though of course if they do run short they can always buy from the "wangan" and have it marked down in the book against their pay. Uncle Mike has also been careful to suggest a good hotel, the Grand View House, where they can stay for a dollar a night.

Next morning they board another train, this time for the trip up through Roxbury and Byron to Bemis, and for the two P.I.'s this trip through the mountains is a real experience after the gentle rolling hills of home. They gawk and get kidded for it, but they are not the only Islanders or the only green hands either. There are men and boys from all three provinces and several states; some, like Harry and Linus, are going in for the first time, others are old hands, while still others are going in not to work but to hunt. The train grinds slowly up over the long grade, the air in the car is blue with pipe smoke, and an occasional bottle gets handed across the aisle to seal new friendships. There is much talk of who's hiring, who's a good man to keep clear of, what it was like at Camp Seven last winter. But it's only twenty-seven miles to Bemis, and soon the boys find themselves at the station, the blue lake before them and the spruce-covered mountains going straight up all around. They are lucky enough to get a boat right out for the trip up Mooselookmeguntic to Cupsuptic Lake. There's a cold wind whipping the lake, even a few flakes of snow from the leaden sky, but the little steamer butts its way along and soon is starting its trip up Cupsuptic River. Five miles of deadwater, the forest closing in more and more on both sides, brings them to the falls and the depot camp, which everyone knows as "the Moocher's Home."

Uncle Mike is there, and glad to see them: "Where the hell have you been? I was looking for you all last week!" They talk of home, and then Mike introduces them to some of the other men around, including the cook, Steve Patterson ("the Moocher" himself), who soon gives them their first taste of lumbercamp food: beans, codfish, biscuits, tea, and (for sweetening) molasses. Maybe they were hungry from the long trip down the lake, but the two boys put away an astonishing amount: "Christ almighty, Mike, we ain't gonna make any money on them two!"

It is decided to send them in to Camp Seven, Arthur Kilfoil's camp, where they need men, and while Linus and Harry are certainly green as grass, they're big and they'll learn fast enough. Next morning Uncle Mike gives them directions, and they start hiking up the tote road, but about an hour later a tote team comes along and offers them a ride on the wagon. They accept, but after about half an hour's jouncing they decide it is a whole lot easier to walk.

About noon the boys find themselves at Kilfoil's camp, and since no one is there but the cook, his helper the cookee, and the barroom-man or bullcook, they have a chance to look around. There are three log buildings: the camp itself, the "hovel" for the horses, and the blacksmith shop. The "camp" is actually two buildings set end-to-end under a common roof but with a space of about ten feet between them (called the dingle, and it's where supplies are kept). Through a low door to the right is the cookroom, containing several long tables and the two big cookstoves. Through the left-hand door (just as low) they enter the men's part of the camp, the barroom (elsewhere called the bunkhouse or just the "men's part"). Down either side run two levels of bunks, pole platforms divided by more poles into something like stalls, two men to a stall. The barroom man sees that each of them gets a blanket (since they'll be bunking together that means two blankets to each two men) and shows them how they can go out around the camp and gather fir boughs for a mattress if they want to. "How about a pillow?" asks Harry. The barroom man laughs. "Sure," he says, "just fold up your coat."

By the light of the kerosene lanterns, they see that along the foot of the lower bunks on either side of the camp runs a long split-log bench, the deacon seat. In the middle of the floor is the woodstove, and above and around it is a rack that the boys will discover is used for drying socks and mittens. For all its roughness and spareness, this room will be home to them for the next four months—and the deacon seat will be all the easy chair they'll know. And they'll share it with about fifty other men.

It has just turned dark. The men are beginning to return from the woods, and soon the boys meet their new foreman. He wanted experienced men, damn it, but they'll have to do, he supposes. He puts Charlie on as a sled tender, since he's had some experience with an ax. That means he'll work as assistant to Jed Cameron, a teamster, also from the Island.

It is still dark next morning when the barroom man yells "Turn out!" and fifty grumbling men rouse, splash a little water on their faces at the washbench at the far end of the room, and go in for breakfast. Then they're out to work, walking a mile or so by lantern-light so that they'll be able to begin work when day comes. Since the big job now is to get the logs cut and yarded before the deep snow comes, each crew consists of head chopper, second chopper (both of whom also work with a crosscut saw), a swamper (sometimes two *swampers if the going is rough), a teamster, and a sled tender. Once the choppers fall and limb out the tree it is the swamper's job (Linus is put to swamping) to make a "road" for the team to haul it out by. The team then takes over, the sled tender's job being to bark and smooth the bottom of the butt end of the log to make it slide along the ground more easily. Sometimes if the logs are particularly big or the ground expectionally rough, they get the butts up onto a bunk sled. Then Jed and Harry throw a chain around the log, secure it with dogs, and drag it off to a place by the side of the main logging road called a "yard," where, with the help of a yard man or two, they stack the logs carefully in great tiers that, when the time comes, will be easy to break down again. But this is the season for cutting and yarding. Jed and Harry bring in their logs and yard them up, and all along the road other crews are doing the same thing. Around noon the cookee comes out with lunch; they build a little fire to boil the kettle, sit or stand around it while they eat, and go back to work. Then in the evening, when it gets too dark to see, they light up the lantern again and head back for camp.*

The snow is late in coming this year, but there's plenty of it when it arrives. The twitch roads from where the cutting is going on to the yards now have to be broken out after every storm. The cutting is a good deal more awkward (and the stumps a good deal taller), but the work goes on just the same. There is a change in the pattern, though; it is time for the two-sledding to begin. Now the logs that have been carefully yarded up must be moved to the banks of the river in preparation for the spring drive. Harry's crew is one of those that is broken up and reassigned for this new work. Harry is still Jed's sled tender, but they are no longer working with a one- or two-horse team twitching logs out to the yard. Now they have a four-horse team and are hauling immense loads of logs on two-sleds (that is, long sleds with a set of runners on each end) three miles or more to the banks of Cupsuptic River, where the logs are repiled in "landings" to await the drive.

It is dangerous work. The yard crews roll the logs off onto the sled bunks, where Harry and Jed must chain them in securely in preparation for the next layer. Let a man slip, and a whole skidway of logs can come down and crush the men on the sled. Once the load is set, the team begins the long haul to the river. The road crew's job is to keep the way open by shoring up soft spots, shoveling out drifts and the like, and keeping the sled tracks iced by running the water-cart along them at night whenever necessary. Downgrades, on the other hand, are not iced but covered with hay or boughs or anything else to slow the sleds down. One hill is too steep for even that, and the sleds have to be snubbed down, that is, held back by a heavy hawser secured to the sled and run around a friction post (better known as a snub-stump) at the top of the hill.

At the landing the logs are taken off the sled and rolled to the edge of the river by the landing crew, who also mark them so that they can be identified later on at the sorting boom as part of the Berlin Mills cut (I.P. and Oxford logs will go on down beyond Berlin, of course). Then the teams head back up the road to the yards. They must work fast to get the entire winter's cut to the landings before the snow disappears and the roads go to slush and mud. Harry hears stories of contractors ruined by early thaws, but this winter all goes well. The entire cut is on the landings early in March, and all hands now break camp and head back to civilization.

Harry and Linus are still together, and they now have several choices open to them. They can go home; they can head back to Rumford Falls and spend their time and money there until it is time to go back up on the drive; or they can go to someplace nearer-by like Oquossoc or Rangeley and do the same thing. They elect to go over to Rangeley; some of the stories they hear of Rumford Falls make them a little shy of it. Someday, perhaps, but not this year. The two go over to Rangeley, take a room at a boardinghouse, and, except for a couple of nights of whooping it up with their friends, they live a rather quiet life until late April, when they decide to hire on to go back up Cupsuptic on the drive.

Once again, it's the old story. Can they "go on logs," they are asked. No, they have to admit they've never driven before. They're hired anyway; they'll just have to learn as best they can! They head back upriver, and notice that the ice is not out of the lakes entirely yet, but it will be, they're told, by the time the drive gets down that far. They go back up almost as far as where they were cutting in the winter, and wait at a driving camp for a few days until the river gets to a good driving pitch. Then the word comes to break in the landings, and the drive is on. With other green hands Harry and Linus are put to the actual breaking work. Once they've knocked out the wedges (they're working on skidded landings) a whole tier of logs

31

should roll off at a time, but usually they have to be prodded and encouraged with peavey and pickpole. Above and below them other crews are breaking landings and, as one man said, "She's running a wooden river today!"

All along the stream men and crews are stationed at strategic spots to keep the logs from jamming. After a few days the landings are cleared and Harry is sent downstream to help "wing up" a small deadwater, which is to say that they let the logs jam in there but keep the main channel free. He stands on the wing, watching old hands do fantastic things on logs. The veteran who is with him points to a rock just downstream where three or four logs have begun to pile up. "Watch!" he says, and hops on a big butt section going by, rides down to the rock, jumps off, clears the incipient jam, jumps on another log, transfers to another, and after leaping to yet another he jumps shore. "Don't you try that just yet," says the veteran with some pride. Harry doesn't, just yet, but in off moments and in quieter water he does try it—and gets soaked. But by the end of the drive, he'll never have to say again that he can't go on logs!

It's been a lucky year. There have been no serious jams and no one even badly hurt. The head of the drive is already in the lake, and now the grinding work of sacking the rear begins. Harry and Linus both are sent back upstream for this nasty job. Now they must sweep everything before them. Logs stranded on the banks must be hauled back to the water; wings that have been laboriously built up in the lagoons and bends are broken up and sent on downstream; every rock that bears a few logs must be visited and cleared; everything goes, and it is wet, backbreaking work. In a matter of some weeks the rear comes into Cupsuptic Lake. Many of the men are paid off here, but Harry decides to stay on for the whole trip to Berlin.

The logs are held at the mouth of the river by means of booms (chains of logs). Towboats come and hook onto these booms and tow them down Cupsuptic to Mooselookmeguntic and down about eight miles of Mooselookmeguntic to Upper Dam. Here the logs are taken out of the booms and sluiced through the dam into Upper Richardson Lake, where they are boomed in again and towed almost ten miles down through the Narrows and Lower Richardson to Middle Dam. They are then sluiced into Pond-in-the-River and from there into Rapid River, where they are driven six mad and dangerous miles into Umbagog Lake. Once again, they are boomed in and towed across to the mouth of the Androscoggin for the last leg of the journey—thirty-five miles to the sorting boom at Milan. Here the drive is "in" and Harry gets paid off.

It's been an adventurous seven months since he left P.E.I., and he has several hundred dollars to show for it. Linus left the drive at Cupsuptic and headed back to the Island, but Harry thinks he'll stay around for a year or two. His older brother likes the farm, and he himself is not really needed at home. If he wants farm work, there's plenty of it around Maine, but there is also plenty of work in the sawmills and paper mills, not to mention construction work in Berlin or Rumford Falls. He likes the woodsman's life and he's no longer a green hand. Maybe after a couple of years of this he'll go home again, but right now, why should he? He's never been so well off. All he has to do is keep off the booze, and hell, he can take care of himself on that score. But that reminds him he hasn't had a real drink since he left Rangeley and. . . .

CLOSE PARENTHESIS

There never was a real Harry McNeill, but there were thousands of Harry McNeills who came to the Androscoggin from their native Island, from the Saint John River, from the Miramichi, from Cape Breton. They came on the heels of a depression and kept on coming in the years of the great spruce boom in a country where magnificent virgin timber still covered the hills. The good old days were still with us, and at night along the deacon seat one could still hear the old songs sung in the old way—hard and clear. Lots of Harry McNeills were good singers, and some of them could even make up new songs in the old way. It was to this country and this life that Joe Scott came sometime in the late eighties, and here he stayed and thus he lived for almost thirty years. The story comes in bits and pieces, but if we see these bits and pieces in the context we now have, they make their own sad sense.

NOTES

1. David C. Smith, *A History of Lumbering in Maine 1861–1960*, p. 82.
2. Ibid., p. 20.
3. Maine, Bureau of Industrial and Labor Statistics, *Sixteenth Annual Report, 1902*, p. 117.

4. James Elliott Defebaugh, *History of the Lumber Industry in America*, 2, p. 69.

5. Smith, *History,* p. 250.

6. John J. Leane, *A History of Rumford, Maine, 1774–1972*, p. 45. One of the nicest features of this little book is its excellent selection of photographs of early Rumford.

3

"The Town of Rumford Falls": The Heart of the Matter

Joe was a redhead. That makes a good place to start, because there is very general agreement on that point. Some speak of his hair as "sandy," others as "auburn," and I am told he himself spoke of it as "a delicate ginger"; but almost all agree that it was red and plentiful. And he had a redhead's complexion, fair and freckled. As might be expected, estimates of his size vary widely, but his hospital record has him down as five feet, five inches, and 129 pounds. If we make some allowances for the fact that he was sick in 1916, we still wind up with a small man.

Yet he was extremely strong and agile. Tom Pollock recalled him as *"about the smartest man I ever see in my life on his feet. . . . When all of us was driving, we just had tents to sleep in and the cook had a outside fire. . . . And I see Joe standing there drying the front of his pants where they was wet, and he struck his hands on his sides that way," said Pollock, slapping his thighs, "and he threw a handspring backwards. And he just give another snap that way and flopped right back in the same place!" Daisy Severy recalled his agility as a kind of physical grace. *"And do you know," she told me, "he had the wonderfullest figure. He really would dance when he walked." And David, her husband, who in his time had been one of the cattiest men on logs the whole length of the Androscoggin, agreed. They also agreed that he was the wrong man to anger or to pick a fight with. *"A fella was trying to get me to dance," Daisy recalled, "and I was saving dances for Joe. Joe came [and] kicked him right through the anteroom . . . where they hang the coats. With both feet, mind you!" Herbert Porter, too, recalled that Joe could turn somersaults as good as anyone he ever saw in the circus. *"He was good at almost

35

anything he wanted to go at," he said. "He was smart with his hands, his tongue, and his feet!"

What this wiry little redhead chose to be good at to begin with was woods work, and there seems to be no doubt in anyone's mind that he *was* good at it. He could handle an ax well and was especially skillful with a cant dog. Cleon Oakes, now living in Detroit, Michigan, remembered loading two-sleds from a yard that had been built up by Joe Scott back in the winter of 1902: "It was the only pile of logs I have ever seen with the butt ends all at one end and even," he wrote. "It contained about 200,000 feet of lumber. . . . Only an expert could have turned those trees so that they were butt end first but Joe Scott was one of the best cant dog men in the country."

He was an expert river-driver, too, and several people have seen him do that old riverman's classic: jumping on a four-foot log and upending it. *"Well, the head of the log was coming floating along down," said Tom Pollock, "and he'd stand on the boom, and he jump and struck the lower end of it and the water took it and up-ended it. And then he come back onto the boom." The great John Ross could do it, Dan Bossy could, too, and Joe Scott was right up there with them. One of my favorite stories about him is the one Fred Campbell told me about Joe using his skill to try to dump a greenhorn:

*Well, we were working building a boom [at] . . . this big eddy [on the Magalloway], and it was right full of logs and we was picking one out occasionally to put on the boom. And there was a place there (there was only about four places on that sixteen miles of water) where they could come to the river to lunch us. They'd come there and they'd boil the kettle and haul our lunch. Joe Scott he started in across this eddy. It was right full of logs, you know, and you could run . . . , step from one to the other. Well, when you do that, you know, the logs starts bobbing in the water. And he thought he was going to kind of confuse me a little, but just about the time he'd leave a log I'd step onto it, and I was getting them right after him. He looked around to see whether I was in the river or whether I was drowned or what happened. And I said, "I'm right to your ass, John Ross!"

He was almost a stranger to me then, see? . . . He never forgot it. Anytime he'd . . . happen to come on me in surprise, why that's what he'd say!"

"I'm right to your ass, John Ross," said Fred, invoking the name of that great Penobscot river-boss. Fred was about eighteen at the time, but he was able to hold his own against an acknowledged expert twice his age, and that, along with Fred's quick retort, must have hit Joe just right, because the two became good friends. As a man among men, Joe got along fine. *"Joe was a nice fellow," said old Joe Wilbur, a man for whom Scott worked for several winters. "Everybody seemed to like him. He was awful comical, you know. It didn't take him five minutes to make up something, turn it right off. I don't mean a lie, but something kind of comical." Fred Lafferty, who had driven with Joe on the Connecticut, spoke of him as *"an awful good fellow. One of the best. Comical, full of the devil." And Leland Nile laughed and recalled the time Joe preached a mock funeral sermon over a drunken buddy: *"I can't remember how he preached it or anything," said Leland, "but this fellow was just as drunk as he could be. We was going in for the log drive. Well, they was a whole mess of us, a whole load went from Rangeley, and this fellow got laid out and they just covered him up with a blanket ('course no danger of a man freezing then anyway). . . . So Joe—we was all drinking and Joe just thought it would be fun to preach his sermon. . . . Right there, right there going in with the team! They hauled us with a pair of horses on a sled. It was in the month of April."

*"Joe Scott was a fellow that was darned well liked," said Nile emphatically. "He was *well liked* and I don't mean maybe! He could be just as drunk [*so that he had*] all he could do to walk the street, and he was the nicest fellow you'd ever see." Remembering as I did that Larry Gorman was anything but well liked, I often tried to elicit this opinion by playing devil's advocate, always without success. I remember leading up to it one time with George Storer in Rumford, finally telling him I'd heard that men often used to take Joe as a character, a kind of joke. *"No sir!" he said. "I never had that impression of Joe Scott. Of course, he did wander around a lot, but he was always a man wherever I knew him. . . . Everyone used to speak well of Joe." Apparently they did, too, for the only exceptions I have ever heard refer to Joe in his last years.

In part, Joe's popularity was due to his abilities as a singer and songmaker, but only in part. Neither of these skills ever made Larry Gorman popular, though they brought him notoriety.[1] Joe's popularity was due much more to his being a good woodsman and excellent company than to his singing and songmaking, though he was well known for both. *"Everyone knew he was a songmaker," said Wesley Smith, who knew Joe well, and apparently this is true, but for the moment it is more important to understand that Joe was very well thought of, a hell of a good man to have in any camp or crew.

Think back for a minute on what Mrs. Merrithew said about Joe's gaiety, his playfulness, and his love of tricks and odd ways. Crossing the border hadn't changed him any, it would seem; but this Joe is a crackerjack woodsman, while the boy in Lower Woodstock wasn't a worker at all. There is nothing very surprising about this. Joe would hardly be the first boy to hate farm work for room and board but at the same time be ready to break his back and even his neck as a sailor or river-driver or gold miner when he got out on his own. If the work was hard, it was no harder than farming, and it offered much more variety. Even if a man stayed the full route on any job, it would never mean more than four months in any one place, and often Joe didn't stay the whole winter on one job. He was a good woodsman, but he was also a wanderer.

Remember, too, that Mrs. Merrithew had said that for all his happy-go-lucky ways, for all his love of making people laugh, *"you could never get near him like to sit down and talk." The men who worked with him have often remarked that he was reserved, even taciturn. *"You wouldn't call him a mixer," said Vance Oakes. "That's the funny thing. He stood away from the rest a little bit. If there was a bunch of men and they didn't have anything to do, he held the floor, but he didn't hold it by force." Nor was he a great joker; in fact, one person told me she doesn't ever recall him laughing right out, though he'd smile. And George Storer, who said Joe was a lot of fun to have around, added that there was *"nothing foolish or anything about him, but he was a kind of a dry-speaking guy." Ned Stewart summed it up: *"No, he wasn't an awful gabber. He talked, but he wasn't one of those kind with his tongue was hung in the middle and switched to both ends. Don't think he had an enemy in the world," he concluded. "He hadn't ought to have."

Men liked him and remember him with real affection, but in spite of their statements that they "knew him well," they were often surprised to discover just how little they actually could tell me about him. If they did know something about his past, they knew it from what someone else had told them, not from Joe. Yet it was pretty generally known that he *had* a past, that he was a man with a story. It was a story of unhappy love all the more romantic because Joe had made it into a song, "The Plain Golden Band." It was the center, the turning point, and (to continue mixing metaphors) in many ways the key to his whole career. It is time now to tell what can be told of it.

The story goes that Joe fell in love with a girl named Lizzie Morse. They were going to get married when Joe came down out of the woods in the spring, but while he was gone a fellow by the name of Sam Learned (pronounced "Leonard") stepped in and won her away from him. When Joe came out of the woods that spring, she gave him back his ring, and the disappointment almost drove him out of his mind. Not everyone had the whole story, but if we put together many different versions, this is the shape of it. Naturally I was skeptical of anything so neat and fitting, but the Rumford town records bore it all out, quietly and all too eloquently. And so did Lizzie's sister, Mrs. David Severy, née Daisy Morse, of Gray, Maine.

Old Matthias Morse had been born in Andover Surplus, but moved to Brunswick (he was related to the shipyard Morses) and finally to Rumford with his family well before there was any town at all at the falls. He was a carpenter, and when that town began to grow in wildcat fashion as the paper industry built up there in the early nineties, he helped put up many of the new buildings, including the hotel. To take advantage of the boom, Mrs. Morse set up a small restaurant and lodging house, and this is evidently where Joe Scott stayed when he came to Rumford. Mrs. Severy told the story this way:

*Joe come in on the train, and my brother—we had a beautiful horse—and he used to take the people from the station over to the hotel . . . [or] wherever they wanted to go, you know, and got paid for it. And Joe came in. He couldn't get no place to board. And he asked my brother . . . if he knew of anyplace, and he says, "Well, if you can't get a place I'll take you home with me." And so he come in. And he told Mother, he says, "Ain't you got a room," he says. "There's a feller out there that I want you to give him a room if you got one. . . . He can sleep in my bed, and I'll sleep on the couch." And so Joe came in. . . . They brought Joe in, trunk and all. Well, of course all of us kids took to him right away, and took to his singing.

She recalled his arrival at the house: *"I remember Mother told me to go up and help him hang his clothes up in the closet. I was only a kid, ten or twelve years old, and I hung his clothes. When he took them out of the trunk, you know, to hang them in the closet, they was all just so. He had a lot of clothes; he had a trunk full of the nicest clothes. He come from awful nice people, Joe did."

The whole Morse family thought the world of Joe, but ten-year-old Daisy seems to have worshipped him as only a ten-year-old girl could worship a handsome, fun-loving man in his mid-twenties. *"I used to like to comb his hair, you know," she told me. "His hair was curly, and Joe'd lay back on the old-fashioned lounge we had and I'd comb his hair and he'd always go to sleep. He was just like a brother to us." Old Matthias enjoyed him, too. Joe used to kid him a lot, something Matthias did not always take kindly to, but he liked it from Joe. Then Lizzie appeared on the scene.

She was just about twenty years old, and several people have told me what a beauty she was, much prettier than the picture we have of her (see fig. 4): petite, with a lovely complexion, auburn hair, and hazel eyes, *"and the fellows was all after her," said Daisy. "She was a great entertainer. She could carry on a conversation, you know, and everybody would pay attention to her and she used to speak a lot of pieces." She'd been away for some little time, Daisy recalls. *"She was away somewhere waiting on tables someplace or somewheres working in a dressmaker's shop, and she come home. And that's how she got acquainted with Joe."

Joe fell hard—no question in anyone's mind about that. How long they went together before they decided to get married we cannot be sure, but Joe did give her an engagement ring. Then on October 19, 1893, they filed their intentions of marriage with the town clerk in Rumford, and five days later (the usual time) they were issued a marriage certificate. But the marriage itself never took place.

At this point I have to surmise a few discreet conjectures. What seems to have happened is this: Joe was a woodsman, and he had to go up into the camps that fall. He probably wanted to marry Lizzie before he went away, but she wanted to wait until spring. He convinced her to take out the license that fall, though, just to seal the bargain. And now imagine Joe Scott lying alone nights in the snoring lumbercamp, the wood chunks falling in the stove and the moonlit wind whirring cold in the spruces overhead. Imagine, too, Lizzie Morse back where the lights were bright (and Rumford Falls *had* electric lights that winter) and men were plenty. Lizzie was not the kind to let herself be lonely, and Sam Learned was in town that winter.

Sam came from Andover, too, and since his mother was a Morse we might suspect that he was some relation to Lizzie, and in fact they

Fig. 4. Lizzie Morse, with her second husband, Ed Martin, presumably photographed shortly after their marriage in 1897. (Courtesy of Daisy Severy, Gray, Maine. NA photo 344.)

41

were second or third cousins. Vance Oakes remembered him as *"a flamboyant fellow, but Sam was a good man, a rugged man," adding that he was a hell of a good worker even if he was on the loud side. He paid court to Lizzie that winter, and he swept her right off her feet. When Joe came back from the woods that spring (1894), Lizzie may have told him how it was. On the other hand, it may not have happened that suddenly, since Lizzie didn't marry Sam for almost a year. But at some point during those months Joe must have found out that it was all over.

*"It all but broke our hearts when she broke up with him," Daisy Severy said, and she remembered that Joe was shaken by it. It isn't hard to believe that Joe was deeply hurt by being thrown over in this way. For whatever wild and irrational action a man might take under such circumstances it would be easy to find plenty of precedent. We will never know just what he did, but there are stories that this was the turning point in his life. *"It ruined poor Joe," Angus Enman of Spring Hill, Prince Edward Island, told me. "He just got to be an old bum after that." Dennis Taylor of Coplin Plantation, Maine, was of the same opinion. *"It just simply knocked him out, 'twas all. That was the whole of his trouble; that was probably the whole cause of his insanity," he said, referring to Joe's condition in his last years. Many people have said that Joe used to cry every time he sang "The Plain Golden Band," and given the proper conditions—a few drinks, perhaps, and the right crowd—it is only too possible that he did; but plenty of men have told me they've heard him sing it and never saw him cry. "Joe'd been a fast one, I guess," "Uncle Joe" Patterson told William Doerflinger, "but this time he'd been burned bad. He was crazy over the girl he wrote the song about, so crazy over her he'd sing it over once, and five minutes later, if another man came into the room, he'd sing it over again. But I guess she was a fly one. She let him down all right. He just made up all that stuff about her saying she was sorry."

Sam and Lizzie were married in West Peru on March 17, 1895. The *Rumford Falls Times* carried the story (April 5, 1895):

A quiet wedding took place in our little village [*West Peru*] on Sunday afternoon, the 17th of March, in the parlor of the residence of W. W. Carver, on High Street. The contracting parties were Miss Lizzie M. Morse, the well-known society belle of Rumford Falls for the past two seasons, and Mr. Samuel M. Leonard of Andover. Rev. W. W. Carver performed the marriage ceremony in a solemn and very impressive manner, wishing the couple a happy and prosperous married life. The bride was attired in a gown of dark blue silk. After the ceremony Mr. and Mrs. Leonard drove to the residence of the bride's parents, Mr. and Mrs. M. M. Morse, of Rumford Falls, where they will reside for the present time. Their many relations and friends wish them a long and happy life attended with great prosperity.

The well-known society belle of Rumford Falls for the past two seasons!" That certainly makes it sound as though Lizzie was something of a "catch," but once she was caught, things did not go well at all. In less than two years Lizzie sued for a divorce, which was granted her on May 12, 1897, the causes being Sam's "confirmed habits of intoxication and nonsupport."[2]

Sam didn't stay around Rumford very long. He moved over the height-of-land to Rangeley, where he married a local girl, Minty Oakes, and evidently buried his past very successfully, since neither she (when I talked to her in 1959) nor anyone else (not even Sam's younger brother) knew anything about his marriage to Lizzie. Of course, plenty of woodsmen knew that he was the one who'd stolen Joe Scott's girl, and since I knew that the two men had worked together at times for years afterwards, I wondered how they got on. Lanson Wilbur had told me that Joe and Sam would never speak to each other, and both Wesley Smith and Ned Stewart claimed that Sam would leave the room when someone sang "The Plain Golden Band." *"Sam would dig for somewhere," Ned said. "He didn't like it, didn't like the sound of it." But Vance Oakes put it this way:

*And of course there was rumors that he [Joe] had a girl that he was going to marry and that while he was gone in the woods she ran away with Sam Learned. . . . But Sam and he used to work there in the same place. . . . I don't think that they were chummy, but Joe Scott was a person that could live with other people. I mean he was one of those people who never caused any trouble between somebody, you know? . . . I don't know who he blamed. It didn't seem as if he blamed Sam Learned, you know. It didn't appear that way to me, because I'd heard the thing then. . . . Some of the fellows would be talking about it, you know. But I never heard it from him nor heard it from Sam Learned.

*"I don't think they had anything to do with each other," concluded Ned Stewart. "Don't remember much about it, and I think he done Joe a good deed. I don't know what the hell ever become of Lizzie."

For a long time I never knew what the hell happened to Lizzie either, but her sister Daisy settled that for me. Daisy claimed (and the records support her) that Lizzie and Sam were together less than a year, even though they weren't formally divorced until the spring of 1897. Then that fall she married a salesman by the name of Ed Martin, and the two moved to Massachusetts, where Lizzie lived until her death in 1948.

What about Joe himself during these years? There seems to be no doubt that he had been terribly hurt, but he stayed around town, and he even continued to board part-time at Morses'. *"We thought an awful lot of that fellow," said Daisy Severy. "The whole family did." Evidently he was extremely fond of the other children. *"Yup, Joe liked all of us kids," said Daisy. "My sister Ruby—she had red hair, dark red hair like my mother's—Joe and her'd take a walk and she'd wipe her nose on his hand and he'd say, 'Child, don't do that!' She was little, you know, a little tot; she didn't know any better. Then Joe'd take out his handkerchief, you know." But as Daisy got a little older, she and Joe became especially close. *"Joe weren't much of a hand to talk about himself," she said, "but I used to understand him a lot, you know. . . . I felt sorry for him. He was really crushed on my sister." He always called Daisy his "little sister," and she remembered that they often went to dances together *"down to the pavilion. Mother wouldn't let me go, you know, with everybody," she said, "but she'd let me go with Joe." Apparently Lizzie even began to wonder what was up. *"She didn't come to herself till I commenced to go round to dances with Joe," said Daisy. "She asked me one day, 'Is there anything serious between you and him?' I said, 'No, he's my brother.' "

Joe probably led a typical woodsman's life for the years immediately following the break-up. He drank pretty heavily, and my hunch is that he also drowned his sorrow with other women. It is very likely that during those years he acquired the syphilis that finally led to his death. There were plenty of whores around to oblige him, to be sure, but we should balance all this by remembering that he kept going back to the Morses and that he took such simple pleasure in Daisy's company or in taking walks with little Ruby.

Then one spring (it was probably 1897 or 1898) when he came down out of the woods or off the drive with his good friend Mike Sutton, Mike introduced him to his sister Helen, and the two saw something of each other during that summer. I talked to Mrs. Casey (that was her married name) in 1958. "My brother used to watch over me like a hawk," she said, "but he'd let me go out with Joe." She thought very well of him, too, and considered him of quite a different stripe from most of the lumberjacks who would hit town. He drank, yes, but not really any worse than the rest. What he loved to do most, she claimed, was go out for long walks with her, and they would spend most of the time talking. One Sunday afternoon he wrote out "The Plain Golden Band" for her, "and he said that that was just how it happened, too. It was pretty clear to me that this girl had broke his heart, and you know," she added, "I always had the feeling he kept that ring with him all the time. I never saw it, but I just think he did."

Joe probably continued to use Rumford Falls as his base of operations until after the turn of the century, going into the woods in the winter, on the drives in the spring, and odd-jobbing it in the summer. In June of 1893 one man recalls that Joe was working in a livery stable in Milan, New Hampshire. Among Robert W. Gordon's papers is a letter claiming that "Scott worked in the woods and on the river around Rumford, me. from 1893 to about 1910."[3] He was very likely in Rumford in May of 1897 when Howard Carrick hanged himself at Annie Siddall's boardinghouse on Canal Street (Dave Severy claimed Joe often stayed at Siddall's), and J. A. Polley said Joe was scaling logs at the sulphite mill (then the Rumford Falls Paper Company) when Guy Reed met his death in September of that year. He was still around in October, when William Sullivan was killed up near Bemis, and in May of 1898 he was probably on the drive over near Berlin, when Benjamin Deane shot his wife. If there is any significance in all of this, it is in the contradiction that Joe Scott was a wanderer who never wandered very far—at least not very far from Rumford Falls.

Then on July 22, 1899, Joe married a girl by the name of Emma Lefebvre. There isn't much to tell about her. Her parents came from Coaticook, Quebec, and after living for many years in Westbrook, Maine (where Emma was born), they and their children moved to the new and building town of Rumford Falls. She was in her early twenties, a good ten years younger than Joe, and the pictures I have seen of her show a dark, attractive woman, a bit on the short side, with direct eyes and a full figure.[4] They were married in the office of Aretas E. Stearns, a Rumford Falls justice of the peace.

The marriage is problematic. What was Joe doing getting married at all? The simplest answer is that he fell in love, and sometimes simple answers are the best, but there are those who claim that Emma forced Joe to marry her. All I will do here is cite the official records, which show that at the time of the marriage Emma already had a nine-month-old son, Henry, for whom she named one Alfred Jotham as father. Then, seven months and a week after they were married, another child was born.[5] Finally, if we consider the additional circumstance of their being married by a justice of the peace although Emma was a Roman Catholic, we have grounds at least for a presumption that something more than Joe's free will was involved.

What were Emma's feelings about it all? Of course there is no way of knowing that now. I have said that simple answers are sometimes the best, but it would be a little too simple to assume that Joe was no more to her than a convenient and available solution to her immediate problem. I think she loved Joe very much and wanted this marriage enough to be willing to put up with the obloquy it evidently generated within her own family. Emma never had an easy time of it; of that we can be certain. I am less sure about Joe's feelings about the marriage, but once he was indeed married he seems to have been willing to give it a good try. He may even have developed a real enthusiasm for the whole idea, seeing it as a start on a new life or something like that. That's pure speculation, of course, but that's the way Joe did things.

In keeping with this idea would be the couple's decision to leave Rumford Falls and head for West Milan, New Hampshire. Emma's family never approved of the marriage, her son Henry told me. Her mother not only didn't recognize it as a real marriage, she wouldn't even let Joe in the house. I am sure the two of them decided that it would be easier to start out elsewhere, and if Emma's mother wanted to keep Henry for a while (which she did) that would help, too.

Tom Pollock had an interesting story to tell about when he was on the main river drive on the Androscoggin with Joe in 1900. *"Many's the night," he said, speaking of Joe and his cronies like Aubrey Blue, "they'd crawl up to me and I'd be under the spread and they'd say, 'We're going out to a dance to West Milan and would you let us have five dollars? You got any money on you?' They'd get five dollars apiece to go out to West Milan where there was a tough house out there, and I knew damn well they wasn't going to dance!" Once the drive was in, Pollock said, Joe went on a bender, *"and when he'd start on a tear that way, drinking and everything, he'd take his lady with him and she'd pass as his wife." Chances are, we can be pretty sure, the lady in question *was* his wife.

Evidently they stayed in West Milan through the winter and spring, and little Blanche was born there in February. But after the drive that year, Joe had a better idea, and it led him and his new family on a trip back to Lower Woodstock.

We should stop and think about that trip for a moment. Rumford to Woodstock (or even Milan to Woodstock) is better than two hundred miles on a straight line; by rail, which is how Joe and his family traveled, it was considerably more than that, involving a couple of changes whatever route they took. Taking a family on a trip like this at that time would have been inconvenient, uncomfortable, and relatively expensive. It does not seem like the kind of venture Joe would have set out on without good reason. I think it is very unlikely he would have gone through all that just for a summer's visit. Now that he was a family man, did he have plans of settling down on the old farm for the rest of his days? Of course, we can't tell for sure, but I think that was the idea.

Old John Scott had just turned sixty-five, and he was not in the best of health. That fall he was going to divide his 300 acres, selling Ensley, Hazen, and Joe a hundred acres each for $500. He needed the money, and he wanted to see the land stay in the family. He and Joe had probably written back and forth about it, and it would not surprise me to know that Emma encouraged Joe to make the trip. Her life had been anything but steady up to this point, and she knew her husband's wandering ways. Perhaps this would settle him down. At any rate, when Joe returned home, everyone concerned may have had hopes he'd stay.

Henry just barely remembered the trip, the way a boy not quite two might remember it—a series of fleeting images reinforced by what his mother told him about it over the years. He remembered getting lost on the train, and the man who found him had something shiny, brass buttons maybe, on his clothes. *"And I remember I was in this house, this large house. There were two women, two men. . . . And they were talking, you know. Then I wandered out [and] got into this cornfield and I got lost. And I was sleeping when they found me, laying there in the corn and I was sleeping. . . . I remember somebody picking me up; I woke up then. . . ." The two men were probably Joe's father and brother Ensley, the two women their wives (Hazen and his wife were in Maine at this time, and Carrie and her husband were probably still living in Edmundston).

Others, too, remember the visit. Clyde Dickinson, who lived just down the road and was about ten at the time, remembers walking by the Scott place with his father one day when Joe hailed them over and introduced them to his wife and two kids. "They were all sitting there in a buggy," said Dickinson, "getting ready to go somewhere. He and my father talked for a few minutes, but I don't remember much about it, excepting that she was kind of dark and French-looking." Two of Ensley's children have told me they just recall the visit, too, and the local papers noticed it. "Joseph Scott, who has been absent about 14 years, returned home Wednesday with a wife and two children," said the *Carleton Sentinel* for July 14, 1900, and four days later the *Woodstock Dispatch* carried a similar item, giving the time of his absence as "twelve or fifteen years."

But it didn't work out. How much they knew about Emma, how much Joe had written them about her, is problematic, but she did not feel welcome. *"She felt that they didn't care much about her on account of her religion, my mother being a Catholic, and that didn't set so good with them people," Henry told me, and considering that the Scotts were staunch Baptists, we can well believe it. She and Joe had not been married by a priest, that is true; but Emma was decidedly French, decidedly Catholic, and had lived all her life in the booming mill towns of Maine. She had nothing in common with the Scotts, and we can be sure no one felt very comfortable. Once Joe had decided to return to Rumford, the Scotts had some idea of keeping Henry with them, but Emma wouldn't stand for that at all. Whatever Joe's other reasons were for deciding not to stay, Emma was ready to leave at any time.

I can picture Joe looking it all over, turning the idea round and round in his mind, leaning on a fence and watching his brother Ensley at work in the fields behind the team. Probably he'd walk down the road to talk with some of the Dickinsons or Dows, standing in the sunlight by the open barn doors, smoking, admiring the new mare—then off again down the road. Perhaps he even took little Henry down to the shore while he helped his father fish the salmon weir, his father all the time talking quietly and earnestly to him about staying on, Joe smiling and noncommittal. No doubt everyone went to church that Sunday, where Joe was welcomed, the children beamed at, and Emma greeted politely as she felt more and more the stranger in this, her new husband's homeland. Then home to Sunday dinner.

And I like to imagine Joe going out behind the house for a smoke after dinner and taking a long look at the pastoral loveliness of the Saint John valley, the slow river sliding by in the afternoon sun. He had an eye for this kind of beauty; it is everywhere in his songs. And it was home and all that home implies to a wanderer. He could swing it all right. His father was willing to go in with him on a mortgage; they'd talked it all out, and he'd decided to take title to the land when his father made it over to him. But he knew another life now, and it was a life with much more color, excitement, and variety than farming. He also had a name there; he was the songmaker, "the celebrated Joe Scott." And he knew Emma was unhappy here. He knocked out his pipe and went back in the house. No. The farm would always be there. Someday, perhaps. But not yet.

Henry recalls that before they left to come back to Maine, Mrs. Scott made one more try. She and Joe went out to a seat under a big tree and sat there most of the afternoon. "My mother said that Mrs. Scott was trying to convince him to cut out his wandering ways and make something more of himself," he said, "and Joe would do everything but promise. Mother said that I walked out to them and climbed up in my father's lap. He took me in his arms and held me for a while, but I wiggled too much and got put down." How long they stayed we don't know. Henry said it was a few days, but it may have been a week or even a month. However long it was, Joe was back in the woods that fall.

That same fall old John Scott did what he had planned to do. He made over his land to his sons just as his father had done with him. The deeds are dated October 20, 1900, and Ensley, Hazen, and Joe each got a hundred acres for which they paid $500. Then on December 1, a mortgage for $300 was taken out on Joe's hundred acres, the mortgagers being listed as "Joseph W. Scott of the Parish of Woodstock in the County of Carleton and Province of New Brunswick and John W. Scott of the Parish of Woodstock in the County and Province aforesaid and Sarah A. Scott his wife," the mortgagee being one Mary J. Hayward. The papers were mailed to Joe in Rumford Falls, and he signed them before a notary on December 26, which probably indicates that he came down out of the woods for Christmas that year. The money was to be paid back $50 in 1901, $100 in 1902, and the balance by December 1, 1905, all at 7 percent interest. My hunch is that this $300 went directly to John and Sarah and represented all of Joe's $500 they were ever to see.

Joe now had title to a farm. It was there if he wanted to go back; all he had to do was pay off the mortgage. If he never went back, and if he never paid off the mortgage, he had lost nothing. He did go back, but the mortgage was never paid off. That part of the story will be told in due time.

The end of Joe's brief marriage seems to have been just about as sudden as the beginning, at least from Joe's point of view. In January, 1901, Joe filed a plea of libel for divorce, claiming not only the general grounds of "gross and confirmed habits of intoxication" and "extreme cruelty and cruel and abusive treatment," but more specific grounds of adultery, naming one man back as far as November 15, 1900, and claiming there had been others whose names he did not know. In typical fashion, Joe never saw the divorce through; it was supposed to come up in February term, 1901, didn't, and was finally dismissed in the October term, 1902, most likely because neither he nor Emma ever appeared in court.[6]

It all sounds pretty final to me, but it is possible that the divorce was dropped because Emma and Joe made up or at least decided to let it all go as a kind of stand-off. Henry claimed that Joe used to turn up every so often over the remaining years. *"He made the world of me when he came home," he said. "Then he'd take off again, you know. He'd always sit me on his knee, I can remember that, singing." That may be, but from all other appearances Joe seems to have kept the marriage as a closed and carefully concealed book forever afterward. Although Joe was never known to talk much about himself, it is still remarkable that with a single possible exception not one of his upriver friends ever knew he had been married.[7] Quite to the contrary, Fred Campbell was sure he'd *never* been married, and Roy Kaulback, who roomed with Joe at John Oakes's boardinghouse in Rangeley about 1910 wrote that "he never told me he had been married and until reading your article [I had sent him a reprint of my 1959 article, " 'Ben Deane' and Joe Scott"] I thought of him as a

bachelor." Nor did George Storer know anything about it, though he
had known Joe well and spent many hours talking to him. *"Joe
never spoke of his children or never spoke of his wife. He never
spoke of anyone," said Storer.

But what about Emma? Twenty-one years old, with two small children, living at home—did she turn against Joe? *"No," said Henry,
"she always thought the world of him, but she felt that her people
turned against her. . . . His people turned against her and her own
people turned against her, too, because, they said, 'You're just
wasting your life. He's never home. You shouldn't have married
him'—things like that, you know." It must have been far from a
happy situation for her, and very lonely. She had another daughter in
April, 1903, born to a father unknown, which suggests that she
turned for comfort to other men, something for which it is hard to
blame her. Five months later she lost this child. Her daughter
Blanche, just recently married, died at eighteen in the flu epidemic
of 1918. And of Joe she had lost all track until she found out he was
dying in the Augusta State Hospital, where she went to visit him.
When he died, no one even bothered to inform her. Five years later,
she herself was dead at forty-four. It is so easy for us to look at the
whole show from Joe's side, but Emma deserves our understanding.
It wasn't an easy time she had.

Henry saw things from his mother's point of view, and he had
heard plenty from his grandmother Lefebvre, but his summing up of
Joe's character is interesting and, if we make allowances for foreshortening, just: *"He was happy-go-lucky. He had everything he
wanted, and he had the brains to go with it—intelligence, you know,
and everything. And he just let things go. Never took anything
serious. Just went with the wind. . . . He always had a nice answer for
anything. Very pleasing, and you couldn't get mad at him from what I
understand. . . . He always had something to say that would make
you forget everything and smooth things over, you know. He was
very clever at doing that. He always had an answer, a good, reasonable, and sensible answer for anything regardless of what it was. . . .
[He had] all the facilities that's required of him right in his hand,"
Henry concluded, "but [he] just seemed to throw them away!"[8]

NOTES

1. See Edward D. Ives, *Larry Gorman*, esp. pp. 183–185.

2. Supreme Judicial Court Records, Oxford Co., Me., May Term, 1897, vol. 26, no. 481, pp. 297–298.

3. J. A. Polley to Gordon, Mar. 2, 1925, Gordon Manuscripts 928.

4. Emma's age on the marriage record is given as twenty-three, but her death certificate gives her birth date as March 13, 1879.

5. This was Blanche, but so far I have been unable to locate a birth certificate for her. Her death certificate gives the place of birth as West Milan, N.H., and the date as February 29, 1900 (the day is clearly a mistake, since 1900, being a centesimal year, was not a leap year; probably February 28 is meant). The town clerk of Milan can find no birth record for her, nor can the Bureau of Vital Statistics for New Hampshire. I also checked the Division of Vital Statistics for the Commonwealth of Massachusetts, since evidently Joe and Emma spent some time there, without success. Considering that Emma never recorded the birth of her son (it was reported some months afterward by the Rumford assessor), it is possible she never reported this birth either; but the date (except for the day) and place are almost certainly essentially correct.

6. Supreme Judicial Court Records, Oxford Co., Me., February Term, 1901, Writ No. 301. For the dismissal, see October Term, 1902, Case No. 133, vol. 29, p. 432.

7. The exception is Angus Enman. See p. 320.

8. At this point I would like to thank Clifford Scott for introducing me to his father.

4

Maker, Minstrel, Magus

Ace woodsman, crack river-driver, and all-round good fellow: Joe Scott was all these things to the men he worked with, but his main claim to our attention is still his songs and songmaking. "A man would get through singing a song, and he'd say 'That was a Joe Scott song,' or 'Joe Scott made that one up,' or something like that," said Irving Ashford, who as a young man had worked in the woods in Charlotte County, New Brunswick, "and that really added something to be able to say that."

Many people remember no more about him than that he was the "man who made up 'The Plain Golden Band,' wasn't he?" James Scott of Mexico, Maine, himself a maker of songs and verses, had been on the river with Joe, and I asked him what he could tell me about his songs. *"Well, he made such good poems that you couldn't say much about them," he told me, "because he was a great poet. If that man had been living today he could have got all kinds of money!" Among woodsmen his fame was not as pervasive as Larry Gorman's, partly because Joe was never as good a press agent as Larry, but he was the only other woods poet in the Northeast who could be said to have that same sort of industry-wide renown.[1]

When did he begin writing songs? We don't know that, nor is it likely that we ever will. He came from a family that loved music, and we know that his younger college-educated brother Wallace had published poetry in the local paper as early as 1889. The first song for which I have anything like a trustworthy date is "Howard Carey," which must have appeared shortly after Howard's death in May, 1897, but it is very hard to believe that anything that skillfully done

53

represents Joe's first effort. It is much more likely that he had fooled around with making songs for many years, but right around 1897 he really began turning them out on a belt, taking it very seriously, and even going into it in a business way.

I have heard two explanations for Joe's turning to songmaking. The first and most common is the one we've already met in the foregoing chapter: that it came about as a result of, or a reaction to, his disappointed love affair with Lizzie Morse. I happen to think that this view is essentially correct, but we'll come back to that later on. Right now it is more important to see that it suggests that people saw Joe's songmaking as a change, a fairly sudden change, in his way of life. And that is exactly the same point that is made by the second explanation, given me by Angus Enman of Spring Hill, Prince Edward Island:

*Well, Joe Scott and a fellow I knew was working [together] in the lumberwoods. He was a Dutchman from River Herbert, Nova Scotia. . . . And Joe was a terrible wicked man. And . . . in them times there was no saws much; we done all with axes, see? We chopped those great big mountain spruce with an ax. And there was a head chopper and a second chopper, and Joe was head chopper. He was the man that led the tree. . . . You had to understand leading. If you didn't they'd lodge in a big birch or something. . . . Well, Joe hung this tree up . . . and he got right under it and he defied the Lord to fall it on him. And he went on . . . calling the Maker names. . . . And this man said that the limb broke like *that* [slapping hands] and Joe just got away with his life. He just took his ax and said, "I'm all done in the woods." He never worked another day in the woods, and he went out and started making those songs. And then he'd come in boarding and we all knew him. And he had copies [of his songs with him]. And he made some awful nice songs.

Whenever it was he started writing songs, and whatever series of events it was that got him going, there is doubt at all that he spent many years peddling his songs from camp to camp. *"Joe made his headquarters in Rumford, Rumford Falls," Angus went on to explain, "and he used to come up around the camps, see? There was a great circle of camps up around Bemis." Hall Grant recalled Joe well:

*Yes, he was around here. He traveled around. He was a fellow never stayed in one place too long. . . . He lived around in those camps and he used to sell his songs. [He'd] have them printed up, you know, the verses of them, on little pieces of paper, different ones—twenty-five cents or something like that as I remember. . . . He'd sell them wherever he was, around camps, wherever he was. . . . I don't know that he ever settled anywhere. He was just one of that kind you might call a woods tramp. He'd work a while and he was always selling his songs. He'd come in, and he was well known, and everyone'd get him to sing, and he'd sing a few songs and he'd sell what he could of them. . . . He always had them in his suitcase. He carried them around with him and he'd come into a camp and if he was out of work, wasn't working anywhere, he'd come in. They might be half a dozen camps within two or three miles of each other. . . . He'd come along and stay a night in a camp maybe—something like that—and he'd sing songs for them and sell some of them, and maybe go to work for a while. Possibly he wouldn't; depended on just how he happened to feel about it. As I say, he was just a kind of vagabond.

A peddler of songs, a wandering minstrel in the kingdom of spruce—of all the pictures I have of Joe, this is one that recurs with great regularity. *"He was known amongst lumberjacks as 'the celebrated Joe Scott!' " said Thomas Hoy of Gorham, New Hampshire, who went on to tell me of his first encounter with him:

*The first place that I met Joe Scott was around 1900 or 1901 (somewhere around there) in a lumbercamp. That was up the Ammonoosuc River on the Kilkenny Railroad up in Kilkenny [*New Hampshire*]. He came in there one afternoon. I was a cookee then; I was only a kid then. And he was selling these songs that he composed. . . . And he sold quite a lot of songs there. He landed there with a little grip or briefcase. . . . And I asked the cook who that fella was. When I see he had a grip [*I knew that*] he weren't no lumberjack!

He says, "That's Joe Scott. Did you ever hear of him?"

I says, "No," so he went on and told me about him.

He says, "He's a composer of songs. He's composed a lot and he's up here probably to sell some."

He stayed there that night and left the next day. . . . Any of the songs they asked him to sing he'd sing them for them. He was a good singer. He'd sing any song that he sold there. And then they'd ask him about other songs [*and*] he'd sing. He knew an awful lot of songs.

He used to get twenty-five cents apiece for [*his songs*]. They were printed on a little paper, just like a little circular you get, you know. He had them typed somewhere. . . . He had a little grip or a kind of a briefcase, a little round grip. . . . And I remember him opening it up and taking out these papers, songs, and passing them around and showing them to them.

Hoy marked him as not being a lumberjack because he carried a grip, though he was dressed like a woodsman; but C. S. Locke remembered Joe being dressed in town clothes when he saw him. That was in the winter of 1898–99. Locke had just come to Maine from the Island and was working for Bean and Whitcomb up in the Cupsuptic country:

*He came into the camp one Sunday afternoon and the only time I was talking to him was about the song ["*Benjamin Deane*"], but he stayed that afternoon, perhaps that Sunday night. Then he went somewhere else. . . . I remember he had on a pair of black pants and a kind of lighter coat—not the same color; but he was dressed up, you know, where the rest of us wasn't. . . . I guess I bought the song from him, and then he sang it. I think he sold them for fifty cents. . . . He sang the whole thing [*for me*], thirty-six double verses, and then I learnt it. It didn't take me long.

Another boy from the Island, John Dignan of Howlan, remembers him coming into Tom Tracy's camp up around Wentworth Location in the winter (he believes) of 1901–2:

*I don't know whether he was there only a short time or for any extended time. I don't think he was. It's quite probable that he had his dinner there (I think it was dinnertime), but I just remember him as he was . . . out at the side of the road going out on that side of the camp. At that time he wasn't mixing up with anyone, apart from the contact I had with him. I remember he had quite a pile of those songs, you know. . . . And he wore a kind of navy overcoat. They were quite common at the time; not very long, just about to the knees. . . . He was selling these songs, I believe ten cents apiece. I think I got possibly three or four of them.

An important point here is that along the Androscoggin Joe was unique. No one else was peddling songs from camp to camp, and no one else seems to have had any reputation as a songmaker. Visitors were not uncommon in these lumbercamps: hunters, tradesmen, and peddlers of various sorts used to stop in from time to time, but there was only one song-peddler and his name was Joe Scott. Nor do people seem to have looked on him as particularly odd; in spite of his singularity, he was obviously well thought of. Remember George Storer's emphatic denial that Joe was looked on as some kind of a nut or a joke for his songwriting and song peddling, and he had known him over a ten-year period. His earliest recollections of Joe come from just after the turn of the century:

>*He come up to Bemis there, and he had a lot of them songs with him. . . . And he was around selling them and 'course he'd stop at the hotel there, and I was boarding there myself, see? So in what we used to call the barroom (it sold no liquor or anything, but it was the place where the men used to come and sit down after supper) and I got acquainted with Joe there first. And from that time on whenever we'd have a meeting we'd always have a conversation about something. . . .

>I knew him when he used to have his songs, when he first came out with them. He had them on a—well, it was a sheet that long [*gesture: three feet*] and he had songs on them, you know, and then if you wanted one song or two songs he'd cut them out for you, see, off'n this long [*sheet*]. . . . He had a long sheet and there was a number of songs on this long sheet, printed up. . . . As I remember it he'd get ten cents apiece for them. . . .

>He would travel in the woods and around. Sometimes he used to work in the woods, you know, and he'd have them in the woods with him. He never was a man that stayed a great while anywhere. He'd just work a while and then he'd move.

I have never seen one of the long sheets George Storer described, but I have seen nine of the original printed songs. Each was neatly printed on a slip about 3½ inches wide and as long as the song required. At the end: "BY JOE SCOTT" and, on a few, "Price 10 cts." The type and format are the same for each of them, which means they easily could have been printed at one time and cut from a long sheet; or it might only mean they had been set by the same printer. Arthur Carr of Boiestown, New Brunswick, remembered Joe having his songs made up into a little book "about the size of a time book" that he would sell for fifty cents, and one or two people have told me that Joe wrote a song off for them longhand. Everyone agrees that there was no printed music but that Joe would sing the song for you to give you the tune once you had purchased the words.

*"Boy, could Joe sing!" said Clyde Dickinson, and on that matter there seems to be almost complete unanimity. "Yes, he was a lovely singer," said John Ross of Rangeley. "He could get it up there so nice and high!" Leland Nile was even more emphatic. *"I've heard Joe Scott sing, for God's sake," he said enthusiastically. "And he could sing, too! And he didn't have to—hell, he'd sit right down! He

wouldn't bother with anything, you know. Sit right down and sing them right off!" Some people say that he had to be coaxed a lot, others claim that all you had to do was ask and he'd sing; but there is no doubt in anyone's mind that he was a fine singer. "Uncle Joe" Patterson told William Doerflinger the following anecdote, which, for all its oddness, makes the point well:

We was in Summit Landing, Maine. The roads was snowed in and the agent at Bemis, three miles down the line, called up for company. He happened to say to the foreman, "I heard some of your boys singin' one day over the phone. Sounded all right!"

"Well," says the foreman, "I'll get ye some singin'," and he called Joe and Joe sang "The Plain Golden Band" over the telephone. Agent said it sounded just like a talkin' machine.[2]

George Storer also recalled that if things ever *"got a mite dull," they could count on Joe to sing for them. Angus Enman claims that Joe not only sang, but used to act his songs out as well:

*He'd act them. . . . And when he'd come in to sing those songs, he'd come in there and we'd be done [*with our work*] and we'd come home and have supper, and then he'd get up and sing them and act them. . . . He'd get up and he'd—well now, this "Norway Bum" I was telling you about there, he'd sing and act it, and it was great. It started,

> Do you think by my dress I would rob a hen's nest
> Or do anything that was wrong—

Well, Joe would act that.

> If you think that I would I will tell you the truth
> You'll strike the nail fair on the head.
> In this dirty pack—

and he'd let on, you know that he had the pack—

> —I just took from my back
> Another one far worse than this.

He'd act it right off. . . . Joe could act and sing it.

It has been difficult to find people who ever saw Joe make up a song or were around when he made one. We get occasional vague reports like "My father remembers that if anything happened during the day Joe would sit down that night and make a song about it," or, as one woman had it, "He'd start singing a song about it, just making it up as he went along." But I have never talked to anyone who could say that he actually watched Joe make up a specific song. The nearest I came to it was with ninety-year-old Tom Pollock. *"Yes," he said, "he'd just sit with a tablet up on his lap, feet hanging down on the bunk, and holding a bottle of ink and a pen. And he'd sit there and write that song off and . . . we'd ask him when he was going to sing it for us. 'I'll tell you when I get the air, the right air!' And he'd be humming that over in the woods and he'd get the right air and he'd tell us tonight he'd sing the song. And he'd just walk the camp floor and sing. Oh, he'd sing! Raise it just as high!" I asked Pollock for the names of specific songs he had seen Joe write, but he could not recall.

Nor does anyone ever seem to have talked to him much about his songwriting, except for Wesley Smith, who one time asked him if he didn't find it hard to compose a song. Scott's answer, said Wesley, was, *"There's days I couldn't compose a song probably no more than you could. But now if I have all the material there's days that I can compose a song as fast as I can write." And that's about all we have by way of eyewitness reports of Joe's songmaking. Careful analysis of all his extant songs will tell us a great deal more about his methods than these few accounts do, but that will be material for later chapters.

Did Joe ever try to do any more than peddle his songs among his fellow woodsmen? Did he ever try anything more "ambitious"? Several people have told me I should look in the old *Rumford Falls Times*, because "all Joe's songs were published there." My careful check has revealed only two, "Guy Reed" and "The Norway Bum," both published in the spring of 1901 within two weeks of each other and both published over the byline "By Joe Scott." Nor have I found his songs in other newspapers until well after his death. Yet there are those reports like the following given me by Tom Pollock: *"He'd just keep making pieces and writing [them] down and going on that way. And when he got the song all composed he would hum over it, you know, an air for it. And he sent it to this here [paper?] once— where they put the poets . . . and he'd get it in print." Unfortunately, Pollock could not recall where Joe sent his songs. Perhaps future search will turn them up.

It has been nothing uncommon for people to tell me that Joe could have been a rich man, if he'd wanted to be. *"They offered him all kinds of money, you know, for a poet, people and companies [did],"

Tom Pollock told me. "Offered him all kinds of money, but he wouldn't take it." There is also the story of Joe being cheated out of a fortune. George Storer told it this way:

*I know he wrote one, and I forget what he called it. Anyway it was a nice song. And . . . he told me that he was working up there on the drive, and he lost the whole day to go down to Bangor. He [*had*] got somebody to kind of promote it for him and everything, and he went down there to hear it after they got the music and all wrote for it. Well then, he said they claimed it didn't take. (And that wasn't really a come-all-ye song, one of those old woods songs. It was a nice song; it had verses and two choruses to it. That's what they used to have years ago and I guess they do yet.) And he claimd they stole that song from him. I remember he used to sing it for me there: "'Twas where the weeping willows wave" and all on like that, you know. It was a nice song. He thought it was going to be a hit. "And I guess it was," he said, "but really they just stole it from me."

It was about 1910 when Joe told Storer of this bit of double-dealing. A few years earlier he had told Joe Wilbur a similar story:

*Well, he was in the woods, way in the woods somewhere alone and he made up this song about the autumn leaf, and when he got out he went down to Rumford to get it [*copyrighted*]. But he wrote in for it, and when he got back there it was [*being sung*] in the theater. 'Course they'd put a few different words into it so that he couldn't do any damage, so he lost. I said, "What'd you do, Joe, when that come on?" He said, "I done just the same as anybody would. I got up and walked out!"

We don't know just when Joe started writing songs, and we don't know how long he kept it up. Interesting as it might be to be able to set limits and say, "Here is Scott's earliest song, here his last," it is much more important to determine where the focus was. And there is no question that his period of greatest activity and success as a songwriter was in the five years from 1897 through 1901, with 1897 and 1898 being the most notable. The reputation that he made in those years stayed with him all his life, and had Joe Scott died in 1901 we would still have all his best-known songs.

However important Joe's songmaking was to him throughout the rest of his life—and we can be sure that it was always of some importance—after the turn of the century we can sense a new emphasis developing. It was not something brand new; rather, it was an intensification of a long-standing interest, just as I am sure his songmaking had been. As we go along, stories of Joe Scott the songmaker are rivaled and even overshadowed by stories of Joe Scott the magician, the clairvoyant, the worker of wonders. Reports run the gamut from card tricks to a pact with the Devil, and the reactions from amusement to terror. A couple of people put the whole thing rather simply: "Joe Scott could do anything, anything at all!" Eighty-year-old Fred MacLean's story is a good place to begin.

Fred, who lived in Magundy, New Brunswick, had worked with Joe up around Ashland, Maine, for part of one summer. They had both hired on with a man who had taken a contract to cut pulp on a burned-over section. He remembered that Joe's job was to catch the four-foot bolts of wood as they came from a portable circular saw and toss them over onto a pile. It was hot, hard work, and no man could stand it for more than a couple of hours straight, but Joe was up to it. MacLean had heard of Joe as being the author of "The Plain Golden Band"; he'd heard the whole story, too, which means that for him Joe was something of a celebrity. He watched him carefully, and what he saw disturbed him. When he talked with me sixty years later, he was still reluctant to talk about it. *"I wouldn't want to say too much about him . . . ," he said. "It doesn't do for one to tell everything he knows about a man. . . . He was good company all right, but he had some ways about him that, you know, was different." And that was as far as he would go for a while. Little by little, though, the story came out.

The picture he gave was of the quiet, reserved Joe Scott: *"He was kind of a quiet man, you know. He'd get up into his berth in the corner and read. . . . After his work, why, he'd come in. He was sort of a quiet man, you know. He'd come in and wash up and if supper wasn't ready he'd maybe lay down in his berth . . . till they called him to supper. But he wouldn't go out around the same as some of the men would together. . . . He was a little mite distant that way, you know."

His distance inspired talk, and MacLean "heard a lot of things" about what Joe could do. What, for instance, I asked. "Well, . . ." I didn't want to put words in his mouth, but I took a chance: "The black art?" He sort of backed off on that. *"Well, I wouldn't want to say anything about that. Wouldn't say a word at all. But he had the appearance, that's all. Did you hear that?" he asked me. I said I had. He shook his head, dubiously. *"Like to tell you something," he said, "but I guess I better not." Then he broke down:

*Well, he was quite a man to read the books, as you say. . . . Yeah, what you said—that he—what was it, the black art? Well, he had the books in there. . . .

I was out one Sunday away from the tent and I was a little late coming in. Well, the cook had called them all in to dinner, but [Joe] he had to finish his little story out of whatever he was reading, and he just took the book and laid it down flat on the floor of his berth. "Well," I says (I had heard something about him and that by then, you know), I says, "I'm just going to have a look at that book. He couldn't see me; he's gone in." So gee, where he had it open, why here was a lot of black cats, pictures of them, you know [with a] lot of reading around them. Then I heard that he read them a lot. He had them on his mind, reading them all the time.

So if you ever hear of him belonging to a—what is it? The black art or something? Well, they said that he had studied them long enough that there were things he could do. . . . They said he read this book so much that he could do almost anything.

I tried very hard to find out specific things that Joe could do, but either MacLean's reticence simply would not let him divulge such dark matter or (and this is perfectly possible) Joe did not actually attempt anything that summer. But MacLean never looked at Joe's books again. *"He had to give himself away, didn't he, for a black art book? Give his soul away?" he asked me. I said I did not know; I had heard something like that, but maybe Joe just bought them. This suggestion did not impress him at all.

*Well, I guess that's the way they all had to do—them that read them books, you see. He just give himself to the Devil, you might say. . . . Oh, I don't know for sure [that he did], you know. But this book, when I see'd that, I knowed that it was different from religion, our religion, that's all. . . . Oh, the whole crew there must have knew it if they thought about it. . . . Some of them would never interfere with [his] things, never go near him at all, because he was kind of a quiet man, you know. He'd get up into his berth in the corner and read.

There is no way of telling what sort of book Joe actually was reading except that it had some black cats in it. But we do know that MacLean did not like what he saw, that he felt that it was "different from religion," and that he was reasonably sure Joe Scott had had to sell his soul to the Devil to get it. Then too, he had "heard things" before he ever peeked at Joe's book, and he probably knew or had heard of the "black book," for legends of the existence and power of such books are fairly common in the Northeast. Whatever MacLean saw, he knew what he thought it was, and, fascinated as he was, he wanted no part of it. Several other people have told me that Joe was supposed to have been possessed by the Devil; even members of his family had heard about his being a "wicked" or "evil" man who had been involved in "unholy practices."

Now, of course, the term "wicked" is often used to describe a man who swears a great deal, especially one who defies God to His face, daring him to "come down here and do this job one bit better than I just done it." Swearing is all very well, but a wicked man is one who just goes a bit too far and says things that no man ought to say (*"It just don't make sense!"*). Joe was such a man, all right. In general conversation he was usually soft-spoken, but at work he could be a wicked swearer. Remember that Angus Enman was told that Joe's wicked swearing almost cost him his life. Wesley Smith, who lived a few miles down the road from Angus, was working on a yard with Joe one time and wondered how any man could swear like that and still put such nice phrases in his songs. Like Fred MacLean, Wesley had "heard things about Joe," but unlike MacLean he had seen the magus in action: one night Joe made a table tip. *"He got a bunch of us men to put our hands on the table and he said, 'Now wish for this table to come up.' And it wouldn't, and he said, 'Those that are agin it, please drop out.' So there was two or three dropped out. And the table, we was all sure the table come right up off the floor!" Wesley laughed as he told me some fifty years after the event. "I didn't care if the old table went through the roof of the camp, that old card table," but he reported that the others were *"the scaredest-looking bunch of men you ever saw! They just sit down. There wasn't a word for I guess half an hour. They thought it wasn't . . . " —Wesley searched for the right word— "wasn't real at all, that it wasn't—it was something out of. . . ." Wesley gave it up: "*You* know!"

"Did he do anything else like this?" I asked him.

*"Oh, he give us cards, you know, a whole bunch around and he give us [*each*] a playing card. [*Then he*] went outside [*and*] told us to pick a card. And when he come in, 'What card did you pick?' [*And when we told him*] he went over to the man and said, 'Give me that

63

card.' So that was the right card, the card we picked. So we thought that he was a little—that there was something about him that wasn't [didn't] belong to this world."

This was about 1911 up around Oquossoc. Wesley was about twenty at the time, and the celebrated Joe Scott was better than twice his age. He remembers Joe as a perfectly pleasant and agreeable person, but *"he was a hard man to get acquainted with—very quiet and reserved." But his interest in magic made everyone uneasy. *"He studied the black art, these books, you know. . . . All that winter he'd just sit in his bunk, you know, after supper, and he'd be reading them books, studying them. He seemed to—he wanted to know all there was, I guess." Did any of the men ever say anything about his being possessed by the Devil, I asked. *"Well, that's what they thought," said Wesley definitely. "I don't know as they said it, but that night [he raised the table] you could tell they didn't want any more of that!"

Tom Pollock had seen Joe "walk a table," even to the detail about his blaming failure on the presence of someone who "hasn't got belief," but he felt it was just a trick. Fred Campbell not only insisted it was just a trick, he claimed to be an accomplice. *"Now, they was another fella there," he said. "His name was George Anderson. . . . And [Joe] he wanted us, George and I, to help him tip this table. And we'd put our hands on it [and] bear down. Well, he made the legs narrow so you didn't have to bear down very hard to tip the other ones [i.e., legs]. Then we'd release it a little and his end would tip up. So that's the way he done it. You didn't have to do much, you know, [just] bear down very easy so they wouldn't notice you."

Campbell was not in the least awed by Joe's "supernatural" powers, simply seeing the table-tipping as another of his tricks, one more way of entertaining the boys in camp. Yet even he had his story to tell:

*We were working on the drive, and I don't know just what happened, but anyway we were laid back there three or four days. And you know how a bunch of men together they'll play jokes on one another and have a lot of fun? Well, Joe wanted to tell somebody's fortune, so nobody wanted their fortune told. I said, "All right, you can tell mine."

So he set me up on something and he got hold of my head. He felt it all over and he said, "This is the Bump of Finatamus," and he said, "You're going to be married very young."

Well, I thought he was just talking, you know. But I *was* married young. Now then, that's followed me all through my life; a lot of that Joe Scott's fortune has followed me all through my life. A lot of it come true. . . . Well, he told me, he said, "You're going to be a farmer, and," he said, "you're going to be—oh, fairly well-to-do—you know, comfortable. And," he said, "pretty religious by times." That all came true.

Parallel to reports of his ability to read the future are reports of his clairvoyance. Harold Rush worked with Joe at what was then known as the Bank Farm, a big sawmill operation not far from Monticello, and he recalled this aspect of Joe's character especially well. Joe worked in the boiler room as a fireman one summer, Rush said. *"and one of the millwrights lost his wrench. Joe was firing there and this fella come up looking. . . . And Joe says, 'What are you looking for?' And he says, 'I'm looking for my wrench. I lost a wrench.' And Joe says, 'Right down there on a beam.' [*The millwright*] he went [*back*] down and found his wrench!" Rush emphasized that as far as he knew, Joe had never been over in that part of the mill at all and in any case could not have actually *seen* the wrench where he said it was. *"There was a fella come in there," said Rush, recalling another time, "and he had twenty-six cents in his pocket. . . . That's what he had and Joe told him just what he had. . . . Never seen him before in the world!" I wondered whether Rush had ever seen Joe do any table-tipping. *"Well, I don't know about the table-tipping," he said, "but I'm going to show you something. Now there's a hat and here's another hat and there's another hat," he said, pointing to three hypothetical hats on the table. "Well, Joe peeled a potato, and he had a stick. . . . And we put the potato under one of them hats. He was blindfolded; he wanted to be blindfolded, see? . . . And now he said, 'I'll tell you which one of them hats that potato's under.' And he just tapped on that table [*with the stick*] and picked out the hat." It may have been a simple "trick," but it left everyone with the impression that there was something uncanny about Joe.

Mixed in with reports of Joe's fortune-telling and clairvoyance come reports (as we might expect) of his attempts at hypnotism. He'd go through the standard steps of getting someone to lie down on the deacon seat, cautioning everyone to be quiet, and then starting the "You are getting verrr-ry slleee-py" routine, but so far I have never heard of his actually hypnotizing anyone. On the other hand, he seems to have been quite successful in relieving pain, although I have only a few examples of his performing this service. Fred MacLean did not think there was anything particularly wonderful about it; "lots of people can do that," he said. But here is his story:

*We was staying in tents, you see, and the cook had his little boy with him, and along in the middle of the night he took the toothache. And his father brought him into our tent where we was all sleeping, you know. Asked him [i.e., Joe] if he could stop the toothache, and he says, "Well, I'll try it, I guess." We kind of riz up, some of us, I suppose (I know I remember it). He just run his finger up in around the little boy's mouth until he touched that tooth. . . . And the little boy went back and went to sleep, went back to his own tent and went right off to sleep! So he could do that. . . . Boy, he was a great thing in there for that little fella. He had a toothache bad; he had quite a time. It was a long ways out to the settlement, you know, [if we'd had] to take him out that night.

According to MacLean, Joe performed the same service for others that summer. And Harold Rush has reason to remember Joe's skill at relieving pain, too:

*I went in there one time, and I got up in the morning and I was sick. I had a kink in my neck. Oh boys, I couldn't move my head! Well, I went in there and Joe was firing there in the boiler room. I went in and he says, "What's the matter with you?" "Well," I says, "I got a kink in my neck." He dropped his shovel and he started rubbing my neck, just like that, you know [demonstrating]. And do you know, I went out and helped a fella put on a load of boards!

Neither Rush nor MacLean makes any point of Joe's gift being supernatural or, for that matter, of its being anything more than something he had learned how to do. Yet obviously Rush thought the cure just short of miraculous. Notice also in Fred MacLean's testimony that the cook brought his son to Joe not knowing whether Joe could cure toothache or not; evidently Joe's general reputation in camp made him appear to be a likely person to turn to in such an extremity. Without wishing to strain too hard to make a point, I find it interesting that the others in the tent "riz up" as if in anticipation of seeing something extraordinary happen. A man who can cure pain with a touch is no ordinary man, and if that same man also reads strange books, can "see ahead" (to use MacLean's phrase for it), and can find lost objects, it is no wonder he was held in some awe.

Joe worked at his magic. It is very likely that the "books" he was seen reading were simply home-instruction manuals of magic tricks and the like, and certainly some of the illustrations in these manuals could panic anyone who had "heard things" and was therefore ready to allow himself to be suggested. A man who sits up in his bunk and reads a lot of the time *is* a bit unusual in a lumbercamp under any circumstances, and if that same man can do even such simple magic as card tricks and making handkerchiefs change color (and Joe could do both), "unusual" would be the mildest term used to describe him.

If these things could be dismissed, by the knowing, as tricks that anybody can do, there were other effects that took more time and practice. For example, Joe had learned how to throw his voice, and although ventriloquism was recognized as a trick, it was acknowledged to be a tough one, and he could and did use it to mystify. *"He'd take a tin dipper," said Harold Rush, "and just stick it right up on the wall and then go back from there and talk from that dipper! I've seen him do that." The best picture of the showman at work was given me by Joe Wilbur, who had hired Joe to work for him in the winter of 1907 or 1908. At the time the incident took place, Joe was working as a yard man, Wilbur said:

*They had a box, the clerk did, nailed up on a tree. [*It was just*] a small box, and they kept their books and stuff in there so they wouldn't get wet, you know. The yarding team had got unloaded and gone back, and it was kind of a cold day, and they were standing around throwing cant dogs [*at a target*], one thing and another. Someone says, "I'd like to know where that team's at, so we can have something to do."

Joe says, "Let's find out." . . . And Joe walked up to this box and rapped on it, you know, and he could talk so's the sound was right in his throat (you know, this throwing your voice). And he called up just as if he was calling up on a telephone, and he asked where the four-horse team was. Then he answers himself, "Just around the bend."

'Course they all listened, you know? All at once they looked down there and see'd the horses coming! And Bernie Steele said, "Well, what do you know about that?"

What are we to make of all this? Was Joe simply a clever backwoods illusionist? That's probably where it all started; Joe, the fellow who was "always full of fun and jokes," learned a few magic tricks. Being quick with his hands, he made a good magician, and before he knew it he had the beginnings of a reputation. No magician is ever unhappy if people believe there really *is* something mysterious about him, and he will often go to some lengths to achieve this kind of notoriety. Joe seems to have done nothing to discourage it, certainly, and if we couple this intentional mystification with Joe's natural reserve when out of the limelight, we get a double reason for mystery.

But having created a mask, did the man himself grow to fit it? Did he come to believe that he really had supernatural power? My hunch is that he did. Many of the practices that Joe was dabbling in— fortune-telling, finding lost objects, and stopping toothache, for example—are traditionally thought of as "gifts," not something one learns except as they are "passed on," say from father to son, especially a seventh son or a "seventh son of a seventh son." Joe may not have been a seventh son, but he was a seventh child, and I think he knew it well. Then too, there was plenty of precedent for him to think about. Both the Saint John valley and the lumberwoods were full of legends of people with power, all the way from bloodstoppers to full-fledged wizards who could shift shape and draw whiskey out of trees.[3] It would be neither surprising nor out of character for Joe to have moved in this direction. *"Sometimes when you'd think about him . . . ," said Mrs. Merrithew of Joe as a young boy, "he was planning to do things maybe that he couldn't ever attain the heights that he wanted to." At the very least, Joe was a deacon-seat mystificator with some interesting second thoughts about himself. At the most, he may have been convinced of his powers and even have reached out his hand to grope for the Prince of Darkness himself. As in all things, the truth probably lies somewhere in between.

If we put it all together—the woodsman, the songmaker, the singer, and the magician—we get a person who would have been notable in anyone's lumbercamp, and being the kind of person he was, Joe was both well known and well thought of. He seems to have been able to turn his hand to a thing and have it go right well for him. Yet by the standards of our society and his, we can't say that he was ever a "success." As Henry Scott said, Joe had *"all the facilities that's required of him right in his hand but just seemed to throw them away!" Why did he never really catch hold? Some people claim he was lazy, but old Herbert Porter demurred. "I can tell you that he was smart of hand, foot, and tongue," he told Josephine McKay, a student of mine. "Yes, that man could do anything. I never saw him do these supernatural things they talk about, but I'll bet he could do them. Folks used to say he was lazy, but that was not so. If a man can do anything, he does not have to stay at one thing. No, a man like Joe didn't have to work too hard."

We know that Joe *could* work hard and work well when he chose to, and no one ever found fault with him as a worker; it is only in his early years back on the farm that we ever heard him described as lazy. Nor will we come any closer to the mark to say it was drink that did him in, although he certainly was a drinker, and the habit got worse and worse in his later years. To blame his unsuccess on alcohol is to call the symptom the disease. The facts seem to be that, like his father, Joe was a dreamer, a maker of plans; but he was restless of mind and body, never being able to settle down long enough to see anything through.

And Joe's restlessness—what was that a symptom of? What pushed, or what pulled him on? The question is important, but the answer lay too deep. It died with Joe, but I think we can be sure of one last thing: Joe would have liked to have the answer, too.

NOTES

1. See Edward D. Ives, *Larry Gorman*, pp. 185–187.
2. Manuscript sent me by Doerflinger, Feb. 27, 1966.
3. For an excellent study of one such wizard, see Roger E. Mitchell, *George Knox*. Mitchell's book is a good introduction to this whole tradition in the Northeast.

5

Farmer and Salesman

It may not be quite fair, and it may even be an example of my inventing evidence where none exists, but I have often wondered why Joe, a dreamer with a loose foot, didn't join the other thousands upon thousands of loose-footed dreamers and head for the Klondike. He was an absolutely free agent in the great gold-rush years of 1897 and 1898, and we know that his younger brother Wallace went there from Montreal in August of 1897 (and Joe must have known it, too). The better I have come to know Joe over the years, the more I wonder that he didn't succumb to the Klondike fever. But that was a big step for any man to take, and just getting together enough money for an outfit could have been a forbidding problem for someone of Joe's station in life. Actually, I have no evidence that he even considered it, though I'm willing to bet he turned it over in his mind a few times. Having raised the question, I now drop it as of no significance, positive or negative. It's just that it's been on the edges of my mind too long not to mention.

Although he moved around a good deal, in and out of the woods and the like, Joe kept Rumford as his base of operations for the first few years after the turn of the century. From here, "the celebrated Joe Scott" took his songs into the woods. Then sometime around 1905 he pulled up stakes and headed back home to Lower Woodstock to try farming again. There are no really hard data to establish just when or why he made this shift, but the circumstantial evidence does show a pattern that makes good sense all around.

First of all, we should remember that Joe had title to a hundred acres of his father's land, and he had probably never entirely dismissed from his mind the possibility of settling down there and farming it. Old John's health was failing him fast, and he was to die March 5, 1905. Joe either went home at that time or (and this is my guess) during the summer before. Both Daisy and David Severy remember that his brother came for him. *"And his brother come up to the boom house to see me, a minister," she said. "We talked a long time. . . . He found out where I was and come up to see me to find out where Joe was. He was hunting Joe up to take him home with him." Her calling him a minister suggests that it was Wallace, but there is very general agreement that having gone to the Klondike in 1897 he never returned to the East again. More than likely it was Hazen, who, while he was not a minister, was an extremely active churchman. At any rate, with Daisy's help, he found Joe. Daisy described the leave-taking to me several times. She was up at the old boom house above the falls:

*He told me, he says, "I'm going home, Daisy, to my people." And he says, "I'm going to write to you if I don't write to anybody else." And he stood with his hand on my head while he was talking to me, and then he kissed me and kissed me, then he shook me and kissed me again. The woman there [*the cook at the boom house*]—'course she didn't know, you know. She thought he was in love with me or something. I says, "No, just friendly."

The fact that the boom house was running makes me think it was summertime, and it seems logical that Hazen had come to tell him how sick his father was and how much he was needed at home. That would make it 1904, but we can't be sure. At any rate, Joe never came back to Rumford. *"I never see Joe after," said Daisy. "He promised to write to me, but he never did."

Almost anyone who knew Joe could have told him that farming was no more his bowl of soup now than it had been twenty years earlier, but that was the way Joe did things. I am sure that as he thought it all over he saw another chance to "start over again," and he returned home full of great plans, resolved to make a go of it. Clyde Dickinson was just a young fellow, but he remembers Joe's return this time even better than he recalled his earlier return in 1900. "This time," he said, "there was no wife and kids and nothing was ever said about any," but it really looked like Joe meant to take hold of things on the farm. He bought a couple of big Clydesdale horses, two-year-olds, and set in to clearing a big patch of ground, probably part of his own hundred acres, which up to then had not been farmed at all. Herbert Porter is pretty sure he remembers Joe building a big chicken-house, too. It sounds absolutely right for Joe.

"Joe never drank much around here," Dickinson recalled. "He was pretty much of a straight citizen, and he really worked hard this time, but he was an awful comical fellow, too. I remember he had a big work frolic once; asked all the neighbors to come help him clear land for a day. Then in the evening he put on a big entertainment for them, with plenty to eat and drink, and he sang and did tricks. A good fellow. He never had to be coaxed to get him to sing," he added, "but then none of the Scotts did." Others remember Joe as being full of fun. One August morning I sat in the parlor of the old Scott place and talked to the present owners, Mr. and Mrs. Ansel Libby of Framingham, Massachusetts. Mrs. Libby is the former Minnie Scott, one of Ensley's daughters, and she remembered Joe well. "He was always full of fun," she told me. "He could play any kind of musical instrument, including the guitar. And he was a wonderful singer, too." She pointed over to the organ. "I've seen him play that very organ," she said, "and if someone would hold a mouth organ for him he'd play that at the same time." She remembered, too, as did others, that he could do queer things like extend his hands over a table or a chair and make it move all around the room. Recrossing the border eastward again hadn't changed Joe much.

Hallowe'en night, a bunch of neighborhood boys went up to the Scott place and took Joe's plow. Clyde Dickinson, one of the pranksters, recalls that they managed to get the plow up in a tree and hung it from a branch so that it dangled right over the road high enough that no one would hit it, yet low enough that everyone would see it as they went by. A few days later he and a couple of the other boys happened to meet Joe in Meductic. "Boys," Joe said, "I know who did that, and it's a pretty good trick. I don't mind a bit, but the only trouble is I can't get it down. Now if you'll all come up and help me get it down, I'll see that we have a little party afterwards." Dickinson said that Joe was as good as his word. They all went up and helped him get the plow down, after which Joe treated them and put on a show for them.

We don't know how long Joe stayed on the farm this time. Estimates vary, but the best guess is that he lasted no more than a year or two. He had cleared a big patch of new ground and built himself a big hen-house. He even bought a big black dog that followed him every place he went. Everything looked fine, but the old problem was still there: the fire in Joe's heels may have smoldered, but it never went out. It was inevitable that he would move on, and when Mary Hayward foreclosed on his defaulted mortgage May 19, 1906, and sold the property to his brother Ensley, Joe was probably well on his way.

Clyde Dickinson did not know why Joe left; all he knows is that one day he just cleared out—sold his two Clydesdales and cleared out. "He was a funny kind of guy," he added. Some years later, about 1910, Joe gave George Storer the following account, which probably refers to his farming:

*He told me how he started farming down in Nova Scotia [*later Storer changed this to New Brunswick*] somewhere. He built a little shack there and he started to plant his garden and everything and—'course I knew that Joe never could stay at anything like that, you know. It was too tame for him. He told me, he says, "I couldn't make nothing of it. It took my vegetables and my products too long to grow. . . . Yeah, couldn't make nothing out of that," he said. So he just closed up his place and everything and started off.

Then we have the account that his nephew Angus Scott had heard in the family. He himself could not remember Joe, but he had heard of him all his life. According to Angus, Joe got the idea that people were turning against him, that they thought he was "different" because he wrote poetry and songs. It got worse; then one day when he came in from the fields he called the big black dog and it didn't come. That evening when the dog still had not come back, Joe was angry. "Well, damn you," he said, "now you've turned against me, too!" And he walked off, never to return to Woodstock again. Always after that, Angus told me, that piece of land he had cleared but never farmed was known as "Joe's Fallow."

That may have been Joe's last trip "home," but it was not the last time he was seen in the Saint John valley. Again, the timetable is unclear, but sometime within the next few years Joe Scott was peddling sewing machines all through the valley from Woodstock north. Possibly he went right to this new venture from the farm, perhaps a winter or more intervened; there's no way of telling for certain now. But his territory covered not only the upper Saint John valley, but the Tobique as well. Ernest Burgoyne, Sr., of Plaster Rock remembers seeing Joe on his rounds with a big pedal-operated sewing machine tied on the back of his wagon:

*Well, what I remember of him he used to drink pretty heavy. . . . I was just a young fella coming up from away down Sisson Ridge for the mail, and I was coming up by . . . this big hill down there. . . . He was off in the ditch there on an awful hot day, pretty well canned, you know. And the horse was feeding. I stopped to watch. . . . Couldn't think what was wrong. And the horse would feed around and never upset that sewing machine, and Joe lay right there, and I must have watched a good half-hour. And then I come on home and he was still there. The horse wouldn't leave him and wouldn't cramp the wagon. He was feeding around and eating grass, him laying there right in the ditch. But that horse would never have upset that wagon. He would just have to have canted the wagon that much, and it would have fallen on the ground. . . . The horse knew just as much as Joe did.

Burgoyne seems to have been more interested in the horse than he was in Joe himself, but evidently the two of them made a notable pair. He recalled seeing them again one day in Plaster Rock:

*Now another time we was in Plaster Rock . . . and he drove down on the railroad track, Scott did, and just as he got right on the railroad track . . . the old horse just stopped as quick as that. And he teamed him and coaxed him and everything. No sir, that horse wouldn't budge. And finally he said wouldn't the train be along pretty soon? And this old Robinson, Ben Robinson his name was, he said, "Yes, it is, and you better get that horse off the track."
"Well," he said, "I can't get him to move." And he jumped out and tried to back him up, and he wouldn't back up one step. "Well, what am I going to do with that horse?" he said.
Ben said, "I'll fetch him out of that!" And he thought he was a great horseman, and he couldn't get that horse [going. He] unhooked him and he wouldn't take a step ahead or a step back, and he'd fight. He kicked. And everybody was watching him, you know, and wondering what could be wrong with that horse. Ben said, "If I could take him up to the barn a few minutes, when I'd bring him back you could hook him on and he'd go!"
"Oh, I don't know," [said Joe]. "Maybe you could, but I doubt it." And all at once he just said something to that horse, and that horse came right around and backed right up into the shafts himself. And he hooked him all up and jumped in. "Well, good day, boys. Git up!" And away went the horse and Scott.

What did he say to that horse, Burgoyne wondered. At any rate, it appeared to him that the whole incident was an elaborate joke on Ben Robinson.[1]

Joe peddled his sewing machines house to house through the valley, and wherever he stopped he seems to have spent as much time talking and singing as he did selling his product. He stopped at the Burgoyne place, and while he did not sell them a machine, he did spend a pleasant afternoon. Was Joe a good singer, I asked. *"I thought it was lovely at the time," said Mr. Burgoyne, "and it's quite a while to remember, but I know the old folks, mother and father, thought he was a lovely singer. And he was a nice man, you know." Did he ever speak of having a family? *"Never heard of him having a family nor a wife nor anything," he answered. "He just seemed to be by himself all the time. . . . He didn't seem to make up with anybody."

"He didn't seem to make up with anybody." That's Joe all right: pleasant with everyone, close to no one. But now the reports of his drinking become more common. Gib Giberson's boardinghouse in Bath was a great hangout for lumbermen and others passing through town, and Charles Bohan remembered seeing Joe there and hearing him sing "The Plain Golden Band." *"I think he was about half cut when he sang the song," Bohan said. "He was quite a boozer, this Joe Scott." Bohan thought Scott was selling parlor organs as well as sewing machines, but he was not absolutely sure. Fred Anderson grew up in the Scottish settlement of East Glassville, and one winter Joe drove up in a horse and sleigh. "He was selling sewing machines," Anderson said, "but he didn't sell one to us, I know. He stayed a while, though; had a few drinks, sang a song or two, and went on his way." Old Herbert Porter laughed about Joe's salesmanship. "I don't know how much he actually ever did sell," he said, "but it wouldn't make much difference to him. Everything always went well for Joe. He didn't seem to worry or care very much about these things."

Fred Campbell, who had worked with Joe over along the Androscoggin, had given up the woods and returned to his home in Arthurette. He had married and settled into being a prosperous farmer. One afternoon he was taking an after-dinner nap on the kitchen couch when someone came in and shook him by the arm. Fred didn't know who it might be; he didn't even look up, just yelled, "Get out of here!" With that, whoever it was yelled, "I'm right to your ass, John Ross!" and rolled him right off onto the floor. *"It was Joe Scott," said Campbell. "He'd come in, you know. My mother was living then and my wife, and they didn't know him then, but I suppose he come in and asked for me, and they told him where I was, and he come right in and pulled me off the couch!" Joe stopped with the Campbells for about five days. Fred's father loved to hear Joe sing and would often ask him to. "I don't know," said Fred, "but I'm pretty sure he had copies of his songs with him for sale then, too." It was a pleasant visit, but it was the last Campbell ever saw of Joe. *"He was a sewing machine agent," he said, "and he must have done that for a couple of years. . . . He stayed in Perth. He boarded at my brother-in-law's; he kept a hotel in Perth, William Johnson."

Joe was known around Johnville, too. Some people say he sold sewing machines, others say organs; Eddie McSheffrey remembers it was pianos and organs. Still others don't recall about Joe's selling anything; he just came home with Jack McGinley sometimes. Jack's daughter Alice remembers that there was a byword around the settlement: "Joe Scott makes the songs, but Jack McGinley sings them!" Yet evidently Joe did some singing there himself, because her uncle remembers hearing Joe sing "The Plain Golden Band" in Tara Hall (the big social hall on the church grounds), he believes as late as 1911 or 1912. However, my guess is that Joe's great business venture was concluded by about 1907.

Once again Joe went back to the woods of western Maine, but he didn't go back to Rumford. He set up his base of operations in Rangeley, about fifty miles over the mountains to the north. He may have passed through Rumford and may even have worked there from time to time (though I doubt it), but he never "lived" there again. Nor, as far as I can tell, did he ever go back to Lower Woodstock, although he was often within a few miles of it when he'd find himself in Houlton or when he'd go up to Johnville with Jack McGinley. But Rangeley became his official "place of residence," and any of several woodsman's boardinghouses there became the home from which he could rove out—and to which he could return.

NOTES

1. For an interesting parallel, see Roger E. Mitchell, *George Knox*, p. 37.

The Rangeley Years:
All Over the Place

*Rangeley . . . in the spring! [*said Leland Nile*]. Why, it was just [*like*]
looking out into a field of grass. Hardly room to take care of all of them. All
of them woodsmen come out here when they finished in the woods. . . .
Might be three weeks, might be a month or something before the drive
would start. Well, they'd gather out here, and they was bootleggers
enough to keep them going. And believe me, sometimes they'd—yes sir!

Long before there was a Rumford Falls, there was a Rangeley,
famous as a resort town and as a jumping-off place for hunting and
fishing trips into the surrounding wilderness. It was an important
lumbering town, too, but for the woodsmen themselves, as Nile
suggests, it seems to have been looked on as a halfway place.
*"There'd always be that crowd of men would come in the spring,"
said Hall Grant. "They'd get out of the woods say around the middle
of March, and the river-drive would start in the early part of April.
Sometimes fifty or sixty of them here in town. . . ." Rangeley was far
enough up in the woods that during the winter men could come into
town weekends if they wanted to, but in no sense could it be
considered a Bangor or a Rumford Falls, a traditional place for the
lumberjack's great downriver spring bender.
    Oquossoc, down on the other end of the lake, had more to offer in
this line. *"They was a big sporting house built right over on the end
of the lake there," said Fred Campbell. "Sixty girls worked there.
You could pick one up any night." Others agreed that this was the
situation. *"They had a fellow had a boardinghouse down there,"
said Vance Oakes. "They called it 'The Dead Rat,' and I'm telling
you, boy, they'd wake up in the morning without a nickel. . . . The

fellow who run it had a livery thing that he'd go in the woods and get them and bring them out there, and they'd stay until their money was gone, and he'd take them back in the woods again."

Not that the main street of Rangeley didn't have its share of problems; not that there were no bloody noses, chawed ears, hooraws, or blind staggers; it's just that Rangeley was not a noted binge town. A man who was that way inclined would be more likely to head down the lake or—more likely yet—downriver to Berlin or Rumford or even Lewiston for his annual conflagration. But if he elected to stay in Rangeley and still felt he had to slake his thirst, several of the woodsmen's boardinghouses could oblige him.

Zelpha Nile, Leland's wife, gave a description of what it was like in her mother's boardinghouse when the camps let out that is just too good not to be repeated, even if simply for its own sake:

*I know they landed about twenty-nine of them down to the house one night for supper, out of the woods. Mother stood up and cooked that supper—twenty-nine!—for them. . . . Well, they happened to be [some] cooks was amongst the crowd, and they helped her. And she cooked I guess twelve dozens of eggs and a big ham, and I don't know how many potatoes she put onto that table. And she didn't know how to make bread, but she made a good nice lot of hot biscuits. They were biscuits, too, let me tell you. You don't get them now every day.

And they stayed there for over a week. I was just a little tot, and oh, I was scared to death. They was drinking and everything else. Well, she'd have a big pot of cold potatoes, and they'd ask me to get them some cold potatoes and some butter and salt. Well, mother would give me a dish to put the potatoes in, a knife and butter and salt, so I'd take it in to them. I'd always have a dime or a quarter or something like that given to me. "Well now, I want some." I was packing cold potatoes all the time. But they was real good. They was very nice. They just wanted a chance—but I don't know. The cold potatoes and homemade butter I suppose tasted good to them.

John Oakes's place, right across the street from the present-day Rangeley Inn, was one of the best known of these boardinghouses, offering rooms, meals, and a place to sit to itinerant woodsmen. John Oakes himself could usually be seen sunning his bulk on the front piazza. *"They claimed he was working one day," said Vance Oakes, "and all at once he said, 'This is crazy.' They say he never worked afterwards, and his wife took in boarders. He was a great big man, fat and big. . . . That's where Will Lovejoy the blacksmith stayed . . . and all those old bachelors and widowers would stay there between jobs." And among the rest, Joe Scott used to stay there when he came to town.

The late Roy Kaulback of New Germany, Nova Scotia, remembered him there:

I only knew him for about a year [*Mr. Kaulback wrote*]. I think it was in the spring of 1910 [*when*] I came out of the woods and came to Rangeley, Maine. I stopped at a boarding house which was run by a Mr. and Mrs. John Oakes, long since passed away. I was young then, only eighteen years old. When I got settled I got acquainted with Joe Scott, as he also was staying there along with several more. I was very pleased to meet him as I had previously heard so much about him from my older brother Reuben. . . . He was always singing Joe's songs and talking so much about him as he knew him real well. . . . So it seemed just like meeting an old friend to me. I slept with Joe as there were four of us in the room in two beds. Joe and I became very good friends even though he was very much my senior.

There not being very much entertainment around Rangeley as it was just a small village, we used to retire quite early to our room, just the four of us (and we usually would have some "oh be joyful" to take). We would get Joe singing his old songs, which he loved to do, and we loved to hear him.

Others recall Joe staying at Oakes's. "He always boarded with my grandmother, Mrs. John Oakes," wrote Mrs. John Farquhar from Newark, New Jersey. "I knew Joe Scott well and was very fond of him. I recall him quite well, a red-haired man and very kind. My sister and I used to listen to him play the piano and sing his songs, especially 'The Plain Golden Band.'" Ray Oakes, John Oakes's adopted son, remembered that his mother used to tease Joe pretty bad sometimes to get him to sing, "but then if she just left him alone long enough he'd go in the parlor and begin to sing anyhow." As to his drinking, some say he drank very little, others that he drank a lot but no more than most woodsmen; we can at least say that he was not a notable drunk around town. Nor do we hear any reports of his magic, except that both Roy Kaulback and Dennis Taylor remembered him working at throwing his voice. It is Joe Scott the singer and maker of songs they seem to remember around town. Of course they remember that "The Plain Golden Band" was about his own life

79

and that Sam Learned (well known around Rangeley then) was the other man, but no one seems to recall Lizzie Morse.

Joe spent most of his summers around Rangeley working as a hand on one or the other of the big farms on the outskirts of town. There were the Ross farms (Sagely, Abraham, and Leonard Ross each had a farm), Gilman's, and (on the south of town) the Ellis Farm; but while he worked at all of them we hear more about him at the Oakes farm, because that's where young Vance Oakes knew him from about age seven to fourteen (say 1904 to 1911).

*Joe came to the farm sometime in June as a rule [*said Vance*]. The woods work was done, the drive was over, so in the summertime it was haying for those fellows. And they'd go through the farms, the same farms, and most always . . . the same fellows would come back every summer and work getting the hay in, you know, and then getting the oats and grain in after the hay . . . or they might cut the wood for you for winter—and sometimes it would be October before all was over. . . .

The ones that I remember of coming to the farm regularly were Sam Learned and Joe Scott and the Bolgers (they was five brothers; they come from Prince Edward Island) . . . , Jim Spinney, Chickamauga Brown, and Billy Powers. And then there were some other people; Andy Stevens always came.

Joe was a good steady workman. *"He wasn't a fellow that asserted himself much," said Vance. "You know what I mean? He always did his work but you'd never notice that he was a good worker. You didn't think about him being a good worker because he always did it and never said anything about it. While he was working he was quiet or humming to himself. He wasn't loud like Sam Learned or domineering like Spinney." Obviously young Vance liked Joe. *"Oh, you couldn't help it," he said. "You couldn't help it because he was so kind to everybody and especially to the women folks. . . . He was a gentleman, you know. Always was. And he was appreciated. Everybody liked him." Yet even a young boy could notice a certain distance, a certain reserve in this man he liked so much. *"Joe Scott was a person that would never talk about himself. . . . He was one of those people that would never ask you any questions about yourself and never talked about himself. And you'd never ask him either. He was one of those persons that you'd never ask." He expanded on this at one point by saying that it always seemed to him that Joe had *"a little bit of sadness in him."

Vance Oakes had a special reason for remembering Joe, though. The first time I walked into his grocery store back in 1959 it was almost an accident that I mentioned Joe Scott at all, but when I did he stopped what he was doing, and smiled: "Joe Scott used to take me on his knee and tell me bedtime stories," he said nostalgically. Neither he nor I could take the time to talk further then, and as luck would have it I didn't see him again until 1965. Then he expanded on this theme:

*In the evenings he would sit out there 'side of our stable there on a plank or a sawhorse or something, you know, and he'd tell stories to all these people. . . . I was just a young fellow, and he'd be telling these stories. And I'd be out there as a kid will, and he'd say, "Come over here, Vance, and I'll tell you a story." Well, he'd tell me a story about Jack and the Beanstalk—and so nice he'd tell it, you know! . . . And then he'd say, "You better [go in]. Your mother'll want you to go in and go to bed." . . .

And I'm going to tell you he could tell it so that anybody'd be interested to listen to it. I'm telling you he was the greatest at description. You'd set there and listen as if you'd never heard it before. He was an artist! . . . He told all those—"The Three Bears" and all those, you know. He had them right on the tip of his tongue. . . . All my family used to hear them. I was at that age when it really impressed me a lot.

Vance didn't always go right off to bed when Joe sent him away, it appears. Sometimes he'd hang around and listen to some of the stories he'd tell to the men:

*I used to listen to some of them. I'll never forget one time when he was telling about being out west and he got into some kind of a fight. It was in a barroom. . . . I don't remember just what it was, but he got cut with a knife and he said, "I went over to this fountain and the moon was shining on the fountain and I was washing the blood off." He didn't know I was listening, see, . . . but you know how a kid will hang around. And I couldn't help [thinking] how descriptive he was making it, you know, and those fellows was just listening to the whole thing, of course. I didn't hear the first of it nor the last of it except how he'd say "and the moon was playing down on the fountain when I was washing the blood off my arm" and so forth, you know? It impressed me. . . .

Two things about this last bit of testimony are problematic. First, to the best of my knowledge Joe had never been out west, but of course he may have gone on a harvest excursion or something of the sort. Besides, Vance may simply have mistaken that part, since he admits he never heard the whole story. Second, here we have a man who would "never talk about himself" talking about himself. Either this story was exceptional, or we should make a distinction between a man who "talks about himself" and a man who can tell good stories about his adventures. The first man can be a fearful bore; the second need not be. At any rate, Vance is not the first to point out that Joe was a good talker and had a way with words that made others listen.

Joe was a very kind person, Vance recalled, giving the following incident as an illustration:

*I had a magic lantern. . . . Somebody give me a magic lantern, I remember, and we used to have a place that we was going to make into a bathroom that was inside with no lights. . . . And I remember the time that Joe Scott and Andy Stevens come in there and I run it for the first time, and I know that I had all kinds of trouble with it, and he was patting me on the shoulder to make me feel good, Joe was. He'd be that kind, don't you know, that he didn't want to see anybody embarrassed. I was putting a show on, you know. I can remember it like it was yesterday.

As I have said, Joe used Rangeley as his base, but he traveled widely through the upper Androscoggin valley. We have already talked about Joe's wanderings through this country when he peddled songs from camp to camp, but we don't want to forget that he probably spent the bulk of his time working like the rest of the men—as a woodsman and driver. He seems to have driven all the different branches of the Androscoggin at one time or another—the Kennebago, the Cupsuptic, and the Magalloway—not to mention the main river-drive into Berlin. Will Bryant was on the Rapid River drive with him one year, and others recall being with him on feeder streams like Sunday, Swift, and Bear rivers.

Joe wandered rather far afield from Rangeley at times, but evidently he always returned there in the summers. Herby Rice said he had worked with him for the Henrys over in Lincoln, New Hampshire, and Fred Lafferty drove with Joe on the Connecticut for at least one and he thinks two seasons. To the eastward, he seems to have worked in the woods and on the drives in various places both along the East Branch of the Penobscot and in eastern Aroostook County: Island Falls, the Bank Farm near Monticello, Oxbow, Ashland, and Patten. We know he must have been working somewhere around Patten in March of 1909, for example, when Norman Mitchell killed himself, but we also know that he was back in Rangeley shortly thereafter. That was his pattern, and in all of these places the man we hear about is the Joe Scott we already know: a good woodsman and crack riverman, a wonderful singer, a magician of sorts, and a showman who yet kept his own counsel. It is only around Houlton that we hear of a different Joe Scott. What we hear is surprising and problematic, and it will help if we know a little more about what kind of a town Houlton was.

Houlton was not only the shire town for Aroostook County, it was also an important center for woods operations in that part of the state, being by far the biggest town on the Meduxnekeag River, and while the Meduxnekeag was no Androscoggin, to be sure, it supported a whole passel of sawmills and the upriver camps that fed them. It also served as a supply center for woods operations in other watersheds, too. Nearby were the headwaters of the Mattawamkeag, one of the larger tributaries of the Penobscot, and in addition men came to Houlton from the East Branch of the Penobscot forty miles away and even from the Allagash. Theoretically, of course, no liquor was to be had in town, but an enterprising woodsman could usually find what he needed. If the town itself failed him, he could always head for "the Boundary Line," where there were three bar-rooms on the Canadian side that would supply him with all the rum required. The point is that Houlton was definitely what Rangeley was not: a well-known watering-place.[1]

Around Houlton, Joe Scott seems to have been a very odd stick indeed. Martin Harkins recalled him well. *"Foolish Crazy Joe Scott," he said. "Yes, I've heard him say that a good many times. 'Foolish Crazy Joe Scott,' he'd introduce himself [as]." Harkins hadn't much use for Joe. *"You see," he said, "when he was around here he was about half shot most of the time. . . . He was just a character. That's about all you could say about Joe. . . . Joe was a dandy little man," he continued, "quite a dresser. Wore a white vest, and it seemed as though they was a design on it. It wasn't just plain white. Some of the boys used to ask him if he was related to the Queen of Scots, and that was a great joke." I asked Harkins if he'd ever heard Joe say he was descended from the great Sir Walter Scott. Yes, he said, but he added that he'd never believed it. Harkins didn't even consider Joe a great singer. *"Oh, he'd sing a little, he said, "but he couldn't sing too much. . . . He was a composer."

The Man

Eighty-year-old James Rush of Houlton had a rather strange story to tell. Rush was not a woodsman; he ran a hay press, which he hired out to the different farms around the area, but he was in town on weekends.

*This Scott was . . . kind of a joke among the fellows. . . . He was very odd, I thought. I was going down there to town one night, and Houlton wasn't lit up in them times like it is [today]. And I heard somebody stealing along behind me, and I turned around. It was Joe Scott! He'd have them kind of queer spells, like. . . . Sneaking right up. You'd think it was just like a cat sneaking up on something. He seemed to be—I don't know. Well, some of the boys used to call him "Crazy Joe Scott."

Interestingly, Mrs. Merrithew remembered how as a boy Joe would *"black his face and come through the woods and crouch all over and walk funny, just to take a rise out of people."2 Such antics may mark a boy as "fun-loving" or (at the worst) "different," but a forty-year-old man who shadows people and jumps out from behind trees at them is going to be considered just plain crazy.

Nor does this seem to be the limit of Joe's antics. "I was over in Houlton one time," said Herbert Porter, "and walked into this barroom for a drink or two. I thought I saw Joe Scott across the room, but I couldn't figure out what was wrong with him; it looked like him, and then again it didn't. Then it came to me: it was Joe all right, but he'd dyed his hair black. Next thing I know, he'd spotted me, and he came over and introduced himself as somebody else: 'I'm so-and-so from—'; I can't remember the name now, but I played along with it and said, 'Oh yeah yeah, sure,' you know. I think he was just trying to duck somebody," said Porter, laughing. "There'd be no harm in it anyhow." Others recall seeing Joe with his hair dyed and his mustache changed. Is it any wonder, then, that people who knew Joe around Houlton thought of him as somewhat gone in the head?

How do we account for Joe Scott's singular reputation around Houlton? Nowhere else do we hear of him consistently referred to as a "character," a "joke" even. Such reports are common in Houlton. It is possible that I happened to talk to people there who just did not like Joe early or late, but that would be too wildly coincidental. It is possible Joe was in Houlton only for short periods before and after the drive, and since both were traditional occasions for binges, Houlton may have seen much more of Joe drunk than sober. But

Joe's actions around Houlton cannot be entirely explained away as the results of booze, and in my opinion that would be calling the symptom the disease. Joe ended his days in the state hospital. We know that for sure. It is very possible that he had "spells" at earlier times, aggravated and even partially brought on by heavy drinking. It is further possible that all the accounts of Joe in Houlton come from a single year—or even part of one—very late in his career. Could it be, for example, that he was in Houlton only during the year or so between his return from Quebec and his commitment to the hospital? That would all make sense, but it can't be offered as more than speculation. We'll leave it there for now in order to move on to Joe's Quebec adventure—his last before the darkness came down to stay.

I first heard about it in March of 1959, when I was up at the Green Farm about fifteen miles north of Rangeley talking to Dennis Taylor and Lanson Wilbur, both of whom remembered Joe Scott well from his Rangeley days. We had had supper and were continuing our talk in Wilbur's room. He had just mentioned how Joe and Sam Learned would never speak to each other, though they often had to work together. Then came the following: *"And he went up to Canady. He was gone from Rangeley about seven or eight years, and then he came back here to Rangeley. . . . He tried to get Rangeley people to go up. 'There's nice places up there.' He said there were awful nice places up in Canady for sporting people. And he tried to get men to go up there and help him build it, but he never could get nobody interested. . . ." That was the first I had heard of anything like that, and naturally I was curious, but neither Wilbur nor Taylor could remember any more about it, except that the name of the place sounded like "Katoots." Knowing as I did that in Maine "Canada" generally means Quebec or points west, I checked all maps, and the nearest I could come to "Katoots" was LaTuque, a hundred miles up the Saint Maurice River from Three Rivers. Had Joe really had some plan of opening sporting camps in this country on the edge of the Laurentians? It didn't sound right, but then. . . .

That summer I went down to Augusta one day to look over Joe's dossier at the state hospital. There was a series of letters to the hospital officials from his sister Carrie (Mrs. Tom Porter), in one of which (October 8, 1917) she asked, "Does he say anything about any property in Quebec?" Shortly thereafter his mother wrote: "We did hear he had taken up a homestead somewhere. But I think he must have property somewhere of his own." It began to appear that Lanson Wilbur had been right. Then I came across a letter from J. O. Gauthier, Privat, Quebec, dated December 11, 1917. Scott, he explained, had a small property in Privat and had also left some furniture there. It was of small value, he continued, but the taxes had not been paid for two years and the property was to be sold for this reason the next spring. There was no doubt, then, that Joe *had* spent some time in "Canady," but in Privat, up by Lake Abitibi more than three hundred miles by rail west of LaTuque. Since that time I have been able to fill in some of the details of this period in Joe's career, and, while I still can't be definitive, I can draw some reasonably good conclusions about why he went, what it was like, and how long he was there.

Before 1900 the whole Abitibi region was terra incognita to all except the Cree, a few trappers, an odd timber cruiser, and an occasional prospector. Geologically it is the bed of an ancient lake. The soil is fertile but thin, and originally the area was covered with dense forest. The summer is cool, the snow comes in early November and does not disappear until the end of April, and during this long winter temperatures of fifty below are common. Yet the region had possibilities, and since the National Transcontinental Railroad would be going through this way, the government had the country surveyed, subdivided into townships and lots, and opened up to colonization. By late 1912 the railhead had pushed its way westward from LaTuque through three hundred miles of wilderness, linking the Abitibi area with Quebec City and the East. Now the settlers began to come in earnest, and among them came Joe Scott.

The records show that Joe purchased lot fifty-eight, range seven, in the township of Privat, near Robertson Lake—about thirty miles east of Lake Abitibi and to the south of the present-day village of Taschereau. He paid the standard three dollars, and his homestead was the usual hundred acres. The date of the purchase was November 18, 1913, but since in his declaration Joe gave his place of residence as Robertson Lake (and since he filled out all the papers in nearby Amos), he had probably been in that country all summer and perhaps even longer than that. Certainly November would have been a very bad time to start a homestead in that subarctic country.

In fact, he had probably already started to build the small log camp that was to be his home, and he may even have commenced to clear some land.

According to the terms of his purchase, he had to put three to five acres under cultivation every year, and since the land was heavily forested and Joe was all alone, we can be sure he had enough to do even to make the minimum requirement. Clearing land was no new thing to Joe; after all, he'd done it before at home. But this was virgin timberland he was clearing, and since there were very few horses around at that time Joe had to grub every stump out by hand with lever and ax. In spite of all that had to be done, Joe evidently found time for other things. He did a lot of hunting; deer and moose were plentiful, not to mention small game like hare and partridge, and nearby Robertson Lake was teeming with big pike, which Joe soon became expert in catching.

At my request, Lucien Rioux of Sainte Irène de Laferté had several interviews with eighty-three-year-old Eugene Brouillet of Taschereau. Brouillet had been the first teamster in Privat and had therefore been much in demand to transport the settlers and their dunnage from the station to their new homesteads. This is how he first met Joe; and the two became close friends. He liked Joe, describing him as cheerful, even jovial. Joe loved to tell funny stories and catch others with his jokes. He also made home brew, and although lots of people used to do the same thing, Joe's was reputed to be the best around. Brouillet couldn't remember Joe doing any magic beyond some card tricks; he often "saw the future in the cards," he said, but he did that only for a joke. I had asked Rioux to inquire about this and perhaps even lead up to the question of possession. He did, and Brouillet laughed. "If Scott had any acquaintance with the Devil, he never told me about it," he said.

Other things that Brouillet said in his carefully noncommittal way sound familiar. "Scott minded his own business," he said, adding that he had a reputation for being very civil and polite. He didn't like people to get in his way when he was doing anything, and those who did were apt to get a rather sharp "Don't bother me!" He was a very proud man, and did not like to be surpassed in anything. All told, the gay, jovial teller of funny stories seems to show the expected balance against the reserved loner. Brouillet recalled one final and characteristic expression. "When someone told him something unusual, he'd show great surprise and say, *'Baptême! Es-tu fou?'* " (which we can translate as a rather curt "Jesus Christ! Are you crazy?").

It may be hindsight, but anyone who knew Joe could have predicted that homesteading was not for him. Years and years of back-breaking work clearing the land, grubbing out stumps; more years of putting in crops, then tending and harvesting them—Joe needed more than that. As I have said, he wasn't afraid of hard work. He probably went at the job with astonishing zeal at first, but he never could stay with a thing the way a homestead needed staying with. Brouillet did not know how long Joe stayed around. All he knows is that one day he left, never to return. Gauthier's letter to the hospital dated December 11, 1917, said that Joe hadn't paid his taxes for two years, which suggests that he left sometime in 1915. My hunch is that that is about right; Joe put in two winters up there and then left.

. . . *The little train clacketed along through the miles of Quebec wilderness. Then the forest opened on a lake gleaming in the late afternoon sun, patches of wind wrinkling its surface. The forest closed in again. Joe looked down the car. That man and woman in the front seat had gotten off at the last stop. He was all alone now. The car was getting chilly. He closed his eyes and tried to sleep.*

NOTES

1. For an excellent description of Houlton around 1900, see Roger E. Mitchell, *George Knox*, pp. 53–54.
2. For a similar story about George Knox, see ibid., p. 24.

7

The Last Days

Joe came back to Rangeley in 1915, although if I have read the signs aright, that might well have been the winter he spent over around Houlton. At any rate, he was back in Rangeley that spring (1916), but the chances are he did not go on the drive that year. He settled in once again at John Oakes's boardinghouse.

Several people had remarked to me that Joe had gone pretty queer at the end, but these remarks are by no means confined to the years after he returned from Quebec. *"Yes, he went insane," Dennis Taylor told me. "It seems as though he said things, you know. Wasn't nothing in it. And he tried to throw his voice. And his eyes went insane. . . . No, he wasn't blind, but you know, an insane man, his eyes changes. He looks wild." Evidently Taylor was not the only one who saw Joe's ventriloquism as evidence of his insanity. "The last winter we were together [1909 or 1910] he was studying ventriloquism and was getting pretty good at it," wrote Roy Kaulback. "Some of the boys used to say he was getting gone in the head, but I couldn't see any difference in him." However we may feel about voice-throwing, a number of men who had known Joe for some years felt that he was no longer entirely in his right mind. *"I think he was deranged quite a bit before he left Rangeley," said Joe Wilbur, "because he stopped to [Mrs. Oakes's] boardinghouse there and someone seen him on the piazza on the side of the house there and he didn't have any clothes on and was out walking around there."

What was wrong with him? Joe Wilbur simply figured that Joe had *"maybe had enough to make a man get twisted around," referring, of course, to Joe's disappointed love life. However, a number of other people knew what Joe's problem was. "Joe got a disease and toward the end of it he couldn't work at all," said Arthur Carr of Boiestown. What disease, I asked. "Well," said Arthur, with an apologetic smile, "you know what it was: syphilis." And that is what it was. It is no use trying to figure out where he picked the disease up; it has always been one of the classic hazards of the lumberman's life. At the last of it, Joe is supposed to have been drinking pretty hard, and nothing could be better calculated to hasten the final, inevitable collapse than alcohol in abundance.

Things began to really fall apart around the twentieth of June, 1916. Joe was working on the road repair crew for the town, but he found he could no longer work, claiming that he was in great pain and was going to die. The general story is that he finally went to the selectmen and told them he was losing his mind and would they lock him up before he hurt someone. He was in the Rangeley jail by June 26, where he was so noisy and restless they finally committed him to Augusta State Hospital on the twenty-ninth. The Franklin County Probate Court appointed Charles L. Harnden, one of the Rangeley selectmen, as his legal guardian. And that was the end of *that* world.

Not quite the end, though, because Joe lingered on for almost two years in whatever warped and fading light still reached him in his ward. He became more and more difficult as a patient as the days passed into months, but that was to be expected. The family back in Lower Woodstock knew where he was all the time; there are more than a dozen letters from his sister Carrie (Mrs. Tom Porter), asking how he is and whether or not they could come and see him. The hospital gently but firmly advised against it, both for their sakes and for Joe's. She inquires about the land in Quebec and in the same letter asks, "Does he take any interest in music? He was a fine singer and could play on any instrument." But evidently Joe is well beyond that sort of thing now.

According to the admission form, the hospital authorities knew that Joe "had a wife," but they made no attempt to contact her. In all fairness, we must remember that Joe was a charity case in terminal care; they were in contact both with relatives and with a legal guardian, which is probably more than could be said for some of the other ward patients. They didn't even know her name, to begin with, and obviously the family back in Lower Woodstock had no intention of involving her, although they certainly knew where she was. In spite of all this, Emma finally found out where her husband was, and in August of 1917 she came over to see him. Henry was at Camp Keyes right nearby and went with her:

*I went to see him. It was during the war. I was at camp at Augusta . . . and my mother came over with my uncle and we went over. . . . He called me Henry, but we didn't know whether he recognized me or not. He asked me how I was and everything, and I said, "You don't look too good, Dad."

"Well," he says, "I haven't et for some time."

I says, "You want me to get you something to eat?"

He says, "No, I'm not hungry any more."

Then Mother told me afterwards that the officials at the hospital told her that he didn't want to eat at all. He had that fear that they were trying to poison his food. . . . He conversed very intelligently and normally, you know, but he still had that particular idea in his mind, that thought that they were trying to get rid of him. He wouldn't eat. He wouldn't dare eat.

. . . Well, he quoted a few sermons, you know. Oh gee, I don't remember just what it was now, but it was salvation and be good to your mother and so forth, and what we have done in the past we must forgive and forget. And then he'd go on to something else; then he'd fall back on that, and I knew that his conversation was varying to a certain extent.

And at the hospital there they told us, "In our opinion it'll just be a matter of time."

Emma went back home to Rumford. Then in January she wrote to ask how Joe was, saying that five months before she had been to see him and at that time had been told he would not live long. The hospital's answer went as follows:

Mrs. Emma Scott
411 Waldo St.
Rumford, Maine

Dear Madam:

Your letter has been received inquiring about the condition of Joseph Scott, and in reply I would state that he is still on the sick ward of our hospital, is gradually failing and of late has not been eating as well as usual. He says that people are trying to kill him and poison him, which probably accounts for the fact that he does not care to eat. He has to be fed by persuasion. He is not showing any serious symptoms at present but is suffering from progressive mental disorder which will later terminate fatally.

Whoever informed you that he had passed away was mistaken and unless you hear reports directly from the hospital you will know that they are groundless. Should he become serisouly ill, I will inform you.

Sincerely yours,

/s/ Forrest C. Tyson
Superintendent.

But he did not inform her. She finally wrote again on March 31, 1919, saying that she hadn't heard anything in a long time and how was he? Three weeks later the hospital wrote that he had died June 22, 1918, that he had been a difficult patient for a long time, and that the remains had been sent to Charles L. Harnden, of Rangeley "at the request of his sister, Mrs. T. H. Porter." Harnden, in his petition for administration of Joe's estate, said that "said deceased left no widow and his only heirs-at-law and next of kin are as follows: Mrs. Thomas Porter. Woodstock, N. B. Sister. There may be other relatives I do not know," continues the document, "but since being guardian I have had correspondence with Mrs. Porter." Harnden can hardly be accused of having any special ax to grind, but the long and the short of it is that Emma had been effectively ignored. Whatever her feelings may have been, Joe was six months dead and buried. There was nothing she could do.

The end came at 2:15 P.M. on the twenty-second of June, 1918. The immediate cause of death was given as pneumonia, but his official death record lists the cause as "general paralysis of the cerebral type," one of the standard euphemisms for syphilis. Evidently the body was sent to Rangeley, and from there to Lower Woodstock, where the funeral was held on Friday afternoon, June 28. Emma Merrithew, who was living in nearby Canterbury at the time, attended the funeral. *"He had a nice casket," she recalled, "but it was never opened. It was sealed up. I thought it would be nice if we could have saw him, you know. We hadn't saw him for years. . . . [But] it was sealed, and none of us ever saw him again." The steel box the coffin arrived in stood out behind the barn for many years. No one is quite sure what finally became of it.

Two details connected with Joe's death are worth comment. Although his obituary in the local paper gives his place of death correctly, several people in the Meductic–Lower Woodstock area, including descendants of the family, had given me to understand that Joe had died "out west." It may well be that this is the story the family decided to tell; they were a prideful lot, these Scotts, and likely would have considered Joe's rather sordid end an embarrassment to them. Often tied in with this "dying out west" is the idea that Joe had left a sizeable estate. "I remember that my Uncle Hazen said there was something like $1800 left when Joe died, but the lawyers had just eaten it all up," Augus Scott, Ensley's son, told me. The fact is that Joe died intestate, but he had left a savings account of $267.82 with the Rangeley Trust Company, all of which went to pay off the expenses of Joe's commitment and death. All that was left over after paying the undertaker's fee and other incidental expenses went to the hospital: $112.47 for almost two years' care! No one got rich on Joe's estate.

Emma Merrithew had heard a slightly different story. *"You know, she said, "just before his body came on, two thousand dollars came to his mother." I came back to this subject some time later in our interview, after telling her what I already knew of Joe's estate. *"She got some money, I know that," she said. "They said it come from Joe, and how much it was we never knowed. They'd say this, that, and the other thing, but she got some money. And I was so glad." Probably all this talk about money is precariously based on that Rangeley bank account. If there ever was more money, he must have sent it home before he went into the hospital.

It was almost inevitable that we would hear about a book of Joe's songs in manuscript. Clyde Dickinson recalls seeing a notebook about four by five by an inch thick ("about as big as a time book") full of Joe's songs, but he doesn't know what became of it; and George Porter remembers that several of Joe's songs were found in an old trunk in the Scott attic, but they were taken to the dump and burned along with other trash a good many years ago. So far as I know, no such trove exists today.[1]

His obituary appeared in the *Press*, one of Woodstock's three competing weeklies, for July 19, 1918. It is a rather full one for the times:

Died at Augusta, Maine, June 22, Joseph Scott, in the 51st year of his age. The remains were brought to his former home at Meductic. The funeral which took place on Friday afternoon of the 28th inst., was conducted from the home of the elder brother, J. E. Scott. The funeral directions were under the efficient management of Delbert Franklin. The funeral sermon which was very earnestly and impressively preached by the Rev. R. L. Foster of Dowville, from 2nd Corinthians, 5th Chapter and

1st verse. The hymns were Lead Kindly Light, Nearer My God to Thee and Lead Thou Me On. The pall bearers were the Messrs Sherman Porter, John Nye, Harley Johnston, and Herbert Marsten, all schoolmates of the deceased. He leaves to mourn his loss his aged mother, Mrs. John Scott, three brothers J. E. and H. B. Scott of Riceville, Wallace Scott of British Columbia; one sister, Mrs. Thomas Porter of Riceville. The large crowd which was assembled at the funeral and which followed the remains to its last resting place, showed the high esteem and loving thought of which the deceased was held by all. Our sympathy goes out to the bereaved family, especially to the aged and widowed mother, for whom we deeply feel in this hour of bereavement. For if one is bereaved of their children they are bereaved indeed, but we know that she has the comfort that soon she will be called to that home where the flowers bloom never more to fade and die. Some glad day beyond the tomb she shall meet them in God's sinless summerland, where good-bye is never known.

Sentinel please copy.

But the *Sentinel* never did.

And so the circle is completed—from the end back to the beginning and now to the end again, not far from the beginning. Joe never found what it was he was reaching for, though he held many things in the palm of his capable hand, only to throw them away. Something always moved him on, but he kept his counsel, and those who were his friends never got beneath that combination of fun and reserve far enough to know what it was—nor do I think he knew himself. But it was all over now.

Ironically, even death did not end Joe's wanderings. When the waters of the Saint John began to flow back from the new Mactaquac Dam, all the graves in the old Porter Cemetery, Joe's among them, were moved to higher ground, a plot on the edge of town where they now stand respectably upright in neat rows. There's a proper fence, and the grass gets mowed all summer. I'm sure it's all right with Joe, but I for one, being of a sentimental turn, will miss the overgrown silences of the old cemetery down across the field, beyond the tracks, where a fox sat on some piled ties, "on the banks of the Saint John."

NOTES

1. For similar stories of the disappearance of a folk-poet's works after his death, see the accounts of John Calhoun and Larry Gorman in Edward D. Ives, *Larry Gorman*, pp. 136–137, 171–172. See also idem, *Lawrence Doyle*, p. 16.

Part

II

The Songs

A Plan to Be Departed From

Insofar as such things are possible, Joe's story has been told in all the available detail, and now in the next eleven chapters we will do the same by each of his songs. Each song presents special problems, and the emphases of each study will necessarily be somewhat different; but in a general way the same subjects will be covered in about the same order each time.

The songs are arranged in their chronological order, as far as I can determine it. If we assume that as a rule a song appeared very soon after the event it celebrated, we can date eight of them with some precision. For the rest, I have used whatever methods appeared most reliable, or I have made some educated guesses.

Each study will begin with a good traditional version of the ballad, including an account of how I came to collect that version. The transcriptions are verbatim unless otherwise indicated, and for each tune I have given a single sample stanza, with significant variations in a note. All tunes have been transposed so that their finals fall on g; the singer's original key and opening pitches are given in a preceding catch-signature. Meters and tempos are given as accurately as possible, but rather than force a tune into a metrical pattern I could not in fact find, I have occasionally resorted to marking a piece "parlando rubato" and simply putting dotted bar lines at the ends of the phrases.

Next will come a consideration of the evidence for Joe Scott's authorship of the ballad in question. There are four basic kinds of evidence to be considered: direct, ascriptive, circumstantial, and stylistic, and I give them in the order of their trustworthiness. I would consider one of Joe's original printed slips or a contemporary newspaper version with his name on it as direct evidence of his authorship. Ascriptive evidence is of various value, depending on how well the person making the ascription knew Joe, and I will try to be quite clear about what weight I give to someone's attribution.

Both circumstantial evidence and stylistic evidence involve my personal judgment in an even more direct way, the former as to whether or not the ballad is about something that could conceivably have been within Joe's purview, the latter as to whether it shows his particular style (I include under style for now not only the question "Was this the way Joe wrote?" but also "Was this the sort of thing he was apt to write about?"). Style alone can never be conclusive, and I will never treat it as though it were. There is a thorough discussion of Joe's style in chapter 21, and rather than preview that discussion here, I will simply refer the reader to it if he feels that at any point I am being arbitrary when I speak of a trait as, say, "vintage Joe Scott."[1] To sum up this matter of establishing authorship, the evidential mix—direct, ascriptive, circumstantial, and stylistic—will be different for each ballad, and if I have any doubts about Joe's authorship of a particular piece I will be very clear about them.

Having established Joe's authorship of the ballad as solidly as the evidence will allow, we need a text that is, if not his original, at least as close to that original as we can get. That text is our *terminus ad quem* for the study of "individual invention," and our *terminus a quo* for the study of "communal re-creation."[2] For nine of the songs I have copies of Scott's original slips. For all the rest, where I have had to settle for something less, I will make clear just how close I feel what I have is to the *Urtext*. Only for "Norman Mitchell" am I without a version that represents to my satisfaction Joe's original work. Which leads me to say something about Bert Thorne.

After seeing "The Plain Golden Band" in the December 11, 1946, issue of the *Family Herald*, Bert Thorne of Jemseg, New Brunswick, wrote the editors to say that their published version had a great many errors. "I roomed with Joe Scott at Simon Oaks Boarding house in the year 1901 at Rangeley Maine," he continued, "and bought several of his songs from him including the plain golden band which I have copied for you."[3] With this letter, Thorne sent carefully written copies of seven more of Joe's pieces, making eight songs in all: "The Plain Golden Band," "The Norway Bum," "Guy Reed," "Howard Kerrick," "Benjamin Deane," "Charming Little Girl,"

"Sacker Shean's Little Girl," and "William McGibbeny." The first two I could compare to "signed originals," and I found them so nearly identical in wording and even punctuation that I had no hesitation in saying that Thorne was copying from Joe's printed slips. He even put the "By Joe Scott" signature in the lower right, just the way it appeared in the originals. And it was with only slightly more hesitation that I was ready to accept his versions of the other six songs as authoritative by extrapolation. Furthermore, if I accepted his date of 1901 as reasonably reliable (and my experience was that a man was seldom off much more than a year or so one way or the other in giving such a date), I had terminal dates for those eight songs, and for three of them ("Charming Little Girl," "Sacker Shean's Little Girl," and "William McGibbeny") those were the *only* assignable dates I had of any kind. Obviously Bert Thorne's versions were very important to me, even in the indirect form in which I had them. If only I could have found the original printed slips themselves! But I had been told that Thorne was dead, and that seemed to be that.

Then in 1974 Neil Rosenberg, chairman of the Folklore Department at Memorial University, Saint John's, Newfoundland, was on leave and doing field research on country music in the Maritimes. Since he was living at the time in Pleasant Villa, New Brunswick, only about six or seven miles from Jemseg, I mentioned Bert Thorne's name to him, saying that if he should come across any of his descendants, he might ask if they'd saved any of his papers. I never for a moment thought he'd be successful, but in mid-December Neil called, saying he'd found Bert Thorne's son, and he still had his father's songbook. The university was still in session, and the weather looked threatening. But three days later I was in Jemseg.

Earl Thorne (his proper first name is Earl Grey, after the fourth Earl Grey, governor general of Canada at the time of his birth) couldn't have been pleasanter or more helpful. He brought out his father's little leather-covered account book and laid it on the kitchen table. Sure enough, there were the printed slips of eight of Joe's songs, just as I had suspected, carefully cut into stove lengths and pasted in with handwritten corrections wherever the original was torn or blurred by time. Interestingly, with the exception of a slip of the Sullivan-Corbett fight ballad and one or two newspaper poems, that's all there was in the book, which may show something about how much Bert Thorne valued Joe's work. Neil and I set right to work photocopying and rechecking the relevant pages, while Earl and his son sat and watched and made friendly talk, and Mrs. Thorne (Bert's widow) brought us great wedges of apple pie and all the homemade bread and butter we could eat and then some. It was an important day for me; it just happens to have been damned enjoyable, too. (My thanks to all present, and gratitude and good rest to old Bert.)

Nine of the ballads covered in the following chapters are about specific and datable events, and for all but one of them ("Norman Mitchell") it is possible to establish "what really happened" through newspapers, court records, and the like, with considerable accuracy. In fact, I am sure that through such records I often have a much better understanding of the event than Joe Scott himself could have had. Such historicism is interesting, and I will indulge in it for its own sake, but for the purposes of this book it is much more important to determine how the event appeared to Joe, and as far as historical background is concerned, this will be my main thrust. Of course, it is not always possible to be absolutely sure what Joe might or might not have known, but through a judicious use of internal and external evidence, a basic assumption that Joe generally wanted to "tell the truth," and a thorough knowledge of traditional forms and content, in all modesty I think I have made some pretty shrewd guesses.

Historical background is only half the story, though, in determining what Joe's "raw materials" were. The other half involves determining what models were available to him through the artistic tradition he had chosen to work in. I have tried to avoid lengthy discussions of, say, the murder-ballad tradition in itself (a huge subject!) by sticking to the narrower matter of what murder ballads Joe Scott would have been likely to know. Again, it is impossible to be certain, but twenty years of collecting and study in the Northeast have given me a good idea of the repertoire, good enough that I can tell not only what models Joe chose to follow but also what models he must have known about and chosen *not* to follow. I have similarly limited my discussion of the tunes, simply referring the reader in a note to more general studies and far-flung parallels.

So much for the *terminus ad quem* of individual invention. Now for the *terminus a quo*. What happened to Joe's ballad as it was passed on through time and space? How far has it spread, and what changes have occurred to it in its travels? Since all such study is based on a whole series of individual texts gathered in various forms and in various ways, it would be worth our while now to consider the various kinds and qualities of versions I have used.

One basic distinction is between the complete version and the fragment. To begin with, when a singer says he has sung us "the whole of it," we have to accept what he gives us as correct and complete. We may know he didn't sing all the stanzas that were in the "original," but of course that is irrelevant; we may also know that he has the stanzas "all mixed up," but that is even more irrelevant. What he knows *is* the song as it exists at that particular moment. We must not speak of fragments when singers speak of whole songs. The only real fragments are versions the singer himself calls incomplete. "*I don't know it all,*" he says, which implies his recognition that there *is* a whole, a complete entity, and the collector should try to determine what conception the informant has of how what he knows fits that whole. Unfortunately, it is very seldom that collectors (myself among them) have ever thought of getting such data.

In the present study, I have held to this basic distinction with one modification only. If a singer told me something like "*There's a couple of verses there I don't know,*" and if my later examination of his version showed that that was indeed how it was, I have generally not counted his version as a fragment. Naturally, I have made statistical allowances, but to have inflexibly applied my own criteria would have been to deny myself for example Angus Enman's version of "Benjamin Deane" (PI.2) simply because he could not recall a stanza and *knew* that he could not recall it. Such splendid rigor would obscure more than it would reveal, but in referring to such versions I have used the weaseling "nearly complete" to save appearances. At any rate, I have based most of my conclusions on the corpus of "complete and nearly complete" versions.

A second basic distinction should be made between versions collected from men who considered themselves singers (and who were so considered by their peers) and versions collected from men who were what we can call the educated audience in that they knew the songs but did not normally perform them in public. The former are what von Sydow called *active*, the latter *passive* tradition-bearers.[4] It is an important distinction, but, since we are dealing with a moribund singing tradition, it is also moot. At this point, it is very difficult to tell which singers are or were which, and therefore I will not force the distinction on my data unless it is obviously appropriate.

The third basic distinction, and one we can easily apply, is between oral and manuscript texts. An oral text is of course one taken down directly from performance, preferably by recording but possibly by dictation. A manuscript text may be of two kinds: first, one that the informant wrote down at an earlier date for his own purposes in a commonplace book or a scrapbook; second, one that the informant wrote down quite recently for the express purpose of giving or sending to the collector. Each has its own kind of value.

In studying a living song tradition, or in studying the place of song in a present-day culture, unquestionably the basis should be those versions that have been recorded in their "natural context" from people who are known as singers. However, that is only a small part of what this book is all about. Essentially we are studying a remembered culture, not so much the way things *are* as the way they *were*. Many of the people from whom I have collected songs had not sung them for as much as forty or fifty years, for example (*"People don't sing much anymore, with the television and all that"*), and that means (among other things) that there is no longer a "natural context" for songs to be recorded in, only the kitchen or parlor where the folklorist plugs in his tape recorder and gets the old man to sing.

I have still put primary emphasis on recorded versions, but to some extent I suspect that is force of habit. Manuscript texts should not be treated as second-class citizens. If a person writes a text out for the collector, it is true that he has time to reflect. One man was writing a song out for me but wouldn't let me have it until he could recall the last stanza; since he never recalled it, I never got the text. But this is not far different from the singer who asks for a little time to think a song over before he sings it (*"Don't think I could get that together now, but I'll sing it for you next time"*). On the other hand, a text written down years ago can also be very valuable. If it was written from memory, it can show us the song as the singer once knew it. More than likely, though, it was written down from another source, a newspaper, for example, or (even more likely) from someone else's singing or dictation. Singers sometimes learned songs this way, and such texts also often served as memory-joggers down through the years. I am not denying that there are differences between oral and written texts, nor am I forgetting that singing is

102

what the whole business was all about to begin with. But for the purposes of this study, manuscript texts must be given their full importance.

Printed texts have a special value, too. First of all, there were Joe Scott's printed slip sheets that he sold around the lumbercamps, and if any versions have a right to be considered "the originals," these do. Versions of "Guy Reed" and "Howard Carey" received national circulation through being printed in Robert W. Gordon's column in *Adventure,* and at least one of Joe's songs ("The Norway Bum") appeared in the "Old Time Songs and Poems" page of the *Boston Sunday Globe.* No doubt other newspapers printed his songs at one time or other, but the *Family Herald,* a weekly rural newspaper that covers all of Canada, has been the most important of them and is worth a special look.

The creation of the *Family Herald* "Old Favourites" column was first announced in the issue for November 12, 1895, and the first feature appeared the following week (November 19), along with the announcement that "this department seeks to provide for readers the words of songs which are out of print, or difficult to obtain in ordinary song collections." It further stated that "in this column of the *Family Herald* there will be published from week to week songs, poems and ballads chosen from the storehouse of English poetry." Readers were advised to preserve these poems, for "by doing so they will secure, at no cost to themselves, a very complete collection of the best English poetry." Readers did clip this column, too, and anyone who had collected songs in the Maritimes (or probably anywhere in Canada) is familiar with the scrapbook or cigar-box bulging with *Family Herald* clippings.

"Many of our songs are not the work of a single hand," said the opening announcement, "but are the growth of time, having received improvements from various hands until they reached their final form." Obviously the department had traditional songs in mind, but the early columns were devoted to classic material from Browning, Tennyson, Bryant, Shelley, and Mrs. Hemans. It wasn't long, however, before traditional songs began to appear in great number, sometimes with their music, and readers began writing in their thanks. One subscriber called the columns "a great boon. They are making some of the old folks feel young again!"[5] With the January 26, 1897, issue, they began publishing requests ("J.A.J. of East

Bathurst, N.B., would like a copy of the words to 'Bloody Waterloo'"—that sort of thing).

The column was a tremendous success and continued in high gear well up into the 1960s, frequently drawing as many as a thousand letters a year from people requesting songs and sending in answers to requests. It not only published songs and requests for songs, but also supplied copies from its files to people who wrote in for them. If the songs had only recently been printed, either in the column or in another source, the reader would receive a clipping or a typescript of the words. In short, the *Family Herald* "Old Favourites" column acted as a kind of folksong clearinghouse for all of Canada, with about thirty thousand songs on file; about three thousand of them were sent in by readers, and the rest were from books, folios, and sheet music. It even published two folios of its own, one in 1898 and one in 1900. The impact that this column has had on Canadian folksong tradition has yet to be measured, but it clearly was an important institution. That it affected the tradition of some of Joe Scott's songs was inevitable, but we'll go into this matter more fully when we come to the individual songs.[6]

One thing more. Throughout the following chapters I make frequent aesthetic judgments, speaking about this or that ballad being "nicely balanced" or about a particular arrangement of stanzas "making sense," and the reader has a right to know the basis of such judgments. No doubt about it, they are my personal opinions and therefore (as the parlance goes these days) "highly subjective." But having admitted that much, I hasten to add that they are in no way arbitrary. After thirty or more years' experience (twenty of them in the Northeast) with ballads of all kinds—listening to them, singing them, studying them, observing which ones persisted in tradition and which ones didn't, and talking with singers and listeners about what it was they liked or didn't like in particular songs—I believe I have as good an inside understanding of the folksong traditions of the Northeast as it is possible for an outsider (and I am an outsider) to have. My aesthetic judgments are based on that understanding, on what I believe is a ballad aesthetic. Frequently I have had to be explicit about what may be only implicit. I talk about symmetry and balance and contrast, although I have never heard a particular ballad praised or even described in those terms. No matter. My aesthetic is still drawn from what I know of ballads, not from the misapplication of my knowledge of elitist literature or (worse yet) from some absolutist concept of True Beauty.

Following each chapter is a list of all the versions of that particular ballad that were available to me, arranged in a roughly geographical west-to-east fashion. First, however, I have listed Joe Scott's own printed slips (JS) and *Family Herald* versions (FH), since both are extra- or super-geographical. Then come versions from the various states and provinces. "Me.1," for instance, is the westernmost version from Maine; but within a state or province it sometimes made more sense to group versions from a particular area (Maine's Aroostook County, for example) than to be hyperconsistent in west-to-east terms. Another inconsistency occurs in the case of versions I collected or received long after the original study was completed, where a complete renumbering of all versions would have meant a mountain of effort to maintain a molehill of consistency; therefore these latecomers are numbered at the end of the list of versions for that particular state or province. For a complete list of abbreviations and catchwords used, see the Appendix.

Now to get on with the study of the songs themselves.

NOTES

1. For further discussion of the usefulness of style as evidence of authorship, see Edward D. Ives, *Lawrence Doyle*, pp. 246–249.

2. See Phillips Barry, "Communal Re-creation," p. 5.

3. Thorne to the *Family Herald*, Dec. 16, 1946. The letter was never published, but it was found in their files.

4. Carl von Sydow, "Geography and Folk-Tale Oicotypes," in *Selected Papers on Folklore*, pp. 44–59.

5. *Family Herald*, Dec. 1, 1896.

6. The staff of the *Family Herald* have been extremely cooperative not only in supplying me with odd copies of songs, but also in making their entire files available to me while I was in Montreal in January, 1966. Especially I would like to thank Sheila Bûcher, who ran the "Old Favourites" column for many years; C. M. LaPointe, librarian; Peter Hendry, editor; and Vernon Pope, senior advisory editor. Edith Fowke is preparing an index to these "Old Favourites" columns.

9

"Howard Carey": The Ballad as Preachment and Prophecy

Wesley Smith had known Joe Scott almost sixty years ago in Maine, when they worked together up around Bemis, but he had learned "Howard Carey" at home in Victoria West, Prince Edward Island, well before he'd gone into the woods. The first time Wesley sang it for me, he was very tired and said afterward that he didn't think he'd done a very good job.[1] That was in 1958, and now, seven years later, I was asking him to try it again for me. *"Oh dear," he said, "I don't know whether I know it or not." He hadn't sung it at all in the intervening years, but if I wanted him to, he said, he'd try it. He sailed right along beautifully until he fetched up on the last line, which wouldn't come and wouldn't come for what seemed like an hour but was actually only a minute of fumblings, silences, and false starts. Then he got it, and we all started breathing again.

Slightly over two weeks later I received a letter from Wesley with an enclosed handwritten copy of "Howard Carey." "Enclosed find this song," the letter said. "I presume you are going to print it and I thought I left some out when I sang it. I made an arse of it anyway. I'd like to have it as near right as I can." The two versions, the one he sang and the one he sent me, were for all practical purposes identical, except for one extra stanza in the manuscript. What follows is the version he sang that afternoon in August, 1965, with the additional manuscript stanza in brackets. I'd like to have it right for him, too.

106

HOWARD CAREY[2]

2. My a-ged par-ents, they be-ing poor, could not main-tain us all, I had to leave my hap-py home, for our lit-tle farm was small; I lived there quite con-tent-ed-ly till the year of eight-y-four, I left my home and par-ents, I ne'er shall see them more.

[1]   My name is Howard Carey, in Grand Falls I was born,
In a pleasant little cottage on the banks of the Saint John;
Where the wild birds chant their notes so true and the rippling
    waters roar,
Where the ivy vine does closely twine round that cottage on
    the shore.

[2]   My aged parents, they being poor, could not maintain us all,
I had to leave my happy home, for our little farm was small;
I lived there quite contentedly till the year of eighty-four,
I left my home and parents, I ne'er shall see them more.

[3]   The day I left my happy home down by the ocean strand,
My poor old aged father he took me by the hand,
Saying, "Don't forget your parents, lad, when in a foreign
    land."

[4]   My mother led me to a seat beneath a willow tree,
With trembling lips bade me sit down for she wished to talk
    with me.
"Do you see on yonder hillside where the grass is growing
    green,
Where the violets and the lilies are plainly to be seen.
Those flowers they are magnificent, attractive to the eye,
But the snake you must remember beneath their colors lies.

[5]   "So when in strange and foreign lands I'd have you be aware,
      Each pleasure hath its poison and every sweet its snare;
      So shun bad company, my boy, and from strong drink refrain,
      Don't patronize those gambling dens, look on them with
          disdain.
      Always remember that old proverb, one that is good and old:
      All are not gems that sparkle, all that glistens is not gold."

[6]   I arose up from my rustic seat, for the dewdrops bright and
          clear
      Had bade the rose a fond farewell, I watched them disappear;
      I kissed my mother's tear-stained cheeks, bade her a fond
          farewell,
      My feelings at that moment no human tongue can tell.
      My brothers and my sisters in a group stood in the door,
      I waved my hand and left them in their cottage on the shore.

[7]   My parents moved to Haverhill, Mass., and sold their little
          farm,
      Four years ago a letter came which filled me with alarm:
      "You mother dear is dying, her heart for you doth yearn;
      She constantly repeats your name, 'Has my wandering son
          returned?'"

[8]   I hastened home, but ah too late, for everything was o'er,
      The curtains they were closely drawn, black crepe was on the
          door;
      And now she sleeps that long last sleep beneath the churchyard
          sod,
      Four years have passed and gone now since her spirit went to
          God.

[9]   Since then I've traveled in the East and in the West also,
      I've traveled in those southern lands where the lofty redwoods
          grow;
      My mother's warnings did not heed, but like a silly fly
      Got tangled in the silken web, and now I'm doomed to die.

[10] [I rue the day I left my home and caused my parents pain,
      I curse the hour that I arrived all in the State of Maine;
      Bad women and bad whiskey they both to me have gave
      A blighted life, disgrace and shame, soon a dark dishonored
          grave.]

"Howard Carey"

[11] Tonight I'm lying in a room in the town of Rumford Falls,
My feverish eyes are rolling round upon its whitewashed walls;
The agony I undergo I cannot long endure,
My limbs are weak and painful, I am dying slow but sure.

[12] My money it has long since fled and my friends they are but few,
I'll snap this tender thread of life, I'll bid this world adieu;
I'll tie this cord unto the hinge upon my chamber door,
There's room enough for me to hang beneath it and the floor.

[13] And when I'm dead this world will roll on just the same as e'er,
The birds will sing, the fawn will play in shady woodlands fair;
The grass will grow up just as green as before I passed away,
What signifies a mortal man when slumbering in the clay?

[14] Here's adieu to earth and all things gay, to home and friends adieu,
Here's adieu unto that girl I love, may God watch over you;
No more we'll roam in woodlands fair to hear the thrushes sing,
You're purer than the lilies that blooms all in the spring.

[15] At twelve o'clock John Durkin came to see his charge once more,
He found his body hanging to a hinge upon the door;
He cut him down and spread the news, and many's the cheek grew pale,
And filled with wonder many's the heart to hear that mournful tale.
So all young men a warning take from this sad tale of woe,
And shun bad company or they will prove your overthrow.

I haven't the slightest doubt that Joe Scott wrote "Howard Carey."
Not only do we have, thanks to Bert Thorne, an original printed slip
with his name on it—evidence enough!—but we also have a number
of ascriptions made by people who were in a real position to know.
Fred Campbell, for example, learned his version from a printed
copy he had bought from Joe, and he had heard Joe sing it a couple of
times up on the Magalloway. *"And then he composed a song about
the fellow that hung himself in the jail up in Grand Falls," ninety-

year-old Tom Pollock told me, and J. A. Polley wrote Robert Gordon
that "Scott wrote a very good song about a friend of his that hung
himself in Rumford in 1895- or 6 named Howard Carrick."[3]

Circumstances support these ascriptions, too. We know that Scott
was around Rumford Falls in the late nineties. In the letter just
referred to, Polley claimed that Scott was working in the sulphite
mill in Rumford at the time Guy Reed was killed, September of
1897, just four months after Howard Carrick hanged himself. Helen
Casey had known Scott well and remembered that Howard had
worked in the woods with Joe and her brother, Mike Sutton. Sutton,
by the way, was one of the men who first discovered the suicide and
cut him down, and Dave Severy added that he is certain that Joe
used to board at Siddall's (where the suicide took place) off and on.
Finally, if we add to ascription and circumstance the fact that the
style of the piece, with its leisurely pathos and freight of traditional
natural description, is Joe Scott right down the line, there doesn't
seem to be any real need for me to plant my usual academic hedge.
Joe Scott wrote "Howard Carey" and that's that. And here it is the
way he sold it around the woods. Material in parentheses represents
Bert Thorne's handwritten restorations of lines and phrases obliterated where the original slip sheet had been folded or torn; the
numbers in brackets (in this and other songs) are my own addition for
convenience of reference.

HOWARD KERRICK.

[1]   My name it is Howard Kerrick,
          In Grand Falls I was born
      In a pleasant little cottage,
          On the banks of the St. John,
      Where small birds chant their notes so true,
          Where the trembling waters roar,
      The ivy vine doth thickly twine
          Round that cottage on the shore.

[2]   My aged parents being poor
          Could not sustain us all,
      I had to leave my native home,
          For our little farm was small;
      I lived there quite contentedly

Till the year of eighty-four,
   When I left my aged parents
For the Bay of Fundy's shore.

[3]   The day I left my happy home
      They took me by the hand,
Saying, "don't forget your parents lad,
      When in a foreign land."
My mother led me to a seat,
      Beneath a willow tree,
With quivering lips bade me sit down,
      For she wished to talk to me.

[4]   "You see on yonder hillside,
      Where the grass in [sic] growing green,
Where the lilies and the violets
      And the wild rose may be seen,
Fragrant flowers numberless
      Of every shade or hue,
They are beautiful for to behold
      All wet with early dew.

[5]   "The dewdrops sparkle in the sun
      Like diamonds rich and rare,
While odors lovely and sweet
      Perfume tne summer air;
Those flowers are magnificent
      And attractive to the eye,
But still remember that the snake
      Beneath their colors lie.

[6]   "And when in strange and foreign lands
      I would have you to beware,
Each pleasure has its poison, too,
      And every sweet its snare;
Shun bad company, my boy,
      And from strong drink refrain,
Don't patronize those gambling hells,
      Look on them with disdain.

[7]   "When you are tempted to do wrong
      Have courage to say no,
Each victory will strengthen you
      The tempter to o'erthrow,

And don't forget that old proverb,
  One that's true and old:
All are not gems that sparkle,
  All that glitters is not gold."

[8] I rose up from my rustic seat,
  For the dewdrops bright and fair
Had bid the rose a fond adieu,
  We watched them disappear,
One by one did fade away
  Beneath the sun's bright ray,
The time had come when I must leave,
  (I could no longer stay)

[9] I kissed my mother's tear-stained face,
  Bid her a long farewell,
My feelings at that moment
  Ah, no mortal tongue can tell.
My brothers and my sisters
  In a group stood by the door,
I waved my hand and left them
  By the cottage on the shore.

[10] My parents moved to Haverhill, Mass.,
  And sold their little farm,
Four years ago a letter came
  Which filled me with alarm,
"Your mother dear is dying,
  Her heart for you doth yearn
And constantly repeats your name,—
  "Has my wandering son returned?"

[11] I hastened home, (but oh to late)
  For everything was(s ore)
The curtains they w(were closely drawn)
  Black crape hung on the (door)
And she now sleeps that long, (long sleep)
  Beneath the churchyard sod,
Four long years have passed and gone
  Since her spirit went to God.

[12] Since then I've traveled in the East,
  And in the South also,
I've traveled in the western lands

Where the lofty red-woods grow;
But my mother's warning did not heed,
    And like the silly fly,
Got tangled in a silky web
    And now I'm doomed to die.

[13] I rue the day I left my home
        (and caused my parents pain)
    I curse the hour that I arrived
        All in the State of Maine,
    For its bad whiskey and bad women,
        They to me have gave
    A blighted life, disgrace and shame,
        Soon a dark, dishonored grave.

[14] To-day I'm laying in a room
        In the town of Rumford Falls,
    My feverish eyes are roving round
        Upon its whitewashed walls;
    The agony I undergo
        I cannot long endure,
    My limbs are weak and painful,
        I am dying slow but sure.

[15] My money it has long since fled,
        My friends they are but few,
    I will snap the tender thread of life
        And bid the world adieu;
    I will tie this cord unto the hinge
        Upon my chamber door,
    There is room enough for me to hang
        Beneath it and the floor.

[16] Farewell to earth and all things gay,
        And home and friends adieu,
    (farewell unto the girl I love,)
        May God watch over you;
    No more we'll rove in groves so green
        To hear the thrushes sing,
    She is purer than the lily fair
        That blooms all in the spring.

[17] And when I'm dead this world will roll on
        Just the same as e'er,

The fawn will play and birds will sing
  In shady woodlands fair,
The grass will grow on just as green,
  The flowers will bloom as gay,
What signifies a mortal man
  When slumbering in the clay.

[18] At 12 o'clock John Derkin came
  To see his charge once more,
He found his body hanging
  To a hinge upon the door,
He cut him down and spread the news,
  And many a cheek grew pale,
And thrilled with wonder many a heart
  To hear the mournful tale.

*   *   *   *

[19] (his remains now lie mouldering)
  By his loving mother's side,
Poor thing, she never lived to know
  The cruel death he died.
And now young men a warning take
  By this sad tale of woe,
Shun bad company, or they
  Will prove your overthrow.

BY JOE SCOTT.

Price 10 cts.

"Howard Carey" is about "something that really happened." According to the death record in the Rumford city clerk's office, Howard Carrick, age thirty-two, laborer, single, was a "suicide by hanging" on May 5, 1897. Place of birth was given simply as New Brunswick, and the names and whereabouts of his father and mother were unknown. The *Rumford Falls Times* for May 7, 1897, told the story in some detail. "TIRED OF LIFE" read the headline, and under that, "Howard Garrick, 33, Hangs Himself While Temporarily Insane":

Howard Garrick, a lumber workman, 33 years old, and home unknown, committed suicide at his boarding house on Canal Street, Wednesday forenoon. He was not found until the noon hour when his absence from the dinner table caused comment. When found he had been dead some hours and medical assistance was useless.

Fig. 5. Rumford Falls as seen from the east in November, 1894. In the foreground is the canal leading to the mill. Facing it is Canal Street. The second house from the right is Mrs. Annie Siddall's boardinghouse. (Courtesy of the Rumford Historical Society. NA photo 500.2.)

115

Mrs. Annie Siddall, with whom Garrick had boarded since he came in town, told the writer that some time past the suicide had been suffering with the grip, and that she had no doubt but that he hung himself during mental aberration. She also added that during the forenoon Garrick stated to her that he was fearful that he should die before many hours. But she paid little heed to what he said, for his mind had not been right for some days, and she was of the opinion that he at the time did not know what he was saying.

About 9 o'clock in the forenoon Garrick again told his boarding mistress that he was soon to die, and expressed regret that one so wicked as he should be obliged to die without being prepared for it. Soon after this Garrick went to this room, and hung himself as soon as he could complete his arrangements. He left no word to any of his relatives or friends.

During the remainder of the forenoon, Mrs. Siddall was busily engaged performing her household duties, and she gave no thought to the where-abouts of her boarder. Twice, however, she went to the room to do the necessary chamber work, but the door was locked, and she, thinking that the occupant of the room was sleeping, made no effort to rouse him.

At the dinner table someone asked where Garrick was and the landlady replied that he had been in his room since early in the forenoon, and asked two of the boarders, Mike Sutton and Jack Weeks, to go to his room. They did and found the door locked. With force they broke in the door and in doing so pushed against the body of the dead man. He had tied a half-inch cord around his neck, and placed the other end over the hinge of the door. He was at once cut down, but life was extinct.

The article goes on to describe "Garrick" as a "sober, industrious fellow" and to say that his acquaintances spoke well of him. It also granted him the distinction of being the first suicide in the history of Rumford Falls, but neither that nor the good opinion of his mates was going to help much, since there was no one to pay for his funeral. The body was turned over to "Undertaker Calhoun," and the selectmen got busy trying to find Howard's family. The word was that his father and two sisters lived in Haverhill, Massachusetts, but a telegram to city officials brought the response that "the relatives of Gerrick could not be found in that city." The law was clear enough in such cases: unclaimed bodies were to be disposed of by the town for dissection purposes. Howard had hanged himself Wednesday morning, and when no kin had been found by Thursday, the Rumford town fathers did their duty by putting his body on the afternoon train for Brunswick, where it would be turned over to Bowdoin College. Howard was on his way to becoming a stiff.

Keep in mind that the *Rumford Falls Times* would have gone to bed late Thursday in order to appear on Friday. As soon as the paper received word of what was to be done with the young man's remains, it sent a telegram off to the *Boston Globe*, asking them to have their Haverhill man look around for the family, and by 3:30 Thursday afternoon came the following reply:

Howard Carrick who committed suicide at Rumford Falls, Me., yesterday, has a father, John Carrick, and two sisters, Mrs. Mary McKinley and Mrs. Adelbert Atwood of this city. The deceased lived in this city three years ago, but suddenly disappeared. He was employed as a farm hand while here. His father says that his death is the first he has heard from his son since he left at that time. His father is a well known citizen in Ward 7, formerly Bradford. His son often suffered from mental troubles and he believes he committed suicide while temporarily insane.

The main story had evidently already been written and set in type, but this telegram was appended to it under its own headline: PARENTS FOUND. Under the headline "SAVED FROM DISSECTION," the next week's *Times* indulged in some self-congratulation. "The discovery of the parents of Howard Carrick," it crowed, "was probably the quickest and most complete piece of work ever accomplished by a newspaper in this section of the state."[4] After an excusable dig at officialdom—"What a police force had failed to do in many hours a newspaper had accomplished in a very few minutes"—it wrapped the story up as follows: "Word was then sent to the chief of police at Brunswick instructing him to stop the body and await instructions. This was done, and on Saturday morning the body of Howard Carrick was sent to Bradford, Mass., and the funeral held from the residence of his parents that afternoon."

The *Haverhill Evening Gazette*, as might be expected, covered the story as well, but it mercifully omitted any mention of the Brunswick business. Its May 8 story was almost verbatim the second paragraph of the Rumford paper's May 7 account ("Mrs. Annie Siddall, with whom . . .") quoted above, but the lead paragraph told of the funeral:

The remains of the late Howard Carrick were brought to this city from Rumford Falls, Me., this afternoon and were buried in Elmwood cemetery, ward 7 [*Bradford*]. The funeral was attended by the relatives and friends, and the services at the grave were conducted by the Rev. J. D.

Kingsbury. The deceased is spoken of highly by his relatives, and the blow to them was a severe one. The report that the deceased had been a tramp was denied, as the relatives state that the deceased had for the past two years been employed at his trade in Rumford Falls. He had not had any work for some time past, and they believe that it was on account of this and the attendant mental worry that led him to take his life.

In the Carrick plot in Elmwood Cemetery, there is a small marker about a foot tall. On the front: DIED / May 5, 1897 / Aged 35 yrs. On the top of the stone in block letters: HOWARD. The name is almost completely obliterated now.

I am not sure I will be pardoned for the trite but efficient transition I have set up for myself here—"The name may be obliterated but his memory . . ."—but the fact remains that there is an oral tradition that has continued alongside the ballad, separate from but in symbiosis with it. First of all, it seems to be common knowledge what Howard's problem "really" was. *"You know what was the matter with him, what killed him?" John Morrison asked me rhetorically. "It was venereal disease that he had. That's why he died. . . . At that time there was no treatment for it like there is today. V.D. can be cleared up, but in them days it couldn't. And that's really actually what Howard Carey was—led up to his end. He hung himself in his bedroom." *"That's what happened to him," Fred Lafferty said. "He got the syphilis. He was rotting right away." Time and time again I have been told this, both by people who knew the ballad and by people who only knew *of* it. Second, James Curtis told Denis Ryan that a friend of his "knew Howard Currie and the men in the camp were taking up a collection for him, for he was quite down and out, when the first thing they heard was that he had taken his life." Finally, the suicide's room seems to have become a legend in its own right. *"I stayed in that boardinghouse," Mike Noonan told me. "Next morning a fellow asked me, 'How'd you sleep last night?' I said, 'Fine. Why?' 'Well, that's the room where Howard Carey hung himself. . . . That hinge on the door, the upper hinge. Same one.'" Arthur Carr of Boiestown, New Brunswick, told me that no one who knew about the business would stay in that room, but he himself used to ask for that room especially, just so he could scandalize the boys back at camp when they'd ask him where he'd stayed.

What was Joe Scott's perspective on the whole sad story? I am sure that he knew Howard, and it is perfectly possible that he himself was staying at Mrs. Siddall's at the time, though that's speculation. He might have been off on the drive somewhere, but in any case Howard and Joe traveled in the same company and worked for the same outfits. Perhaps Joe had seen the newspaper accounts, but I doubt it, largely because had he seen them he likely would have corrected his spelling of the name from "Kerrick" to "Carrick." Aside from that detail, it is really immaterial whether Joe had seen the papers or not, because there is nothing in the ballad that couldn't have easily come from more direct sources: common talk among friends and even from earlier talks with Howard himself (it is easy to imagine the two young men from the banks of the Saint John sitting down in the parlor at Siddall's and comparing notes). It remains, then, for us to see how Joe took what he knew and combined it with traditional materials and attitudes in order to come up with a satisfactory ballad.

Laws pigeonholed "Howard Carey" under "Ballads about Criminals and Outlaws,"[5] but if there was ever an example of a *faute de mieux* classification it is this one. Although in a very general, and I mean *very* general, way this ballad does resemble other ballads in this category, its hero is neither a criminal nor an outlaw; he is simply another victim of the roaring life whose only distinction was choosing a dramatic way of ending it all. The ballad is a preachment, yes, but only against boozing and whoring as evils in themselves, not— and this is the more usual approach—because they have led the hero to commit a murder or some other deed of crime.[6] "Howard Carey" is unusual in this respect, then, and it is further unusual in being the only suicide ballad I know of in which the act is precipitated not by an unhappy love affair but by sickness and despondency. In other words, in writing this ballad on his friend, Joe Scott had no immediate model he could easily adapt to his purposes, and he had only the vaguest kinds of parallels to draw on. He had a lot of work to do.

In general outline, the ballad looks something like this: an introductory stanza (1); the leave-taking, beginning with a simple statement (2), followed by the mother's advice (3–8), and concluding with a good-bye (9); his mother's death (10–11); his confession (12–15); a farewell (16–17); the discovery of the suicide (18); and a conclusion, including a warning (19). There's nothing especially remarkable about this structure: a young man warned against sinning sins and suffers the consequences. But when we consider the proportions of the different sections, we do find some unusual things. Let's take each section up separately.

The opening stanza has its facts right, to begin with; Howard was born in Grand Falls, New Brunswick. It is also a very traditional formula, the naming stanza, and we can get our first good look at one of Joe's most characteristic traits, if we compare his stanza to a more standard development of the formula in, for example, "Peter Emberly":

> My name is Peter Emberley
>> As you may understand
> I was born on Prince Edward Island
>> Near to the ocean strand.
> In eighteen hundred and eighty,
>> When the flowers were a brilliant hue,
> I sailed away from my native isle
>> My fortune to pursue.[7]

Notice that this ballad gets the name and birthplace taken care of in half a stanza and then gets on to other matters. Joe Scott, on the other hand, extends those lines into a whole stanza by bringing in four lines of completely gratuitous and conventional natural description:

> Where small birds chant their notes so true,
>> Where the trembling waters roar,
> The ivy vine doth thickly twine
>> Round that cottage on the shore.

By so doing, he helps create the picture of happy childhood, the Eden from which the hero is to fall. This emphasis is continued all through the leave-taking stanzas that follow. The "aged" parents are more traditional than factual, though: John Carrick would have been fifty-five in 1884, and his wife, Elizabeth, would have been only forty-four. They could not have been described as "young," but even in the 1880s "aged" would have been a bit much. Of course there is no way of being sure that that *is* the year when Howard left home, but given other facts we *do* have, it is probably pretty nearly correct. At that time Howard himself would have been about nineteen. As for his going to the "Bay of Fundy shore," Joe Scott is probably being factual here and working into his ballad something that his friend had told him about, say, his first job. I can't think of any other reason for Joe's bringing this material in at this point.

Parental, usually maternal, advice is common in balladry. Before Harry Dunn goes on to his death in the woods of Michigan, for example, his mother tries to keep him home:

> The morning that he went away his mother to him did say,
> Saying, "Harry, dear, take my advice and on the farm do stay.
> You'll leave your poor old mother, likewise your sisters three—
> There's something tells me that your face no more on earth shall see."[8]

In "The Texas Rangers," it appears in this form:

> Then I thought of my dear mother, who in tears to me did say,
> "You're going among all strangers, you'd better with me stay;"
> But I thought her old and childish and the best she did not know,
> For I went bent on roving, and a-roving I would go.[9]

The advice is always unheeded. Structurally it could be said to be the interdiction that has to be violated or there is no story; but that may be a little heavy-handed, since the violation is always implicitly obvious without any direct statement.[10] At any rate, it is an extension of the Eden theme, the that-which-might-have-been, the good life lost. How important this theme was to Joe Scott can be deduced from the fact that the leave-taking scene takes up seven stanzas, and five of these are devoted to maternal advice. That's better than a third of the ballad—if we take it together with the two introductory stanzas it's almost half—and no other ballad that I know of has anything like those proportions. Yet it is developed by a combination of traditional formulas, phrases, and proverbial expressions that make it all sound right and natural. Joe begins, for example, by setting the talk beneath a tree, a scene that almost certainly suggested by one in another ballad current in lumbercamp tradition, "The Irish Patriot."[11] The fact that both ballads are sung to the same tune is something we will return to later. The next two stanzas (4–5) are vintage Scott: the kind of stylized traditional natural description for which it is easier to find parallels in his own than in other ballads, although traditional analogues can be found for almost every phrase and adjective.

Back in 1834, a man by the name of Horatio Richmond Palmer had published a song called "Have Courage, My Boy, to Say No!," which

was entirely made up of parental advice to a young man starting on
"life's journey," and it was popular enough that Joe might well have
known it. He might also have known "Oft Times I Wonder," a version
of which was collected in Vanceboro, Maine, containing the following stanza:

> Now my poor ancient mother oft-times cautioned me
> To leave off my drinking, shun bad company,
> "For my boy you are young and they'll lead you astray,
> You will think of my words when I'm cold in the clay."[12]

In other words, it is neither the presence nor the purport of the
parental advice that is surprising; it is the sheer abundance of it. Joe
developed his ballads in an extremely leisurely manner, and in this
section, even the two stanzas that are not part of the mother's speech
show this emphasis: one (8) being simply more natural description,
the other (9) being a long good-bye.

The third section of the ballad (sts. 10–11) begins with the family's
move to Haverhill, Massachusetts, and ends with the mother's
death. As far as I can establish them, the facts are straight enough.
According to the *Haverhill Gazette*'s account of Howard's death,
John Carrick and family had moved to Bradford (which became Ward
Seven of Haverhill) "eleven years ago," which would be 1886.[13]
More than likely he came there like so many others to work in the
shoe factories that were then booming (Haverhill was one of the
world's largest producers of slippers), though he seems also to have
worked as a farmhand from time to time. Elizabeth Carrick died of
"heart disease" December 22, 1891, which would have been six, not
four, years before Howard's suicide, and Howard not only returned
home at this time, but evidently stayed around for about three years,
working as a farmhand. Mrs. Carrick is buried in Elmwood Cemetery, Bradford, not in a churchyard; but the churchyard is part of the
tradition.

The fourth section, which I have called the "confession," includes
stanzas 12 through 15. Howard tells us that he has knocked around a
lot, has been a bad boy, is now sick, and is planning to kill himself.
There is no way of checking the extent of Howard's travels. According to his family he disappeared suddenly about 1894, and while they
admitted they hadn't heard from him for three years, they denied
vehemently the rumor that he had been a tramp. That's understand-

able, of course, and any of us would likely have done the same thing for a member of our own family, but in the ballad Joe Scott is probably working with what he knew firsthand or, at the least, secondhand, which is to say that Howard *had* been a tramp. It is also understandable that neither the newspapers nor the official death record would say anything about syphilis. As a matter of fact, not even Joe mentions it by name. It's just that everybody who knew anything about it seems to have known that, and there is no doubt in my mind that that *is* what Joe is talking about in stanza 15. The door-hinge, of course, was a detail that was common knowledge.

Once he has Howard confess his problem and state his intentions of suicide, we get two very traditional farewell stanzas, but once again they are developed in typical Joe Scott imagery and with typical Joe Scott leisureliness. Stanza 16 is a pretty straight "adieu," the sort of thing John Calhoun extended to four stanzas in "Peter Emberly." Although we can't say so with finality, the girl is almost certainly the poet's invention. Perhaps he was working with something Howard had told him, but it is more likely that she is a creature of ballad convention, heightening the sense of the good life lost. The theme of stanza 17 is a traditional one, but Joe has taken what is usually done in four lines and extended it to eight. Again "Peter Emberly" offers the parallel:

> For the world will roll on just the same
> When I have passed away,
> What signifies a mortal man
> Whose origin is clay?[14]

By bringing in the birds, the fawn, the grass, and the flowers, he makes Howard's last words just that much more poignant.

G. Malcom Laws, Jr., said of the first-person ballad that "death may be fearfully anticipated, but it cannot be dramatized, and thus such ballads are not neatly rounded off."[15] Scott neatly rounds this ballad off by the direct and simple expedient of shifting his point of view from first to third person. As I have said elsewhere, it is more common for a ballad to tell its story "from a fairly consistent single point of view in time and space, but there are enough exceptions to make it clear that such consistency was not a matter of style."[16] No traditional singer has ever suggested that this shift was a flaw, though several of my literary friends have, which makes it a splendid example of how the standards of one tradition do not always apply to others.

Two details should be mentioned. First, Joe knew who cut Howard down, but neither John Derkin nor any of the names in other extant versions of the ballad resembles Jack Weeks or Mike Sutton at all: John Durgan, Doc Durgin, Jack Jordan, Jack Coggins, and so on. According to the death certificate, the physician's name was J. F. DeCosta. Why did Joe alter the facts of the case? Why did he not have Sutton and Weeks discover him? The only answer I can come up with is one that I'm not really very satisfied with: a doctor making his round would have been a logical person to discover a suicide.

Second, although Joe certainly knew that Howard's body had been sent to his family in Haverhill, he could not have known where exactly he was buried. It must have been his sense of what was artistically fitting and appropriate that led Joe to place Howard at his mother's side for the long sleep. In point of fact, Howard is buried not at his mother's side (his brother Eli has that position) but about eight feet behind and to the right of her. That's getting pretty fussy, though. The point is that given the mother's importance in this ballad, Joe puts Howard right where he *ought* to be, at her side.

It remains only to comment on the four concluding lines, which make up the warning, and these are so commonplace and conventional as to make detailed comment superfluous. As the naming stanza frames the story at one end, the warning frames it at the other, and it lets us feel that our interest in Howard's case has not been just prurient.

"Howard Carey," then, tells a true story, which means that it is true in the main. Scott was working from the best sources available to him: what friends (like Mike Sutton) might have told him and what he might have learned directly from Howard himself. His facts are straight enough, but his emphasis is unquestionably on scenes that were necessarily almost entirely imaginative: Howard's leave-taking from his mother and his final soliloquy. We can also see Joe's love of traditional natural description, since a quarter of the ballad is devoted to birds and flowers and dewdrops. But the truly remarkable thing in "Howard Carey" is the importance given to the mother, who appears as the dominant figure—either the speaker or the one spoken about—in thirteen of the nineteen stanzas. We'll have more to say about that after we see what subsequent singers and seventy years have made of Joe's creation.

"Howard Carey" has been extremely popular, and one measure of its popularity is that it was a song frequently asked for in the *Family Herald* "Old Favourites" column: a dozen requests, the earliest in 1916, the latest in 1952. For the present study I was able to bring together forty-nine versions of the ballad, thirty-one of them complete (*"That's the whole of it"*) or nearly complete (*"There's a verse or two missing, I think"*). Aside from Joe's original print of it, the song seems to have circulated almost entirely by oral tradition. The *Family Herald* never printed it, although they evidently sent out typed copies from time to time. Robert W. Gordon reprinted "Howard Curry" in his "Old Songs That Men Have Sung" column in *Adventure* magazine for December 8, 1926,[17] but I have never had anyone tell me that is where he learned it, nor is there any evidence to show that that version affected the song's tradition in any way. The geographical distribution is, as we might expect, entirely limited to Maine and the Maritime Provinces, but within this area it moved easily and freely. It had its start and was a standard fixture in lumbercamp tradition; but there are plenty of examples of people who learned it "at home," so it was well established in local tradition as well.

The first thing that is clear from an examination of the "complete" versions is that the ballad has been shortened. The average length is a little over thirteen stanzas, but it is more meaningful to point out that more than half of the versions have between fourteen and sixteen stanzas. Interestingly, though, it seems to have been less de rigueur with this ballad than it was with "Benjamin Deane" to speak of it as a "long" or "tough" one, even though it was just about as long in most cases and (if my statistics mean anything at all) just about as tough. Let's look now at what got remembered and what didn't.

To begin with, "Howard Carey" has kept the heavy emphasis on the mother. With only one exception,[18] she is present, either expressly or by implication, in more than half the stanzas. But that's not really very surprising; if the ballad was to survive at all it would have to keep that emphasis. It couldn't change *that* much and still be "Howard Carey." However, certain other proportions and emphases *could* change without destroying the ballad, and change they did, but not as much as we might expect. For example, while Joe devoted a quarter of his ballad to natural description, the median proportion for the extant complete versions is more nearly a fifth, but that's still a lot in proportion to other ballads in northern tradition. It would appear, then, that in "Howard Carey," as in several of his other ballads, Joe's innovations were essentially acceptable, even if slightly modified.

As might have been predicted—in fact I *did* predict it—the seven-stanza leave-taking (3–9) was shortened, but it still kept its importance. Joe's original 37 percent was reduced to a median of 33, that's all. Every complete version has the third stanza, with its picture of mother and son beneath the willow tree, followed by some sort of advice, but not as a rule four whole stanzas of it. Three stanzas would be more like it, and there are almost never fewer than two, which is really pretty remarkable. What frequently happens (in eighteen of the thirty-one complete versions, to be exact) is that stanzas 4 and 5 get compressed; the flowers-dewdrops-perfume lines drop out and the advice stays, leaving something like this:

"So you see on yonder hillside where the grass is growing green,
The lilies and the violets and the wild rose might be seen;
Those flowers are magnificent and pleasing to the eye,
Remember that the snake always beneath those blossoms lie."[19]

There is some tendency, then, toward economy through a pruning of Joe's more luxuriant passages, but as tendencies go it is a pretty faltering one. It looks more to me as though people liked Joe's ballads *because* they were florid, and that is borne out by the fact that the only addition I can find that anyone ever made to "Howard Carey" was an extra stanza of motherly imprecation set between Joe's stanzas 8 and 9, thus:

I then arose from off my seat, I could no longer stay;
"You'll think of what I've told you, lad, when mouldering in the clay.
And when I'm dead and in my grave, you'll kindly think of me;
And what I told you as a boy, beneath this willow tree."

That's from the *Family Herald* version, and their occasional mailing out of copies (as I said, they never published it) may account for the appearance of that second line in three other versions,[20] but the stanza can't be said to have caught on at all.

"Howard Carey"

If stanzas 10 and 11—the move to Haverhill, the mother's death, and Howard's return home—were to be omitted from the ballad, it would change the story line very little, and I was sure that these two stanzas would frequently be omitted. I couldn't have been more wrong; more than 80 percent of the complete versions have retained them. And their position is very stable, which is to say that if they are in a particular version they always appear at just this point. But then the events they narrate could hardly come earlier or later.

Stanzas 12 through 17 show a good deal less stability, in terms of both the order and the frequency of appearance of the individual stanzas. Stanza 12, which tells of Howard's wanderings and getting caught in the web, occurs in more than 90 percent of the versions, while Howard's curse on Maine (13) appears only 60 percent of the time. Both stanzas 14 and 15, telling of his suffering and his intention to kill himself, are in almost all the complete versions. On the other hand, the farewell stanzas (16–17) are by far the most unstable in the entire ballad, appearing in fewer than half of the versions, often out of sequence (though always within this group of stanzas). The next stanza (18), in which the suicide is discovered and the body cut down, is always present, while the final stanza (19), bringing Howard to rest at his mother's side and pointing the moral, occurs about 60 percent of the time.

To sum up for the moment, we can say that singers of "Howard Carey" have kept Joe Scott's original plan and proportions almost without change, cutting down only a little on the heavy freight of maternal advice but somewhat more on Howard's farewells and philosophizing. Within these two sections, the sequence of stanzas may alter some, but only within very definite limits. Overall, the ballad has held up very well, and it has remained the way Joe made it: lush and leisurely.

The tune tradition for this ballad has been very stable. Of the thirty-one tunes I have collected, all but five are clearly sets of the same air. Wesley Smith's tune is a good representative of it, and so is Edmund Doucette's (Pl.6), which follows:

127

hand, Say-ing, "Don't for-get your par-ents, lad, when in a for - eign

land." My moth - er led me to a seat be - neath a wil-low tree,

With quiv-'ring lips bid me sit down, for she wished to talk to me.

In classic modal terminology, this would be described as Mixolydian (with evidence of incipient chromaticism in the frequent raised seventh of the cadence); but it is even more important to notice that the second degree is usually either entirely lacking or present only occasionally in unaccented passing positions. The tune has a range of a major ninth or (if the inflected seventh is counted) a minor tenth. The melodic contour is undulating, while phrasal structure is ABCD, the first phrase rising to the fifth and returning to the final, the second rising to the octave and resting on the fourth (usually, as in Doucette's rendition, above) or the fifth (less frequently, as in Wesley Smith's), the third rising to a ninth in the first half and ending on the octave, and the fourth phrase rising quickly to the seventh or the octave and descending at the end, of course, to the final. In spite of its being a progressive tune it has a cyclic feel, because the cadences of the A and D phrases are always identical, a descent from the fifth to the final that omits the second and anticipates the final in the next-to-last measure, thus:

All of which is to say that this tune shares many of its characteristics with other double or come-all-ye tunes, yet is entirely distinctive and identifiable in spite of a host of variations. Sometimes, for example, we get a ABCA progression with the A phrase this way:[21]

parlando rubato

or the mid-cadence (end of the B phrase) is approached this way:[22]

Jim Brown's tune (NB.14) is unique in having an ABBC phrase pattern and a range of a major tenth; yet I would still call it a set of the same air:

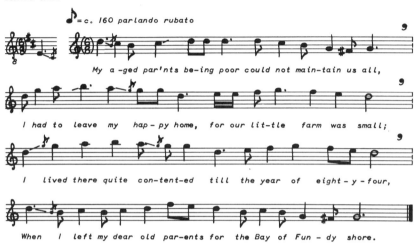

My a-ged par'nts be-ing poor could not main-tain us all,

I had to leave my hap-py home, for our lit-tle farm was small;

I lived there quite con-tent-ed till the year of eight-y-four,

When I left my dear old par-ents for the Bay of Fun-dy shore.

This tune is widespread in Irish-American tradition. One strain of it is the standard tune for "The Texas Rangers," while in the Northeast along the Miramichi River we find two local songs to slightly varying sets of it.[23] Obviously, it is a tune that Joe Scott would have known as part of standard woods repertoire, and since it is so clearly *the* tune for "Howard Carey," I am perfectly ready to say that it is the one Joe had in mind for it on that basis alone. But there is a more cogent argument I can add as a clincher. In Maine and New Brunswick a long ballad called "The Irish Patriot" is always sung to this tune. A ship's captain lands on "India's burning shore," where he meets an elderly Irishman who tells him the story of how he revenged himself on a cruel English lord who murdered his wife and child. The second stanza begins as follows:

> The old man led me to a seat,
>   it being a fallen tree
> And at his request we both sat down
>   for he wished to speak to me.[24]

129

Since those are virtually the same lines Joe used in his third stanza to introduce the mother's speech, it is just possible that this is where it all began: he wanted to make a ballad about his friend's death; he recalled something Howard had told him about how his mother had given him such good advice (in his last days Howard was feeling pretty lugubrious, and it's the sort of thing he might well have brought up); the scene from "The Irish Patriot" came to mind, and Joe was off and running. That's speculation—it's also possible the scene was suggested by the tune—but I have no doubt at all that Joe got his tune from "The Irish Patriot."

How about the five "nonstandard" tunes? When I asked Omer McKenna (Me.2) about "Howard Carey," he doubted that he could get it together. After fumbling around a bit he started off, using the same tune he had just used for "Benjamin Deane." After two stanzas he shifted over to both the tune and the words to "Peter Emberly," but he caught himself, laughed, and quit. In other words, he didn't remember the song very well, but he wanted to oblige me. When Judson Armstrong sang the ballad for Helen Creighton (NS.1), he used the standard tune for "Guy Reed," which may or may not have been a mistake (though we have no right to assume it is) similar to the one Phil Walsh of Northwest Bridge, New Brunswick, made when he sang "Howard Carey" for me in 1963 (NB.15).

Phil had been wanting to sing it for me for over a year, so one evening I stopped by his place and said how about now. He was on his way out, but since I was leaving town the next day he took the time. When he got into it, I was surprised to hear him using the tune to "Peter Emberly," which I had never heard to "Howard Carey" before. He paused awkwardly before the second stanza, and later on even mixed in a line from "Peter Emberly," though he caught himself. I was interested but didn't want to say anything at the time, figuring I'd catch him again. Later that summer I met Phil in downtown Newcastle and asked him to sing over a stanza of "Howard Carey" for me. He did, this time using the standard tune. I checked him again when I saw him at the Miramichi Folksong Festival the next year, and again he used the standard tune. What it all comes to is that in his hurry that evening Phil got started on the wrong tune but for any number of reasons figured he'd just go ahead with it. Had I not been suspicious, I might have enshrined his error as a unique version. There is a moral in that for folklorists.

"Howard Carey"

Leo Gorman's tune (Pl. 1) is very unusual, a two-phrase affair repeated over and over:

My a - ged par - ents, they be-ing poor, could not main - tain us all, I had to leave my lit - tle home, for our lit - tle farm was small.

Since his version was the shortest one I found that had any claim to completeness—six stanzas, which Leo felt was pretty much the whole of it—it may be a bit suspect, but there it is. The version Joe Walsh of Morell, Prince Edward Island, sang for me, though, is something else again. Is it truly a different tune, or is it just one more variant of the standard one? The modality is different, whether we call it Dorian or simply point out that the third and (with two exceptions) the seventh degrees are "flatted"; and the phrasal pattern is different, being ABBC. Yet compare his B phrase with the standard C phrase, and add to that the presence of the descending cadence that avoids the second degree in both his A and C phrases. It may be cowardly, but having pointed out the differences and similarities, I am going to let the matter rest and simply give the tune as Joe sang it for me:

The day I left my hap-py home, they took me by the hand, Say-ing, "Don't for-get your par-ents, lad, when in a for - eign land." My moth-er led me to a seat be-neath the old oak tree, With trem-bling lips bade me sit down, for she wished to speak to me.

131

In sum, "Howard Carey" shows an amazingly stable tune tradition—further evidence of the ballad's strong oral tradition. The exceptions are minimal, and those that exist can be minimized even further.

How do we account for "Howard Carey's" great popularity? Before launching into more abstruse and high-sounding explanations, I would like to point out that it is a good ballad, well put together and full of beautiful language. It sings well, and what sounds mawkish to elevated literary tastes does not sound at all that way when the ballad is performed by a good traditional singer like Wesley Smith, Jim Brown, Joe Walsh, or Fred McMahon. In other words, it was popular because it is a fine piece of balladry. That may sound simpleminded, but I consider it a good place to begin.

One approach to this problem of popularity would be to ask people why they liked "Howard Carey," and I have frequently done so. The most common response has been that "it was true, it was about something that really did happen," but several people went further than that. Irving Ashford of Andersonville, New Brunswick, said that he liked the old songs because they had a moral. *"That 'Howard Carey' now," he went on, "that had a real moral to it for the young, if they'd listen." John Morrison of Charlottetown, Prince Edward Island, had more to say on that point: *"Yes, I always liked it. I mean there seemed to be a lesson to it, and I think if the songs today were more like them there that the younger people would take a—well, they'd know the pitfalls that there is in this life. You can't tell them. . . . No, they couldn't tell me either, not up until a certain age, but I did after I got out around and realized that those things could happen, and today I see it more than ever."

I don't think it is unkind to suggest that such statements involve a good deal of hindsight, telling us more about why an older man approves of a song than about why a young man learned it; yet at least one explanation for the ballad's popularity certainly lies in this direction. It is not that anyone who sang the song seriously believed that his audience would eschew broad and bottle for hearing Howard's tale of woe. I don't think even Joe Scott believed that; the moral tag in "Howard Carey" seems like even more of an afterthought in this ballad than it does in most, something *comme il faut*, and singers appear to have felt this gratuitousness because these lines are dropped in almost half the versions (and the same can be said of stanza 13, the only other direct reference to whiskey and bad women). It is rather that through singing this ballad or hearing it sung one could momentarily subscribe to or participate in a code of conduct and view of life that everyone recognized as right. One should listen to the wisdom of his elders, beauty and pleasure are suspect and probably bad, and self-denial is good. Though given a solid start in life, Howard falls and is punished, which is as it should be; and all hearing the ballad can assume virtue, though have it they may not, and feel better for it.

There's a paradox here. "Howard Carey" got its start and lived most of its life in lumbercamp tradition, and there probably wasn't a man-jack in the woods who couldn't in some way identify with its unfortunate hero. All had left a home, even if only for the winter, and the song tells lovingly and nostalgically of home and mother and all they represent. The woodsman's life was a notoriously roaring one; all had roared a bit (or intended to, perhaps), and certainly all knew of men who had suffered in some way the consequences of roaring. Each man could see in Howard's story something of his own life or something close enough to it to be recognized as a perpetual possibility, and through Howard's "cruel death" each could achieve a vicarious expiation. One could, then, subscribe to the prevailing moral code and see Howard's death as his just desert, while at the same time he could identify with the sinner, feel sorry for him (and of course for himself), and suffer with him. Small wonder that on hearing the news "many the cheek grew pale / And filled with wonder many the heart to hear this mournful tale."

Since I am already so deep into psycholiterary speculation, there is no reason not to go deeper yet and suggest an even more latent pattern: the setting-out and return, and what is set out from and returned to is the mother. I have spoken before of the tremendous importance of the mother in this song and of how the Haverhill stanzas (10-11), with their temporary return to her, have been kept in the ballad, though they could have been dropped without hurting the story. Now in the end the restless wanderer sleeps at his mother's side in an almost classic Freudian death-as-return-to-the-womb resolution. In a life that was full of restless wanderers, that cluster of associations must have been compelling.

Finally, since whatever else this book may be it is a book about Joe Scott, think of what Howard's fate must have meant to Joe. Here was a man from his native Saint John valley, a man five years his senior who had hanged himself in a fit of despondency coming on the heels of an unpleasant bout with secondary syphilis. Joe, as we know, entered the hospital with what was clearly tertiary syphilis in 1916, and that stage of the disease may take as long as twenty years to manifest itself. It is entirely probable that when Howard died Joe knew he had the same disease, and while he could not foresee his own cruel death, he must have had at least a looming of things to come. In any case, we can be sure that when he wrote of Howard Carrick, he was also writing about Joe Scott. It was a kind of autobiography; it just happens to have been prophecy, too.

LIST OF VERSIONS

JS   Original printed slip, as obtained from the notebook of Bert Thorne, Jemseg, N.B. 19 sts.

FH   *Family Herald* version. No source given, n.d.; 17 sts. This was never published, but some copies were typed up and sent out.

NH   William H. Monroe, ca. 70, Monroe N.H., Sept. 3, 1957; in a letter, typescript, 14 sts., very irregular. On Sept. 11, 1965, Monroe tried to sing the tune for me, but couldn't get it straight; see NA Ives tape 65.16. Knew it was by Scott. His title: "Howard Kerwick."

Me.1   Edward Gavel, Sanford, Me., Aug. 29, 1966; in a letter, manuscript, 17 sts. "This is as I remember it. Thought there were eighteen verses. Maybe I forgot one." His title: "Howard (Carrey?)." On Aug. 25, 1966, he recited eleven stanzas and sang one; see NA Ives tape 66.10. Thinks he learned it on the drive over on the Mattawamkeag in the 1920s. Did not know it was by Scott.

Me.2   Omer McKenna, ca. 80, Rumford, Me., Sept. 28, 1965; NA Ives tape 65.19, sung, 3 sts., fragment. McKenna doubted that he could get it together. Using the same tune he used for "Benjamin Deane" (Me.2), he sang two stanzas, then shifted both tune and words to "Peter Emberly." *"That it?" he said doubtfully. "That's that other fella that you were talking about," he laughed. Learned it back home on P.E.I.

Me.3   Pearl Longley, Mexico, Me., Sept. 29, 1965; from a manuscript book, NA 248.025–027, 12 sts. Taken down from singing of her late mother, Gertrude Bradbury, as she had learned it around Bridgewater, Me. Knew it was by Scott.

Me.4   Roy Lohnes, ca. 70, Andover, Me., Aug., 1958; taken down by Anna Thurston and sent me in a letter, recited, 18½ sts. Knew it was by Scott. His title: "Howard Kerry."

Me.5   Isaac Gardner, Allagash, Me., Nov. 19, 1962; collected by Ronald Jean, NA 207, sung, 5 sts., fragment. Gardner sang four stanzas, then said, "That's not all of it," and sang one more. Then he did not go on. Did not know it was by Scott.

Me.6   Eldin Colsie, Staceyville, Me., July 15, 1941; collected by Helen Hartness Flanders, Flanders Collection D–347b2, sung, 2 sts., fragment.

Me.7   Arthur Corey, Westfield, Me., Sept. 21, 1962; collected by Beatrice Field, NA 128.038, recited, 3 sts., fragment.

Me.8   Emma Turner, Bucksport, Me., Oct. 9, 1941; collected by Marguerite Olney, Flanders Collection D–257a, sung, 3 sts., fragment. "I used to hear it sung here in Bucksport," Mrs. Turner said.

Me.9   Merle P. Weymouth, Ellsworth Falls, Me., Mar. 16, 1957; NA Ives tape 1.9 and ATL 2142.5, sung and recited, 7 sts., fragment. Did not know it was by Scott.

NB.1   Phyllis Woodside, Milltown, N.B., July 5, 1964; in a letter, manuscript, 5½ sts., fragment. Learned from the constant singing of her mother. See notes to version NB.15 of "The Plain Golden Band." Knew it was by Scott.

NB.2   Wilfred Woodard, ca. 80, St. Stephen, N.B., Aug. 18, 1964; NA Ives tape 64.7, sung, 1 st., fragment. Knew it was by Scott.

NB.3   Michael Noonan, 77, St. Stephen, N.B., Aug. 18, 1964; NA Ives tape 64.7, recited, 6½ sts., fragment. Did not know it was by Scott.

NB.4   Mrs. Trueman Scott, Honeydale, N.B., June 19, 1964; in a letter, manuscript, 16 sts. On Aug. 23, 1964, Mrs. Scott sang it for me from a version in her scrapbook (from which the manuscript copy she sent me was probably taken); see NA Ives tape 64.9. She says she got the words to this song from her brother-in-law, Charles Vernon Scott, in 1928. Her title: "Howard Kerry."

NB.5   Harry W. Stevens, St. George, N.B., June 27, 1964; in a letter, manuscript, 18 sts.

NB.6   Thomas Cleghorn, 86, Harvey Station (York Co.), N.B., Aug. 22, 1964; manuscript, 19 sts., and sung in part, NA Ives tape 64.6. His daughter, Mrs. Karl Byers, copied it for me from his notebook. His title: "Howard Carrick." Knew it was by Scott. Learned it in the woods in Maine.

NB.7   Thomas Pollock, 90, Harvey (York Co.), N.B., Aug. 23, 1964; NA Ives tape 64.8, recited, 2½ sts., fragment. Knew it was by Scott.

NB.8   Eddie McSheffrey, ca. 80, Bath, N.B., Aug., 1964; in a letter from Alice Flynn, Allegany, N.Y., manuscript, 6 sts., fragment. Second version sung and recited for me, Bath, N.B., Aug. 20, 1964; NA Ives tape 64.8, 6 sts., fragment. Knew it was by Scott.

NB.9   Joe McCullough, Mineral, N.B., Aug. 21, 1964; NA Ives tape 64.8, sung, 1 st., fragment. Said he had known it all once, and learned it down in Island Falls, Me., about 1923.

NB.10 Harry Keenan, 72, Woodstock, N.B., May 11, 1962; NA Ives tape 1.122 and ATL 3129.7, recited, 10½ sts., then 1 st. sung. Does not recall where he learned it.

NB.11 Fred Campbell, 81, Arthurette, N.B., Aug. 19, 1964, sung at Seventh Miramichi Folksong Festival, Newcastle, N.B.; NA Ives tape 64.7, sung, 16 sts. Campbell had previously sung and recited the song for me on Aug. 13, 1963, during the Sixth Festival, 15 sts. On July 17, 1965, he recited it for his daughter, Kathleen Campbell; see NA 80.045–048. His title: "Howard Carrick." Learned it from Joe Scott's printed version.

NB.12 Lloyd Belyea, Brown's Flats, N.B.; July 19, 1964; in a letter, manuscript, 15 sts. Did not know the tune. It was written down "by someone I can't remember who in some camp where I worked." Did not know it was by Scott.

NB.13 G. W. Elder, Sussex, N.B., 1958; collected by Helen Creighton, NMC CR–196–2, 245, sung, 3½ sts., fragment.

NB.14 James Brown, 80, South Branch, N.B., July 12, 1963; NA Ives tape 1.137 and ATL 3144.5, sung, 14 sts. Brown sang it again the next day with minor variations but with identical musical phrase patterns; see NA Ives 1.144 and ATL 3151.2. Learned it in the Maine woods some fifty years ago. Did not know it was by Scott.

NB.15 Philip Walsh, ca. 55, Northwest Bridge, N.B., July 11, 1963; NA Ives tape 1.136 and ATL 3143.2, sung, 14 sts. Sung to the tune of "Peter Emberly." Learned locally. Did not know who it was by.

NB.16 Ernest McCarthy, Blackville, N.B., July 17, 1965; collected by Kay Hayes, NA 193.014–017, sung, 14 sts.

NB.17 Fred McMahon, ca. 70, Chatham, N.B., Aug., 1948; Beaverbrook Collection, sung, 16 sts. See Manny and Wilson, *Songs of Miramichi*, pp. 111–114.

NB.18 Harold Whitney, Strathadam, N.B., sung at Third Miramichi Folksong Festival, Newcastle, N.B.; NMC CR–213–2, 675, sung, 1 st., fragment. Whitney was simply demonstrating how an evening might have been spent when he was a boy at home: "The evening would continue with my brother Bill, who would sing 'Howard Currie.' "

NB.19 Wilmot MacDonald, 59, Glenwood, N.B., July 10, 1963; sung, 1 st., fragment. Claims he never knew all the words; felt he could probably get about half of it together but couldn't be sure where the stanzas came in.

NB.20 Herbert Eddy, Gloucester Co., N.B., 1926; Gordon Manuscripts 1520, manuscript, 17 sts. Published by Robert W. Gordon in *Adventure*, Dec. 8, 1926, pp. 206–207. "Communicated by Mr. George Hirdt, who obtained it from Mr. Herbert Eddy of Gloucester County, N.B."

NB.21 Anna L. Murray, Campbellton, N.B., June 25, 1964; in a letter, manuscript, 10 sts. At the time of writing, Mrs. Murray was living with her daughter, Mrs. H. St. Onge, Niagara Falls, Ont., who took the song down from her mother's dictation. Did not know it was by Joe Scott.

NB.22 George Fulton, ca. 75, Salmon River, N.B., Oct. 13, 1974; collected by Neil Rosenberg, his tape 74–5 (to be deposited at MUNFLA), sung, 13 sts. Had never heard of Joe Scott. (See also NB.23 below.)

NB.23 Marjorie Stillwell, Chipman, N.B., 1974; collected by Neil Rosenberg, photocopied from Mrs. Stillwell's songbook, type-script, 16 sts. From Rosenberg's notes: "From singing of her father, Fred Fulton, now deceased. . . . Fred Fulton was George Fulton's brother [*see NB.22 above*]. So here are two versions of 'Howard Carey' from the same family."

NS.1 Judson Armstrong, Sherwood (Lunenburg Co.), N.S., June, 1949; collected by Helen Creighton, NMC CR–1–4, sung, 12 sts.

NS.2 L. P. Corbett, Pembroke, N.S., letter, June, 1964; in a letter, manuscript, ca. 4 sts., fragment.

NS.3 Jack Turple, Upper Kennetcook, N.S., July, 1952; collected by Helen Creighton, NMC CR–97, 974, sung, 11 sts.

NS.4 Patrick Pentecost, Sydney, N.S., June 11, 1964; in a letter, manuscript, 16 sts.

NS.5 James Curtis (b. 1898), Cape North (Bay St. Lawrence), Cape Breton Island, N.S., 1975; collected by Denis Ryan, MUNFLA 76–345, sung, 19 sts. Learned from his uncle Tom Brown, who had worked with Scott in the Maine woods.

PI.1 Leo Gorman, 70, St. Charles, P.E.I., Apr. 1, 1968; NA Ives tape 68.2, sung, 6 sts. Gorman learned the song locally. Did not know it was by Scott.

PI.2 Joseph Walsh, 72, Morell Rear, P.E.I., June 17, 1964; in a letter, manuscript, 9½ sts. On Sept. 1, 1965, Walsh sang it for me; see NA Ives tape 65.12, sung, 9 sts. Third version, Apr. 1, 1968; NA Ives tape 68.3, sung, 9 sts. Learned locally. See Ives, *Lawrence Doyle*, pp. xv–xvi, for the circumstances. Did not know it was by Joe Scott.

PI.3 John Morrison, 53, Charlottetown, P.E.I., Feb. 3, 1965; in a letter, manuscript, 13 sts. When I visited him Aug. 30, 1965, he sang the tune for me; see NA Ives tape 65.8. Says he learned it from Asaph Walfield when the two of them worked in a lobster factory near his home in Conway about thirty-five years earlier. Did not know it was by Joe Scott. See also Dibblee and Dibblee, *Folksongs from Prince Edward Island*, pp. 59–60, for another version; 11 sts. with tune. Although the stanzas differ considerably in detail, both versions are alike in leaving out the Haverhill stanzas (10–11) entirely.

PI.4 John O'Connor, ca. 65, Hope River, P.E.I., Aug. 31, 1965; NA Ives tape 65.11, sung, 14½ sts. On Mar. 12, 1965, he had sent me a manuscript version, almost identical to the one he sang. Says he learned the song "from some lad in the woods" over on Burnt Hill in Miramichi in the winter of 1919, "the winter the flu was so bad." He also said he had heard others singing the song around Hope River. Did not know who wrote it.

PI.5 Wesley Smith, 66, Victoria West, P.E.I., Aug. 18, 1958; NA Ives tape 1.40 and ATL 2165.3, sung, 14½ sts. Smith had to stop several times to figure out what came next. Second version, Aug. 28, 1965; NA Ives tape 65.9, sung (last line recited), 14¼ sts. This version is given at the beginning of this chapter. On Sept. 11, 1965, Smith sent me a manuscript version, 16½ sts. Learned it locally, but also heard it sung in the Maine woods. Knew it was by Scott.

PI.6 Edmund Doucette, 69, Miminegash, P.E.I., July 14, 1963; NA Ives tape 1.145 and ATL 3152.1, sung, 8 sts., fragment. Learned it locally. Did not know who wrote it.

PI.7 Grattan McHugh, 60, Tignish, P.E.I., Aug. 25, 1965; NA Ives tape 65.4, sung, 11 sts. He learned the song in Tignish from Bert Provost about 1930. Did not know who wrote it.

PI.8 Malvina Doucette, 65, Tignish, P.E.I., Aug. 26, 1965; NA Ives tape 65.5, sung, 11 sts. Had not sung the song in twenty-five years. Learned it in Palmer Road, where she grew up, from Jim Poirer. She had no idea who wrote it.

PI.9 Emile Arsenault, Tignish, P.E.I., Aug. 26, 1965; NA Ives tape 65.7, sung, 1 st., fragment. Said he did not know the song but had heard it sung. He was just giving me the tune.

"Howard Carey"

NOTES

1. For an account of this meeting, see Edward D. Ives, *Twenty-one Folksongs from Prince Edward Island*, p. 62.

2. Tune variations are as follows: In st. 3 the first half of l. 3 is the first half of the C phrase, while the second half of l. 3 is the second half of the D phrase. In st. 4, ll. 5–6, repeat CD, and the same for ll. 5–6 in sts. 5, 6, and 15.

3. Polley to Gordon, Mar. 2, 1925, Gordon Manuscripts 928. Others who have attributed the song to Scott include Bill Monroe, Roy Lohnes, Phyllis Woodside, Thomas Cleghorn, Eddie McSheffrey, James Curtis, and, of course, Wesley Smith.

4. *Rumford Falls Times*, May 14, 1897.

5. G. Malcom Laws, Jr., *Native American Balladry*, p. 187.

6. A quick survey of Laws's categories E and F in *Native American Balladry* and category L in *American Balladry from British Broadsides* will support this point.

7. Louise Manny and James Reginald Wilson, *Songs of Miramichi*, pp. 160–161.

8. "Harry Dunn" (Laws C–14). The present example is from Edith Fowke, *Lumbering Songs from the Northern Woods*, p. 123.

9. "The Texas Rangers" (Laws A–8). The present version is from Helen Hartness Flanders et al., *The New Green Mountain Songster*, p. 37. See also n. 23 in this chapter.

10. See Alan Dundes, *The Morphology of North American Indian Folktales*, esp. pp. 61–72. See also Roger Abrahams and George Foss, *Anglo-American Folksong Style*, pp. 92–131, and in particular the comments on the "morality mode."

11. Edward D. Ives and Sharon Sperl, *Folksongs from Maine*, pp. 81–84.

12. NA 331.032b.

13. *Haverhill Gazette*, May 6, 1897.

14. Manny and Wilson, *Songs of Miramichi*, p. 162.

15. Laws, *Native American Balladry*, p. 29.

16. Edward D. Ives, *Lawrence Doyle*, p. 163. For further references, see ibid., p. 165, n. 6. "The Butcher Boy" (Laws P–24) offers a beautiful example of this kind of shift.

17. NB.20.

18. PI.1.

19. NB.14. See also PI.5 at the beginning of this chapter.

20. Me.1, NS.1, NS.3.

21. PI.4. The same pattern is found in NS.3 and Me.5. See also the D phrase of NB.17 as it is transcribed in Manny and Wilson, *Songs of Miramichi*, p. 111.

22. NB.4. Also PI.4, NS.3, Me.5, NB.18.

23. See Manny and Wilson, *Songs of Miramichi*, pp. 52–53 ("The Banks of the Miramichi"), and James Reginald Wilson, "Ballad Tunes of the Miramichi," pp. 24, 71–72 ("Kate Dennis"). For further tune analogues, see ibid., p. 24 (No. 19), and Fowke, *Lumbering Songs*, pp. 123–125, esp. the notes under B on p. 125. It is also worth remarking that when Lewis Lund of Jacksonville, Me., sang "The Texas Rangers" for me in 1959, he called it "The Howard Rangers," but he did not know that there was a ballad called "Howard Carey." Is this simply an interesting coincidence?

24. Ives and Sperl, *Folksongs from Maine*, p. 82.

10

"Guy Reed":
The Ballad as Lament

"We ought to have *something* to treat Phil with," Nick Underhill said to me. "I thought you had a bottle."

"I thought I did, too," I said, "I swear I had some in there. I *know* I did. But that's no help now," I added, fumbling for a last time in the offending glove compartment as though conceivably there might be a pint lurking behind the flashlight. "Sure as hell nothing in there now to do a man any good."

"And the liquor store's closed," said Nick hopelessly (it being Saturday afternoon). "Well, we really ought to have something to treat Phil with." Then he brightened. "Wait," he said, and got out of the car to go back in his house.

We had only just come out. For about an hour Nick had been singing for me in that unique style that no one who has attended a Miramichi Folksong Festival can ever mistake or forget: very slow, many rests, and a way of hanging on to the high notes that made you wonder where in that little man there was that much breath. But Nick was tired this afternoon, and besides, there was a neighbor he wanted me to meet who knew a lot of old songs, too. His name was Phil Walsh, and we were just on our way over when the present contretemps occurred.

Nick came back out carrying a bottle. By shape it was neither a whiskey bottle nor a rum bottle; if I had to put a name to it, I'd call it a medicine bottle. It bore no label, but the contents looked suspiciously satisfactory. Nick climbed into the car and battened the bottle safely between his feet. "That ought to do it," he said.

"I'll replace that for you Monday," I said apologetically.

"Guy Reed"

"I'd appreciate that," Nick said. And we drove over to Phil's.

Walshes' was a big house, one of the biggest in Northwest Bridge, and it obviously had been and still was alive with children and grandchildren and neighbor children in and out all day, and now a junketing folklorist to see Phil. We went into the parlor, and while I set up the tape recorder Nick and Phil had a treat. Then I had one, and we were ready to begin. Phil knew what song he wanted to sing and got right to it.

Guy Reed

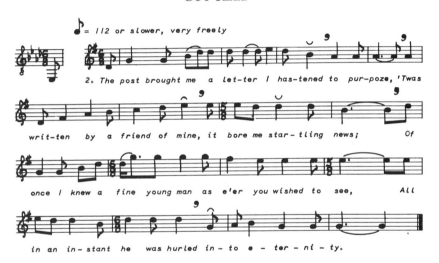

♪ = 112 or slower, very freely

2. The post brought me a let-ter I has-tened to pur-poze, 'Twas writ-ten by a friend of mine, it bore me star-tling news; Of once I knew a fine young man as e'er you wished to see, All in an in-stant he was hurled in-to e - ter - ni - ty.

[1]   Oh, well do I remember one dark and stormy night,
The rain it fell in torrents and the lightning flashed so bright;
The moon and stars above me could not their light reveal,
Dark clouds so gloomy their welcome light concealed.

[2]   The post brought me a letter I hastened to purpose [*pronounced "pur-POZE"*],
'Twas written by a friend of mine, it bore me startling news;
Of once I knew a fine young man as e'er you wished to see,
All in an instant he was hurled into eternity.

[3]   While him and his companions where the waters they do roar,
Were breaking in a landing on the Androscroggam shore;
They worked the face of one of them from the bottom to the top,
Till thirty feet this landing had a perpendic'lar drop.

141

[4]   To work the face much longer 'twould be a foolish part,
      When a jar so slight you see it might that lofty landing start;
      Then all the crew decided that one of them should go
      To roll a log from off the top to start the logs below.

[5]   This young man he among them with a heart so stout and
         brave,
      Not thinking that before night he'd be all straightened for his
         grave;
      Not thinking that the almighty hand was soon to lay him low,
      To leave the ones he loved so dear in sorrow, grief, and woe.

[6]   Oh, a log he quickly canted, the landing creaked below,
      Until it sped unto the verge, it would no further go;
      Then this young man he approached the verge of landing high,
      While all the crew with pale cheeks and trembling limbs stood
         by.

[7]   Up went the shout of warning to warn him of his fate,
      And for an instant he did pause, he seemed to hesitate;
      He rolled the log 'bout halfway off when the landing broke like
         glass,
      And quick as thought he disappeared into that rolling mass.

[8]   The logs they quickly canted from off his mangled form,
      The birds were sweetly singing and the sun shone bright and
         warm;
      Strong men knelt down beside him, their grief could not
         command,
      Unhidden tears that fell like rain and rolled into the sand.

[9]   His comrades [*pronounced "comraids"*] bore him gently and
         laid him on the green,
      Beneath a spreading spruce that stood beside the burbling
         stream;
      The burbling sparkling water fled o'er her rocky bed,
      It seemed to sweetly softly say farewell unto the dead.

[10] This young man he was buried by the order of K.C.,
      A funeral more attended you would very seldom see;
      The church and yard was crowded by people young and old,
      Once more to view that face so fair now forever pale and cold.

[11] His mother she died early when he was but a child,
      They laid her down to slumber near that forest fair and wild;

142

A sister and a brother's now's sleeping by her side
In the village churchyard near that river's dancing tide.

[12] His poor old aged father he's stricken now with grief,
The joys of earthly pleasure cannot bring him no relief;
His untold gold and silver, procession wealth in store,
Sunny skies or music sweet cannot the dead restore.

[13] The blackbird and the swallow, the sunshine and the rain,
The robin and the thrushes in the springtime come again;
The songbird and the sparrow in foreign lands may soar,
But loved ones in death that sleep will come again no more.

[14] Come all ye friend kidren [*sic*] pray for him who's dead and
gone,
To a better home in heaven far away beyond the sun;
Of him you loved most dearly you'll never again see more,
Until you cross death's valley to that great eternal shore.

"Want to hear that back?" I said, when he had finished and we all had another drink. He said he did, so I ran the tape back and once more we listened to the story of this young man's hard death on the river. When it was over, I stopped the machine and looked up at Phil to see what he wanted to sing next. His face was running with tears. "Sorry," he said, "but that song always gets me." He excused himself for a minute. When he came back we went on to more cheerful things like "The Wild Colonial Boy" and "The White Cafe."

There is almost no doubt that Joe Scott wrote "Guy Reed," and as far as I am concerned his title would be perfectly clear, were it not for one awkward problem for which I have no final solution and for which there probably never will be a final solution. It's a nice scholarly sort of problem, but before I go into it we should have a look at the ballad in the form in which Joe originally sold it. Fortunately, Bert Thorne's notebook contained a copy of the original slip, and I reproduce it here:

GUY REED.

————

[1] How well do I remember
One dark and stormy night,

The rain it fell in torrents,
　　The lightning flashed so bright.
The moon and stars above me
　　Did not their light reveal,
For dark clouds so gloomy
　　Did their welcome light conceal.

[2]　The post brought me a letter,
　　I hastened to peruse,
T'was written by a friend of mine,
　　But bore me startling news.
For one I knew, a fine young man
　　As you would wish to see,
In an instant he was hurled
　　Into eternity.

[3]　He and his companions,
　　Where the waters they do roar,
Were breaking in the landing
　　On the Androscoggin shore;
They had picked a face on one of them
　　From bottom to the top,
Fully thirty feet this landing had
　　A perpendicular drop.

[4]　To work the face much longer
　　Would be a foolish part,
A jar so slight, you see, it might
　　This lofty landing start.
There were a few among them
　　Did volunteer to go
To roll a log from off the top
　　To start the logs below.

[5]　This young man he among them
　　With heart so stout and brave,
Not thinking he e'er night would be
　　All straightened for the grave,
Not thinking that death's cruel hand
　　So soon would lay him low,
To leave those ones he loved behind,
　　In sorrow, grief and woe.

[6]　This log they quickly started,
　　The landing creaked below,

And on it sped unto the verge
    But would no further go.
This young man now approaches
    The verge of landing high,
While all the crew with pallid cheeks
    And trembling limb stood by.

[7]   Up went a shout of warning
      To warn him of his fate,
And just an instant he did pause,
    He seemed to hesitate.
He rolled the log just half way o'er,
    The landing broke like glass,
And quick as thought he disappeared
    Into the rolling mass.

        *   *   *   *

[8]   Those logs they rolled carefully
      From off his mangled form,
The birds were singing sweetly,
    The sun shone bright and warm.
Strong men knelt down beside him
    Who could not their grief command,
Unbidden tears burst from their eyes
    And fell into the sand.

[9]   Tenderly they bore him,
      Gently laid him on the green
Beneath a shady tree that grew
    Near by a purling stream.
The bubbling, sparkling waters
    Stealing o'er its sandy bed,
Seemed to murmer [sic], sweetly, softly,
    A farewell unto the dead.

[10]   His remains were buried
      By the order of K. P.,
A funeral more attended
    You would seldom ever see.
The church and yard were crowded
    With people young and old,
Once more to see that face once fair,
    In death now pale and cold.

[11]   His casket was decorated
   With roses sweet and fair,
  His pillow, too, with every hue
   Of flowers bright and rare;
  His brothers of the Order,
   As they marched two by two,
  On the casket a spray let fall,
   A token of adieu.

[12]   His mother she died early
   When he was but a child,
  They laid her down to slumber
   Near a forest fair and wild;
  His brother and his sister
   Are sleeping by her side
  In a quiet country churchyard
   Near the river's dancing tide.

[13]   This young man's name was Guy Reed,
   His age was twenty-three,
  On September the eighth was killed
   In a town known as Riley.
  In the little town of Byron
   Was laid beneath the earth,
  He sleeps beside his kindred
   Near the spot that gave him birth.

[14]   His poor feeble father
   Is stricken now with grief,
  The joy of earthly pleasures
   Will bring him no relief.
  For untold gold or silver,
   Position, wealth in store,
  Sunny skies or music sweet
   Will not the dead restore.

[15]   The robin and the swallow,
   The sunshine and the rain,
  The cuckoo and the sparrow
   With the spring will come again.
  The blackbird and the thrushes
   From foreign lands will soar,
  But loved ones that in death doeth sleep,
   Will come again no more.

"Guy Reed"

[16]   Kind friends and loving kindred
       Of him who's dead and gone
       To a better land in heaven,
       Far away beyond the sun,
       The one you loved so dearly,
         You will ne'er again see more,
       Till you pass through death's dark valley
       To that bright celestial shore.

                                    BY JOE SCOTT.

The direct evidence of Joe's authorship is clear enough. In addition, the ascriptive evidence is just about unequivocal. Those members of the Reed family that I have talked to all claim Joe Scott was a friend of Guy's and wrote the song about him. Other people who were around at the time and were in a position to know also claim the ballad for Joe. J. A. Polley, for example, in response to Robert Gordon's request for information about "Guy Reed" when he published it in *Adventure,* wrote Gordon that "the song was wrote by a lumber jack named Joe Scott a few weeks after Reed was killed," adding that "at the time Scott wrote the song he was scaling logs on the bed of the Sulphit Mill at Rumford, Me."[1]

Furthermore, Dave Severy says he happened to visit Joe while he was composing the song. *"I went up in the Steam Laundry when he was writing up a song," he said. "That was the Guy Reed song. . . . It was just a rooming place, the Steam Laundry, and they let rooms. [*It was*] on Canal Street" (and just up the street from Mrs. Siddall's). Add to this the fact that Joe was around the area in May, when Howard Carrick hanged himself, and in October, when William Sullivan was killed, and there doesn't seem to be much doubt that he would have been around in September, when Guy Reed met his death. Finally, the style is in every way typical of Joe's work. Why, then, should there be any question of his authorship?

The question is raised by a single version (NB.5) found among Fannie Hardy Eckstorm's papers at the University of Maine. Entitled "The Death of Will McClinton," it is identical in every way with "Guy Reed," except for normal traditional changes, the placing of the accident on the "North Brook" rather than the Androscoggin shore, and the omission of stanzas 10 and 11 (which describe the funeral) and stanza 13 (which gives Guy Reed's name, date of death,

147

and place of burial). The text as we have it exists only in a typed carbon copy with this heading: (COPIED FROM NOTEBOOK OF GEORGE H. O'MAR- RIVER DRIVER ON WASSATAQUOIK 1884–5– OAK HILL, ST. STEPHENS, NEW BRUNSWICK). In Phillips Barry's hand there is a penned-in note, presumably to Mrs. Eckstorm: "O'Mar said you had the notebook," he wrote, and then he asks her to check certain matters of spelling. As a headnote to the ballad, evidently following O'Mar's orthography, is typed "The Death of a young man a Friend of Mine, Will McClinton by name over 40 years ago. Please Fit the Headlines to it in your own way." As a footnote Barry has typed, "The homestead of Will McClinton is next to where George E. [sic] O'Mar now lives. Mrs. Eckstorm said she had heard this sung as the death of Guy Reed on the Androscoggin but O'Mar said he had heard this sung as the death of Will McClinton long before he ever heard of Guy Reed." The original notebook itself has disappeared.

George H. O'Mar supplied Phillips Barry with a number of texts and fragments in 1926 and 1927, and the notebook in question he presumably either sent to Barry or gave to him when Barry visited him in 1927.[2] His dating of McClinton's death as "over 40 years ago" would put it in the 1880s, and this just happens to agree nicely with the information given by Myron H. Avery in an article on the Wassataquoik.[3] According to Avery, the firm of Tracey and Love, under contract with T. H. Todd of Saint Stephen, New Brunswick, began cutting on the Wassataquoik in the fall of 1883 and continued work until 1891. He then gives the following details:

The graves of men drowned in the early operations were marked by inscriptions on rocks along the stream or on the tote-road, which marked the burial place of a skeleton found in a gravel bar two or three miles below Orrin Falls, presumably that of Charles Stewart of Little Ridge, N.B., who was drowned in 1888 at Orrin Falls, was so chipped by the Wassataquoik fire that the letters have disappeared. Lee's Rock marked the site of the drowning of Charles Lee, two miles below Old City camp. The drowning, a year later, of a McGinnis at Ledge Falls, two miles above Old City, *and of a Will McClinton at the mouth of Pogy Brook a short time before,* were similarly marked by rocks.[4]

The italics are mine. The time sequence is not clear enough to allow us to pinpoint a date for McClinton's death, but it is safe to place it in the mid- to late eighties. Since Guy Reed was killed in 1897 on the

Androscoggin, the acceptance of O'Mar's version as genuine would push the origin of this ballad back a good ten years and at least 150 miles to the north and east.

I can see four solutions to the "Guy Reed–Will McClinton" problem. The first and least likely is that both ballads are reworkings of some as-yet-undiscovered original. A second solution would be that Scott simply took a ballad that someone else had written about Will McClinton and added a few stanzas about the funeral to make it fit Guy Reed. A third solution would have Joe Scott as the author of both versions. That is perfectly possible. Joe would have been about twenty years old at the time of McClinton's death. Tracey and Love was a Milltown, New Brunswick, firm and, as Avery points out, "Many of the lumbermen were old acquaintances and employees of Tracey and this first operation had a decided New Brunswick atmosphere."[5] Joe's home was only about fifty miles from Milltown, and he could well have gone on that operation and therefore been on hand to tell of McClinton's death. Then, some ten years later, he could have refurbished his old song for Guy Reed.

Of these three solutions, I find the third the most acceptable, but none of them in any way accounts for the fact that O'Mar's "Will McClinton" is unique, even in Charlotte County, New Brunswick, where I was able to find five versions of "Guy Reed".[6] Why did "Will McClinton" die so ignominiously, while "Guy Reed" flourished even on Will's and O'Mar's home ground? A fourth solution does account for this: George O'Mar did a little creative remembering. He admits that he had heard "Guy Reed," but "he had heard this sung as the death of Will McClinton long before." Quite simply, Will was a friend of his, and O'Mar wanted there to be a song for him. He adapted "Guy Reed," and when the folklorist from the States questioned him on the similarity, O'Mar defended himself. In other words, "Will McClinton" is a local adaptation of "Guy Reed"; it was the creation of George O'Mar, and it existed only in his notebook, where Barry found it. All four solutions are speculative, but obviously I take my stand on the last one, which means that I will consider "Will McClinton" as merely another version (NB.5) of "Guy Reed," albeit a special one. We'll leave it at that for now.

It may not be directly relevant, but it is at least of sentimental value to put down what we know about Guy Reed himself, especially since we are lucky enough to have a photograph of him (see fig. 6).

The Reeds were old settlers in the Byron area. Abram Reed, who had come to West Byron from Freeport in 1815, had seven children by his first wife and two by his second, one of whom was Joseph, born in 1830. Joseph married Remember Mitchell of Roxbury, and the couple had ten children before her untimely death at age forty-one in 1875. Guy was the last-born, just a year old when his mother died, and he grew up to be a tall, handsome, well-built lad with blue eyes, a fiery temper, and an eye for the ladies. One niece, describing him as her favorite uncle, remembered that all the youngsters in the neighborhood thought he was great. He cut quite a figure, evidently; she recalled him driving around town in a buggy with an orange rug on the floor, and he liked to drive fast. He was impetuous, always ready to take a dare, and it was on a dare that one day he rode a log through the rips behind the present Rumford Library. One look at that water will give anyone the measure of the man: a young buck, hot-blooded, with the world in his pocket and everything going for him. It must have been a great way to be twenty-three.[7]

We can get a pretty clear picture of what actually happened to Guy Reed. First of all, we have a photograph of the Androscoggin at Riley that sets the scene for us (see fig. 7). The railroad went along the river here, but between it and the shore was a steep bank. Logs were brought in on cars and unloaded on this bank, where they were piled in great landings. Then, when logs were needed at the mill, these landings could be "broken in," which means that a crew of men armed with peaveys and pickpoles would go up and roll the logs into the river to float down to the mill. Young Guy was working with such a crew.

There were two kinds of landings, those that were skidded and those that were not. On a skidded landing a bed of logs was laid down and then poles placed rail-fashion on top of them. Then another layer of logs was put down on these "skids," then more skids, more logs, and so on upward. The "face" or forward edge of such a landing was apt to be quite square, and each tier of logs was held in place (that is, kept from rolling off the end) either by "fids" stuck upright in the ends of the skids or by cutting shallow notches in the skids for the front log to lie in. Then, when the time came to break the landing in, the fids would be knocked out or that front log would be started out of its notches and a whole tier would be rolled in at a time. Then the skids could be removed and the next tier started.

Fig. 6. Guy Reed, who met his death at Peterson's Rips on the Androscoggin River and about whom Joe wrote the ballad. (Courtesy of Mrs. Wirt Virgin, West Peru, Maine. NA photo 113.)

On the other hand, if the landing was not skidded, the logs were simply piled up loose. My old friend Jim Brown described it very well. *"Sometimes they'd skid the landing," he said, "and sometimes they'd be just put over rough and—nail-kegged, they'd call it. . . . Like a nail keg. That's when they'd put it over rough and tumble." There wouldn't be anything like a perpendicular face; it would slant back more or less shallowly in whatever form gravity and the shape of the bank allowed. When the crew came to break the landing in, the men would start at the bottom, rolling the logs nearest the river in first and working their way back up the bank. Neither system was perfect. On a skidded landing a rolling tier could take a man with it, and on a "nail-kegged" landing the uncertain pile could let go at any time and crush a man working below. Neither of these fates was exactly Guy Reed's, as we shall see, but for the moment let it be said that breaking in landings was dangerous work. However, like much dangerous work of the type, it became routine.

The conformation of the landings in the photograph makes it appear that Guy and his friends were working on nail-keg landings. Now, there is no guarantee that the landings pictured are the very onces he was working on, but if we look at what the ballad says happened and listen to what family tradition has to say, we can be pretty sure that this is how it was. It was late summer, September 9 to be exact, almost fall. That means that the landings they were working on had probably been there since spring and had had plenty of time to settle in. According to family tradition, the foreman's name was Thomas, and the crew had been hard at work all day. Some of the men wanted to quit, but Thomas wanted to take one more landing; the work went ahead, though there was some grumbling and tempers were running short.

This landing presented problems. Notice that the song says that they "picked the face" from "bottom to the top." That is, they began with the log nearest the river and worked back, expecting logs would slip down as the crew moved up, and the face would stay well slanted. But that wasn't the way it worked out this time. The logs did not slip down, and as the men picked their way back up the bank they soon discovered they had a face that was almost straight up and down. Thirty feet sounds like a bit much, but when I asked Ned Stewart, who had done that kind of work, he wasn't entirely ready to say it couldn't have been. *"I don't know," he said, "as long as I wasn't

Fig. 7. Logs landed on the banks of the Androscoggin about 1900, in the approximate area where Guy Reed met his death. (Courtesy of George Storer, Rumford, Maine. NA photo 342.)

153

there. The song *says* 'full thirty feet.' I've seen 'em do it just the same." However high it was, it easily could have looked like thirty feet to the men working it, and no matter how high it was, it presented a dangerous situation. It is hard to tell what was holding those logs together in that unnatural position. It happened that way sometimes when everything was just right (or, more like it, just wrong), and at any moment a wrong move could cause the whole pile to break suddenly. When that happened, a couple hundred sawlogs would explode down the slope, and anyone in the way stood very little chance. Thomas got Guy and the rest of the crew out of the way at this point.

What to do now? There were several possibilities, but the method selected was a perfectly standard one: send a few men up the bank and have them start a log or two from the top (that is, the back), in the hope that as these sticks rolled over the edge they would start the whole pile. Guy and a couple others probably volunteered; it was a risky job, and while that kind of risk was commonplace on the river, it was still something one volunteered for, as a rule. They went up the bank, got hold of a suitable log with their peaveys, and started it on its way.

Evidently the log went as far as the verge, or top front edge of the landing, and hung there. It might have been a good idea to start another one and see if that would take the first one with it, but as I have already pointed out, it was late in the day and the whole crew was edgy. Guy was notably short-fused anyway, and presumably this hung log was all that was needed to make him blow. He grabbed a peavey and charged out to free that log. The landing was making noises as though it were going to break, and his companions yelled at him to be careful, but he got a hold on the log with his peavey and yanked.

That was all. The whole landing collapsed, and the song is not exaggerating in saying that Guy simply disappeared into that churning mass of huge sawlogs. As his obituary said, "One stick which scaled about 350 feet struck him on the chest, crushing it in. Another hit him on the back of the head, crushing the skull."[8] He never stood a chance. "Mick Denny cried every time he told me the story of Guy Reed," a woman from Johnville, New Brunswick, remembered. "Mick was the one who pulled him out from under the yard of logs. Mick said the body was so badly crushed they just rolled it in a blanket."⁹ The newspaper says he died instantly, but family tradition claims that although he was unconscious, he was still breathing when they dug him out. That's probably the way it was, since they sent for a doctor.

They must have known Guy was doomed. The nearest doctor was in Rumford Falls, almost twenty miles upriver, and the fastest way to get him to Riley would have been down the rails by handcar. The odds were worse than poor, but as long as breath was going out and in, his friends knew Guy deserved the best shot at life they could give him. The desperate call went out. "When the news reached Rumford Falls," said the *Times*, "Dr. DeCosta was called and sent down on a car. He only reached Gilbertville however before he learned that a trip to Riley would be useless. The remains were brought to relatives in Peru, where the doctor received them and gave a burial certificate. Undertaker Calhoun took charge of the body."

That was on Thursday afternoon. The funeral services were held in the Methodist Episcopal Church in Rumford Falls on Saturday afternoon, the Reverend G. B. Hannaford officiating, and the obituary described it this way: "Mr. Reed was a member of Metalluc Lodge, Knights of Pythias, and this order attended the funeral services in a body and accompanied the remains to Byron where the burial services of the order were observed at the grave. The floral tributes were many and beautiful."

There used to be a community at West Byron. A niece remembered going to school right across from the cemetery and how hard it was to look over and see Uncle Guy's grave there. The cemetery is all that's left now, seven miles back in the woods on the Ellis Pond road, and even that has been vandalized. But Guy Reed's stone is still standing—inscribed "GUY L. REED / Jan. 27, 1874 / Sept. 9, 1897. / 'Tis the Lord who hath bereft us / Of the one we loved so well"—with a Knights of Pythias emblem atop it. Always when I have visited that spot, there has been a small K. P. flag in a standard next to the stone.

More than likely Joe attended the funeral, since it was held right in Rumford, and he could easily have gone along with the party out to the burial in West Byron; but the chances are he was not an eyewitness to the accident itself. That crew would have been based in some nearby place like Chisholm or even Riley, or downriver in

Livermore Falls, and Joe was twenty miles upriver in Rumford that year. That part of the river was not Joe's bailiwick anyhow, but Guy was a friend of his. The two men had probably worked in the woods and on the drives together, and it is reasonable to assume that Joe, much possessed by death in any case, would have been hard hit by the dark news. Doubtless he talked to mutual friends who had been there. His information is just that kind of information.

Within the Reed family, there was a tradition that Guy had had a premonition of his death, and the newspaper account of the accident is interesting in this respect:

One of the workmen who was working with him, informed the TIMES that Mr. Reed had been feeling very much depressed in spirits all the morning and expressed himself as not feeling at all like work, and not long before the accident occurred he remarked "They won't have me here much longer."

Ed Filardeau informs the TIMES that the night previous he dreamed of seeing Mr. Reed walking on drift wood and saw him killed. All the morning he had a presentment [sic] that something was going to befall some of them and tried to laugh off the feeling, calling it childish.

Aside from this business of premonitions, though, there was less of an independent narrative tradition coexisting with this ballad than there had been for "Howard Carey." Obviously, Mick Denny used to tell the story up in Johnville, but most accounts I have arose *from* the song as explanations of this or that detail. They do not *add* anything like the business of what was "really" the matter with Howard Carey; nor does the place where it all occurred seem to have excited any curiosity or special concern the way Howard's suicide room did. For all practical purposes, we can say there was only the song. And the same could be said about almost all ballads I know about death in the woods.

Ballads about men who died on the river-drives were a tradition unto themselves. Laws lists eleven in his syllabus, and Edith Fowke adds three more in her collection of Ontario woods songs.[10] It would not be hard to expand this list, but even a cursory examination of these fourteen pieces will make the point: if a man died in a river accident, a ballad would make a most acceptable form of memorial. Not only was the subject traditional; but once a man had considered making such a song, he had a very traditional structure to work with and a common stock of formulas, themes, and images with which he could flesh that structure out.

The structure is not at all startling, being simply an adaptation of the more general pattern used in many disaster ballads, but it is very consistent. First came the opening, an invitation to listen followed by a general statement of the subject. "The Jam on Gerry's Rock" is typical:

> Come all of you bold shanty boys,
>   And listen while I relate,
> Concerning a young riverman
>   And his untimely fate,
> Concerning a young river boss,
>   So handsome, true and brave,
> 'Twas on the jam on Gerry's Rock,
>   He met his watery grave.[11]

"John Roberts" shows the same pattern, using the "long-meter" stanza often found in earlier disaster ballads, rather than the more common and later double stanza:

> Come all you friends pray lend an ear
> A melancholy tale to hear;
> One of our mortal members he
> Has gone to long eternity.[12]

Next came the description of the accident itself, beginning with a couple of lines to localize the event:

> We were camped on the Wild Mustard River
> Just below the old Tamarack Dam.
> As we rose from our blankets one morning,
> We saw on the rocks a big jam.[13]

Then the accident is given in varying amounts of detail, usually in two or three stanzas, but sometimes, as in "The Wild Mustard River," half a dozen or more. Invariably this section is followed by the search for and recovery of the body. Again we have "The Jam on Gerry's Rock":

> Now when the rest of the shanty boys
>   The sad news they did hear,
> In search of their brave comrades
>   To the river they did steer.

157

> Meanwhile their mangled bodies
> Down by the stream did flow,
> While dead and bleeding near the bank
> Was that of young Munroe.[14]

Descriptions of the body are common, and while such generalities as "bruised" or "mangled" usually suffice, sometimes we get more detail. Many versions of "The Jam on Gerry's Rock" have it that only Munroe's head is found, for instance, but no one went further in this direction than the author of "The Wild Mustard River":

> Every bone in his body was broken,
> O flesh in long strips it hung down.[15]

The older ballad of "John Roberts" has this section as follows:

> We searched the stream from shore to shore
> His lifeless body to secure;
> Trusting in God to guide the way
> Unto his tentament of clay.
>
> 'Twas on the third day at three o'clock
> When Mr. Filsber took his boat,
> And with a grapple in his hand
> He raised him from his bed of sand.[16]

It is perhaps not quite right to speak of the fourth section as a section at all, since it may include several diverse elements; it represents a sort of classical "falling action," though "aftermath" is a better word for it. Usually the loved ones left behind are mentioned, as in "Jimmy Judge":

> Oh, the lass that loved him dearly, she cries, "Now I'm undone."
> Likewise his aged parents, they cries, "My darling son."[17]

This is usually followed by a description of the funeral or, if not a funeral, the burial. "John Roberts" has it:

> And in due time a bier was made,
> And on it was his body laid;
> Born to the grave where he shall lie
> Till Gabriel's triumphs shall rend the sky.[18]

So does "The Wild Mustard River":

> We buried him there by the river,
> Where the lark and the nightingale sing.[19]

And that remarkable piece from Ontario, "The Haggertys and Young Mulvanny":

> Now far away up the distant river
> Their graves were dug by the rolling tide
> Beneath the branches of swaying treetops
> Moved by the breezes from every side.
> Yes, far away up that distant river
> No sound could reach any mother's ear,
> And raindrops fell on them from the branches
> Instead of parents' lamenting tears.[20]

The ballad is usually concluded with a pious wish or prayer, as in "John Roberts":

> We fellow men, we too must die
> And go to our long eternity;
> So let us live while here below,
> Love God and all his paths pursue;
> And let us live in Christian love
> And go with him to reign above.[21]

or "The Wild Mustard River":

> Here's adieu to the Wild Mustard River,
>   Where my Johnny lies under the sod,
> For here on earth lies his body,
>   And we hope that his spirit's with God.[22]

Invitational opening, description of the accident, discovery of the body, aftermath (including mention of loved ones, a funeral or burial scene, and a closing prayer): that pattern is present even when the balladist decided to depart from it in some way. The author of "The Jam on Gerry's Rock," for example, had the hero's sweetheart present at the finding of his body, then went on to tell of the purse that was made up for her, and concluded with her death and the famous double burial:

They gave him a decent burial, it being on the sixth of May
Let the rest of ye young shantyboys for your dead comrades pray.
In less than three weeks after, this maid was called to go,
And her last request was that she might be buried with young
    Monroe.

On a little mound by the riverside there grows a hemlock tree:
The name, the date, the drowning of our hero you may see.

The shantyboys cut the woods all round, two lovers here lie low:
Here lies Miss Clara Fenton and her lover, young Monroe.[23]

In spite of this departure, all the elements of the basic pattern are present. And whoever it was that wrote the local Ontario ballad "The Haggertys and Young Mulvanny" kept pretty close to it in spite of his florid and elaborate four-stanza "As I walked out . . . I spied a maid weeping" opening.[24] It might be objected that what I am calling a structure is simply the natural way to tell the story ("*How the hell else would you do it?*"). I don't want to labor that point by suggesting alternate possibilities, because at the moment the important thing for us to see is that when a man wanted to write a song about someone who died on the river he had a pattern right to hand. In addition, he had a diction (that of the come-all-ye or broadside tradition), stanza forms (basically the double stanza), and tunes that not only were available to him, but that his prospective customers, the singers and their audience, would have expected to find in any such song. Obviously a certain amount of innovation was acceptable; the songs are *not* simply carbon copies of each other. But most authors of these songs stayed pretty close to their models.

When he set about to write a song on the death of his friend Guy Reed, Joe Scott knew this pattern well. It is simply impossible that he didn't. He could have rejected it and chosen some alternate pattern (which, as we shall see, is what he did when he wrote the murder ballad "Benjamin Deane"), but he decided not to. What he did was to elaborate it and combine it with popular tradition of the time.

Rather than choose one of the standard come-all-ye tunes for his ballad—and any of them would have fit perfectly well—Joe chose one from a well-known popular song, George F. Root's "Bright Eyed Little Nell of Narragansett Bay." First published in 1860, the song continued to be popular for many years, and we have Phillips Barry's word that " 'Little Nell' was much sung in the woods."[25] It is worth giving in full at this point (Root's original is in F major):

BRIGHT EYED LITTLE NELL OF NARRAGANSETT BAY

Moderato

1. Full well do I re-mem-ber My boy-hoods hap-py hours,   The
   I had a dear com-pan-ion But she's not with me now,   The

"Guy Reed"

cot-tage and the gar-den Where bloomed the fair-est flowers, The
li-ly of the val-ley Is wav-ing o'er her brow, And

bright and spark-ling wa-ter O'er which we used to sail With
I am sad and lone-ly And mourn-ing all the day For

hearts so gay, for miles a-way Be-fore the gen-tle gale.
bright eyed laugh-ing lit-tle Nell Of Nar-ra-gan-sett bay.

CHORUS:

Toll, toll the bell at ear-ly dawn of day, For love-ly Nell so

quick-ly passed a-way, Toll, toll the bell a soft and mourn-ful lay, For

bright eyed laugh-ing lit-tle Nell of Nar-ra-gan-sett bay.

Full well do I remember My boyhoods happy hours,
The cottage and the garden Where bloomed the fairest flowers,
The bright and sparkling water O'er which we used to sail
With hearts so gay, for miles away Before the gentle gale.
I had a dear companion But she's not with me now,
The lily of the valley Is waving o'er her brow,
And I am sad and lonely And mourning all the day
For bright eyed laughing little Nell of Narragansett bay.

CHORUS: Toll, toll the bell at early dawn of day,
For lovely Nell so quickly passed away,
Toll, toll the bell a soft and mournful lay,
For bright eyed laughing little Nell of Narragansett bay.

I loved the little beauty, My boat, it was my pride.
And with her close beside me What joy the foam to ride,
She'd laugh with tone so merry To see the waves go by,
And wildly blew the stormy wind And murky was the sky.
Tho' lightnings flashed around us And all was dark and drear,
We loved to brave old Ocean, And never dreamed of fear
'The Arrow bounded onward And darted through the spray
With bright eyed laughing little Nell of Narragansett bay.

CHORUS: Toll, etc.

One day from us she wandered, And soon within the boat
The cord was quickly loosened And with the tide afloat,
The treacherous bark flew lightly And swift before the wind,
While home, and friends, and all so dear, Were many miles behind.
Next day her form all lifeless Was washed upon the beach,
I stood and gazed upon it Bereft of sence [*sic*] and speech
'Tis years since thus we parted, But here I weep to day
For bright eyed laughing little Nell of Narragansett bay.

CHORUS: Toll, etc.

Why did Joe choose this tune? We can't know that now, but
however the parallel suggested itself to him, once he had it in mind
we can see that more than just the tune came over into his ballad.
The "full well do I remember" opening, the "bright and sparkling
water" of stanza 9, the storm and lightnings of the first stanza, all
these were probably suggested by "Little Nell." Having pointed out
the facts behind the song, the pattern it follows, and the source of the
tune and some of the images, it now remains for us to see the
remarkable way Joe put them all together. But first a digression.

From a literary perspective, ballads often do crazy things. I have
already shown how "Howard Carey," in shifting from first to third
person, was treating point of view in a most traditional way, which is
to say ignoring it. Anyone interested in such elegant and harmless
pursuits can have a lovely time discovering "absurdities" in
folksongs, and he may begin with my favorite example, "The Two
Sisters" (Child 10), in which a girl who is pushed into the ocean
floats downstream into a millpond. It seems incredible that over the
centuries someone didn't notice this howler and "correct" it; but
while it may have been noticed, it obviously wasn't considered an
important matter at all. It raises the question of what singers and
listeners "hear" or "see," because it is obvious they can't be "following the story," not "logically," anyhow, and a ballad that requires
close listening may suffer for it. [26] What seems to come across most of
the time is a very general story line developed through a series of
images relating less to exactly what happened than to how we are to
feel about what happened, which is what Coffin called the "emotional core." [27] A violent death, followed by quiet lament that such
things must be: that is what "Guy Reed" is really about.

"Guy Reed"

All of this leads us to Joe's first two stanzas, which constitute his come-all-ye or introduction. If we look at these stanzas logically, they are absurd: in the midst of a dark and stormy night a letter arrives that tells the narrator of Guy Reed's death. The mails don't behave this way now, and they didn't in 1897 either, but no singer of this ballad has ever suggested to me that it is absurd; nor in fact has anyone ever even noticed it until I have pointed it out. As a matter of fact, I didn't notice it myself until I "studied" the stanzas rather carefully. But no matter. What Joe wanted here was the gloomy, foreboding quality of a violent storm, and that is heightened by the darkness and the clouds blotting out the stars and moon. The ballad opens ominously, and ominous things follow.

The letter that brings bad news is not a standard opening for a traditional ballad, though of course letters are far from unknown.[28] There were popular sentimental songs like "The Letter Edged in Black"—copyrighted, by the way, in 1897, the year Guy Reed was killed—in which the cheerful postman hands Jack a letter telling of his mother's death:

> But he little knew the sorrow that he brought me,
> When he handed me that letter edged in black.[29]

Whether that is the particular song Joe had in mind is hard to say, of course, but we can be sure the letter is entirely fictional, an artistic device. Joe was in Rumford Falls, about twenty miles upriver from Riley, and he probably got word of the accident the same day it happened. Possibly he got the news at night, possibly there was a storm, too. That's speculation, and not particularly important. What Joe wanted was the sudden dark opening; the storm-and-letter combination gave him that very well.

We have already discussed the second section in our consideration of the historical background, but a few points deserve repeating and reemphasizing. First, while Joe was not an eyewitness to the accident, he probably had his account of it from someone who was, and as an old river-driver himself, he was thoroughly acquainted with what was involved. He had picked faces, rolled from the top, and heard landings creak ominously under his own feet—and he had probably stood by with pallid cheek and trembling limb while someone else risked *his* life as he had risked his own. Joe was writing about what he knew from the back and from within, and he tells it in characteristic detail: five full stanzas. He sets his scene very carefully, bringing us to see how precarious the situation is; then a few of the men "volunteer to go" (a line that can't help sounding like an echo of "The Jam on Gerry's Rock"):

> Till six of our Canadian boys did volunteer to go
> For to break the jam on Gerry's rocks with their foreman, young
>   Monroe.[30]

In stanza 5, Joe leaves direct description of what happened to step in with a stage aside, a foreshadowing of the death to come. Such asides are common enough in traditional balladry. Joe uses the same technique twice in "Benjamin Deane," and the Ontario author of "Vince Leahy" says of Vince's mother early on in the ballad, " 'Twas little she was thinking that's the last she'd see him smile."[31] But usually all we get is one line, or at the most two, while Joe in typical form develops it into a whole stanza. Then he gets back to the job.

Stanzas 6 and 7 are carefully worked out, so carefully it is tempting to think of them as a kind of movie scenario. The volunteers start the log; the landing creaks, and we follow that log to the verge. We turn again to Guy, who "approaches" the log, which is to say he didn't just run out, but moved very carefully. Then we cut to the watchers below, tense and fearful. One of them shouts a warning (or they all do), and Guy pauses; then he goes back to work, and the end is very sudden. I submit that that is pretty good writing by any standard one wishes to apply. Literary blokes, for example, can admire the skillful detail of having Guy pause for a moment. He becomes very much alive just before he dies.

Where did Joe get his details? There are two possibilities. First, his eyewitnesses might have furnished them: *"The whole landing was creaking like it was going to break any minute, but that log went right out to the edge and hung there, and Guy got mad and went out to free it. All of us was scared to death and yelled at him for Christ's sake to get back, but you know Guy. He just kind of stood there a minute, then he got a hold on that log and that was it. Landing broke and. . . ."* That's the sort of thing Joe was working from, I'm sure. Since he would have wanted to "have it right," I doubt that he would have chanced inventing details for something that happened in full view of so many potential critics (*"Naw, Guy just charged right out there and bang! Didn't pause nor nothing. 'Course that sounds good, I suppose. Joe just put that in"*). Of course, Joe *could* have invented. I doubt that he did, but that's the second possibility, and I'll simply have to allow it.

The third section, the finding of the body, raises the same problem, and I offer the same solution, although certainly Joe would have been permitted a little more leeway—a little more license to bring "how it was" in line with "how it should have been"—in an emotion-charged scene like this. He begins, however, by leaving something out, not putting something in. For the condition of Guy's body he could have had all the details he wanted; the newspaper had no trouble in that department, and the tradition allowed for plenty of vivid writing here. But Joe contents himself with speaking of Guy's "mangled form," which must have said all that was necessary to his woodsman audience. Then, after the violence of the accident and the recovery of the body,

> The birds were singing sweetly,
> The sun shone bright and warm.

This violence/tenderness, death/life contrast is vintage Scott, and he develops it at some length.

First, Joe presents a chorus of mourners. Since Mick Denny cried when he told of it years later, it is anything but too much to imagine strong men kneeling around whatever was left of Guy and weeping at what they saw. But he arranges them carefully, and, second, he has animated Nature, with "shady tree," "purling stream," and "bubbling, sparkling waters," to surround and support their mourning. It is probably a pretty accurate description; it was early September, and the trees were shady, the grass along the bank green enough, and Peterson's Rips (where it all occurred) bubbling and sparkling in fine shape. That is to suggest again that the ballad is good reportage, but the language and imagery are highly traditional. The "laid him on the green" may well come, as Louise Manny opined, from "The Bonny Earl of Murray" (Child 181),[32] but for the most part the diction is the stuff of popular and sentimental song, some of it right out of "Little Nell" itself. Finally, it should be pointed out that Joe takes his time, spending two full stanzas on what is more commonly covered in a word, a phrase, or even a gesture.

As I have already pointed out, the fourth section usually contained certain elements—burial, loved ones left behind, and a pious wish or prayer—but the balladist was at considerable liberty in the way he might combine these elements. Joe includes them all, and characteristically takes seven stanzas to describe the funeral, balancing the dead hero in his casket with crowds of people on one side and masses of flowers on the other, and framing the whole scene with the Knights of Pythias ceremony. Then follows a stanza on Guy's mother, who died when he was only a year old, and she and two of her children form part of the scene in that "quiet country churchyard" where Guy was buried.

Next comes a rather unusually placed naming stanza, giving the particulars of the case and pointing up that Guy has returned to sleep "beside his kindred." Joe had the date wrong; Guy was killed on the ninth, not the eighth, a simple mistake (that's all it could have been) that probably was an embarrassment to Joe if anyone pointed it out to him. Stanza 15 gives the stock figure of the poor old father (who in fact went on to live for a good many more years with a new wife) followed by a series of what might be called life-images—gold, silver, sunny skies, sweet music—that are useless against death. This leads naturally into the pious closing, a rather remarkable picture of the finality of death, first (in st. 15) through a lyrical comparison to returning spring and then through a mix of otherworld images—land beyond the sun, through the dark valley, bright celestial shore. It makes a fitting end to this final section that has all along been playing the beauty of life against the sleep of death.

So much, then, for what Joe Scott wrote. How has "Guy Reed" fared in the seventy-odd years it has been in tradition here in the Northeast? First of all, like the rest of Joe's work, it has stayed in the Northeast: Maine, northern New Hampshire, and the Canadian Maritimes. Second, with the exception of the original printed slip, it has circulated almost entirely by oral tradition. The version printed by Robert W. Gordon in his *Adventure* column for March 30, 1925, and the truncated version printed by the *Family Herald* on September 9, 1942, do not seem to have had any marked effect on the tradition, and I never heard a single singer cite either as his source. The fact that the tune tradition is just about a hundred percent stable is one more argument in favor of the ballad's solid oral quality. Third, and finally, it has been extremely popular. I have been able to bring together fifty-one versions for this study, thirty-seven of them complete, and twenty-five of them with tunes. Like "Howard Carey,"

"Guy Reed" won a very solid place for itself in northeastern tradition.

If we take a look now at the thirty-seven "complete" versions of the ballad to see what changes subsequent singers may have worked on substance and structure, we will find no surprises. It has been shortened some, only nine versions having all sixteen stanzas; and all but four of those came to me in manuscript form.[33] But since "Guy Reed" was more nearly within the limits of what the tradition seems to have been able to accept than was "Howard Carey," it suffered less shrinkage. Some descriptive passages drop out of this version, others out of that one, but in no complete version has enough dropped out to alter the basic tone much. "Guy Reed" is always a slow, sad lament.

There is an interesting contrast, though, in what has happened to the first and second halves of this ballad in tradition. While more than half the versions have the first nine stanzas entire and in proper order (and only a few lack more than a stanza or so), fewer than a quarter are complete for the last seven, and of these the only ones that maintain Joe's original sequence are those I am sure come directly from his printed slip. The difference between the two halves is easily explained: the first tells the story, while the second is mainly commentary on that story covering a number of discrete matters (funeral, mother's fate, naming, father's fate, preachment), with no time sequence to lock them in place and make one stanza suggest the next.

While we are on the subject of sequence, stanza 13 ("This young man's name was Guy Reed") deserves special notice. Joe's original version places it between a stanza on Guy's mother's death and his father's grief. The only versions that keep this order are those noted above as coming directly from Joe's printed slip. In all the rest, the naming stanza is either dropped or moved to some other position, thus bringing the mother/father stanzas together. Obviously singers found the original sequence awkward and improved on it, and if we are going to talk about a "folk process," here is a good example of how it works. But we should keep in mind that this same process accepted the "midnight mail" of stanzas 1 and 2, since not one complete version omits these stanzas, and some fragments are composed of little else. That "absurdity" was not seen as a problem; the misplaced naming stanza was. It is a question of aesthetics.

In spite of all I have said about confusion and shortening in the second half of the ballad, it should not be forgotten that almost every complete version of "Guy Reed" has its ample share of these lyrical stanzas. I see no evidence that they were disappearing or that the ballad was becoming significantly more spare, more purely narrative. The balance between the violent action of the first half and the sentimental calm of the second seems to be what people liked about "Guy Reed," and balance is the right word for it, since Joe arranged it all with the fulcrum in those remarkable lines in stanza 8, just halfway through his ballad:

> Those logs they rolled carefully
> From off his mangled form,
> The birds were singing sweetly,
> The sun shone bright and warm.

Give or take a stanza, the only complete version that doesn't maintain that balance is the one printed in the *Family Herald* (FH), which is an enigma anyway. Omissions, yes; shifts in structure, yes; but alteration of the ballad's essential whatness, its emotional core, no, not at all.

The maintenance of this balance is all the more remarkable when we consider how very innovative Joe had been in this ballad. He followed the basic structure of the death-on-the-river ballads, but he yanked it all out of shape, as we have seen. There is no other ballad in this tradition that has anything like these proportions, and it would be reasonable to assume that singers would have tended to "normalize" them. But clearly Joe knew what he was about, and just as clearly the tradition approved his work.

I have emphasized how innovative Joe Scott was, but we should not get the idea that he was introducing his audience to something totally foreign, something utterly new. As we shall see elsewhere, songs like "Little Nell," "The Letter Edged in Black," and "When You and I Were Young, Maggie" were very popular among the same people who sang and enjoyed "The Jam on Gerry's Rock." Present-day collectors have often complained—in print and in private—how these sentimental or Tin Pan Alley pieces have tended to crowd out the "good old songs," or how singers "naively" failed to discriminate between them. Whether or not some kind of Gresham's Law was in operation, and obviously many observers feel there was, it is clear that the two types of song could and did exist comfortably side by side. What Joe Scott did was to *combine* them in a special way.

An interesting example of how Joe worked out this combination and how his audience basically accepted but modified his work can be seen in the tune. To begin with, Joe chose a "popular," not a "traditional" tune for his ballad, "Little Nell of Narragansett Bay," although, as I have already pointed out, any standard come-all-ye tune would have fit his words perfectly well. Unfortunately, we can't determine in just what form Joe knew the tune (that form would be the "original" tune). For instance, did he sing it without the chromatic touches in the cadences of the A and C phrases, or is that a change made by later singers? The chromaticism is definitely absent in all of the twenty-five tunes I have brought together. At whatever point the change was made, though, this modified form of "Little Nell" is clearly *the* tune to "Guy Reed," and the modification is a standard one for tunes in folk tradition.[34]

The tune has shown great stability, to be sure, but there are many small variations. Frequently the opening phrase may begin on the third rather than on the tonic, after an upbeat on either the fifth below or the fifth above, and in a number of versions there is a leap downward of a full octave to the fifth below at the midpoint of the D phrase (on the word "hurled," for example, in the first stanza). The meter is always duple. About two-thirds of the versions show a basic 2/4, while the other third is in 6/8, though sometimes the decision as to which is which gets academic, since there are numerous infixes and a good deal of liberty is taken with time values in woods tradition anyway.

Two versions show an interesting drift that raises the old question of when a tune is the *same* tune and when it is a *different* tune. Eighty-year-old Gertrude Toothaker (who had known Joe Scott) sang "Guy Reed" (Me.6) for me as follows:

The post brought me a let-ter / has-tened to per-use, 'Twas written by a friend of mine and bore me start-ling news; For

one I knew a fine young man as you would wish to see,

In an in - stant he was hurled in - to e - ter - ni - ty.

Her first and third phrases are the standard C phrase, and her final phrase is perfectly standard, too, which gives her tune an ABAC structure rather than the usual progressive ABCD pattern. That repetition, together with her variant B phrase, brings her tune close to that of the old cowboy favorite "When the Work's All Done This Fall." Over on the Miramichi, Fred McMahon sang "Guy Reed" (NB.15) to a tune that resembled the cowboy song even more closely. What seems to have happened here is that both singers had heard that very popular song via radio and record more frequently and more recently than they had heard "Guy Reed" sung to its "proper" tune, and the one influenced the other. If that is true, it's a wonder it didn't happen more often than it did.[35]

Any ballad of this type was a memorial to its hero, who died doing his job, and singing about such a death ritualized it and made it more meaningful for his companions and counterparts, for whom any moment might be *their* next when the jam they were picking hauled or their batteau got sucked over the pitch to be smashed to splinters on the rocks below. "Guy Reed" served this function, certainly; it is very particularized, very much Guy Reed's special song. But even more than other river ballads, it became a universal lament that such things must be, that a fine young man should die such a hard death on a sunny afternoon. It does not rage, though. It accepts, and gives us that death as death ought to be and so seldom is: heroic, the result of daring, with companions kneeling and weeping, with a fine funeral, with the promise of sleep at home with the family, and with the hope of eternal life on that bright celestial shore where we shall all meet again. Small wonder, then, at Phil Walsh's tears. It was Phil he mourned for.

LIST OF VERSIONS

JS.1   Original printed slip, as obtained from the notebook of Bert Thorne, Jemseg, N.B. 16 sts. This is the version reproduced near the beginning of this chapter.

JS.2   Joe Scott's original as published in the *Rumford Falls Times*, Mar. 30, 1901; 16 sts. Reprinted ibid., Nov. 20, 1915, with the following headnote: "The following poem was written by the woodsman poet, Joe Scott, and published in the *Rumford Falls Times* of March 30, 1901. It tells of the awful death of a Byron young man while starting a log jam at Riley, Ed."

FH   *Family Herald*, Sept. 9, 1942; no source given, 10 sts.

NH.1   Orlon Merrill, Charlestown, N.H., Oct. 16, 1931; collected by Helen Hartness Flanders, Flanders Collection, cylinder 46, sung, 15 sts. Published in Flanders et al., *The New Green Mountain Songster*, pp. 55–58. Merrill was originally from Maine and had worked for many years in the woods.

NH.2   William Monroe, Monroe, N.H., Oct. 9, 1957; in a letter, manuscript, 6½ sts., fragment. Set down as prose in eight paragraphs. "This is a song I don't know who composed it."

NH.3   Fred C. Wiggett, Plymouth, N.H., Nov. 25, 1957; in a letter, manuscript, 4 sts., fragment. Actually, sixteen lines, irregularly spaced. Wiggett knew Scott and knew this song was by him.

NH.4   James Custeau, Lincoln, N.H., July 27, 1964; in a letter, manuscript, 15½ sts. Did not know it was by Scott. Learned it in 1926. *"I guess that was based on a true story. . . . I learned that one from—when I was up in Berlin. . . . It was a girl there by the name of Helen Egan; she used to sing that song. . . . She wrote it down for me." He wrote the present version down from memory, though. Did not know the tune.

NH.5   Jack Rodgerson, 67, Berlin, N.H., Sept. 10, 1965; NA Ives tape 65.15, sung (with guitar accompaniment), 14 sts. Knew it was by Scott. Learned it as a boy in Crapaud, P.E.I. Had not sung it for years and was really amazed that he knew it that well.

Me.1   Mabel Worcester, 86, Hanover, Me., July 7, 1964; in a letter, typescript, 15 sts. What she sent me was a typed copy she had had around for some years. On Sept. 12, 1965, she sang the first five stanzas for me. Knew it was by Scott.

Me.2   Omer McKenna, ca. 80, Rumford, Me., Sept. 28, 1965; NA Ives tape 65.19, sung, 8½ sts., fragment. Knew it was by Scott. Learned it back home in Waterford, P.E.I., when he was about thirteen.

Me.3   Florence Knapp, 71, Mexico, Me., June 16, 1964; in a letter, manuscript, 4½ sts., fragment. Knew it was by Scott, whom she remembered as a sometime boarder at her mother's in Houghton.

Me.4   John Brown, Mexico, Me., July 11, 1964; NA Ives tape 64.4, recited, 14 sts. Knew it was by Scott. Learned it from his older brother back in Chipman, N.B., before he came to Maine in the 1900s.

Me.5   Gertrude Bradbury, Mexico, Me., written down from recitation by her daughter, Pearl Longley, in a notebook lent to me Sept. 29, 1965; manuscript, 7 sts., fragment. Knew it was by Scott.

Me.6   Gertrude Toothaker, 80, Rangeley, Me., July 29, 1959; NA Ives tape 1.60 and ATL 2180.6, sung, 14 sts. Knew it was by Scott and thinks she may have heard him sing it back home in Rangeley. Her tune is transcribed in this chapter.

Me.7   From Gray, *Songs and Ballads of the Maine Lumberjacks*, pp. 24–28. "Taken down for the editor in 1916 by A.B.H., at the time a student in the University of Maine." Set down as 32 ballad stanzas, which is 16 sts. No mention of who it is by.

Me.8   Hollis Tedford, Millinocket, Me., Sept. 30, 1940; Flanders Collection, typescript, 15 sts. Typed out by Mrs. Tedford as her husband sang it and sent to Helen Hartness Flanders. No mention of authorship.

Me.9   Alton Irish, Island Falls, Me., July 10, 1940; collected by Helen Hartness Flanders, Flanders Collection, cylinders 206–207, sung, 16 sts. In a headnote to the typescript of the song: "Of it, he said it was 'taken from facts. It happened he lived in the town of Byron.' Mr. Irish learned it from Hollis Tedford—'he wrote it off for me,' he said."

Me.10 Cora Hogan, Houlton, Me., May, 1962; NA 181.027–028, typescript, 8½ sts. Copied from a collection that belonged to her father, who came from Millville, N.B., and used to work in the woods.

Me.11 James Rush, Sr., 82, Houlton, Me., Aug. 24, 1964; NA Ives tape 64.9, recited, 12½ sts. Thought it was by Larry Gorman. Knew he had left something out, but felt that this was almost the whole of it. Learned it from Jack McGinley.

Me.12 Charles Finnemore, Bridgewater, Me., Aug. 30, 1942; Flanders Collection, D–573A, sung, 15 sts. In a headnote to the transcript of the song: "Learned it from his son Stanley Finnemore, who learned it when working in the woods." Nothing mentioned about authorship.

Me.13 Stanley Finnemore, Bridgewater, Me., Aug. 30, 1942; collected by Marguerite Olney, Flanders Collection, D–566A, 2 sts., fragment. See note to Me.12.

Me.14 John Hafford, ca. 70, Allagash, Me., Nov. 19, 1962; collected by Ronald Jean, NA 207.007–009, sung, 15 sts. After st. 2, l. 2, a long pause; then he starts up again. Between his stanzas 10 and 11 (Scott sts. 13 and 10, respectively): "I'll have to quit it, I guess. That ain't the half of it."

Me.15 Thomas MacLeod, ca. 80, Baring, Me., Jan. 29, 1957; in a letter, typescript, 7 sts., fragment. On June 5, 1957, he sang me one stanza; see NA Ives tape 57.1. Had heard it was by Joe Scott.

Me.16 Edward Gavel, 72, Sanford, Me., Aug. 25, 1966; NA Ives tape 66.10, sung and recited, 16 sts. Did not know it was by Scott, but always liked the ballad. *"It kind of, it always kind of made me . . . kind of broke me up a little bit."

Me.17 Ned Stewart, 88, Rumford Point, Me., July 28, 1967; NA Ives tape 67.1, ms. 46–48, recited, 5 sts., fragment. Knew it was by Scott. *"That 'Guy Reed,' that was one of the best songs that I ever heard. Gee, it was good. Don't know where he got his tune or [if] he made the tune up or not." Had also known Guy Reed himself.

NB.1 Michael Noonan, ca. 80, St. Stephen, N.B., Aug. 18, 1964; NA Ives tape 64.7, recited, 6 sts., fragment.

NB.2 Carl Bryant, 67, Bayside (St. Andrews), N.B., Aug. 18, 1964; NA Ives tape 64.7, recited, 14 sts., then 1 st. sung. Did not know who wrote it. Learned it in the woods on the St. Croix somewhere.

NB.3 Mrs. Trueman Scott, 58, Honeydale, N.B., Aug. 23, 1964; NA Ives tape 64.9, sung, 16 sts. On June 19, 1964, Mrs. Scott sent me a manuscript version; when I asked her to sing it for me, she took the manuscript version and sang from it, making minor word changes. Got the song from Tracey Scott, also of Honeydale, her first cousin. He wrote it out for her in 1925. Did not know who wrote it.

NB.4 Sedgefield Gregory, 90, Rolling Dam, N.B., Aug. 23, 1964; NA Ives tape 64.9, sung, 14 sts. Says he learned the song in New Hampshire, near Gorham about 1908 from a man named John Carter who came from up above Woodstock, N.B. Did not know who wrote the song.

NB.5 George H. O'Mar, Oak Hill (St. Stephen), N.B., n.d. (probably in the 1930s); Eckstorm Papers 329–330, typescript, 13 sts. This is "The Death of Will McClinton," discussed earlier in this chapter.

NB.6   R. A. Cross, St. George, N.B., Oct. 20, 1924; Gordon Manu-
       scripts 773, manuscript, 13 sts. Printed by Robert W. Gordon in
       Adventure, Mar. 30, 1925, p. 191. "I have sent you my original
       copy, spelling and all," Cross wrote to Gordon. The copy is in a
       different hand from Cross's letter, with a note at the end,
       presumably to Cross, "Please let me know if you get this all right I
       am laid up with a sprained knee / From / Cobb."

NB.7   Harry Keenan, 72, Woodstock, N.B., May 11, 1962; NA Ives
       tape 62.1 and ATL 3130.4, sung and recited, 11½ sts.

NB.8   Victoria Costigan, Littleton, Mass., June 16, 1964; in a letter,
       manuscript, 13 sts. At a later date, she sent me a tape with the
       tune. Did not know it was by Joe Scott. Learned it about 1912 in
       South Knowlesville (Carleton Co.), N.B.

NB.9   Alice Flynn, Allegany, N.Y., Aug. 1, 1964; typescript, given to
       me in Bangor, Me., 16 sts. Sang 5 sts. for me that day to give me
       the tune; see NA Ives tape 64.7. She is Jack McGinley's daughter,
       originally from Johnville. She and her brothers (who live in the
       Boston area) have tried to remember how their father sang it.
       *"We've been two years getting 'Guy Reed' together. . . . I knew
       part, they knew part, and we kept writing back and forth. And
       then I got Gray's book with 'Guy Reed' in it. His version is
       different from ours." Knew it was by Scott.

NB.10 Fred A. Campbell, 82, Arthurette, N.B., July 17, 1965; NA
       80.039–044, recited, 16 sts. Collected by his daughter, Kathleen
       Campbell, who adds the following note: "Mr. Campbell first
       heard this poem by Joe Scott on October 28, 1913. He was
       pleased to recite it and added this small verse that he'd always
       heard with this poem. Short is our longest day of life, and soon its
       prospects end. Yet on that days uncertain date . . . eternal years
       depend."

NB.11 Joseph Pagett, 68, Markhamville (Sussex R.R. 5), N.B., Oct. 12,
       1965; NA Ives tape 65.22, sung, 10 sts. On July 31, 1964, Pagett
       sent me a manuscript version. Differences between the two
       versions negligible. Learned the song about 1920 from Ora Wal-
       lace on the Big Salmon River drive.

NB.12 Mrs. Joseph Mercer, R.R. 3, Sussex, N.B., Dec. 13, 1957; in a
       letter, manuscript, 4½ sts., fragment.

NB.13 John Nicholson, 58, Jordan Mountain (Sussex R.R. 2), N.B., Oct.
       12, 1965; NA Ives tape 65.23, sung, 13½ sts. On June 16, 1964, I
       received from him a manuscript version in a letter; adds st. 11, ll.
       1–2, omits st. 9, ll. 3–4, and st. 11, ll. 3–4. Learned it about 1921
       from his uncle King Scott, who lived in Upham. Thinks he recalls

him remarking that the man who made up the song was a *Joe Scott*, but can't be sure.

NB.14   Clarence McCarthy, Tracy, N.B., Aug. 5, 1966; in a letter, manuscript, 13 sts. Learned it from Bob Lindsay "one night in a driving tent on the West Nerepis." Did not know who wrote it.

NB.15   Fred McMahon, 68, Chatham, N.B., Oct., 1948; Beaverbrook Collection, NMC MAN–23–76, sung, 13½ sts. Did not know who wrote it. Printed in Manny and Wilson, *Songs of Miramichi*, pp. 104–107.

NB.16   Philip Walsh, Northwest Bridge, N.B., July 22, 1961; NA Ives tape 1.96 and ATL 3103.3, sung, 14 sts. This is the version given at the beginning of this chapter.

NB.17   Manny Monzelle, 60, Dalhousie, N.B. (collected in Young's Cove), July 13, 1965; collected by Ethel Hamilton, NA 194.008–010, sung (but tune not submitted), 9½ sts., fragment. Monzelle was aware that a portion was missing toward the end.

NB.18   Charles Chesser, Campbellton, N.B., June 10, 1964; in a letter, typescript, 13 sts. Learned it about 1939, while working in the woods.

NS.1   Peter Glode, Pubnico, N.S., n.d.; typescript from William Doerflinger, as collected by him, 5½ sts., fragment.

NS.2   Judson and Allister Armstrong, Sherwood (Lunenburg Co.), N.S., June, 1949; collected by Helen Creighton, NMC CR–1–5, sung, 16 sts.

NS.3   Jack Turple, Upper Kennetcook, N.S., July, 1952; collected by Helen Creighton, NMC CR–96–956, sung, 15 sts.

NS.4   James Curtis (b. 1898), Cape North (Bay St. Lawrence), Cape Breton Island, N.S., 1975; collected by Denis Ryan, MUNFLA 76–345, sung, 16 sts. Learned from his uncle Tom Brown, who had worked with Scott in Maine.

PI.1   Mrs. Underhill Coughlin, Brooklyn (Alberton R.R.), P.E.I., Aug. 23, 1965; NA Ives tape 65.3, sung and recited, 11 sts. Manuscript sent me June 17, 1964, almost identical. She learned the song locally years ago and had not sung it for thirty years at least.

PI.2   Angus Enman, 78, Spring Hill, P.E.I., Aug. 18, 1958; NA Ives tape 1.39 and ATL 2164.4, sung, 4 sts., fragment. Knew it was by Scott.

PI.3   Wesley Smith, 66, Victoria West, P.E.I., Aug. 18, 1958; NA Ives tape 1.40 and ATL 2165.4, sung, 14 sts. This version was published in Ives, *Twenty-one Folksongs from Prince Edward Is-*

land, pp. 63–68. On Aug. 28, 1965, he added one more stanza, st. 9.

PI.4   Mrs. Arthur Bowness, Charlottetown, P.E.I., June 22, 1964; in a letter, manuscript, 16 sts. "While going through some old papers, I found a tattered copy of Guy Reed. I have copied it off and am enclosing it." Almost verbatim Scott's original version.

NOTES

1. Polley to Gordon, Mar. 2, 1925, Gordon Manuscripts 928.
2. Phillips Barry, Fannie Hardy Eckstorm, and Mary Winslow Smyth, *British Ballads from Maine,* pp. 95, 381, 430. See also Eckstorm Papers, pp. 97, 98 verso, 127, 441, 444.
3. Myron H. Avery, "The Story of the Wassataquoik."
4. Ibid., pp. 95–96.
5. Ibid., p. 87.
6. NB.1, 2, 3, 4, 6.
7. For the information in this paragraph I am grateful to Mr. and Mrs. Joseph Reed of Roxbury, Mrs. Wirt Virgin (née Madeline Reed) of West Peru, and David Severy of Gray, Me.
8. *Rumford Falls Times,* Sept. 17, 1897. All subsequent quotations are from the same source. Most of the article can be found reprinted in Edward D. Ives, *Twenty-one Folksongs from Prince Edward Island,* pp. 63–64.
9. Mrs. Leo Kilfoil, Johnville, N.B., July 21, 1965, as told to Eugenie M. Lenehan. NA 246.001.
10. Laws C–1, 3, 4, 5, 6, 7, 9, 10, 12; dC–33, 35. I have omitted, somewhat arbitrarily, C–2, "The Banks of the Little Eau Plaine," as fictional, and C–11, "The Lost Jimmy Whelan," as a special case. Both are peripheral or (better) tangential to the tradition I am referring to. See also Edith Fowke, *Lumbering Songs from the Northern Woods,* pp. 138–142 ("The Haggertys and Young Mulvanny"), 146–149 ("The Cold Black River Stream"), and 154–155 ("Vince Leahy").
11. Louise Manny and James Reginald Wilson, *Songs of Miramichi,* p. 115.
12. Edward D. Ives and Sharon Sperl, *Folksongs from Maine,* p. 39.
13. See G. Malcolm Laws, Jr., *Native American Balladry,* p. 149.
14. Manny and Wilson, *Songs of Miramichi,* p. 116.
15. Ibid., p. 307.
16. Ives and Sperl, *Folksongs from Maine,* p. 38.
17. Fowke, *Lumbering Songs,* p. 105.
18. Ives and Sperl, *Folksongs from Maine,* p. 38.
19. Manny and Wilson, *Songs of Miramichi,* p. 307.
20. Fowke, *Lumbering Songs,* p. 141.
21. Ives and Sperl, *Folksongs from Maine,* p. 38.
22. Manny and Wilson, *Songs of Miramichi,* p. 307.
23. Fowke, *Lumbering Songs,* p. 98.
24. Ibid., pp. 138–141.
25. Helen Hartness Flanders et al., *The New Green Mountain Songster,* p. 58. Barry cites a set of the air as sung by F. L. Tracy of Brewer, Me., and a copy of the text in M. C. Dean, *Flying Cloud,* p. 119. The tune given here is taken from the original sheet music.

26. See, e.g., "Fogan MacAleer," especially Art Cahill's statement about it, in Edward D. Ives, *Lawrence Doyle*, p. 42.

27. Tristram P. Coffin, "The Traditional Ballad as an Art Form."

28. See, e.g., "The Soldier's Letter" in Ives and Sperl, *Folksongs from Maine*, pp. 41–44.

29. See Sigmund Spaeth, *Weep Some More, My Lady*, pp. 38–39. Several other letter songs are included ibid., pp. 36–40.

30. Fowke, *Lumbering Songs*, p. 96.

31. Ibid., p. 155.

32. Manny and Wilson, *Songs of Miramichi*, p. 107.

33. Me.9 (sung), Me.16, NS.2 (sung), NS.4 (sung), NB.3, NB.9, NB.10, NB.14, PI.4. The last three were clearly written off from Joe's original printed version.

34. See Anne Cohen and Norm Cohen, "Tune Evolution as an Indicator of Traditional Music Norms," p. 41. It is also worth mentioning that Joe used only the melody for the stanzas, omitting that for the chorus, which goes along with the Cohens' observation that there was a "tendency to simplify elaborate musical patterns" (p. 42). But the same problem arises here as with the chromaticism: was Joe working from a "folk" version of "Little Nell" or from the original? Did *he* do the simplifying, or had it already been done for him? Once again, we suffer for lack of a Ouija board.

35. For "When the Work's All Done This Fall," see Carl Sandburg, *The American Songbag*, pp. 260–261. For Fred McMahon's singing of "Guy Reed," see Manny and Wilson, *Songs of Miramichi*, p. 104. Joe Hickerson of the Library of Congress Archive of Folk Song (with some help from the indefatigable Gus Meade) made a quick check and was able to find at least a dozen pre-1930 recorded releases of this cowboy ballad by such well-known artists as Carl Sprague, E. V. Stoneman, Alton Ray ("The Dixie Cowboy"), Vernon Dalhart, and the Cartwright Brothers. For a discussion of "When the Work's All Done This Fall" see John I. White, *Git Along, Little Dogies*, pp. 85–87, 193–195.

11

"William Sullivan":
A Notable Unsuccess

"There's no music in me," said Roy Lohnes, "no music at all. I can't sing a note, but I learned all them songs so that I could say them over for myself, and I still know a lot of them."

We were talking through the screen door of his Andover, Maine, boardinghouse. Anna Thurston, then of Farmington, Connecticut, had written me about him, saying that he was a friend of her father's and knew a lot of songs. I asked him if he'd be willing to recite some of his songs over so I could tape-record them. Sure, he said, he'd be glad to, but his landlady wasn't happy about strangers, so why didn't we drive down to Thurstons'. Anna was home now, and we could sit on the porch there.

It turned out to be a wonderful suggestion, and an even more wonderful front porch. We sat there—Anna, Roy, and I—all of a sunny August afternoon with the swallows glinting in and out of the eaves and the peaceful noise of a tractor coming and going as the man across the way mowed his field. Roy held the mike; he insisted on that. "Ready?" he'd say, and I'd nod and turn the machine on. He'd recite "James Bird" or whatever it might be, and when he came to the end, "Shut her off," he'd growl, and then we'd talk a bit, until he hit on what his next song was going to be.

Roy hadn't known Joe Scott personally, but he'd heard a lot about him and knew several of his songs: "Howard Carey," "The Plain Golden Band," and "The Norway Bum," to begin with. Later in the afternoon he recalled that he knew another one. "It's called 'William Sullivan,' but I don't know all of it. I never wanted to learn all of it. You know how Joe was," he added, "and how he was always putting

178

in stuff about the bubbling brooks and the flowers?" I nodded.
"Well," he continued, "the whole first third of this song was like that,
so I just never bothered to learn that part. But I'll go over what I
know of it for you, and it's still pretty long." He cleared his throat.
"Ready?" he asked, and when I said I was, he started in.

I had never heard the ballad he recited, but all the elements were
familiar enough: a mother trying unsuccessfully to persuade her son
not to leave the old home, a death in the lumberwoods, and a return
home to final rest, all told in that lush, leisurely fashion that I had
come even in 1958 to identify with Joe Scott. Roy's voice was
pleasant, and the mower came and went in the afternoon sun as the
swallows swooped and twittered. It was an almost perfect way to
listen to a Joe Scott ballad. Then it ended. "Shut her off," Roy said.
I shut her off.

I never heard that ballad again. Lots of people told me they'd
heard of it and knew there was such a ballad, but no one knew it. I
had completely given up ever finding out what those stanzas might
be that Roy never bothered to learn; then in 1976 rescue came from a
familiar quarter. Neil Rosenberg wrote that one of his students,
Denis Ryan, had collected "Willie Sullivan" from a Cape Bretoner by
the name of James Curtis, who had learned it from an uncle who
spent many years in the Maine woods and had known Scott. It is
Curtis's version that I give here, but I have marked with an asterisk
the stanzas that Roy Lohnes knew, and I have bracketed stanza 13,
since that is one Roy had that Curtis did not.

WILLIAM SULLIVAN

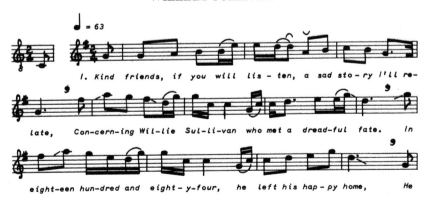

1. Kind friends, if you will lis-ten, a sad sto-ry I'll relate, Con-cern-ing Wil-lie Sul-li-van who met a dread-ful fate. In
eight-een hun-dred and eight-y-four, he left his hap-py home, He

left his friends and kind re-lates in dis-tant lands to roam.

[1]   Kind friends, if you will listen, a sad story I'll relate,
        Concerning Willie Sullivan who met a dreadful fate.
        In eighteen hundred and eighty-four, he left his happy home,
        He left his friends and kind relates in distant lands to roam.

[2]   The day he left his happy home nearby the ocean strand,
        His poor old aged father he took him by the hand,
        Saying, "Son you're going to leave us now, in distant lands
            you'll roam. .
        I would have you remember the old folks here at home.

[3]   "We are growing old and feeble now, our hair is turning gray;
        Our forms will soon be mouldering in the cold and silent clay.
        And you to go and leave us now would hasten on," he said,
        "Those gray hairs you see gathering in your poor old father's
            head."

[4]   His poor old aged mother she stood there by his side,
        And the tears rolled down her wrinkled cheeks, and bitterly
            she cried:
        Saying, "Willie, dearest Willie, why do you from us stray?
        It almost breaks my poor old heart to see you go away.

[*5]   "It's well do I remember and it seems like yesterday,
        But it is three long and dreary years since Douglas went
            away;
        He never returned in life again," with quivering lips she said.
        "They brought your brother home again, my son, but he was
            dead.

[*6]   "And there is Rob, another; who but one year ago
        Who went to seek his fortune in some distant land you know.
        But oh, alas, poor Robert all the fortune that he found
        Was a grave beside his brother in the silent churchyard
            ground.

[*7]   "And yet there is another, for you're going to leave us now.
        No wonder there are traces of sorrow upon my brow.
        No wonder that my eyes are dim; my hair is turning gray.
        Remember, son, you may have children of your own some
            day."

180

[8]   They were standing at a cottage on a pleasant summer's
        morn,
        And the glorious sun was setting o'er the place where they
        were on.
        Where the wild perfume of roses bore upon the mountain air,
        Caressed the group that lingered round that little cottage
        there.

[9]   "This little farm you bought for us, you paid your money free,
        That we might have to call our own, contented for to be.
        You might as well remain with us contented here at home.
        Remember what the poet wrote about the rolling stone."

[*10]   "I know, dear mother, you are old, your head is bending low.
        I know your hair is turning gray, your steps are getting slow.
        My prospects here look dark and drear, last night my tears
        did flow.
        In vain I would tarry with you, now, but Mother I must go.

[*11]   "In the town of Richibucto, a maiden fair do dwell,
        I love that comely creature more than a mortal tongue can
        tell.
        She loves me, dearest Mother, and her words are not in vain;
        She slights me for my poverty and slights me with disdain."

[*12]   Up speaks his aged mother and her words were very true:
        "The girl that loves you for your gold is not the girl for you.
        The girl that loves you for yourself, that love will always last,
        While rivers flow and crickets sing in the fields of waving
        grass.

[*13]   ["But if you're bound to leave us now, to try you to detain,
        For if your mind is bent on roving, my words would be in
        vain."
        She reared her eyes toward Heaven and with favrunt [fer-
        vent?] heart did pray
        That God would guide her wandering son in a land so far
        away.]

[*14]   He kissed his mother tenderly, he grasped his father's hand.
        He kissed his sisters o'er and o'er as they stood on the strand.
        Then turning round he waved his hand and to his brothers
        called,
        "Farewell, dear brothers, I am bound for the town of Berlin
        Falls."

[*15] Three long and dreary years he spent in many lands did
      roam.
But yet he never did forget the loved ones left at home.
He intended to return again, I think that coming fall.
But oh, comes death untimely and it puts an end to all.

[*16] He was chopping off a spruce the wind had blown across the
      way;
The wind had blown it from its roots, so I was told one day.
And when the top it was chopped off the roots so large they
      say,
Instead of tipping back to place it tipped the other way.

[*17] It buried him in an instant, in a mass of earth and stone,
Completely covered him from sight and he was all alone.
His comrades loud his name did call, but not a word was
      heard,
But the echo of their voices or the song of some wild bird.

[*18] Until at last, they found the spot where his lifeless body lay.
They quickly dug it from the mass of roots and earth and clay.
It's gently they bore his form in blankets to the train.
Where a little casket was prepared and in it he was lain.

[*19] He was taken by John Norman to the town of Berlin Falls,
And gently laid all in his house with strong and narrow walls.
He was taken then to Rumford Falls as far as Brien's Pond,
Where his brother-in-law he bore him to his distant home
      beyond.

[*20] It was in the town of Bemis, Maine, where gently flows the
      rills,
Where the echo of the woodsman's ax awake the silent hills.
On the twentieth of September on a Thursday afternoon,
Where Willie Sullivan met his fate, when scarcely in his
      bloom.

[*21] On the bonnie, bonnie banks of Boss, all leaved in ruby
      green,
Where winding streams and valleys low and rippling rills are
      seen.
Where winding streams flow gently on o'er mountain, hill
      and dell
There stands a little cottage where an aged couple dwell.

[*22]   This pleasant little cottage was the home of Sullivan
Whose worldly cares are over and whose work on earth is done,
Who sleeps beside his brothers where the golden flowers grow,
Where the birds of spring, their notes do sing in the valleys far below.

There is no direct evidence that Joe Scott wrote "William Sullivan," but it has been attributed to him by several people, among them Fred Campbell and George Storer, both of whom knew Scott well, and of course Roy Lohnes and James Curtis. The ballad is set in country Joe knew very well—he'd worked in and around Bemis for years—and it is about something that happened at a time when we know he was still working out of Rumford Falls, the fall of 1897, only a little more than a month after the death of Guy Reed. Stylistically, the ballad is full of touches that are Joe Scott right down the line. In sum, the ascriptive, stylistic, and circumstantial evidence for Joe Scott's authorship of "William Sullivan" is, as far as I am concerned, compelling, and there is nothing to gainsay it.

Since we do not have Joe Scott's original version of "William Sullivan," we must be content with a reconstruction, but my reconstruction is simply Curtis's version with the addition of a single stanza from Lohnes's. That means we cannot be sure we have all the stanzas (although I think we do). Nor can we be sure that the stanzas we have are in their proper order. I am certain, for example, that the present stanza 20 should come between stanzas 15 and 16, both because it makes better sense there and because that is where Roy Lohnes had it. But since neither argument is necessarily conclusive, as we have seen in our consideration of "Guy Reed," I have left the stanza where Curtis had it. I have also resisted the temptation to "correct" patent errors in geography and diction, but some of them are worth comment.

The geographical errors in the two versions are what we might expect. Curtis, a Maritimer, has the girl living in Richibucto, quite near Bass River, while Lohnes, a Mainer, has it incorrectly as Richburg. We can be sure that Joe Scott would have had it right. Conversely, Lohnes has the body put aboard the train at Bryant Pond (it would have been the nearest Grand Trunk Railroad stop to

Rumford Falls), which is correct and the way Joe would have had it. Again, I am sure Lohnes's version is closer to Joe's in correctly having the body taken to the undertaker in Rumford Falls rather than to Berlin Falls, some forty miles by road or rail to the west. Each version mistakes Bass River differently, but Lohnes's "banks of Bash, all robed in leafy green" is certainly closer to Joe's original than Curtis's "banks of Boss, all leaved in ruby green." Finally, at the end of the leave-taking scene, Lohnes has Sullivan address his *dead* rather than his *dear* brothers, a touch I like but can hardly insist on. With the exception of these details, however, I am willing to accept the reconstructed version as both complete and very close to Joe's original.

If we make allowances for just a little poetry, Joe had his facts remarkably straight. The settlement of Bass River is in a beautiful, gently rolling section of Kent County, New Brunswick, about twenty miles up the Richibucto River from the sea. The grant map for that area shows that a William Sullivan held a lot of about one hundred acres on what was known locally as the Easter Road, and in the local Presbyterian cemetery there is a monument to this William (1830–1904), his wife, Mary Ann Robertson (1836–1902), and their five sons. Samuel, the oldest (1861–1927), evidently stayed home and took care of the farm, and John Alexander died in childhood (1863–65). But John Douglas (1868–91), Robert (1870–93), and William (1872–97) all went away to seek their fortunes elsewhere, and all three came home dead. "This is the third time in the short space of six years," said the *Moncton Daily Transcript* in reporting William's death, "that they [*the Sullivans*] have had a son brought home coffined for burial."[1] Assuming that in the original ballad Joe had William leave home in 1894 (when he was twenty-two) rather than in 1884 (when he would have been twelve), Douglas would have been dead for three years at that time, Robert for one. The father and mother would have been sixty-four and fifty-eight respectively, which in the 1890s required only a little poetry to qualify as aged.

The accident was a freakish one, as several people have been at some pains to explain to me. The tree Sullivan was working on had been blown down and uprooted by the wind. What he did was to cut the butt away from the exposed roots, thinking that when he did so the stump and the roots would naturally fall back into the hole they had left; but evidently they were already tipped too far, and instead of falling back into place the stump and the ton or so of dirt, rocks, and roots attached to it fell over on top of him. When the rest of the crew came to look for him, all they could see was a hand (some said a hand and a foot), all the rest of him being buried under the toppled stump.

The *Rumford Falls Times* for October 22, 1897, told the story of Sullivan's death on page 5, under the heading "A FATAL ACCIDENT":

Tuesday afternoon soon after returning to work from dinner William Sullivan, Jr., a foreman for the Berlin Mills Co., in their logging business near Bemis, was working a little distance from the rest of the crew, on the steep mountain side where the wind of Saturday night and Sunday had uprooted several trees. He had the snarl partially cleared out and cut a tree off at the but [*sic*] when the stump with tons of dirt tipped forward onto him. The crew soon missed the sound of his axe and called to him without response. They went to the place and saw one hand and foot that were not buried. They ran to the camp for shovels and removed the earth and roots. One side of his head and face was crushed in and his neck broken. He was also considerably bruised about the body. He was brought to Rumford Falls and taken to Calhoun's undertaking rooms where he was prepared for burial. Dr. C. M. Bisbee viewed the body and gave a burial permit. Wednesday morning the remains were taken to Beaver Brook, N.B. Mr. Sullivan was twenty-four years old and a native of Bass River, N.B.

"Beaver Brook" is probably a reportorial error, since the only community of that name is on the Miramichi River about fifty miles to the north of Bass River and in a totally different part of the world. The remains most likely came by rail to Harcourt, only ten miles away.

Joe may have used the newspaper article as one of his sources for this ballad, but, as with "Howard Carey" and "Guy Reed," it is more likely he was depending on barroom authority for his description of the accident. It is of course possible that Joe was working out of the same camp with Sullivan, or even in the same crew, which would make him the next best thing to an eyewitness, but I doubt it. I think we can take at face value his statements in stanza 16 that this is what he was "told one day" and that it is what "they say." Besides, had Joe been part of the crew, I see no reason why he would have told this part of the story in the third person rather than in the more dramatic first-person plural.

It wouldn't have been hard for Joe to pick up the story via the bush telegraph anyway. An oddball death like Sullivan's is something that gets talked about, and even sixty years after the event I have found it much easier to find secondhand oral accounts (that is, *not* from eyewitnesses) of the accident than to find versions of the ballad Joe Scott made up about it. Frequently these accounts surface because I have asked someone like George Storer what ballads Joe made up. *"Oh well, by gorry, it was so long ago," was Storer's apologetic response. "There was one, I know, called 'Bill Sullivan.' He was killed up to Summit there in the woods . . . and Joe made up a song about it. . . . Well now, this tree it was blowed down. . . ." But Storer did not remember the ballad itself. Only Lohnes and Curtis remembered that.

For the rest of the ballad, Joe's information is too accurate to have come from simple barroom authority, and my guess is that it came from Sullivan himself. The two New Brunswickers were about the same age (Joe thirty, Bill twenty-four) and worked for the same outfits in the same area. It would be surprising if they hadn't known each other, and the central detail (for the ballad, that is), that Bill was the last of three brothers to die in the past five years, is something Joe is much more likely to have learned directly from him than from gossip. This assumption is partially supported by the fact that none of the oral accounts I have heard mentions the brothers at all.

But there is another source Joe might have used for these family details: John Norman. The *Moncton Daily Transcript* described Norman as "a native of Bass River, who was working with the deceased at the time and who had the remains taken down to Rumford Falls, dressed, and inclosed in a neat casket."[2] The grant maps for Bass River show a John Norman—more than likely the father of our John Norman—living less than a quarter of a mile from Sullivan's home, and we can be sure that Norman would have known about the brothers and how Bill's parents implored him not to leave home. He might also have known about the girl in Richibucto (assuming she is for real). A detail like young Bill's having bought the farm for his parents is a little more likely to have come from someone like Norman than from Sullivan himself, partly because it doesn't seem like the sort of thing a man would tell about himself and partly because it is wrong. It doesn't matter, really, whether these details came from Norman or directly from Sullivan or (what is just as likely) from a combination of the two. The point is that they did not come from the newspaper, and it is unlikely they would have been part of the general talk. They had to come from an inside source.

The ballad's structure is remarkable, a little too remarkable, it turns out, and a quick reading of it immediately suggests a parallel with "Howard Carey." As the discussion of that ballad demonstrated, a leave-taking scene whose main feature is parental advice is a common feature of broadside balladry. But if "Howard Carey" was unusual in devoting a third of its stanzas to such a scene, what are we to say of "William Sullivan," where it makes up well over half of the ballad? If we take it together with the opening stanza—a very straight and traditional one—we have a ballad whose action doesn't really begin until stanza 15, practically two-thirds of the way along. In the meantime, we have had both paternal and maternal advice, the sad history of his brothers, and the suggestion that it is a hopeless love for a local lass that impels his venture. The parallel with "Howard Carey" is made even closer by the heavy emphasis both ballads give to the mother. Howard died in May, 1897, Sullivan in October, less than six months later. The earlier ballad would still have been fresh in Joe's mind, and, working on the assumption that nothing succeeds like success, he may have decided to follow the same pattern. It didn't work this time, but we'll come back to that in a minute.

Stanza 15 parallels the motif of Howard Carrick's wanderings, but the denouement to follow is entirely different. Howard came to a bad end; Sullivan's death was caused by an accident that occurred while he was doing his job, and at this point Scott swings right over into the structure of ballads on that classic theme. In stanzas 15, 16, and the first half of 17, he describes the freak accident. He goes on in the second half of 17 and all of 18 and 19 to give us the finding of the body and the equivalent of a funeral, the sending of the body home. I have already said that I believe stanza 20 is out of place, belonging between stanzas 15 and 16. The final two stanzas (21–22) close out the ballad in a spate of typical Joe Scott nature imagery, bringing Sullivan home to his parents to sleep beside his brothers.

"William Sullivan" was written right in the midst of the time when Joe was making his best ballads, and we can assume it was marketed right along with the others. Why didn't it catch on, then? Any answer to that question is going to have to be highly speculative, but I do have an answer. Joe Scott had recently written two very successful ballads on the death of friends. In May of 1897 Howard Carrick had died, and in the ballad he made about him Joe told the story from the inside. It is the monologue of a young man at death's door, taking us step by step from his happy childhood to his present state of sickness and despondency. Even the shift to third person in the final two stanzas does not detract from the psychological focus of the drama. Then in September, Guy Reed met his death, and Joe made a ballad about him in which the drama is entirely one of events; the focus is on *what* happened.

In October of that year a third friend, Bill Sullivan, died, and in making a ballad about him Joe seems to have tried to combine elements of both his earlier successes: the leave-taking of "Howard Carey" and the detailed accident scene of "Guy Reed." But it didn't work. On the one hand, he went absolutely overboard with the leave-taking scene; it is simply too long, even in Roy Lohnes's cut version, where it takes up only half rather than two-thirds of the ballad. On the other hand, the accident is not adequately explained. It was a freak accident to begin with, difficult to describe under any circumstances, even when the person describing it can use his hands (*"See, that tree was setting there this way, and the roots was up this way, and Bill he tried to cut it off right here, see, and . . .").* When we consider that in "Guy Reed" Joe took four full stanzas to detail a familiar kind of death, the six prosy lines he devotes to the task here not only fail to make clear what happened, they also fail to counterbalance to emotional weight of the leave-taking scene. It's a matter, then, of too much and not enough.

In "Howard Carey" the long leave-taking scene is entirely appropriate for making us empathize with Howard's final wretchedness; in "Guy Reed" the detailed description of the accident makes us see it—and therefore feel it—more vividly. It is possible that the two could have been made to work together, but in my opinion Joe never really made up his mind what kind of ballad he wanted "William Sullivan" to be, and I offer the following as the course of his indecision: an unfortunate accident like Sullivan's seemed to call for the "Guy Reed" approach; yet Joe knew all about the dead brothers and aged parents back home, and that seemed to call for the "Howard Carey" approach. Here was a friend, only a few years younger than he, the last of his line, going home to rest in what was Joe's homeland, too, and Joe identified with him just as he had with Howard

Carrick. Considering Joe's psychological state at the time,[3] it was almost inevitable that he would try to make a "Howard Carey" out of what might better have been a "Guy Reed."

One final point remains. Roy Lohnes claimed that there was about a third of "William Sullivan" he never bothered to learn, and it turns out that his estimate is perfectly correct. But it is interesting to compare what he chose to omit with what he *said* he chose to omit, which was "stuff about the bubbling brooks and the flowers." Only stanza 8 fits that description, and he kept stanzas 21 and 22, both of which fit it too. I find his omission of stanzas 1 and 2 surprising, since it leaves him with a rather confusing *in medias res* opening. Essentially what Lohnes did was to cut the opening and leave-taking sections down from two-thirds to a mere half of the ballad while omitting only a stanza and a half of maternal advice! It is the father's advice that gets cut completely. That brings "William Sullivan" still more closely in line with "Howard Carey," but even with this kind of editing, the ballad never caught on at all.

If "William Sullivan" was as bad as all that, it may seem a wonder that it was remembered by even two men. For James Curtis, the very fact that it was a song by Joe Scott seems to have made it something special, and his five Scott ballads were heirlooms from his uncle Tom Brown. Roy Lohnes had always been interested in Joe's ballads, too, but beyond that—or rather, including that—was his interest in local songs and poems of all kinds, a number of which we went over and talked about that swallow-filled August afternoon. Like the rest of these poems, "William Sullivan" was about country Roy knew well, and he'd heard the story, too, about how they'd found poor Bill by the one hand and foot that were still uncovered. "There's no music in me," Roy said, and that may have been. Roy's patron was Clio, not Euterpe. But all the Muses were Memory's daughters.

LIST OF VERSIONS

Me.   Roy Lohnes, ca. 70, Andover, Me., Aug., 1958; NA Ives tape 1.33 and ATL 2159.3, recited, 16 sts. This version is a fragment in that Lohnes admitted he did not know all of the ballad; but since he deliberately did not learn certain stanzas, it represents all of what he intended to know.

The Songs

NS   James Curtis (b. 1898), Cape North (Bay St. Lawrence), Cape
        Breton Island, N.S., 1975; collected by Denis Ryan, MUNFLA
        76–345, sung, 21 sts. Learned from his uncle Tom Brown, who
        had worked with Scott in Maine.

NOTES

1. *Moncton Daily Transcript.* Oct. 29, 1897. I would like to thank Agnes
Campbell of Bass River for her help in finding the Sullivan monument.
2. Ibid.
3. See pp. 429–433.

12

"The Plain Golden Band":
The Ballad as Autobiography

Jim Brown was from South Branch, New Brunswick, down in Kent County, but every year he came up to sing in the Miramichi Folksong Festival, and he always stayed with Tommy Whelan down in Chatham.[1] We'd often get together down at Tommy's for some wonderful singing, and once in a while Jim's friend Dan Shortall would be along, and then we'd have some reciting of pieces like "The Days of Duffy Gillis." But the first time was in August of 1959, and there was just Jim and me.

We were sitting in the front parlor, a bottle of Black Diamond "Demi" Rum between us, and Jim was singing some wonderful songs about Waterloo and life in the lumberwoods. Though he was in his seventies, his voice was strong; and his style, though traditional, was one of the most individual I had ever heard, a sort of pulsating staccato that made a line sometimes sound as though there were rests between each syllable. He sat there, thumbs in galluses, rocking back and forth a little, sometimes reaching slowly up to scratch the back of his head. His face was an intense mask, but every so often he'd smile, not at anything in the song but all to himself, as though he were just plain glad to be singing. And he did love to sing. I don't think he was ever happier than when he was singing. That afternoon he sang "The Plain Golden Band" for me. And I was glad to be listening.

The Songs

THE PLAIN GOLDEN BAND

♩ = 116

3. She was love-ly and fair as the ro-ses in spring, She ap-peared like some god-dess or some Gre-cian queen; Far fair-er than the li-lies that have bloomed on the shore, She's the pride of the val-ley, the girl I a-dore.

[1]   Oh, I been thinking today, love, on the days past and gone,
As the sun glimmered over the hilltops at morn;
And the dew drop from heaven like diamonds did glow,
They were kissing the roses in the valley below.

[2]   Oh, the clear purling waters so mild and so blue,
And the green drooping willows where the birds sang so true;
Where the wild roses bloomed on the rocks by the shore,
Where I parted with Lizzie, the girl I adore.

[3]   She was lovely and fair as the roses in spring,
She appeared like some goddess or some Grecian queen;
Far fairer than the lilies that have bloomed on the shore,
She's the pride of the valley, the girl I adore.

[4]   The day that we parted I ne'er can forget,
For I in fancy I see those sad tears falling yet;
How my poor heart did ache and in sorrow did ring,
When she drew from her finger that plain golden ring.

[5]   Saying, "Take back the ring which I fain would retain,
For wearing it only has caused me pain;
I have broken the vows which we have made on the strand,
So take back, I pray you, that plain golden band."

[6]   "Oh, renew the engagement, fair darling," I cried,
"Remember you promised you'd be my bride;

"The Plain Golden Band"

My love it was true and ne'er can grow cold,
Retain, I beseech thee, that plain band of gold."

[7] "Oh, dear laddie, I know that your love it was true,
I know that you've loved me and that I have loved you;
And I know you deceived me that night on the strand,
When you placed on my finger that plain golden band.

[8] "On a clear starry evening as the moon it shone bright,
All nature was wrapped in its rich mellow light;
When a gentle cool vapor blew o'er the wild moor,
As I strayed from my cottage to roam on the shore.

[9] "Oh, a young man appeared and him I knew well,
He told me false stories, false stories of you;
He vowed that he loved me and offered his hand,
Then I put a stain on your plain golden band."

[10] "Fare you well, my fair darling, fare you well and adieu,
Although you've deceived me, it's to you I'll prove true;
Some day think of one while you are roam on the strand,
That has placed on your finger that plain golden band."

[11] Oh, she fell in my arrums and cried in despair,
While the gentle breeze ruffled her dark wavy hair;
And the sunlight from heaven shone on her fair hand,
And the same light shone bright on the plain golden band.

[12] "Oh, forgive me, forgive me, fair darling," she cried,
"Ere they lay me to rest in some cold silent grave;
And a fond cherished letter penned by your own hand,
Lay'em on my bosom with the plain golden band."

[13] In some green shady forest [though in] far far away,
Where the deer loves to ramble and the child loves to play;
While all in its nature though it seems wild but grand,
The author you'll find to "The Plain Golden Band."

Kipling's "Conundrum of the Workshops" has special poignance for folklorists, for the Devil always whispers at about this point, "It's pretty, but is it a folksong?" Without getting involved in a full-dress definition of folksong, I can point out that authorities have differed. "There are some songs that are so obviously folksongs that a fellow can't very well mistake them for anything else, such as The plain golden band which is of Nova Scotian origin," wrote George Hirdt of

193

Nouvelle, Quebec, to Robert W. Gordon back in 1927, when he sent Gordon a copy of that song along with several others.[2] But Hirdt's instinct was at variance with that of at least one noted collector, Helen Creighton, who wrote me in 1957 that she had heard the song but had been "doubtful if it was actually a folk song."[3] In addition, G. Malcolm Laws, Jr., the ballad scholar and canonist, had misgivings about it, being very skeptical of William Doerflinger's claim that it had been "composed by a New Brunswick logger,"[4] though he later included it as number H–17 in his revised edition of *Native American Balladry* under the rubric "Ballads on Various Topics." We can see now that Gordon's unlettered correspondent was correct, and we can pick up our lead from Laws and ask just what evidence there is for the claim that Joe Scott did in fact write "The Plain Golden Band."

First of all, we have not one but two of Joe's original printed slips—almost identical but clearly different printings. Both have his name on them, and while that is pretty conclusive evidence in itself, there is plenty more. "The Plain Golden Band" is attributed to him more often than any other single song, both by people who knew him well and by people who knew no more about him than that "he was the man who made up 'The Plain Golden Band.'" Many of these attributions are based on reports of Joe Scott's own claim. Peter Jamieson's story is typical, if a bit dramatic. He had left his home in Bathurst, New Brunswick, to work in the woods for Henry and Company in the Lincoln valley in New Hampshire, where he met Scott. "After knowing him about a month," he wrote, "one night as him and I were talking one of our crew started to sing The Plain Golden Band. He stopped talking to me, and as I turned to look he was sobbing and tears running down his cheeks. After a while he turned to me and said, 'I am the author of that song and you have found me right where the song said you would. Still true to the vows I made. . . .'"[5] Finally, as Jamieson's statement suggests, the song fits perfectly with the facts of Joe's life. Doubts seem academic at this point.

Not that I haven't seen counterclaims of sorts. B. H. Rix of Kamloops, British Columbia, sent in a version of the ballad to the *Family Herald*'s "Old Favourites" column. There is no date on the covering letter, but external evidence would place it in the mid-forties. It included this note:

I was quite surprised and pleased to see in your old favorite page to see Joe Scott's Plain golden band in print again must be getting popular never had any idea it would be when Joe and I composed and wrote it together and sang it many times, out in that logging camp on Beaver Brook in Northern New Hampshire of course Joe was the better half. But there I've gone and done it and told you my secret I've kept locked up for years . . . your correspondent who wrote and sent you Joes song got his wires crossed some not bad I'm sending you Joes song as we wrote it I should know as I had a finger in the pie as some people say.

To be sure, Rix is not saying he wrote the song, merely that he helped Joe, and that could mean anything from suggesting a minor change in wording on up. Fred Campbell said that his older brother Alec told him *he'd* helped Joe write "The Plain Golden Band" one winter in the woods up near Bemis. Joe would make up the verses in the woods during the day; then at night Alec would help him write them down, he said. When I asked him what that meant, Campbell wasn't sure, but said that was what his brother had told him, anyhow. Once again, it is a vague claim of assistance, not of authorship.

As far as I know, the only out-and-out claim of authorship was made by Jack Scott of Salmon Arm, British Columbia, in a letter to the *Family Herald* dated November 18, 1957: "I am sending in the words of The Plain Golden Band composed by me on a river drive in Maine in 1902 or 3. I gave the song to Joe Scott who put the music to it and often sang it. I never saw Scott again. . . . It don't matter who composed the song at this date." I don't think there is any need to take this claim seriously, even though the only argument I can use to refute it is the rather flimsy one that several men claim that they learned the song well before 1900. To sum up, I am satisfied beyond reasonable doubt that Joe Scott was indeed the author of "The Plain Golden Band."

In order to study the way in which Joe blended tradition and fact, we should have a version of the song that is as close as possible to what he wrote. As with "Howard Carey" and "Guy Reed," we have printed copies of the ballad as he hawked it around the lumber-camps, but we are embarrassed by riches this time, in having not one but two distinct versions. The first (JS.1) was given me by Daisy Severy of Gray, Maine; the second (JS.2) was in Bert Thorne's notebook. They are almost identical, but they are also quite clearly different printings, and the variations include minor shifts in wording and punctuation. Many of them could be explained as the sort of thing that would have happened had Joe Scott taken a copy of one version to another printer and said, "Let me have a couple hundred more like that one"; but some of them might also represent his own editing. There is simply no way of telling which way it was—or if it was both ways—at the present time; nor is there any way to tell which (if either) version is the "original." Possibly there were other printings, too, and, as a final disturbing thought, it may well be that Joe thought of the ballad entirely in oral terms and therefore couldn't have cared less how the printers set it, as long as he had a copy of "the words" to sell.

I don't know any way of settling any of these matters, but we can at least say that the slips had Scott's tacit approval in that he sold them. And it would be fussy beyond fussiness to question that they represent "The Plain Golden Band" essentially as Joe conceived it. What follows is the complete text, *literatim et punctatim*, of Daisy Severy's version (JS.1). Where Bert Thorne's copy shows significant variations I will comment on them as I go along, and *all* variations are given in full under JS.2 in the list of versions at the end of this chapter.

THE PLAIN GOLDEN BAND.

——————

[1]   I am thinking tonight of the days that are gone,
When the sun clambered over the mountain at morn,
When the dewdrops of heaven like diamonds did glow,
Were kissing the rose in the valley below;
[2]   Where the clear waters flowing so mild and so blue,
Where the green willows wave and the birds sing so true,
Where the wild roses bloom on the banks by the shore,
There I parted with Lizzie, the girl I adore.

[3]   The day that we parted I ne'er can forget,
Oh I fancy I see those sad tears falling yet;
My poor heart was sad and with sorrow did sting
When she drew from her finger that plain golden ring.
[4]   "Take back the ring that I fain would retain,
For wearing it only causes me pain,
I have broken the vows that we made on the strand,
Then take back I pray you the plain golden band."

196

[5]   "Retain the engagement ring, darling," I cried,
       "Remember you vowed you would soon be my bride,
       My love it is true and will never grow cold,
       Retain, I beseech you, that plain band of gold.
[6]   Dear lady, I know that your love it is true,
       I know that you love me and that I love you."
       "And I know I deceived you one day on the strand,
       Then take back I pray you the plain golden band."

[7]   "One fine starry night when the moon it shone bright,
       All nature was wrapped in her pale mellow light,
       And a soft gentle breeze blew o'er the wild moor
       As I strayed from my cottage to roam on the shore;
[8]   A young man appeared and him I well knew,
       He told me false stories, false stories of you,
       He vowed that he loved me and offered his hand,
       Then take back I pray you that plain golden band."

[9]   She threw her arms round me and cried in despair,
       While a gentle breeze ruffled her dark wavy hair,
       And the moonlight of heaven fell on her fair hand,
       The fair light shone bright on the plain golden band.
[10]   "Forgive, oh forgive me, my darling I crave,
       E'er they lay me to sleep in a cold silent grave,
       With those fond cherished letters penned by your own hand
       And on my cold bosom that plain golden band."

[11]   "Farewell, my own love, farewell and adieu,
       Tho' our vows they are broken to you I'll prove true,
       Sometimes think of one when you roam on the strand
       Who placed on your finger that plain golden band;
[12]   In a cool shady forest so far far away,
       Where the deer loves to roam and the child loves to play,
       Where all nature is gay and the scenes wild but grand,
       There the author you'll find of the plain golden band.

                                                    BY JOE SCOTT
       Price 10 cts.

We have already covered the "facts" behind "The Plain Golden
Band" in chapter 3, and we can see that those many informants who
have told me that this song is about "something that really happened" were right. Joe Scott *was* jilted by Lizzie Morse, no question

about it. On this much the record is clear, but what we've been talking about is for the most part background to the song itself. If we are going to study the transmutation of reality into art, what we need to know is exactly what happened that "day" when Joe and Lizzie parted; what we need are the "and-he-said-and-then-she-said" details, and these we do not and cannot hope to have now. But we can be sure that this poem, like any other, is a distortion, that the poet has reshaped "what happened" for an aesthetic end. For example, even those who have been most insistent that "the song tells all about it" would not, I am sure, carry that insistence to the point of maintaining that Joe and Lizzie spoke to each other in rhyme or even that the speeches in the song represent their actual words at the time. Thus the point for distortion is made by a reduction to absurdity; the actual words and speeches are adjusted to the requirements of the artistic tradition within which Joe was working. We can make some pretty good guesses at the relationship between these two orders, truth and tradition, as we come now to the closer analysis of the song itself. This will allow us to see not only how good a traditional songmaker Joe Scott was, but also wherein he was being most original.

The stanza form that Joe chose is a double form of a very common four-line stanza: triple-time, with four beats to the line (or a predominantly anapestic tetrameter, to put it more formally). A glance through any folksong collection will show parallels aplenty for the four-line version of this stanza,[6] but very few for the double form, although we do find it in "Bendemeer's Stream." Interestingly, the tune that we find to this ballad, which is certainly the one Joe had in mind when he wrote the song, is a four-phrase tune; we'll have more to say about that when we discuss the tune and the effects of oral tradition on the ballad.[7]

"The Plain Golden Band" begins with a backward look. The reminiscence, the "I'm thinking tonight" opening, is not one of the most common devices of folksong; it is found more in popular songs like "Blue Eyes" and "Slavery Days."[8] Joe uses it in a much more leisurely fashion than do his "sources," if sources they were. In fact, he spends his whole first stanza (1–2) describing a rather literary landscape seemingly for its own sake, not getting around to the real point of it all until the last line—a sixth of his song simply on the backdrop! Another woods poet, W. N. "Billy" Allen, began his

198

"Banks of the Little Eau Pleine" with a similarly leisurely nature scene, but his imagery is much more concrete, much less pastoral, and not a little tongue-in-cheek:

> One evening last June as I rambled
>   The green woods and valleys among,
> The mosquito's notes were melodious,
>   And so was the whip-poor-will's song.
> The frogs in the marshes were croaking,
>   The tree-toads were whistling for rain,
> And partridge's round me were drumming,
>   On the banks of the Little Eau Pleine.
>
> The sun in the west was declining
>   And tinging the tree-tops with red.
> My wandering feet bore me onward,
>   Not caring whither they led.
> I happened to see a young school-ma'am.
>   She mourned in. . . .[9]

Joe's imagery here is, as I have said, more literary, more "beautiful." It is certainly not an accurate description of the Androscoggin valley just above or just below Rumford Falls, although there were the requisite mountains, flowing waters, singing birds, and probably even some roses and willows. The point is that it could be *any* valley, idealized by memory and described in largely traditional terms. It is difficult to pinpoint specific phrases, but "The Rose of Tralee" has the correct tone:

> The pale moon was rising above the green mountain,
>   The sun was declining beneath the blue sea,
> When I strayed with my love to the pure chrystal fountain
>   That stands in the beautiful vale of Tralee.
>
> She was lovely and fair as the rose in the summer,
>   Yet 'twas not her beauty alone that won me,
> Oh, no, 'twas the truth in her eye ever dawning,
>   That made me love Mary, the rose of Tralee.
>
> The cool shades of ev'ning their mantle was spreading,
>   And Mary, all smiling, and list'ning to me,
> The moon thro' the valley her pale rays was shedding,
>   When I won the heart of the rose of Tralee.
>   Though lovely and fair. . . .[10]

Joe's second stanza (3–4) begins the real business of the ballad; the first half (3) is narrative, the second (4) is Lizzie's first speech. His third stanza (5–6) is mostly devoted to the narrator's imploring her not to break the engagement. However, in the last two lines, Lizzie explains further, going on in the fourth stanza (7–8) to tell how she has betrayed him. Once again, notice that we have three full lines of traditional nature imagery, the "wild moor" of the third line being a splendid case in point, since there are no moors, wild or otherwise, within a hundred miles of Rumford. Her plea for forgiveness comes in the fifth stanza (9–10), after a bit of narrative telling how she fell in his arms and wept. Honesty compels me to point out that Joe shifts the scene here from daylight to moonlight, though honesty further compels me to point out that I never noticed this until I sat down to "study" the ballad. As a final honesty, I am further still compelled to point out that Bert Thorne's version (JS.2) has it as "sunlight," which brings us back about to where we started before all this honesty got in the way. The last stanza (11–12) is devoted to the narrator's final speech. He says good-bye, asks her to think of him, and says that he will spend the rest of his days in the forest, which he describes once again in general traditional terms.

There are several noteworthy things about this song as Joe wrote it. The first we have referred to several times already: the high proportion of natural description, all of it rather generalized, pastoral, and "poetic." In fact, almost a third of the ballad is devoted to such description. Second, two-thirds of the ballad is dialogue between the two principals, and the only direct ascription we get is in the first line of Joe's third stanza (5), although a reasonably careful reading, following Joe's punctuation, makes it perfectly clear who is speaking at any time. It is only when the ballad is sung that any problem arises. More about that in due time.

The most remarkable thing about "The Plain Golden Band" is the sympathetic treatment accorded to Lizzie herself, because here we find Joe moving well beyond anything offered him by folk tradition, and I don't know of anything quite like it in the popular songs of the day either. The "hero" is a stock figure, the jilted lover remembering the sad occasion of his jilting; but the girl in such songs usually does not come off so well as Lizzie Morse does here. Lizzie weeps, begs forgiveness, says she still loves him, even claims she had been told false stories; in fact, the narrator does everything he can to portray her as a lovely young girl unhappily caught in an emotional crossrip. To what extent does this conscience-stricken girl, so tearful and full of self-reproach, represent the real Lizzie Morse? Is this the way she really did act, or is Joe Patterson right that Scott "made up all that stuff"?

As I suggested earlier, there is no way of *knowing* now, but my educated guess is that Lizzie *did* act just about the way the ballad says she did. After all, she had been in love with Joe, and she certainly knew that what she was going to do would hurt him terribly. She probably was still very fond of him, but, bedazzled as she was by big blazing Sam Learned, she had to settle the matter. A breaking-off, a "Dear John" scene, always tears at the heartstrings, and this one must have been especially difficult. It would be surprising if an emotionally volatile girl like Lizzie did not at least get in some really vintage weeping, and she probably did a good deal more than that. She may have been quite dramatic, may even have enjoyed it (back of hand to forehead, "Ah God! The pain of it all!"). But however deep and sincere or however shallow and phony her feelings may have been, they must have been obvious, especially to Joe.

How about the ring, the "plain golden band"? I had always wondered about that, since the description fits a wedding ring better than an engagement ring; yet Joe specifically refers to it in the song as an engagement ring. However, at least one contemporary book of etiquette claimed that while "a jeweled ring has been for many years the sign and symbol of betrothal," the general preference is now for "a plain gold circlet, with the date of the engagement inscribed therein."[11] I also checked this out with Mrs. Severy, and she assured me that that's just what it was, a plain band of gold. She further claimed that when Lizzie tried to return the ring, Joe really did refuse to accept it, insisting that she keep it with her, which she did. Ironically, her second husband, Ed Martin, took to wearing it. *"He wore it on his little finger," she said, "and they—we was all in swimming to Old Orchard Beach and the plain golden band went into the ocean. He said he lost it off'n his finger."

The ballad's content, then, is an interesting blend of the traditional, the factual, and the innovative. The setting—backdrop, scenery, and lighting—is purely traditional, and so is the diction (Lizzie never used the word "fain" nor Joe "adieu," I am sure). Yet

201

through the romantic haze these traditional trappings generate, we are seeing something pretty close to what actually happened. The haze is given a richer glow by two further considerations. First, this is a memory poem. We do not know how long after the event Joe wrote this ballad—it was probably at least three or four years—but however long it was, memory had gotten in its work of heightening drama and softening outlines. Second, the narrator, the persona, is portrayed as a man still in love, and such a man will see the past by the light of the torch he carries. It is artistically irrelevant, I suppose, that Joe himself *was* probably still in love with Lizzie when he wrote the song, but we can be sure that Joe *is* the narrator, that persona and poet are one. Thus, in a lush arcadian landscape we see through the aureate air two figures moving. Their gestures are stylized and their speeches mannered, but we can still recognize them as Joe Scott and Lizzie Morse.

If we assume that the slip sheets represent Joe's original (and I have assumed that), we know where the whole thing started. This is the form in which Joe Scott sold his song from camp to camp in the upper Androscoggin valley in the late 1890s and early 1900s, and the ballad quickly became a part of the standard repertoire for traditional singers in the Northeast. We have discussed its birth and parentage; what follows will be its biography. What has happened to "The Plain Golden Band" in the past seventy years?

I will base this life history on the fifty-seven extant versions of the ballad I have brought together. Since a complete descriptive list of every version can be found at the end of the chapter, I will confine myself here to a couple of generalities on the quality of the texts. To begin with, forty are complete, and seventeen are fragments ranging all the way from one to eight stanzas. Most of my statistics in the following pages will be based on the forty complete versions, but the fragments will be discussed where they are relevant. More than half of the complete versions were collected in manuscript form, and we can parallel this with the fact that most of the people who sang the song for me were older people who had not sung this or any other song for many years. We are dealing with an item of remembered, not living, culture.

As for geographical distribution, this ballad's tradition is, like all the rest of Joe Scott's ballads, almost entirely confined to Maine and the Maritimes. Three of the four exceptions (NH.1, BC.1, and BC.2) are not really exceptions at all; Colebrook, New Hampshire, is about twenty miles out of Maine but still part of the same culture area, and both of the British Columbia informants learned their versions in the Maine woods. The fourth exception (NF) is a surprise, being the only version of any Joe Scott song to have been collected in New-foundland, but the tune and text indicate almost certainly that the singer learned it from print. Efforts to locate versions of the song elsewhere, in Michigan or Wisconsin, for example, have so far been unsuccessful.

Within the central area, the tradition is twice as strong in the Maritimes as in Maine and New Hampshire, and it is especially strong in New Brunswick; more oral versions come from that province than from all the other areas put together, and the four best renditions I have collected are all from New Brunswick. We seem to have here a Maine-to-Maritimes movement, and while we should remember that Scott also sold his songs in New Brunswick along the Saint John valley, it is likely that most of the Maritimes versions were brought back from Maine by returning woodsmen. We have, in fact, a number of statements that this is exactly what did happen. But it is also clear that the ballad was pretty well established in *local* Maritimes tradition, too; that is, while the song may have originally come from Maine, the singer learned it in New Brunswick or on Prince Edward Island. For example, Charles Budge wrote me that he had learned the song locally in Victoria County, Nova Scotia, from a man who "in his younger days worked in the lumberwoods in Maine."

Fewer than half of the people who contributed versions of the ballad knew that it was by Joe Scott. One man told me he thought it was by Larry Gorman (everything gets attributed to Gorman, it seems, by someone), but most singers simply had no more idea who wrote this song than they did who wrote any of the other songs they knew. "I have heard all the songs that you had mentioned in your enquiry," wrote William Bergin of Moncton, New Brunswick, "but lumberjacks never seemed to be very concerned as to the author of the songs they knew." True enough, and even among those who *did* know that the ballad was by Joe Scott, only about a third knew or had heard that it was about his own life. However, these figures should be balanced against the fact that a lot of people who did not know the ballad but had heard it or knew something about Joe identified him as "the man who made up 'The Plain Golden Band.'" For instance, one afternoon I was in Meductic, New Brunswick, only a mile or so down the road from the old Scott farm in Lower Woodstock. I stopped at Cummings Brothers Store for a pie and a bottle of pop, and the conversation got around to what I was doing. When I mentioned Joe Scott's name, Cummings said, "Oh yes. That's the fellow who made up 'The Plain Golden Band.' He lived right up here and that was all about his own life, you know." I looked interested, and the next thing I knew, another man, a customer, joined the conversation. "Yeah, that's what I heard, too," he said. "Joe Scott made that up and it was true, about himself." Another customer nodded approval, saying that's how it had been told to him, too. These were all younger men, and none of them knew the song; but they knew the story.

The point is that there is the song and there is the story about the song; they were sometimes known to the same people, but we cannot say that the story is in any way an integral part of the song's tradition. Except for the fact that it is now in print I am sure the story would have disappeared completely in another generation or so. Not that people would consider the song a fiction—all the evidence shows that traditional singers usually believe that the songs they are singing are true, even if they cannot tell where or when the chronicled event took place, and almost all the people who sang "The Plain Golden Band" for me considered it to be a true song. Joseph Pagett of Markhamville, New Brunswick, for example, told me that he had heard that the song was true and that it had originated in Ireland.[12] Thus, within the short span of seventy years not only was the story behind "The Plain Golden Band" being forgotten, but the song was well on its way to becoming just another traditional song, anonymous but "about something that really happened."

What part has print played in the life history of "The Plain Golden Band?" The most obvious printed tradition has, of course, been the printed slips themselves—the ballad as Joe Scott wrote it and peddled it. Only one version can be shown to come directly from this source, that of Lucy Morse of Norway, Maine, who evidently typed it off from a copy of JS.1. Others have told me they bought the song from Joe, and one woman recalls that he wrote it out for her (though she had since lost it). The printed slips may be where it all began, but they disappeared rather swiftly.

"The Plain Golden Band"

The *Family Herald* seems to have done its part in getting "The Plain Golden Band" around. The first request for the song appeared on January 5, 1916: "H.B. (N.B.) would like an old favourite called 'The Plain Golden Band.'" There were further requests, one from New Brunswick on February 8, 1922, and one from Nova Scotia on October 14, 1925, followed by a general appeal on December 28, 1927: "Several requests have been made for the 'Plain Golden Band.' Will someone please supply." Finally the song itself appeared as follows on May 2, 1928, "supplied by W. Sharpe, Dee Side, Quebec, and others":

THE PLAIN GOLDEN BAND

[1] I am thinking tonight of the days that are gone,
Where the sun slumbers sweetly on the valley at morn;
And the dewdrops from heaven like diamonds did glow
While kissing the rose in the valley below.

[2] And the clear waters flowing, so mild and so blue.
There came a low whisper to you I'll be true;
The flowers bloomed brightly upon the dark shore.
When I parted from Lizzie, the girl I adore.

[3] She was lovely and fair as the roses in June,
She appeared like some goddess or some gracious queen,
Fair as the lilies that bloom by the shore,
She's the pride of the valley, the girl I adore.

[4] The day that we parted I ne'er shall forget,
I fancy I see those sad tears falling yet;
How my poor heart did ache and with sorrow did ring
When she drew from her finger the plain golden ring.

[5] Saying, "Take back this ring, which I fain would retain,
For wearing it frequently causes me pain;
Our vows are all broken that we made on the strand,
So take back, I beseech you, this plain golden band."

[6] "Retain our engagement, my darling," I cried,
"You know that you promised you'd soon be my bride;
My love, it is true, it shall never grow cold,
So retain, I beseech you, this plain band of gold."

[7]   "My darling, I know that your love it is true,
I know that you love me and that I love you;
But you know I deceived you that night on the strand,
When you placed on my finger the plain golden band.

[8]   "One bright starry night when the moon it shone bright,
All nature looked gay in its pale yellow light,
It was there a dark stranger crept o'er the moor,
As I strayed from my cottage to roam by the shore.

[9]   "A young man appeared, and him I well knew,
He told me false stories, false stories of you;
He vowed that he loved me and offered his hand
I placed then a stain on the plain golden band."

[10]   "Retain our engagement, my darling I crave,
E'er you lay me to sleep in my cold silent grave;
With those fond cherished letters in my right hand,
And on my cold bosom the plain golden band."

[11]   In some dark shady forest so far, far away,
Where the deer loves to ramble and the child loves to stray;
Where all nature looks gay, the scene wild and grand,
That's the altar you'll find to the plain golden band.

Eight years later, on May 6, 1936, the same version was printed again; then again on October 6, 1943, this time with a note that it was "by Joe Scott of Bangor Maine." A little over a month later (November 24), they published an excerpt from a letter by B. H. Rix of Kamloops, British Columbia, who said that he had been "working with Joe in a logging camp on Beaver Brook, a tributary of the Magallaway River, when he wrote that song." The ballad was printed once more on December 11, 1946, again with a brief biographical note. As I said, each time the paper reprinted the 1928 version, although they had received at least four others in the meantime. I have frequently found these *Family Herald* clippings in people's scrapbooks, though often the people who kept the scrapbooks were not themselves singers. If "The Plain Golden Band" ever appeared in newsprint elsewhere, I have no record of it, although a couple of people have told me they are sure they saw it in the *Boston Sunday Globe*, and I remember seeing a request for it there dated October 23, 1921.

For many people, "The Plain Golden Band" was simply another song they had clipped from the *Family Herald;* for them it was a bit of print, not a song they had heard. Most people I have talked to, though, clipped it because it was already familiar. They had heard it sung (*"I remember my father used to sing that a lot"*), or they had once sung it themselves but had forgotten it or no longer sang at all. Still, the important question remains, just how much influence can this *Family Herald* version be shown to have had on oral tradition?

We can best answer that question by rephrasing it: can we demonstrate that any singer's version was influenced by the *Family Herald* version? Of course, we have to remember that this influence may run an entire gamut, all the way from the printed version's being the direct source of a singer's words (though I have never had a singer admit he learned the song this way) to its being a simple memory-jogger, enough to cause a man to recall the song as he had originally known it. I know of no way to determine how effective the *Family Herald* version may have been as a memory-jogger (though it may *help* explain why this ballad is well known); but it is comparatively easy to see where it has served as a source, partial or complete, immediate or secondary, since it contains a number of unique details, three in particular. First, there is the second line of stanza 2: "There came a low whisper to you I'll be true"; second, stanza 8, line 2, has a "dark stranger" rather than a "soft gentle breeze" going o'er the wild moor; and in the final line it is not the "author" but the "altar" one will find to the plain golden band. For the moment I am not considering the third stanza as diagnostic, since it presents a special problem that we will take up in due time. Using these three details as a base, let's see what we can determine about the influence of the *Family Herald* version on individual extant versions of the song.

Sam Jagoe of Newcastle, New Brunswick, sang "The Plain Golden Band" for me on the morning of August 21, 1959 (NB.2). He sang it again that evening at the Second Miramichi Folksong Festival, and these singings were all but identical, the changes amounting to such trivia as "this" for "that." In 1963, and again in 1967, Sam told me that he had learned the song while on a harvest excursion to Saskatchewan. That was in 1923, and on the train home he heard a man named Piccard from the Gaspé sing it a couple of times, he said. He got the tune and most of the words from him, but later on he got more words from other people he heard sing the song. Sam claimed never to have seen any printed versions of the song, but his second line of stanza 2 is "There came a low whisper, 'To you I'll be true.' " Then in stanza 8 it is a "dark shadow" that creeps o'er the moor, and in the final stanza he had "That's the altar you'll find to this plain golden band," though it is a little difficult to be sure he isn't singing "awter." Sam stays very close to the *Family Herald* version in several other details, too, making it abundantly clear that that verison has influenced him either directly or indirectly. And I know Sam has learned other songs from printed sources.

William Doerflinger sent me two manuscript versions (NS.2 and NS.3) he had received from Nova Scotia, both of which show clear evidence of *Family Herald* influence, if not derivation. Ethel Hamilton of Dalhousie, New Brunswick, submitted a version (NB.8) from her mother's manuscript book of old songs. Since all three telltale details are present, there need be no question of the source. And Kathleen Campbell submitted a version (NB.11) in 1965 that she said she took down from the recitation of her father, Fred A. Campbell of Arthurette, New Brunswick. Campbell had known Scott well, but when I interviewed him in 1963 he claimed he did not know "The Plain Golden Band." One look at the version his daughter claimed her father "remembered quite well" and recited to her makes it clear that he must have read directly from a *Family Herald* clipping.

When John O'Connor of Hope River, Prince Edward Island, sang the song for me on August 31, 1965, he had a clipping of the May 6, 1936, printing in his hand, which he referred to from time to time, and his rendition not surprisingly showed some *Family Herald* influence (PI.2). I asked him about the clipping, and he said he had found it only the other day; his wife, who had been cleaning out an old trunk, found a copy of the *Family Herald* with the song in it, and he clipped it. It is interesting to compare this clipping-in-hand singing with a manuscript version Mr. O'Connor had sent me six months earlier, well before he had found the newspaper. The manuscript version was incomplete, as he recognized when he sent it, but it still has traits in common with the *Family Herald* version. Yet O'Connor claimed he had learned the song locally from Gabe Warren somewhere around 1925. What probably happened is this: he did learn the song from Warren, but sometime after 1936 he found the *Family Herald* version and occasionally used it to refresh his mind. In later years he did not sing much, and the paper got put away, only to be rediscovered in the summer of 1965, after he had written me, but before he sang the song for me.

Finally, the version from Newfoundland (NF) shows all the *Family Herald* traits, and while it is clear that the singer, Mike Kent, was performing from memory (not singing from a text), I am sure that that was his source. It is probably safer to say that if Mike Kent didn't learn it from the *Family Herald*, whoever he learned it from did, and the fact that his version is sung to an entirely different tune from the one found in Maine and the Maritimes is further evidence that his version had its source in print.

At this point we should take up the problem of the "extra" stanza, extra in that it does not appear in Joe's originals. It does appear in the *Family Herald* version but is not at all peculiar either to it or to versions that can otherwise be shown to derive from it. When present it usually appears as the third stanza, and in four manuscript versions it is clearly labeled as "chorus," in three of them to be sung after a double stanza and in one presumably after every single stanza. Here it is as it was sung for me by Mrs. Lidelle Robbins of Hudson, Maine (Me.3):

> She was lovely and fair like the roses in spring;
> She appeared like some goddess or some gracious queen.
> She was pure as the lily that grows by the shore,
> She's the pride of the valley, and the girl I adore.

Possibly this stanza was written by Joe Scott and left out of the original slips by accident; possibly it was added later by someone else; but I think it most likely that Scott added it himself to later versions that he sang or wrote out for people, intending it to be sung as a chorus after every double stanza. Yet where it did catch on, it was sung only as a new third stanza; and since the ballad was already in circulation without that stanza, and that stanza added nothing significant to the story, it was left out about as often as it was included. However it may have gotten into the ballad, there is no question that it has become part of the tradition, although, as I have suggested, it is the least stable stanza in that tradition. Of the fifty-seven versions of the song I have been working with (a figure that includes all versions, complete and fragmentary), it occurs in only twenty-two, and by far the largest number of these are manuscript versions of one sort or another. It occurs in all of those versions influenced by the *Family Herald,* and its occurrence in print certainly helped spread it around.

One final point should help make it clear that "The Plain Golden Band" was passed on by a predominantly oral tradition. Had singers learned this ballad from print without ever having heard it sung, they would have had to supply their own tunes, and by all odds that means we would find "The Plain Golden Band" sung to different tunes. But with the single exception of the Newfoundland version discussed above, the tune tradition is very stable. And that sums up all we can discover about the influence of print on this ballad's life history. It is a clear but minor influence that has created some interesting eddies in the mainstream of oral tradition without changing its course significantly. It remains for us to see what changes that oral tradition has worked on Joe's original production.

To simplify matters, I will refer to the stanzas by the numbers I have given them in Joe's original version (pp. 196–197). The ballad can be thought of as consisting of four main "movements" or sections: the introduction (sts. 1 and 2 plus the "chorus"); the first exchange of speeches (sts. 3–6); Lizzie's explanation (sts. 7–8); and the final exchange of speeches (sts. 9–12).

The first section, the introduction, is found in every version that makes any pretense at even halfway completeness, and only Bill Cramp of Oakland, Maine, got all the essentials into one stanza (Me. 1):

> I'm thinking today of the days that are gone
> When the sun clambered over the mountains at morn;
> Where the bright golden lilies they bloom by the shore,
> There I parted with Lizzie, the girl I adore.

However much we may feel such economy to be a virtue, it is obvious that traditional singers of this song enjoyed the lush, full treatment. Thirty-three of the forty complete versions give us both stanzas 1 and 2, and of these, twenty-two add the chorus as an additional stanza. Only four versions have fewer than two stanzas, and of these, only Bill Cramp's is very satisfactory. Even when we turn our attention to the fragments, we find that this section has been exceptionally memorable, but we should expect that the first stanza or two of any ballad would be the ones most often remembered (what traditional singer does not have a score of such opening stanzas cluttering around in the back of his mind?). Even when we get down to the details, these two stanzas are amazingly stable. The variations are limited to such small matters as the sun "clambering," "clouring," "climbing," "rising," or "slumbering" over the mountain; and the versions are about equally divided on whether it is a "gracious" or a "Grecian" queen (with one vote each for "greater" and "generous") in the second line of the chorus. The only really significant variation in these stanzas is one I have already discussed: the telltale "to you I'll prove true" found in stanza 2, line 2, of *Family Herald*–influenced versions.

The second section, made up of stanzas 3, 4, 5, and 6, comprises what I have called the first exchange: a narrative stanza setting the scene (3), Lizzie's offer to return the ring (4), his plea that she keep it because he still loves her (5 and the first two lines of st. 6), and her statement that she has deceived him (the last two lines of st. 6). No complete version omits this section; at the very least they all get across the idea of the broken vows and the ring being returned. In fact, most of the versions have everything just about as Joe meant it to be, until we come to stanza 6, where it is hard to be sure just what he intended. JS.1 has it this way:

> ["]Dear lady, I know that your love it is true,
> I know that you love me and that I love you."
> "And I know I deceived you one day on the strand,
> Then take back I pray you the plain golden band."

JS.2 is identical except that it has "Dear laddie" rather than "Dear lady," which makes it appear as though the whole stanza is spoken by Lizzie; yet the punctuation clearly indicates a change in speaker. It would be a mistake to give *too* much weight to Joe's use of open and close quotes (why a close quote at the end of stanza 6, for example, when there is no change of speaker, or none at any point after the hero's final speech?); but it is hard for me to believe that their use in the present instance didn't have *some* significance for him. And that is as far as I can go.

Whatever Joe's intention may have been, subsequent singers have almost to a man interpreted that whole stanza as Lizzie's speech. It is not that there is anything unusual either about unin-

211

troduced dialogue or about a stanza in which the first two lines are spoken by one party, the last two by another. In fact, such stanzas are common in the so-called Child ballads, where their presence evidently offered no problems of interpretation. But if Joe intended a division of that sort here, he had made a distinction in writing that could not possibly be maintained in singing. Sing it how you will, it still comes out feeling that the whole stanza is a single speech, and that is exactly what singers have made of it. Almost all the versions in which this stanza is present (about three-quarters of the complete versions) have it as Lizzie's speech. Most have the word "laddie" in the first line of stanza 6, but a few have "my darling," probably following the *Family Herald*'s lead. It seems a bit much to speak of "communal re-creation" in this matter; I suggest instead the term "communal clarification."

The next section, stanzas 7 and 8, consists of Lizzie's explanation of what happened. Only one version omits this section entirely,[13] and of the rest all but four have both stanzas in full. It is amazingly stable in its details, but there are two changes that are worth mentioning. The first is the substitution of the "dark stranger" for the "breeze" or "zephyr" that crosses the moor; this is one of those changes in the *Family Herald* version already discussed. The other involves a change in the last line of stanza 8. Taking it in conjunction with the preceding line, we find that Joe Scott wrote:

> He vowed that he loved me and offered his hand,
> Then take back I pray you that plain golden band.

It is given this way in both JS.1 and JS.2. Though there is no suggestion that Lizzie did anything but change her mind, tradition has been harsher on her than Joe would have liked, changing that line to "Then I put a stain on your plain golden band." With the exception of the version that derives directly from the original slip (Me.13), almost every other version has this more suggestive line. Whether it is an "improvement" or not is a matter of opinion, but there is no doubt that this line has replaced Joe Scott's original and the folk have once again had their way. Its occurrence in the *Family Herald* version certainly helped establish it, but is too widely known to be explained simply as an incursion from print.

At this point I should mention one of the more unusual versions (BC.2), that sent in to the *Family Herald* by Jack A. Scott of Salmon

Arm, British Columbia, who claimed to be the author of the song.
We should remember, however, what Fannie Hardy Eckstorm said:
"A woodsman would claim 'Hamlet' if he added four doggerel lines to
the Soliloquy."[14] Here is the way Jack Scott worked out the central
sections of the song:

> A young man he came to me one I knew well
> He told me false stories false stories of you
> He vowed that he loved me and offered his hand
> There I put a stain on that plain golden band.
>
> He who made the bold eagle made also the dove
> All the beauty in nature tell of his love
> His kindness and mercy should teach us to live
> To be kind to each other and freely forgive
>
> I know my dear laddie but my vows were untrue
> I knew that you loved me and that I loved you
> I know I deceived you that night on the strand
> So take back I pray you that plain golden band.

Evidently Lizzie speaks the first and third of these stanzas and the
narrator speaks the second. It is not an entirely bad touch, but it
never caught on.

That brings us to the final section, stanzas 9, 10, 11, and 12. It
includes a descriptive narrative stanza (9) telling how Lizzie threw
herself into his arms and wept; her final speech, a plea for forgiveness (10); the narrator's farewell (11); and his final statement of where
he may be found. This is a diffuse section in a pretty diffuse ballad. If
there is a trend toward economy in oral tradition, a trend that causes
stanzas unnecessary to the story line to be forgotten more easily than
others, we should be able to see it operating here, if anywhere.
Unfortunately, the evidence is equivocal. Take stanza 9 of Me.3, for
example:

> She threw her arms 'round me and cried in despair
> While the gentle breeze ruffled her dark wavy hair,
> And the moon light from heaven shone on her small hand,
> It glittered and gleamed on the plain golden band.

It adds little if anything to the story, being almost entirely lyrical and
descriptive, and while it occurs in 75 percent of the complete
versions, it is still one of the stanzas most frequently omitted. But

that hardly establishes a trend. On the other hand, stanza 11 is more cooperative, turning up as it does in fewer than 60 percent of the complete versions. Here, from Me.1:

> Fare you well my own darling, farewell and adieu,
> Though the vows you have broken, I'll always be true;
> Sometimes think of me when you roam on the strand,
> Where I placed on your finger the plain golden band.

In my opinion, something is gained by the dramatic shift that occurs when it is omitted (as in Me.4):

> "Forgive, oh forgive me, my darling I crave
> E'er they lay me to rest in that cold silent grave;
> With those fond cherished letters penned by your own hand
> And on my cold bosom the plain golden band."

> Now in the cold shady forest so far far away,
> Where the deer love to ramble and the child loves to play;
> All nature is glad and the scenes wild but grand,
> There you'll find the author of the plain golden band.

Traditional singers seem to have shared my opinion, because of all the complete versions (not counting Joe's original), well over half end in this way, even though in three of them stanza 11 is present earlier in the ballad.[15] That stanza 11 is easily forgotten is further borne out by the fact that it occurs in only one fragmentary version—and that a long one (NB.15). On the matter of economy, then, the best we can say is that this section offers some support for it, but a very qualified support.

The final stanza, as we might expect, occurs in every complete version and in more than half the fragments. It is always the final stanza, too, never occurring elsewhere in the ballad. The only significant variation is the change in the last line of stanza 12 of "author" to "altar," which we find in those versions influenced by the *Family Herald*. But once again we have the question of what Joe Scott may have intended, as compared with what singers have made of it. If we look at Joe's original versions, we find that the end of stanza 11 has no close quote. In fact, as I have already pointed out, there is no close quote for this speech anywhere in either JS.1 or JS.2. Did he want us to see the last four lines (that is, st. 12) as part of the narrator's final speech to Lizzie? In such a circumstance, it is difficult to know just how he meant us to construe the final line; but if this *was* his intention, then he was once again making a distinction in print that it would be impossible to convey in singing. The whole stanza makes much better sense as an epilogue, a return to the time level of the introduction. Then it is not the narrator speaking in time past to Lizzie about where she will find him; it is, rather, the narrator speaking in time present directly to the listener about where the narrator now *is*. In this way the final line makes perfectly good sense, too, and this is how most singers I have talked to about it interpret the stanza. When stanza 11 is omitted, and we have just seen that it often is, that is the *only* way the final stanza makes any sense. The point I would like to make here is that while Joe Scott's handling of the final stanza as it is represented by the printed slips leaves some doubt about his intentions, there is no question at all about its meaning in subsequent versions. It is an epilogue and that is that. Once again, communal clarification.

Having now completed this rough statistical survey, I would say that for a ballad as diffuse and lyrical as "The Plain Golden Band," it is remarkable that so many versions have retained the original structure pretty much intact. Yet I do not want to overemphasize the narrative element in this ballad, because while it is undeniably there, the important thing is the overall tone, the general feeling of sadness over the parting of lovers, remembered sorrow in a lovely landscape. Even when all the stanzas are in "correct" order, the singers I have talked to are not always certain how to assign a speech, nor, I must confess, was I until I sat down one day and figured it all out. With a couple of dubious exceptions,[16] I know of no versions that have gone the whole way to becoming lyrics; the story line is present in every version I have that is given as complete. Were I arranging folksongs along a narrative-lyric spectrum, I would place "The Plain Golden Band" toward the center but somewhat on the narrative side.

As I have said, most of the versions follow the original order of stanzas, but there are alternative ways that turn up and still make sense. Stanzas 6 and 9 for example, have a certain free-floating quality about them and may appear at different points in the song. F. L. Tracy of Brewer, Maine, contributed a version (Me. 11) in which Lizzie's plea for forgiveness (sts. 9–10) occurs before she tells her story (7–8), which makes perfectly good sense. So does the manuscript version contributed by Lloyd Belyea of Brown's Flat, New Brunswick, in which Lizzie asks the narrator to take back the ring (3–4) and tells her story (7–8), whereupon he pleads with her to retain the ring (5), she says she knows his love is true but she has deceived him (6), and she begs his forgiveness (9–10). One of my favorite renditions, that of Joseph Pagett of Markhamville, New Brunswick (NB.16), simplifies the whole thing by being the only version to omit Lizzie's confession. It works out very nicely:

THE PLAIN GOLDEN BAND

[1] I'm thinking tonight of the days that are gone,
As the sun clambered over the mountains at morn;
And the dewdrops from heaven like diamonds glow,
While kissing the roses in the valley below.

[2] 'Neath the clear flowing waters so mild and so blue,
Where the wild willows wave and the birds sing so true,
Where the wild flowers bloom by the banks of the shore,
There I parted with Lizzie, the girl I adore.

[3] The night that we parted I ne'er shall forget,
I fancy I see those sad tears falling yet;
My blue eyes were dim and with sorrow did sting,
As she drew from her finger that plain golden ring.

[4] Saying, "Take back the ring that I vain would retain,
For wearing it causes me sorrow and pain;

216

The vows they're all broken we made on the strand,
So take back I pray thee that plain golden band."

[5]   She threw her arms around me and cried in despair,
As the gentle winds ruffled her dark wavy hair
And the bright stars from heaven shone on her small hand
And the moon it shone bright on the plain golden band.

[6]   "Farewell, my old sweetheart, farewell and adieu,
The vows they're all broken, to you I'll prove true;
Sometimes think of me when you roam on the strand,
Who placed on your finger that plain golden band."

[7]   In the green shady forest so far far away,
Where the deer loves to roam and the child to play;
All natures seem gay and the scene wild but grand
There the author you'll find of the plain golden band.

Joe Pagett's version does change the story, but since the narrative element is quite subdued in "The Plain Golden Band" to begin with, we can hardly say that any of these changes through omission or changing the order of stanzas makes much difference. Nor can we show that any clear local versions or oicotypes have developed for this ballad, but it is through such changes as we have been describing that oicotypes would presumably develop in time.

Not only is the basic structure of "The Golden Band" surprisingly stable for a ballad so lyrical, but the structure of the individual stanzas is, too—so stable that we can speak of the stanza as the basic unit. Of all the stanzas in all the versions, only about 6 percent are composites like Bill Cramp's opening stanza, and that figure is even lower (only 4 percent) if we consider only complete versions. Predictably, almost all the composite stanzas break at the midpoint, one couplet coming from one stanza, the other from another. But in every case, the first couplet is always from the first part of the stanza, the second from the second part. Probably this has been aided by the fairly consistent rhymes with "band" in the second half of the stanzas. To recap, then, even though we must keep in mind that seventy years is a relatively limited time (we are often dealing with only one link in the chain of oral transmission, and probably never with more than three or four), I would still say that the words to "The Plain Golden Band" have shown an amazing resistance to change.

If the words have shown an amazing resistance to change, it is hard to know just how to characterize what has happened to the tune. With one notable exception (NF) and one not so notable (Me.15), "The Plain Golden Band" is always sung to the same tune, and it is the only song I have ever found that *is* sung to that tune. It is straight major with a range of a ninth from the second above to the octave below the final (two versions, one of them Joe Pagett's, stretch that to a minor tenth). The meter is usually 3/4 or 6/8, with an occasional 2/4 or 4/4 infix. Even in those versions sung parlando rubato it is still possible to see this basic meter throughout. The phrase pattern is progressive (ABCD), and the tune is an undulating one that stays consistently below the final except for those stressed high notes in the second and fourth phrases. All in all, there is nothing in this description that gainsays the tune's traditional quality. As a matter of fact, James Wilson considers it a set of the standard "Villikins and His Dinah" tune, and in conversation Norman Cazden suggested to me the same similarity.[17] I can hardly deny that there is a resemblance; but if it is truly in this family, it seems to be a subfamily all to itself. The stressed high seconds and the fact that it rises rather than descends to its final particularly seem to set it apart from other versions of this tune. It may well be a traditional tune, but I still have suspicions (and that is about as specific as I can be) that it is a late-nineteenth-century popular tune that Joe heard somewhere.

If my sixth sense is right and this *is* a popular tune, or even if it is the tune to some other traditional song, it is remarkable that I have not found the original. I have whistled my way through scores of song collections with no success; I have all but gone hoarse singing it for people who should have recognized anything there was to recognize, only to be rewarded with a puzzled smile, perhaps a statement that it sounds "familiar," and some measure of support for my suspicion that it is a popular tune. I have never collected another ballad sung to this same tune, nor has any traditional singer ever described it as "the tune to such-and-such." Wherever I have found it, it has been the tune to "The Plain Golden Band."

Is it possible that Joe Scott *composed* this tune? Several people have told me that he did, and we might recall that Jack Scott of Salmon Arm, British Columbia, who claimed that he himself wrote the words, claimed also that he "gave the song to Joe Scott who put the music to it and often sang it." Since I do not credit Jack Scott's claim to have authored the words, I have no reason to credit his claim that Joe wrote the tune. None of the other attributions is especially authoritative either. But suppose Joe Scott did in fact "write" this tune. What would that mean he had done? Just as with the words, he would have used the patterns and formulas that his tradition offered him and would probably have come up with a tune that sounded very much like many others, while yet being distinct from them. He may have deliberately made up a new tune, unaware that all he was really doing was varying a tune he already knew, the well-known "Villikins and His Dinah." But I don't think this is what happened. As a rule, songmakers took an old tune and created new words to it, and I see no reason to believe that Joe Scott was any exception. It would certainly be ridiculous to assume that he wrote this tune merely because I have not been able to find his source, be it folk or popular. We cannot prove that he wrote it, and I doubt that he did. But it is just possible. We'll have to leave it at that.

There is one more matter to be dealt with in our consideration of the tune. I pointed out earlier that in both JS.1 and JS.2 the words are printed in an eight-line stanza form, while the tune has only four phrases. Could Joe have had a different tune in mind, one with eight phrases, when he wrote the song? The Irish tune for "Bendemeer's Stream" or "The Mountains of Mourne" would fit perfectly, for example, and there is that intriguing coincidence (unless it *is* echo, which I doubt) of the latter title in the second line, which has the sun coming over "the mountains at morn." "The Rose of Tralee" would (with a little shoving) fit, too. Eight-phrase tunes frequently break down in oral tradition into two four-phrase tunes, and often only one of the two will be used in some versions of the song. It is possible that something like this happened to "The Plain Golden Band," but I think it is highly unlikely. For one thing, whenever we find that an eight-phrase tune has become a four-phrase tune, we usually find some versions of the song that still use the eight-phrase tune.[18] This we never find with "The Plain Golden Band." It is always sung to the same four-phrase tune. Then too, I have talked with a number of people who heard Joe Scott himself sing the song, and none of them has ever made the point (even when I asked about it) that he sang it to a different tune than the one we hear today. I am positive that the tune we have to this ballad is the one Joe Scott meant to be there. Whatever his reasons may have been for having the song printed in six eight-line stanzas rather than twelve four-line stanzas, he was once again making a distinction in print that would be impossible to convey in singing; and while some of the manuscript versions have kept the eight-line stanzas, none of the oral versions does. Those who sang the ballad can be said, then, to have worked a change, though it is again more a change in how the singer sees or hears the song in his head than it is a change through omission, addition, or alteration of material.

One final problem remains. I have made the general assumption that Joe's songs were written soon after the events they chronicled. That would place "The Plain Golden Band" back in 1894, making it by three years the earliest song of Joe's we have. Why did I not take it up first? Why do I feel it is an exception to my general assumption? To deal with the second question first, what is really assumed is that a ballad will appear at a time when public interest in its subject is high, which usually means right on the heels of the event itself. Since in the case of "The Plain Golden Band" there was no public event, there was no public interest to exploit, and the rule does not apply.

Then are there any reasons for believing that Joe did not write this song until three or even four years after the jilting? Yes, I believe so. First of all, "The Plain Golden Band," as I have already pointed out, is written as a memory song, telling about something that happened in "the days that are gone," though how *far* gone those days are is not clear. Now, of course this backward look could have been a purely poetic device, a point that I will concede without contest; but it seems unlikely that a man like Joe Scott would have chosen this way of telling the story at a time when the whole affair was still painfully immediate to him.

Second—and this is far more important in my mind—since the whole break-up was so traumatic for Joe, clearly the central event of his whole life, I very much doubt that he could have written about it at all for some time. It could easily have taken him a few years to get the kind of distance necessary to write about it as he did, with balance and without rancor. It would not surprise me, either, to know that he had to wait until Lizzie had left for Massachusetts after her marriage to Ed Martin in 1898; and while I think this is the way it was, I have to admit it is conjecture, and even conjecture on conjecture. But my conviction stands: the event was shattering, the song is composed, and the rebuilding of one's world that that implies takes (among other things) time. The "days that are gone" may be a poetic device, but it is also a statement of fact, and "The Plain Golden Band" is both art and autobiography.

LIST OF VERSIONS

JS.1   Original printed slip, obtained from Daisy Severy, Gray, Me., July 21, 1966. 12 sts. (or 6 double sts.). This version is given on pp. 196–197.

JS.2   Original printed slip, as obtained from the notebook of Bert Thorne, Jemseg, N.B. 12 sts. (or 6 double sts.). This printing is identical with JS.1 except as follows: st. 1, l. 1: to-night; st. 2, l. 4: Lizzie the; st. 4, l. 2: pain.; st. 5, l. 4: Retain I beseech you that; st. 6, l. 1: laddie; st. 7, l. 2: in a pale; st. 9, l. 1: arms around; st. 9, l. 3: sunlight; st. 9, l. 4: band,; st. 10, l. 2: E're; st. 10, l. 3: hand,; st. 11, l. 1: my own true love; st. 11, l. 4: band.; [*signature:*] By Joe Scott.; [*price:*] 10 cents.

FH   *Family Herald,* May 2, 1928, "supplied by W. Sharpe, Dee Side, Quebec, and others"; reprinted May 6, 1936, Oct. 6, 1943, and Dec. 11, 1946. 11 sts.

NH.1   Belle Richards, Colebrook, N.H., Nov. 21, 1941; collected by Marguerite Olney, Flanders Collection, D–316, sung, 11 sts. Someone prompting her at the beginning, but no indication who or from what.

NH.2   C. S. Locke, 90, Berlin, N.H., Sept. 9, 1965; NA Ives tape 65.14, sung, 1 st., fragment. Locke had known Scott, and knew this song was by and about him.

Me.1   Bill Cramp, 83, Oakland, Me., Oct., 1964; collected by George Keller, NA 225.021, sung and recited, 10 sts. Knew it was by Joe Scott and about his own life. Sang all but the last two stanzas, which he recited. But then said that these two stanzas were so good that he wanted to sing them, and he did.

Me.2   Omer McKenna, ca. 80, Rumford, Me., Sept. 28, 1965; NA Ives tape 65.19, sung, 2 sts., fragment. Knew it was by and about Joe Scott.

Me.3   Mrs. Lidelle Willey Robbins, ca. 70, Hudson, Me., assisted by Vera Robbins (her daughter-in-law), Feb. 8, 1957; NA Ives tape 1.4 and ATL 2138.11, 11 sts. Learned from her brothers, who used to work in the woods. Knew it was by Joe Scott. Mrs. Robbins had dictated the words some weeks before to her granddaughter, who typed them out. Mrs. Robbins was too nervous to sing alone, so her daughter-in-law sang along with her. Only stanzas 1–3 sung; rest in manuscript.

Me.4 Ray Lohnes, ca. 70, Andover, Me., July, 1958; taken down from recitation by Anna Thurston, 10 sts. Lohnes knew the song was both by and about Joe Scott.

Me.5 Gordon Frazer, ca. 72, Caribou, Me., Sept. 19, 1962; collected by Lorina Wakem, NA 412.049, recited, 1½ sts., fragment. Learned about 1914 up on Chase Brook from Christopher Columbus Davenport. Same item collected from same man by Marion Porter, NA 320.061.

Me.6 Gertrude Bradbury, Mexico, Me., written down from recitation by her daughter, Pearl Longley, in a notebook lent to me Sept. 29, 1965; manuscript, 9½ sts. Knew it was by Joe Scott. Mrs. Longley had begun writing her mother's songs down shortly before the latter's death; this was some years before I met Mrs. Longley. Mrs. Bradbury had lived most of her life around Monticello, and her husband had worked with Joe Scott on the Bank Farm near there.

Me.7 Evelyn Smith, Rangeley, Me., manuscript version taken from the singing of Bob McKinnon, ca. 1925; collected by Lillian Williams, Rangeley, Me., Apr., 1960, NA 414.046–050, 12 sts. Both McKinnon and Smith knew it was by and about Joe Scott.

Me.8 Bessie Lary, Dover-Foxcroft, Me., manuscript sent me June 13, 1964; 11 sts. Miss Lary's note: "This is a copy by Fred L. Barrows, Oakfield, Maine, (deceased)." Did not know it was by or about Joe Scott.

Me.9 Mrs. Jerry Desmond, Island Falls, Me., version mailed to Helen Hartness Flanders, July 19, 1940. Her husband, Jerry Desmond, sang it for Flanders Collection, cylinder C–211, 9 sts.

Me.10 Dennis Taylor, 85, Green Farm (Coplin Plantation), Me., Mar. 30, 1959; NA Ives tape 59.1, fragment. Taylor had known Scott and knew this song was by and about him. He recited it as a kind of rhythmic prose.

Me.11 F. L. Tracy, Brewer, Me., manuscript sent to Fannie Hardy Eckstorm, Feb. 19, 1934; Eckstorm Papers, 12 sts. Written on the sheet in F.H.E.'s hand: "Probably composed by Joseph Scott, of Androscoggin region, who sold printed songs to woodsmen about 1900."

Me.12 Elwell Field, Westfield, Me., Nov. 19, 1962; collected by Beatrice Field, NA 128.039–041, manuscript, 13 sts. "Bill Hallett sang it on Burntland Stream in 1911." Did not know it was by or about Scott.

Me.13 Lucy Morse, ca. 80, Norway, Me., typescript sent to me, Sept. 23, 1966; 12 sts. (6 double sts.). Knew it was by and about Scott.

This version is identical in every way to Scott's original slip, JS.1.

Me.14 Edward Gavel, ca. 70, Sanford, Me., Aug. 25, 1965; NA Ives tape 66.11, sung, 1 st. On Oct. 3, 1966, he sent me a manuscript copy of all the words he could recall; 9 sts., fragment.

Me.15 Wilbert Morrison, 77, Orland, Me., Jan. 9, 1969; collected by Bonita Freeman-Witthoft, her tape number 69.1, sung, 3 sts. Says he learned it locally. Collector had asked him in November if he knew this song, and he said he'd have to put it together. The tune he sings begins like "When You and I Were Young, Maggie," but never settles down into being anything. My impression (and the collector's) is that he did not really remember the tune at all, but put this together to oblige her.

NB.1 James Brown, 76, Chatham, N.B., Aug. 20, 1959; NA Ives tape 1.64 and ATL 2183.3, sung, 13 sts. Believes he got this written down from someone and learned it from the written copy. Originally thought it was by Larry Gorman. Brown is from South Branch (Kent Co.), N.B., but was staying with Tommy Whelan in Chatham while he attended the Miramichi Folksong Festival. This is the version given at the beginning of this chapter.

NB.2 Sam Jagoe, 62, Newcastle, N.B., Aug. 21, 1959; NA Ives tape 1.66 and ATL 2185.2, sung, 11 sts. For Jagoe's second singing of it, see NA Ives tape 1.83 and ATL 2201.6 (see also Manny and Wilson, *Songs of Miramichi*, pp. 164–65). For the tune to an earlier singing, see Doerflinger, *Shantymen and Shantyboys*, p. 247. More information on NB.2 appears on pp. 207–208.

NB.3 George Duplessis, ca. 60, Newcastle, N.B., Sept. 15, 1958, at First Miramichi Folksong Festival; NA Ives tape 1.52 and ATL 2176.6, sung, 12 sts. Duplessis comes from Eel River Bridge, N.B.

NB.4 William J. Bergin, Moncton, N.B., June 21, 1964; in a letter, manuscript as recited by a young man named Vincent Cashen, Blissfield, N.B., and taken down by Bergin's sister at least forty years before, 12 sts., written without any breaks between stanzas. Did not know it was by Joe Scott.

NB.5 Gordon Mountain, Blackville, N.B., as written down by Hugh U. Crawford and given to me June 9, 1957; 11 sts.

NB.6 John A. Jamieson, 85, East Bathurst, N.B.; words as sent in to *Family Herald*, n.d., but probably early 1950s. Tune collected by E.D.I. in East Bathurst, June 12, 1957; NA Ives tape 1.27 and ATL 2153.7, sung, 12 sts. "I learned this song over 50 years ago in Lincoln, N.H., by a man who knew Joe Scott, the author" (J.A.J. in note to *Family Herald*).

NB.7   Peter Jamieson, 75, East Bathurst, N.B., Mar. 4, 1957; in a letter, manuscript, 11 sts. Had met Joe Scott and knew it was by him. Source not clear.

NB.8   Margaret Hamilton, River Charlo, N.B.; copied out from her notebook and given to me July 24, 1965, by her daughter, Ethel Hamilton, NA 194.026–027, 11 sts. "Another of the songs my mother had written out years ago." See p. 208.

NB.9   Thomas Cleghorn, 86, Harvey Station (York Co.), N.B., typescript given me by his daughter, Mrs. Karl Byers, Harvey Station, Aug. 22, 1964; 13 sts. (6 double sts., with chorus). That same evening Mr. Cleghorn sang six stanzas from the typescript; see NA Ives tape 64.6. Had known Joe Scott and knew this song was by and about him.

NB.10   Ansel Libby, ca. 65, Lower Woodstock, N.B., Aug. 22, 1964; NA Ives tape 64.4, sung, 6 sts., fragment. Learned in northern Maine from the singing of Norman McDold, a sailor who was putting in that winter in the woods. Knew the song was both by and about Joe Scott. Says he has seen this song printed in the *Boston Globe* with Scott's name to it. Libby was simply singing what he remembered of it at my request. He is married to Scott's niece, and we were sitting in the parlor of the old Scott homestead.

NB.11   Fred A. Campbell, 82, Arthurette, N.B., June 17, 1965; collected by his daughter, Kathleen Campbell, NA 80.049–051, 11 sts. For a discussion of this version see p. 208.

NB.12   Fred Anderson, ca. 55, Juniper, N.B., Oct. 9, 1965; NA Ives tape 65.21, recited, 12 sts.; then at my request he sang the first two stanzas. Learned from Jack Underwood of Blackville up on Elliot Brook, a tributary of Burnt Hill, about thirty-five years before. Knew it was both by and about Joe Scott, but understood the girl was from Island Falls, Me. See also the version dictated to Frederick Welch, July 20, 1965, NA 431.6–13.

NB.13   Alice Flynn, Allegany, N.Y., as put together by her sisters and brothers remembering how their father, Jack McGinley of Johnville, N.B., used to sing it. Given to me in Bangor, Me., Aug. 1, 1964; 3 sts., fragment. Knew it was by and about Joe Scott; father had known both Joe and Lizzie, she said.

NB.14   Mabel Carr, ca. 60, Canterbury, N.B., July 18, 1965; written down from her recitation by Ruth Collicott, NA 79.2, 1½ sts., fragment.

NB.15   Phyllis Woodside, Milltown, N.B., July 5, 1964; in a letter, 6 sts., fragment. Learned from her mother. Joe Scott "taught these songs to my grandmother and my mother, who was a young girl at the time. My mother sang the songs so often I learned them well."

NB.16   Joseph Pagett, 68, Markhamville (Sussex, R.R. 5), N.B., Oct. 12, 1965; NA Ives tape 65.22, sung, 7 sts. Learned from Ora Wallace "on the drive on Big Salmon River," about forty-five years before. Never knew who the author was. Believed it to be a true song that originated in Ireland. Earlier, Aug. 31, 1964, Pagett had sent me a manuscript version, very similar to version he sang, but lacking present stanza 4; this version is given on pp. 216–217.

NB.17   Lloyd Belyea, Brown's Flat, N.B., July 19, 1964; in a letter, 13 sts. (6 double sts., with chorus). "I can't remember any other place that I heard it only from my father and he had a copy of it." Exact source of his manuscript copy is not certain.

NB.18   Spurgeon Allaby, ca. 70, Passekeag, N.B., July 14, 1964; in a letter, 5 sts., fragment. Did not know who wrote it. Heard it sung by several different people but recalls specifically a man named William Cronk from St. Martins, N.B., with whom he worked in a portable sawmill around 1908.

NB.19   Wilfred Woodard, 78, St. Stephen, N.B., Aug. 18, 1964; NA Ives tape 64.7, sung, 1 st., fragment. Had known Scott and knew this was by him.

NB.20   Wilmot MacDonald, 59, Glenwood, N.B., July 10, 1963; NA Ives tape 1.131 and ATL 3138.2, sung, 2 sts. fragment, Wilmot never cared enough for the song to learn it, but used to hear his sister Ann singing it.

NB.21   Walter M. Campbell, Daytona Beach, Fla., and Whitefield, N.H., Dec. 15, 1968; in a letter, 5 sts., fragment. Learned in St. Croix area between 1903 and 1910.

NB.22   Marjorie Stillwell, Chipman, N.B., 1974; photocopied from Mrs. Stillwell's songbook by Neil Rosenberg, typescript, 11 sts. From Rosenberg's notes: "From singing of her father, Fred Fulton, now deceased."

NS.1   Joseph Patterson, Caledonia, N.S., as recited to William Doerflinger, summer, 1930; 11 sts. Same version is printed in Doerflinger, *Shantymen and Shantyboys*, pp. 248–249, except that there stanza 9 is omitted. Learned from Joe Scott at Summit Landing, Me., about 1905.

NS.2   Peter Glode, Pubnico, N.S., n.d. Sent to William Doerflinger, who describes it as identical to NS.1 except for the following: "In another copy, by Peter Glode, and too exactly similar to Joe Patterson's to be worth printing here, the hint as to the author in the final stanza is quite lost, and it is an 'altar' which is to found in the deep woods. In this version the chorus appears as a regular stanza, used only in one place."

NS.3   John Bartlett, Scarsdale, N.S., sent to William Doerflinger in 1930–31; 5½ sts.

NS.4   Clifford Beeler, Scarsdale (Lunenburg Co.), N.S., as collected by George Hirdt and sent to Robert W. Gordon, when the latter was writing his column for *Adventure;* Gordon Manuscripts 2710, 9 sts.

NS.5   MacOdrum Collection, pp. 205–208; 11 sts.

NS.6   Charles W. Budge, New Haven (Victoria Co.), N.S., June 15, 1964; in a letter, 12 sts. Learned from a man who "in his younger days worked in the lumberwoods in Maine."

NS.7   James Curtis (b. 1898), Cape North (Bay St. Lawrence), Cape Breton Island, N.S., 1975; collected by Denis Ryan, MUNFLA 76–345, sung, 12 sts. Learned from his uncle Tom Brown, who had worked with Scott in the Maine woods.

PI.1   Edmund Doucette, Miminegash, P.E.I., July 14, 1963; NA Ives tape 1.146 and ATL 3153.4, sung, 8 sts., then added a stanza he had left out. Was not sure of all of it. Learned it locally from Fred Daigle about fifty years ago.

PI.2   John O'Connor, ca. 65, Hope River, P.E.I., Aug. 31, 1965; NA Ives tape 65.11, sung, 11 sts. Learned locally from Gabe Warren about forty years ago. For further information see pp. 208–209.

PI.3   Philip Cameron, ca. 70, Wellington, P.E.I., Aug. 28, 1965; NA Ives tape 65.6, sung, 1½ sts., fragment. Learned about fifty-five years ago from an uncle, Michael Cameron, who used to travel to the States to work in the woods. Cameron says he never learned the whole of it. Also had sent me a manuscript of the same fragment in a letter, Mar. 9, 1965.

PI.4   Mrs. Underhill Coughlin, ca. 65, Brooklyn, P.E.I., Aug. 23, 1965; NA Ives tape 65.3, sung, 3 sts., fragment. Learned locally.

PI.5   William J. Ballum, Summerside, P.E.I., May 22, 1959; in a letter, 6 sts. "This may be the complete song and there may be another verse or two. It has a lovely tune to it."

BC.1   B. H. Rix, Kamloops, B.C., in a letter to the *Family Herald,* n.d., but in the mid-forties; 11 sts. For further information see pp. 194–195.

BC.2   Jack A. Scott, Salmon Arm, B.C., in a letter to the *Family Herald,* Nov. 18, 1957; 12 sts. He claims he made it up on a river-drive in Maine in 1902. For further information see pp. 195, 218–219.

NF   Mike Kent (b. 1895), Cape Broyle, Newfoundland, 1950; collected by MacEdward Leach, MUNFLA, Cape Broyle, Leach I, 10A, #7, sung, 10 sts. See pp. 203, 209.

NOTES

1. Most of this chapter was published earlier as part of my essay "A Man and His Song: Joe Scott and 'The Plain Golden Band,'" pp. 86–132.
2. Gordon Manuscripts 2710.
3. Creighton to Ives, Sept. 11, 1957.
4. G. Malcolm Laws, Jr., review of *Shantymen and Shantyboys*, p. 437.
5. Jamieson to Ives, Mar. 5, 1957.
6. See, e.g., "The Old Elm Tree" in Phillips Barry, *The Maine Woods Songster*, p. 34.
7. For easily available versions of the tune to "Bendemeer's Stream," see William Cole, *Folk Songs of England, Ireland, Scotland, and Wales*, pp. 78–79, or Margaret Bradford Boni, *The Fireside Book of Folk Songs*, pp. 20–21.
8. For "Slavery Days," see Edward D. Ives and Sharon Sperl, *Folksongs from Maine*, pp. 45–48.
9. Franz Rickaby, *Ballads and Songs of the Shanty-Boy*, p. 26.
10. Manus O'Conor, *Irish Com-All-Ye's*, p. 80.
11. John H. Young, *Our Deportment: Or the Manners, Conduct and Dress of the Most Refined Society*, p. 201.
12. See NB.16. For further discussion of singers' belief that songs are "true," see Herbert Halpert's introductory essay, "Truth in Folk-Songs—Some Observations on the Folk-Singer's Attitude," in John Harrington Cox, *Traditional Ballads and Folk-Songs Mainly from West Virginia* (q.v.).
13. See NB.16, given in full on pp. 216–217.
14. Fannie Hardy Eckstorm and Mary Winslow Smyth, *Minstrelsy of Maine*, p. 36.
15. See, e.g., Jim Brown's version at the beginning of this chapter.
16. Me.15, NB.14.
17. James Reginald Wilson, "Ballad Tunes of the Miramichi," p. 25. For some of the permutations of the "Villikins" tune, see Phillips Barry, "Notes on the Ways of Folk-Singers with Folk-Tunes."
18. For examples of this phenomenon, compare "The Boys of the Island" as it is found in William M. Doerflinger, *Shantymen and Shantyboys*, p. 218, with the same song as it appears in Edward D. Ives, *Larry Gorman*, pp. 123–124. See also "The Old Elm Tree" as reported by Barry in the *Journal of American Folklore*, 27 (1914), 69–70, and as it appears in his *Maine Woods Songster*, p. 34.

13

"Benjamin Deane":
Crime Passionnel in the White Mountains

It was 1957, and I was over in Brewer, Maine, talking to Billy Bell. Bell was seventy-five and had had "the darned asthma" for too many years to allow him to sing easily, but he had sung over a couple fragments of a Larry Gorman song for me (he'd known Larry) so that I could "get the air." His voice was cracked and uncertain, and he was a bit ashamed of it, but I "got the air" all right. We talked for a while longer, and then, apropos of almost nothing, his sister asked him if he still knew "that one about 'slowly they sank 'neath Virginia's dark waters." Billy laughed. "Yeah," he said, "but that's long as a sleigh track!" Would he try it for me, I asked. We both coaxed him, and he finally agreed to give it a try, saying he'd sing as far as he could and then recite the rest for me.

> Oh shipmates, come rally, and join in my ditty
> Of a terrible battle that happened of late;
> Let each good Union tar shed a tear of sad pity
> As they list to the once-gallant *Cumberland*'s fate.

That was not the voice I had heard earlier. It still wavered a bit and cracked here and there, but it had an integrity I was not prepared for, and it seemed as if Billy gained strength with every line. He sat there on the couch, singing slowly, looking out at nothing. I watched him some, but mostly I looked out at nothing, too.

He sang it right to the end. It was my first taste of real traditional singing, and while I have heard many wonderful things in the years since that evening, none has been more wonderful than that. "And

228

that's all the singing you're going to get out of me tonight!" he said happily. He hadn't sung for twenty years, but that had been his favorite song. I had watched a miracle happen.

We went back to talking about Larry Gorman and old songs. Then I remembered something. About a month before, a Bangor druggist by the name of James Leeman had mentioned a song called "Ben Dien" (that's the way he spelled it for me) that he thought had been written by Larry Gorman, and not more than a week after that Herby Rice had told me that it was one of the songs written by a man named Joe Scott. I asked Billy about it. Yes, he knew it. Would he sing it for me, I asked. In spite of his renunciation of a few minutes earlier, he agreed to try:

BENJAMIN DEANE

[1] Good people all both great and small read these lines penned
       by me,
      These lines were written by a man deprived of liberty;
      Who is serving out a sentence for a deed that I have done,
      And it's here I fear I will remain till my race on earth is run.

[2] My name is Benjamin Dee-un and my age is forty-one,
      I was born in New Brunswick in the city of Saint John;
      Nearby the Bay of Fundy where the seagulls loudly call,
      As they rock with pride on the silvery tide as the billows rise
         and fall.

He stopped here. *"That's all I can sing," he said, but he went ahead and recited the rest, doing such a beautiful job that I found as much pleasure in his easy and sensitive speaking of the words as I had in his singing.

[3]   My parents reared me honestly, brought me up in fear of God,
But long have they been slumbering beneath their native sod;
Side by side they slumber in a quiet cemetery
Where the willows bow before the breeze from off the deep
    blue sea.

[4]   Farewell unto my happy home, I ne'er shall see it more,
No more I'll watch the billows break upon its rockbound
    shore;
No more I'll watch those ships go by with sails as white as
    snow,
Bound for some port far o'er the sea before the winds that
    blow.

[5]   When I arrived in Berlin Falls some twenty years ago,
The town was then about one-half as large as it is now;
And laboring men of every nationality were there,
For work was plenty, wages good, each man could get a share.

[6]   The businessmen of Berlin then were making money fast,
I thought that I too would invest before the boom had passed;
A building leased on Mason Street, and into business went,
I kept a fruit and candy shop, likewise a restaurant.

[7]   My business proved successful for I did the right by all,
I gained the favor of the great, the rich, the poor, and small;
To my surprise before a year had fully rolled around
In glittering gold I did possess more than a thousand pound.

[8]   The coming year I wed with one, the fairest of the fair,
Her eyes were of the heavenly blue and light brown was her
    hair;
Her cheeks were like the dawn of morn, her form graceful and
    fair,
Her smile as bright as morning light, her step as light as air.

[9]   She was born of good parents and they reared her tenderly,
'Twas little did they ever think she would be slain by me;
The night I gained her promise and her hand to me she gave,
It would have been better far for her if she lay in her grave.

[10] I own I loved my fair young bride, which proved a prudent wife,
'Tis little did I think that I one day would take her life;
But as the years rolled swiftly by upon the wings of time,
I found the paths of pleasure had led to the fields of crime.

[11] I soon began a wild career caused by the thirst for gold,
My property on Mason Street for a goodly sum I sold;
I bought a building on Main Street which cost a handsome sum,
I ran a free-and-easy house and went to selling rum.

[12] My fair young wife would often beg me my steps to retrace,
She told me that the path I trod led to death and disgrace;
Had I but heeded her warning I wouldn't be here now,
And she might still be living with no brand upon her brow.

[13] I soon began to associate with men of low degree,
And my business kept me constantly in their base company;
I quickly went from bad to worse, did many a deed of crime
That never will be brought to light in future years of time.

[14] My fair young wife then fled with one whose name I will not write,
Whose character was blacker than the darkest hour of night;
To persuade her to return to me it was my whole intent,
So to the house where she then dwelt my steps I quickly bent.

[15] I cautiously approached the house and opened the hall door,
I found the way to my wife's room upon an upper floor;
The sight that fell upon my gaze is stamped upon my mind,
For on the bosom of a man my fair wife's head reclined.

[16] The very fiends of hell it seemed my being did possess,
I drew a loaded pistol and I aimed it at her breast;
And when she saw the weapon 'twas loudly she did cry,
"For God's sake do not shoot me, Ben, for I'm not fit to die."

[17] The bullet pierced her snowy breast, in a moment she was dead,
"For God's sakes, you have shot me," were the last words that she said;
The trigger of that weapon either moved too fast or slow,
Or else another would have passed with her to weal or woe.

[18]   The last time that I saw my wife she lay upon the floor,
       Her long and light brown wavy hair was stained with crimson
           gore;
       The sun shone through the window on her cold and lifeless
           face,
       As the officers led me away from that polluted place.

[19]   I have two daughters living, they're orphans in a way,
       And should you chance to meet them, treat them kindly I
           pray;
       Don't chide them for their father's sin, for on them there will
           rest
       A crimson stain long after I am mouldering back to dust.

When Billy had finished, I asked if he knew who wrote the song.
*"They claim that Benjamin Deane made that himself while he was
serving time," he said. "But that's supposed to be a true song made
by Benjamin Deane himself." He had learned it back on his native
Prince Edward Island (he came from Enmore) more than fifty years
ago, he told me later. *"I got that wrote down upstairs," he said, "but
it's just a little different from that," referring to a copy that someone
had given him after he came to Maine. He went upstairs later to look
but could not find it.
    Billy Bell died in 1967. During his last months in the hospital he
recognized no one, not even his wife or sister; but as the end came
on, he sang the old songs once more, going over and over his
favorites, among them "The Cumberland Crew" and "Benjamin
Deane." No friends traveled further into that night with him than
they.

    Did Joe Scott write "Benjamin Deane"? Yes, I am certain that he
did. Not only do we have (thanks to Bert Thorne) a printed slip with
his name on it, but the circumstantial and ascriptive evidence is
compelling, too. That is, "Benjamin Deane" was written about
something that happened in a town and a part of the country where
Joe Scott had worked and lived at a time when we know he was
there. The spring drive was evidently passing through Berlin at just
about the time the murder took place, and I have the word of several
men that Joe had worked on the Androscoggin drive down as far as

232

Berlin and probably below. I cannot prove that he was on the drive in the spring of 1898, but it is at least even money that he was. In addition, several people claim that they bought or learned the song directly from him. C. S. Locke, for example, was working in the woods up around Cupsuptic in the winter of 1898 when Joe came into camp selling his songs, and one of the songs Locke bought from him at that time was "Benjamin Deane." I have also been told that Jack Garland, the third party in the ballad's triangle, was pretty sore at Joe for making up that song, even though it never mentioned his name. *"He said he'd kill that Joe Scott if he ever got him, you know," Thomas Hoy told me. "He didn't like it because he made up that song about him. . . . He said, 'I'll break his neck if I ever get hold of him.' . . . No, it didn't mention his name . . . but of course they knew who it was and everybody knew that he was the one who was connected with it."

Joe Scott wrote "Benjamin Deane," then, and he wrote it shortly after the murder took place on May 4, 1898, when interest in the affair was running high. It is less certain in my mind that he was actually in Berlin at the time; since Ben Deane himself was well known to woodsmen all through the upper Androscoggin area, it is perfectly possible that the "bush telegraph" and perhaps (though I doubt it) a copy of the May 8 edition of the *Berlin Reporter* made their way to Joe upriver or down in Rumford. But I still say it is even money, or better than even money, that he *was* on the main river-drive that spring and in or near Berlin when the murder took place.

Here is "Benjamin Deane," taken from Joe Scott's original printed slip as I found it in Bert Thorne's notebook:

BENJAMIN DEAN.

----

[1]   Good people all, both great and small,
        Read these lines penned by me,
    These lines are written by a man
        Deprived of liberty;
    Who is serving out a sentence
        For a deed that I have done,
    And here I fear I will remain
        Till my race on earth is run.

The Songs

[2]   My name it is Benjamin Dean,
       My age is forty-one,
   I was born in New Brunswick
       In the city of St. John,
   Near by the Bay of Fundy,
       Where the sea gulls loudly call
   As they rock with pride the silver tide
       As the billows rise and fall.

[3]   My parents reared me honestly,
       Brought me up in the fear of God,
   But they have long been slumbering
       Beneath their native sod;
   Side by side they slumber
       In a quiet cemetery,
   Where the willows bow before the breeze
       From off the deep blue sea.

[4]   Farewell unto my native home,
       I ne'er will see it more,
   No more I'll watch the billows break
       Upon it's rock bound shore,
   No more I'll watch those ships go by
       With sails as white as snow,
   Bound for some port far o'er the sea
       Before the winds that blow.

[5]   When I arrived in Berlin Falls
       Some twenty years ago,
   The town then was about one-half
       As large as it is now,
   And laboring men of every
       Nationality were there,
   For work was plenty, wages good,
       Each man could get a share.

[6]   The business men of Berlin then
       Were making money fast,
   I thought that I, too, would invest
       Before the boom had passed.
   A building leased on Mason street
       And into business went,
   I kept a fruit and candy store,
       Likewise a restaurant.

"Benjamin Deane"

[7]   My business proved successful,
     For I did the right by all,
   I gained the favor of the great,
     The rich, the poor and small.
   To my surprise before one year
     Had fully rolled it's rounds,
   In glittering gold I did possess
     More than two thousand pounds.

[8]   That coming year I wed with one,
     The fairest of the fair,
   Her eyes were of a heavenly blue,
     And light brown was her hair,
   Her cheeks were like the dawn of day,
     Her form graceful and fair,
   Her smile was bright as morning light,
     Her step was light as air.

[9]   She was born of good parents,
     And they reared her tenderly,
   But little did they ever think
     She would be slain by me.
   The night I gained her promise
     And her hand to me she gave,
   'Twould have been better far for her
     Had she laid in her grave.

[10]   I own I loved my fair young bride
     Who proved a prudent wife,
   Oh, little did I think that I
     One day would take her life;
   And as the years rolled swiftly by
     Upon the wheels of time
   I found the paths of pleasure
     That lead to the fields of crime.

[11]   My wife would often plead and beg
     Me my steps to retrace,
   She told me that the paths I trod
     Led to death and disgrace.
   Had I but heeded the warning
     I would not be here now,
   And she might yet be living
     With no brand upon her brow.

[12]   I soon began a wild career,
        Caused by the thirst for gold,
    My property on Mason street
        For a goodly price I sold.
    I bought a building on Main street
        That cost a handsome sum,
    And ran a free and easy house
        And went to selling rum.

[13]   My former friends of decent grade
        My company did shun,
    But still I was content to lead
        The life I had begun,
    For gold and silver like a brook
        Came flowing in to me,
    By its glitter I was blinded
        And my danger could not see.

[14]   I soon began to associate
        With men of low degree,
    My business kept me constantly
        In their base company.
    I quickly went from bad to worse,
        Did many a deed of crime
    That never will be brought to light
        In future years of time.

[15]   Kind fortune that had been my friend
        Began to frown on me;
    Twas then my eyes were opened,
        I could see my destiny.
    Black clouds were gathering o'er me,
        That with fury soon would break,
    I fain then would retrace my steps
        But, ah, alas, too late.

[16]   All I possessed in real estate
        To my wife it was made
    Over in legal writing,
        When kind fortune's smile did fade.
    But her regard and love for me
        Did gradually grow cold
    When she found my heart and soul
        Were bound with glittering gold.

[17] The storm it came; the house I built
        Upon the sands did fall,
      With it my name, my wife and children,
        Ill got wealth and all.
      And on the verge of deep despair
        I saw them drift from me
      Upon the tide of justice
        Towards the sea Eternity.

[18] Then under forty thousand
        Dollar bonds I soon was placed,
      To respect the laws of man
        That I had long disgraced.
      And then to add unto my many
        Troubles that had come
      Were four indictments that appeared
        For selling beer and rum.

[19] My fair wife she had fled to one
        Whose name I will not write,
      Whose character was blacker
        Than the darkest hours of night.
      To persuade her to return to me
        It was my whole intent,
      Unto the house where she then dwelt
        My steps I quickly bent.

[20] I cautiously approached the house
        And opened the hall door,
      I found my way to my wife's room
        Upon the upper floor.
      The sight that fell upon my gaze
        Is stamped upon my mind,
      For upon the bosom of a man
        My fair wife's head reclined.

[21] The very fiends of hell it seemed
        My being had possessed,
      I drew a loaded pistol
        And I aimed it at her breast.
      And when she saw the weapon
        It was loudly she did cry
      "For God's sake, do not shoot me, Ben,
        I am not fit to die."

[22] The bullet pierced her snow-white breast
    In a moment she was dead;
"My God, Ben, you have shot me!"
    Were the last words that she said.
The trigger of my weapon
    Either pulled too hard or slow,
Or else another soul would passed
    With her's to weal or woe.

[23] The last time that I saw my wife
    She lay upon the floor,
Her long and wavy light brown hair
    Was stained with crimson gore.
The sun shone through the window
    On her cold and lifeless face,
As the officers led me away
    From that polluted place.

[24] I have two daughters living,
    They are orphans in a way,
And should you chance to meet them
    Treat them kindly I pray.
Don't chide them for their father's sin,
    For on them there will rest
A crimson stain long after
    I am mouldering back to dust.

[25] And now, young men, a warning take
    By this sad tale of mine,
Don't sacrifice your honor
    For bright gold or silver fine.
Let truth and honor be your shield,
    You'll find that you will climb
The ladder to success and fame
    And not be stung by crime.

BY JOE SCOTT.

As a work of art, a ballad of this sort is the sum of two vectors: the "facts" and the poetic tradition. "Benjamin Deane" is about something that "really happened" (as many singers have pointed out), and it is clearly in the broadside confessional tradition. In order to see more clearly how the artist adjusted these two orders of things to make of them something that was at the same time neither and both, we should look at each of them in some detail. First, let's look at the facts.

It may be revealing for the reader to follow the story as it unfolded itself for me back in 1957. I was in the western part of Maine late in July, and since I had nothing particular to do for a day, I decided to head across the border to Berlin to see what I could find. I remember very well that it was a hot day when I arrived, and I stood there on a street-corner looking down Main Street wondering where to start. Actually, I didn't even know that the murder had taken place; the whole thing could have been fiction, or even if it actually had taken place, it could have happened anywhere, since I knew ballad names had a way of shifting around. Yet I felt pretty sure of myself; the record was just too consistent.

The problem was where to begin. After about an hour of Stan Laurel head-scratching, there came to me one of those magic moments of sudden insight: if a man had murdered his wife, there would doubtless be a death record for the wife, what? Not a little pleased with myself, I went to the city clerk's office and was further delighted to find a splendidly complete cross-indexed vital statistics file; but even with the able and interested help of two clerks, Mary Morgan and Rosa Jutras, I was unable to turn up references to anyone named Dien, male or female. Saddened, I turned to go, but Miss Jutras saved the day. "You don't suppose it could be *Dean,* do you, instead of Dien?" she asked. Back to the files we went, and after a few minutes' digging we came up with something. An Elizabeth Deane, the record said, married, occupation "housekeeper," died in Berlin on May 4, 1898, at the age of thirty-five. Cause of death: "Internal Hamorhage from Boulet."

That sounded right, and if it was, I now had a date to work with. I went over to the office of the Berlin *Reporter,* but since this was printing day and the old files were down by the presses, they asked if I would come back later, though they were dubious that I would find anything that far back. It turned out to be several days before I could return, but when I did I quickly became just as dubious as they had been, since the old papers had lain in a basement cabinet on a damp bottom shelf and had been badly mouse-eaten. Worse yet, the file was both disordered and incomplete. But after about half an hour of musty thumbing I came across the May 6, 1898, edition. "SPAIN'S ASIATIC FLEET IS DESTROYED. DEWEY TAKES THE PHILLIPINE

ISLANDS," shouted the headlines, and right alongside that lead article was what I was looking for. Since we will have occasion to refer to it later on, I reprint most of it here.

A FATAL SHOT
Benj. F. Deane Kills His Wife
The Terrible Climax of a Life of Infelicity

Our city had scarcely recovered from the shock caused by the fatal shooting of Telesphore Gagnon, three weeks ago, ere the angry bullet of the murderer again finds a victim, and another crime is added to the history of Berlin.

Various causes, some apparent and others only hinted at, seem to have led up, step by step, to the murderous deed of Tuesday [sic] afternoon that left five motherless, and in all probability fatherless, children to grope their way through a none too charitable world, in the shadow of a deadly sin.

About 3:45 on Tuesday afternoon Mrs. Shaver, Mrs. Deane and John Garland were sitting in Mrs. Shaver's sitting room, when Deane quietly entered, and approaching his wife said to her "Lizzie, are you coming home with me?" She replied, "No, Ben, never." Deane then stepped toward his wife, drawing a revolver. She cried out, "Oh, God, don't, Ben, don't." Garland, who by this time was on his feet, grappled with Deane. In the struggle a shot was fired, and Mrs. Deane cried, "Oh, my God, you've killed me," reeled and fell on the lounge, and died in about five minutes.

The police had been summoned in the meanwhile, and Deane, who had been held captive at the point of his own revolver by Garland, who wrestled it from Deane, was given into the hands of the officers, who at once took him to the lock-up.

After the shooting, Deane, who did not even have the hackneyed excuse of being "intoxicated," in answer to Garland's command to remain absolutely quiet, said, "No, Jack, I have done all I want to," thus clearly showing a premeditated determination to avenge his actual or imaginary wrongs with death. . . .

Long before 9 o'clock, the hour set for the hearing, the public building and Mechanic Street in the immediate vicinity were packed with a jostling, curious crowd, eager to gain admission to the courtroom.

At the appointed hour, Judge Rich called the case and read the complaint to the prisoner, in which he was charged with "murder," and to which he pleaded "not guilty."

The rest of the article is given over to the sworn testimony of Dr.

Cobb, the examing physician, and the two witnesses, Mrs. Shaver and Jack Garland. For our purposes, the only new material added is in Garland's statements that Mrs. Deane's daughter was also in the room with them and that after it was all over Deane turned to Mrs. Shaver and said, "Shaver, Shaver, Shaver, I blame you for the whole business." The item concludes as follows:

> Deane was about 40 years of age and is a native of Massachusetts.
> Mrs. Deane was about 35 years of age, and was born in Berlin, and was the daughter of Joseph Blodgett. She leaves five children, the oldest being between 15 and 16 and the youngest two years.
> The funeral services will be held on Saturday.

Over the next decade I was able to consult the rather complete records of Deane's trial, which included a detailed eight-page statement by County Solicitor Herbert I. Goss on the prosecution's reasons for accepting a plea of "guilty of murder in the second degree." Through these and whatever incidental public records I was able to find (deeds, tax records, vital statistics, and the like) I have reconstructed a tolerably accurate picture of the murder and the events leading up to it.

Benjamin F. Deane was born in Saint John, New Brunswick (not in Massachusetts, as the newspaper had it), on May 6, 1854. Within a year, however, his parents moved to Portland, Maine, and that seems to be where Ben spent his younger days. There is no way of establishing just when he arrived in Berlin Falls, but since his first child was born there in 1881, we can pretty safely accept the ballad's statement that he had been in Berlin for about twenty years.

The 1880 census gives the population of Berlin Falls as 1,144, but by 1900 that had increased better than sevenfold to 8,886. Work *was* plenty, too, as the pulp and paper industry began to boom. The Forest Fiber Company, the first chemical pulp mill in Berlin, opened its doors in July of 1877, to be followed in 1883 by the White Mountain Pulp and Paper Company, and the Glen Manufacturing Company in 1885 (a big one); then in 1888 the Berlin Mills Company—parent of the present Berlin colossus, the Brown Company—began work. In addition to the thousands these new mills employed, men were needed to work in the woods, build streets and houses, and provide the many services needed in the new town. The ballad is perfectly correct here: the town *was* growing.[1]

This is the booming Berlin Falls that Ben came to in the late 1870s. Unfortunately, for documenting Deane's own business career we have very little to go on. The parcel of land he bought in 1883 was out Green Street near the tracks, not far from where his wife's family lived. He sold this property in 1891, and I doubt that he ever had a store on this land; it just wouldn't have been a very good place for one. However, on March 13, 1893, together with one John Sheridan, he bought "lot numbered 40 with the buildings thereon according to the plan of the Mason estate" for $600. Less than a month later he bought Sheridan out, using a $400 mortgage to do it. This may be the place on Mason Street referred to in the ballad, although it was actually on Saint Giles Street (present-day Granite Street) about a hundred feet from the end of Mason Street. This thickly populated, heavily Irish Saint Giles neighborhood could have been a good place for a store—there is today a small store nearby on the corner of York Street—but I am doubtful about a restaurant.

It is much more likely that Ben lived here and had his store and restaurant downtown. Several people recall that Deane had a store and restaurant on the corner of Main and Mason streets, and court records indicate that in early 1896 he was "the proprietor of a certain restaurant situated on Main and Mason Streets." He never owned this place, and there is no record to show how long he leased it, but information gleaned from the birth records of his children show that in 1881 and 1884 he was a "laborer," in 1886 and 1888 he was an "overseer at mill," in 1892 and 1893 he was a "merchant," while in 1894 and 1895 he was a "fruit dealer." This jibes interestingly with a series of 1896 suits for nonpayment of bills, which show that he was in the fruit and candy business at least as early as 1895, and we can be pretty sure that he had been in it for some years before that. That he sold more than fruit and candy is clear enough from a series of four indictments for illegal selling of spirituous liquors in 1895 and 1896, which cost him $100 in fines and a six-month suspended jail sentence.

Let me sum up Deane's career as I see it to this point. He came to Berlin before 1881 and went to work in one of the mills as a laborer. He continued in the mill, working his way up to an overseer's job, until about 1890 or 1891, when he moved his family into a house on Saint Giles Street. At about the same time he leased a place on the corner of Main and Mason, where he "ran a fruit and candy store, likewise a restaurant." But all this occurred more than ten years after he came to Berlin and at least ten years after his marriage. Furthermore, neither common sense nor the records suggest that he ever made a large fortune. He was behind in his bills, he was behind in his taxes, and he had a large family of girls. At the very best, he probably did little better than the rest of us, which is to say he barely managed to stay solvent; at worst he was one jump ahead of the sheriff and the town marshals. And he had already been on the dark side of the law for selling rum. Clearly, then, there are considerable differences between what happened and what Joe Scott *said* happened.

It is not certain just when Ben married, but since his first child was born August 6, 1881, we can assume it was around 1880 shortly after he arrived in Berlin, or perhaps (though I doubt it) even before he came. His wife's name was Lizzie, Mary Elizabeth Blodgett, and she was nine years younger than Ben, which means that she was married when she was seventeen or even younger. The couple had seven children, five of whom were alive at the time of the murder and would have ranged in age from three to fourteen. There is nothing in the record to indicate what kind of person she was or how smoothly the marriage went, except for a statement in the court records that there had been "trouble between them as much as two years prior to the homicide" arising out of conduct that Deane "alleged was in violation of her marital duties." More about that in due time, but I think it is safe to assume the couple had an increasingly tough time of it, financially and maritally.

It was probably sometime in 1896 that Deane gave up his business at Main and Mason streets and began keeping a boardinghouse on Main Street up above where the present post office stands and just about where the Potluck Restaurant is. County Solicitor Goss's statement describes it as follows: "Their [*i.e., the Deanes'*] boarders were mostly common laborers and woodsmen, some of the woodsmen being at Deane's only during the time they were not employed in the woods, but making Deane's boarding house their home where they kept their clothing. Deane kept a bar where liquors were sold more or less, sometimes only malt liquors were dispensed and sometimes both malt and spiritous. During some of the time too, women of questionable character were harbored upon the premises."

That sounds like what could be called a "free and easy house" all right, but if gold and silver flowed his way he never used it to pay his old candy-store debts, because he was sued by five creditors in late 1896 for debts totaling nearly four hundred dollars. Ben probably never lived far from the edge of a desperation that became increasingly less quiet.

His health was failing him, too. He seems to have been in good shape for most of his life, but in December of 1897 he had particularly bad attacks of rheumatism and entered Maine General Hospital in Portland for treatment, remaining there for several weeks. After his return, he could get around only on crutches until April, when he was "able to do some light work about his house." Most of his boarders agreed, says Goss, "that whereas previous to his rheumatic attack he was generally sociable, pleasant and ready for conversation, that after his return from the hospital, he was cross, irritable, and undisposed to converse with anyone." He went in in December; he returned home in February. The murder took place in early May.

Solicitor Goss's statement of what happened is not substantially different from the newspaper account, but he goes into more detail about the events leading up to the murder. About a week previous, Ben and Lizzie had a fight that was serious enough to occasion his ordering her to leave, which she did. Goss could never determine exactly what she did or where she was for all of the next four days, but on Saturday evening Ben asked his neighbor, Mrs. Shaver, to go look for her. She found her down by the old Grand Trunk House—hardly the best address in town—and took her home with her. Next day Ben came around and they went home together, apparently on good terms, too, but it didn't last more than a few hours. Goss tells the story:

Among the boarders who were then boarding at Deane's boarding house were two men by the names of John Scott and John Garland who roomed together. It appears that Scott on this Sunday was somewhat under the influence of liquor and was assisted to his room by Garland; soon afterwards Garland left the room but later the room was entered by Mrs. Deane who was found there sitting on the bed, as Deane claimed, by the side of Scott who had his arm more or less around her waist, there upon Mr. Deane again ordered her from the premises and as a result both Scott and Garland left. Mrs. Deane returned to the house of Mrs. Shaver where she remained until the day of her death. Garland returned to Deane's and boarded there a day or two but his room having been occupied by other parties he went away and took up his residence at M. J. Holland's. He seems to have been on friendly terms with Deane and so far as we are able to ascertain Deane never had any feeling against him.

That was on Sunday. Monday and Tuesday seem to have passed quietly enough. Then on Wednesday, Jack Garland was downtown and saw Ben across the street. Ben hallooed him and offered to buy him a drink, whereupon Jack crossed over and the two men went into Brooks's Drug Store for a couple slugs of gin. Leaving here, Jack went up the street, and when he was in front of Mrs. Shaver's place he was invited in (he was no stranger there; Mrs. Shaver used to do his laundry). He went in, and there were Mrs. Deane and her small daughter.

Deane, on the other hand, went downtown after having his drink, bought a revolver in one store, some cartridges in another, and then headed for Mrs. Shaver's. What happened then has already been so adequately described in the newspaper account there is no need to repeat it here: Ben shot his wife, and it was all over in five minutes.

The rest of the story is easily told. Deane was indicted for murder at the October term of the Supreme Court, Southern Judicial District, Coos County, held at Lancaster, but the case was carried over to the April, 1899, term, trial to commence May 23. However, before that date, defense indicated that a plea of "guilty of murder in the second degree" would be made if counsel for the prosecution would accept such a plea. It was accepted, and on May 23 Deane was sentenced to twenty-five years in the New Hampshire State Prison at Concord, sentence to begin immediately. He was evidently a model prisoner, for on March 6, 1907, just under eight years later, Governor Charles M. Floyd, in response to a petition signed by the mayor and twenty-two officials and leading citizens of Berlin, granted Deane a full pardon. He returned to Berlin, remarried (her name was Georgiana Mercier), and until his death in 1924 he ran a small store in Berlin Mills, just across from where the Brown Company now has its offices.

Here, then, is the story as it is revealed in the official and public records of the time. It is as close as we will ever come to "what really happened," and while it is not without its ambiguities, obviously it tells a story that is at considerable variance with the ballad. To be sure, it shows us Ben Deane moving from the proprietorship of a fruit and candy store to that of a questionable boardinghouse; but he

obviously never made much money, and his "wild career" seems to
have gone little beyond penny-ante bootlegging and not being too
curious about what his lodgers did upstairs. He was also a sick man,
in constant and nagging pain. As for Lizzie, the newspaper account
says nothing about how much provocation she might have offered
Ben; the court records, while they give nothing specific, at least
show that Ben had had his suspicions for some time and suggest that
he may have had some reason. From the conditions of his pardon and
the fact that he returned to Berlin to lead what appears to have been
an exemplary life, I think it is safe to infer that public sentiment was
far from being mobilized against him. Finally, when we come to the
murder itself, the record shows that it took place in Mrs. Shaver's
sitting room, where Jack Garland just happened to be at the time,
lying on the couch holding Ben's four-year-old daughter—not his
wife—in his arms. And Garland, rather than being lucky to get away
with his life, wrestled the pistol from Deane and held him at gun-
point until the police arrived.

As might be expected, the oral record is considerably more
melodramatic, and while it shows a good deal of variation, it has its
own emphases. First of all, the general run of gossip seems to have
been that Ben had provocation enough from his wife, but several
people emphasized that even for that Ben had only himself to blame.
*"I'll tell you," Fred Lafferty said, "they blamed him entirely be-
cause she was a nice woman, but I'll tell you what happened. You
know, he wanted her to play up to these woodsmen, you know, to a
certain extent. And that was it." Herbert Sullivan of Worcester,
Massachusetts, was a young man in his twenties living in Berlin at
the time of the murder, and he recalls what a sensation the murder
caused. "Some people blamed Deane," he wrote me, "for going into
the liquor business and letting his wife serve it, bringing her in touch
with the type of men that gather in such places. And of course others
blamed her for allowing these drunks [to] fool around [with] her."
Tom Pollock of Harvey, New Brunswick, remembered the place and
thought very well of Mrs. Deane:

*Yes, it was all right. That was a nice house and she was a nice woman,
Benjamin Deane's wife was, and they kept a boardinghouse and a good
one. And the boys would go in there and have their dinner and it was nice
as could be. And then he got running wild after he had the barroom down
in the basement. . . . Had a bunch of toughs [whores] from the lead-mine

246

tough house there, and Ben he was running with them. He had them, you see, chambermaids and waiting on tables. And that's what started the whole thing. And she left him.

On whatever other matters the gossip may have varied, it consistently makes Jack Garland the third member of the triangle. Big, handsome, reputedly very much a lady-killer, Jack was a woodsman who regularly stayed at Ben's place, and it is almost universally claimed that he and Mrs. Deane were having an affair. *"This big fellow come along," said Fred Lafferty, "and she kind of found—as though she liked him a little bit," he said delicately. "So she started—he was raising the devil all the time anyway—she started going out with him, and that's what caused the jealousy." As we have seen, the official record makes it clear he was in the room at the time of the murder, but the gossip compromises him considerably more, having him holding Mrs. Deane on his lap or even claiming Ben *"caught them on the bed together." Some claim that Jack saved his own life by escaping out the window, but more generally people claim, as Fred Campbell said, *"[Ben] got excited, and he held the revolver too tight that Jack Garland got to him and jerked it out of his hand." It is widely accepted that Ben fully intended to shoot both of them.

The memory lingered on, the crimson stain remained. Lots of people remember Ben as he was after he came back from prison and opened his store up in the Mills. Jack Keating remembers that he and the other youngsters were fascinated by him, having heard all about the murder, and though of course they had been told by their parents to "stay away from there," they often went in and bought candy from him. Others remember being scared to go in, and when they even went by his place they'd walk on the outer edge of the sidewalk, kid fashion. But it wasn't only the children who kept the memory alive. Old Arthur Carr of Boiestown, New Brunswick, told me that one day, a considerable time after the murder, he was walking down Main Street in Berlin, when a fellow he knew came out of a doorway and grabbed him by the arm. "Hey, Art," he said, "would you like to see the blood mark where Ben Deane shot his wife?" Carr followed his friend into the room; a piece of carpet was pulled back and he looked down at that stain, no longer crimson but still clear.

In establishing the facts behind the ballad, the problem is just the reverse of what it was with "The Plain Golden Band": here we know infinitely more about what went on than Joe Scott did. What, then, did Joe probably know about it all? What were *his* "facts"? Now, of course there is no way of establishing this, but we can make some pretty good guesses, and my first is that he did not have the newspaper account at hand. He may have read it, but I'd be willing to bet he hadn't even done that. His material is an interesting mixture of generally correct (Ben's being a New Brunswicker and his shifting from fruit-and-candy merchant to boardinghouse-keeper) and just plain wrong (all that business about his being placed under bond and his possessions being signed over to his wife, and especially the matter of the murder having taken place in his wife's room). Joe probably knew Ben slightly and might even have stayed at his boardinghouse from time to time.

That would have started it, but from there on, Joe's facts are almost exactly the sort of information one would gather from barroom experts of the "I-was-right-there" or "Hell-I-knew-him-well" variety. I don't think it is too imaginative to picture Joe sitting by the fire of a river-driver's camp near Berlin shortly after the murder listening to one or two such authorities expatiating gleefully to all the eager rest. Possibly someone there has a copy of the newspaper, from which he reads; then the experts jump in and set it all straight. However it may have been, I am sure that Joe wanted to tell it like it was, and to that end he used the most authoritative sources available to him. He is just too laboriously factual in places for me to see it any other way. To be sure, he made the picture these facts created fit the frame of traditional broadside-ballad morality and worldview, and it is to this frame that we should now turn our attention, both for its own sake and for what it reveals about Joe's conception of the facts.

For the telling of this story, Joe chose a very traditional form indeed: the criminal's confession. Beginning with a general statement of crime committed, such a ballad has the criminal tell his own story. He often begins with his childhood and leads up to the crime from there, but always the crime itself is told about in some detail. The ballad ends with regrets and a warning to other young men to shun the path he trod. It has been a particularly popular form for ballad makers on both sides of the ocean, as a glance through Laws's two syllabi will show.[2] We will have to turn to the psychologists for any detailed explanation of why murder is such an interesting subject; in general terms, the confessional form we have just described allows the singer and his audience all the excitement of a vicarious life of crime in a setting that is indisputably moral and didactic. There is nothing very new or startling in this technique, and we can see a continuation of it in the "true confession" magazines of today. The confessional ballad simply capitalized on this technique of making murder moral.

The stanza form—the double stanza, with four seven-foot lines (basically fourteen syllables) rhyming *a a b b*—is unquestionably the most common one for the confessional ballad. This is especially true in Maine and the Maritime Provinces, where, in fact, it is the single most popular form we find for any kind of traditional song. If we take Helen Creighton's *Songs and Ballads from Nova Scotia* as a fairly representative sample, we find this double, or come-all-ye, stanza in almost a third of the songs; and if we take it together with its closest rival, the "Villikins" type—a stanza with four four-foot, predominantly anapestic lines rhyming *a a b b*—we find that the two forms account for more than half. Obviously, there need be no question that Joe Scott used a traditional form in making his ballad.

The center of interest in "Benjamin Deane" is the murder itself, to be sure; but notice that the murder does not occur until stanzas 20 and 21, with 80 percent of the ballad behind us. Now, there is nothing particularly surprising about this; it is standard narrative technique to have the climax occur toward the end of the story. Yet most confessional crime ballads do not follow this structure; the crime itself will come earlier in the ballad, a good deal more space will be devoted to it, and it will be followed by stanzas devoted to arrest, conviction, regrets, and farewells on the model of "James MacDonald" (Laws P–38) or "The Wexford Lass" (Laws P–35). Our ballad is much closer in structure and tone to those well-known pirate ballads "The Flying Cloud" (Laws K–28) and "Charles Augustus Anderson" (Laws D–19), both of which chronicle the sorrowful downfall of erstwhile good men, but even these ballads spend much time directly on the crime itself. In short, I know of no murder ballads that are constructed in quite the way Joe Scott constructed "Benjamin Deane," although at first look it is "just like a dozen others." While staying within the limits of the tradition, he has been inventive.

Further evidence of Joe's inventiveness is the leisurely pace of the

entire ballad, which he achieves not only through the way he
structures the whole thing, but also, as with "Howard Carey,"
through his elaboration of traditional devices and imagery. The
opening stanzas are a case in point, and for comparative purposes,
here are the parallel stanzas from "The Flying Cloud":

> Come all you rambling sailor lads and listen unto me.
> I'm heavy bound in iron chains, to die for piracy.
> With eighteen more I am condemned in sorrow to complain
> For plundering and burning ships down on the Spanish Main.
>
> My name is Edward Anderson, as you will understand.
> I was born in the town of Waterford in Erin's lovely land.
> My parents raised me tenderly, in the care of God likewise,
> But little did they think I'd die 'neath Cuba's sunny skies.[3]

It's all there: the exhortation to listen or read, the allusion to present
confinement and punishment to come, the naming and mentioning
of place of birth, and the statement that the criminal was brought up
by good God-fearing parents. Joe's first stanza is perfectly straight,
but not his second one. He spends four lines on absolutely gratuitous
and conventional natural description, just the way he did in the same
place in "Howard Carey":

> Near by the Bay of Fundy,
>   Where the sea gulls loudly call
> As they rock with pride the silver tide
>   As the billows rise and fall.

The next two stanzas (3–4) continue the same emphasis, slowing
the pace even further by the use of additional conventional natural
description. Once again, Joe has taken traditional formulas and
elaborated on them. The "my parents reared me tenderly" formula,
to begin with, occurs in so many crime ballads as not to require
citation; but usually the next line points up the lad's errant ways, as in
"The Girl I Left Behind" (Laws P–1A):

> My parents reared me tenderly, they had no child but me.
> My mind was bent on rambling, but with them I could not agree.

The tender parents and the gentle upbringing are obviously formulaic concepts, and they are usually expressed in any of several line
or half-line formulas, such as "brought me up in the fear of God"; but

I know of no other ballad here in the Northeast or anywhere else that expands this concept into a full stanza. Joe gives us four lines describing in fully traditional terms that willow-bemused cemetery by the sea. We can be sure that this scene is entirely from Joe's imagination; at least I find it very hard to believe that he knew anything about Deane's upbringing or about where his parents were buried (and we know they were *not* buried in Saint John). No matter; this is the way it *ought* to have been.

The fourth stanza is an entirely formulaic concept—we can call it the "farewell"—that is usually expressed in perfectly formulaic language. "Peter Emberly" offers a close parallel:

Here's adieu to Prince Edward Island, that garden in the seas,
No more I'll walk its flowery banks to enjoy a summer breeze;
No more I'll view those gallant ships as they go sailing by
With streamers floating in the breeze above the canvas high.

Of course, it is not always a *place* that the narrator says adieu to; it may be mother, father, or sweetheart. ("Peter Emberly" manages to get them all in in the longest series of adieus I have ever seen—Joe Scott was not the only ballad writer willing to try something a little different, it would seem.)[4] Yet even though this stanza is thoroughly traditional in its conception, its position is very unusual. As a rule such a stanza (or group of stanzas) appears after the climactic action of the ballad, or at least toward the end. "Charles Augustus Anderson" (Laws D–19) is a notable exception, and it may be where Joe got his idea for bringing this material in near the beginning, where it further slows the pace and increases emphasis on the lost childhood.

Thus in the first four stanzas nearly half the lines are devoted to highly conventional natural description. Joe probably built the whole business up from simply knowing that Deane was born in Saint John, because while the descriptions *are* reasonably correct for that area (rocks, billows, ships, willows), they give us less a picture of Saint John than they do a picture of what a seaside home should be if we are going to feel about Benjamin Deane the way Joe wants us to feel.

This same leisureliness can be seen in the next section of the ballad, stanzas 5 through 11, which details for us Ben's honest rise in the world. Structurally this has its parallel in a single stanza in "The *Flying Cloud*":

My father bound me to a trade in Waterford's fair town.
He bound me to a cooper there by the name of William Brown.
I served my master faithfully for eighteen months or more,
Then I shipped on board the *Ocean Queen*, bound to Valparaiso
    shore.[5]

Joe takes seven stanzas to do about the same thing, recounting Ben's
rise as an honest merchant and his marriage to a lovely girl. Viewed
another way, it takes Joe almost half the ballad to establish the state
of innocence, the Garden of Eden, from which the hero will fall.
Stanzas 5 through 7 are fairly straight reporting of Ben's business
success, and of course they make Ben's rise just that much more
straight-line and dramatic than it actually was. However, although
Joe certainly enlarged on that two thousand pounds of glittering gold
to accord with the ballad world's tendency to overstatement, these
stanzas are too strictly reportorial for me to believe that he was trying
to do anything but tell it like it was. And it is just the sort of thing he
would have gotten from barroom authority. (*"Why hell, I've known
Ben for years. He musta come here about twenty years ago and first
thing he did was open up a fruit and candy store right there on the
corner of Main and Mason, and there was a little restaurant attached to it, too. Awful nice place, and he was an awful nice fella,
too, and he really made a bundle. . . ."*)

The stanzas on Ben's marriage (8–11) can be considered the final
touch in Ben's success story: not only has he made a fortune and won
the respect of all, he has married a beautiful girl as well. Joe's
description of her beauty is entirely traditional in concept, but when
we get down to the actual words and phrases we find that his
language is startlingly fresh for broadside balladry. There is a good
deal more of Stephen Foster's "Jeanie" about the "fair young wife"
than there is of more typical ballad heroines whose "cheeks were like
roses," whose "teeth were like the ivory white," whose "skin was like
the lilies fair," and whose "hair hung down in ringlets."[6] Once again
we should remark the emphasis on description; it is unusual for a
ballad to devote six full lines to describing the heroine.

The prefiguring of the crime in these marriage stanzas ("little did
they ever think . . .") is a standard fixture in crime ballads, and so is
the pure, sweet, lovely heroine-victim, but this second point needs
some comment. As we have already seen, there was a broad spectrum of opinion on just how culpable Mrs. Deane may have been for

what happened, and it is almost impossible, especially when we consider his probable sources, that Joe Scott had not heard plenty of uncomplimentary talk about her. Possibly he ignored it because he did not believe it, but I think there are two more likely reasons. The first is artistic. The emphasis he wanted was on Deane's downfall, and a loving wife practically driven into the arms of another man by Ben's life of crime suited his purposes. Besides, female murder victims are notably more sinned against than sinning. The second reason is more speculative. In the world he was creating in his songs at this time, there was no place for "bad" women—especially, I might add, when their names were Lizzie. They may be weak, but essentially they are pure. Both reasons come to this, though: if we cannot say that Scott *changed* reality to make a better ballad, we can at least say that he was very selective of the material he had available.

Scott then turns to Deane's "wild career" and spends a good quarter of his ballad describing it in detail. Again we have "The *Flying Cloud*" as a structural parallel, and again we can be sure that Scott was following his barroom authority. His information is an almost perfect mixture of right and wrong, correct and garbled—just what one would get from such authority—yet it is all so carefully and factually told that I cannot imagine Joe including all these untraditional details unless he felt they were the truth.

All this was very important to Joe; we may assume that from the amount of time he spends on it. I think his reasons are clear enough. He wanted to show Ben as a man reduced to desperation, and he does that by the end of stanza 18. Through his "thirst for gold" Ben has lost everything: name, wife, children, wealth. In the next stanza he will make a gesture of contrition, but it is too late. Clearly, for Joe Scott this was *not* a murder ballad so much as it was another moral preachment. As with "Howard Carey," the paths of pleasure lead to death, be that death suicide or murder; but in "Benjamin Deane" he emphasized one particular path: avarice. It may just be that "The *Flying Cloud*," also about how the lust for gold brought a good man to his death, was the perfect model for what Joe wanted to do in "Benjamin Deane."

Now we come to the climax of the ballad—the murder itself. Stanzas 19 and 20 deserve a very careful look, because they can reveal some interesting things both about Joe's intent and about his use of sources and models. First of all, he says that the fair young wife fled *to*, not *with* someone; I am certain Joe had Mrs. Shaver in mind here, not Jack Garland. We know from the newspaper article that Ben implicated Mrs. Shaver ("Shaver, Shaver, Shaver, I blame you for the whole business"), and the gossip may have been even more pointed. At any rate, it would have been in keeping for Ben to have assigned her a "black" character, and he would certainly then have approached her house "cautiously." Having her flee to Mrs. Shaver would also make the shock of Ben's seeing his wife with another man more intense (after all, if she had fled with another man, he should have expected something like what he saw, not that it wouldn't have been a shock anyway). Second, Joe follows the gossip by having Ben find his wife and the other man alone together in an upstairs room, a rather more compromising situation than that reported in the papers, where they are in a downstairs sitting room together with Mrs. Deane's daughter and (possibly) Mrs. Shaver herself.

It is at this point that Joe comes as close to excusing Ben's actions as he ever does, by having him say that the "very fiends of hell" possessed him at that moment, which suggests that he went temporarily insane. We might also say that the wife's claim that she is "not fit to die" implies her guilt and further exculpates Ben; but since the phrase is formulaic and is often used by utterly innocent female murder victims in ballads, I doubt that Joe Scott intended it to be interpreted this way—though of course I am less sure that singers and audiences may not have so interpreted it.[7] But it is Joe's intentions that concern us now. He has gone to considerable trouble to show us the fair young wife, pure and much beloved, pleading with Ben to change his ways, and finally all but being driven into the arms of another man by Ben's life of crime. Along with this, he has Ben detail his "wild career," the whole song being essentially his confession of guilt and wrongdoing. It changes nothing to have Ben commit the murder in blind rage or to have the wife make the traditional plea for her life. It simply allows more room for our sympathy and understanding to enter the balance.

And it is the balance of this ballad that I find remarkable. When we consider the opportunity Joe had for allowing Deane to indulge in either lugubrious breast-beating or pious outrage (both of which would have had traditional sanction), we have to admire his restraint. After the deed he simply gives us a leisurely (almost a whole stanza!) last look at the dead wife that contains a line notable, as broadside balladry goes, for its sensitivity and expressiveness: "The sun shone through the window / On her cold and lifeless face." Without excusing Deane's actions, Scott has successfully maintained his tone of sorrow over a good man's fall.

The same tone—and the same leisureliness—is kept through the concluding stanzas, which allow the ballad to come to a quiet close. Deane's plea that the listener not throw his crime up to his daughters has no traditional parallel that I can find, although it serves about the same function that a "farewell" stanza would at this point. On the other hand, the final stanza is about as traditional as we can get: a warning stanza that points the moral to be gleaned from our sad tale. It is the sort of moral anyone could subscribe to, and its comfortable presence allows the singer and listeners to feel that their interest has not been in murder and gore, but in morality and right conduct.

To conclude this part of the study, then, we can see much more clearly not only how Joe Scott blended his facts with ballad tradition, but also in what ways he has been innovative. First of all, for both his facts and his general attitudes toward what happened, he depended entirely on gossip, on what I have called barroom authority; but his intent was to tell the story as factually and as straight as he possibly could. Second, while he used the basic structure and conventions of the confessional ballad, he did not use other murder ballads for his immediate model, but rather a pirate ballad like "The *Flying Cloud.*" Finally, he developed his material in an extremely leisurely manner, frequently indulging his love of conventional description in the same way we have already seen him do in the other ballads we have considered. That the final result of all this, the ballad of "Benjamin Deane," was approved by a couple of generations of singers is evident from the ballad's popularity. But the approval was not without its reservations, and that is material for the next few pages.

Since "Benjamin Deane" was the first ballad of Joe Scott's I ever found, and since for that and other reasons it has always been in the front of my mind, I always assumed it was Joe's most popular ballad—but it is not. "The Plain Golden Band," "Guy Reed," and "Howard Carey" seem to be about twice as well known, and "The Norway Bum" is almost as well known. However, it is still correct to speak of it as a ballad that had made a very strong position for itself in northeastern tradition. Of the twenty-eight versions I have found, fifteen were given as complete and nine more as all but complete (the informant claiming he had forgotten a stanza or two, perhaps), about equally divided between oral and manuscript versions. Its geographical distribution is about the same as that of the other ballads we have looked at: Maine, northern New Hampshire, and the Maritime Provinces of Canada, the one exception coming from way-upstate New York from a man who had learned the song in Maine. Since the ballad was written in northern New Hampshire or northwestern Maine, obviously its general movement has been from there eastward to the Maritimes, being carried there by men like Augus Enman of Spring Hill, Prince Edward Island, who told me he learned his version in a western Maine lumbercamp. But every version that moved in this direction can be matched with one that moved the other way. Billy Bell of Brewer, Maine, for example, whose version stands at the opening of this chapter, learned it back home on Prince Edward Island, and Omer McKenna of Rumford learned his version back on Prince Edward Island from his brother, who in his turn had learned it originally in a Maine lumbercamp. Suffice it to say, then, that this ballad was well established in local tradition throughout the limited area of the Northeast, moved easily within it, but never got beyond it.

"Benjamin Deane" has gone further down the road to complete anonymity than has "The Plain Golden Band," partly, I suppose, because it hasn't got that ballad's immediate connection with Scott's own life. Fewer than a third of my informants attributed the ballad to him, most of them having no idea who wrote it and caring less. Several people, of course, like Billy Bell, were convinced that Ben Deane himself made the song while he was in prison, and I was told by at least one man that Larry Gorman had made it up. But for the most part it is just one more come-all-ye.

What part did print play in getting "Benjamin Deane" around? Very little, so far as I can determine. I cannot find, for instance, that it was ever published in any newspaper or magazine. The *Family Herald* published several requests for it between 1919 and 1951, but it wasn't until the fall of 1951 that they received a version from someone signing himself simply "A reader" from Kennetcook, Nova Scotia (NS.1). From this, they prepared a printed copy, making many small "corrections" that helped smooth out the diction and the meter considerably. They never got around to publishing it, but they did have a batch of offprints prepared, copies of which they sent out to correspondents requesting this ballad. Aside from this offprint, Joe's original slip sheet, and whatever manuscript versions may have passed around, "Benjamin Deane" circulated entirely by oral tradition.

The most striking thing that has happened to this ballad in tradition is that it has been shortened. In all its glory, "Benjamin Deane" is twenty-five stanzas long and would take almost fifteen minutes to sing; but I have never heard a version sung or recited that had more than nineteen stanzas, and the average is nearer seventeen.[8] Yet even these shortened traditional versions are often spoken of by the singers as long or "hard" ones. We should have been able to predict this shortening, however. If we compare "Benjamin Deane" to other ballads in northeastern tradition that have a reputation for length, we find that nineteen stanzas is just about the top limit, and even that is very rare. "The *Flying Cloud*" has seventeen stanzas at the most, and even "Meagher's Children" (Laws G–25) cannot claim more than nineteen. That should help us form an idea of what singers and their audiences would tolerate when it comes to the length of a song, and Joe Scott went so far beyond that limit in "Benjamin Deane" as to make shortening inevitable. A look at Billy Bell's version at the head of this chapter, especially at his stanzas 11 through 14, can give us the clue to just *how* it got shortened.

The central section detailing Ben's life of crime (12 through 18 in the original) may have been important to Joe, since he devotes almost a quarter of the ballad to it, but it has just about vanished from tradition. Its function is maintained by stanza 12, which gets Ben into the rum-and-women line, and 11, which shows his wife pleading with him to reform (and the two stanzas are usually in this order, by the way); but obviously singers considered all that detailed business about bad company, failure, and legal actions superfluous. Its appearance is limited almost entirely to a few manuscript versions, except for an occasional single stanza like 13 in Bell's version ("I soon began to associate . . ."). The only other stanzas that are left out with anything even approaching the same consistency are stanza 4 (that unusually placed "farewell") and the opening and closing stanzas (1 and 25), but the appearance or nonappearance of these three stanzas seems to be more gratuitous than anything else. I would hardly say that that abstraction we call "the tradition" was rejecting these stanzas; it simply doesn't seem to have made much difference one way or the other. On the other hand, there is no question about what was happening to stanzas 13 through 18.

So much for subtractions. How about additions? Have any new stanzas ever appeared? Whenever Wilmot MacDonald of Glenwood, New Brunswick, sang the song for me (NB.8), he included the following as his third stanza, between the "decent rearing" and the arrival in Berlin Falls:

> 'Twas on a summer's evening strange thoughts came in my mind,
> That I should leave my native home, likewise my friends behind;
> I steered my course for New Hampshire, strange visits for to call,
> And I landed in a pleasant town, they called it Berlin Falls.

That makes excellent sense and supplies a neat transition at a point where I always felt one was needed, but the stanza is unique with Wilmot. To the best of my knowledge, no other new stanzas ever appeared.

It might be expected that all kinds of changes would take place on the level of phrases and single words, and they do, but there is only one that is of any real significance. When Ben's wife finally leaves him, Joe puts it this way in stanza 19:

> My fair wife she had fled to one
> Whose name I will not write,
> Whose character was blacker
> Than the darkest hours of night.

But about half of the traditional versions have it this way:

> My fair wife she had fled to one
> Whose name will not appear.
> I do not think it necessary
> That I reveal it here.

I have no explanation for that change, but there it is, a clear departure from what Joe wrote. Furthermore, as I pointed out earlier, I think Joe intended the "one" to be Mrs. Shaver, not Jack Garland, but no one interprets it that way. At least, everyone I have ever asked sees it as a clear reference to the "other man," whether or not they know his name was Jack Garland. And, just to reinforce this, traditional versions are about equally divided on whether Mrs. Deane fled *to* or *with* this "one." If I am correct about Joe's intentions, the shift was inevitable because it would have required a special knowledge of the circumstances to have maintained his original sense. If I am wrong, then his original sense has been maintained, and I have been weaving the wind.

Whatever stanzas may be left out and whatever minor changes may have been made, the ballad shows great stability when it comes to the order in which stanzas appear. The farewell stanza (4) may be present or omitted; but if it appears it always appears at this point, never, say, toward the end, where farewell stanzas are equally traditional. The only significant inversion I have found is that in most versions where we find both stanzas 11 ("My wife would often plead and beg . . .") and 12 ("I soon began a wild career . . .") their order is reversed; Ben starts his life of crime, and then she tries to straighten him out. That makes a little better sense, it seems to me, and it forms a nice transition to the next stanza in most versions, the one in which the fair young wife flees (19).

What tune did Joe Scott use for this ballad? There is no way of knowing that for sure, but since ten of the fifteen tunes I have collected (or that others have collected) are essentially the same as Billy Bell's, it is likely that that was the tune he had in mind.[9] It is a standard come-all-ye tune with its ABBA phrase pattern, though its range of a twelfth is somewhat greater than we usually find. Modally it contains no particular surprises, but it is a neat example of how contour predominates over mode in giving a tune its identity. Bell's version is Dorian, while five others are Mixolydian, and three more are hexatonic, lacking the third degree that would establish them as either Dorian or Mixolydian altogether; yet that rise to the ninth in the B phrase and the approach to the cadence from below in the A phrase (to name only two salient features) are clear in all of them. Even as elaborate and inflected a version as that sung by Wilmot MacDonald still shows its lineage:

The bus-i-ness-men of Ber-lin Falls are mak-ing mon-ey fast,

thought I would in-vest a home be-fore the boom had passed;

bought a house on the Main Street, I in-to bus-iness went, Where I

run a fruit and can-dy store, like-wise a res-tau-rant.

Wilmot's singing of this ballad is interesting for another reason. The first time he ever sang it for me, he broke down about half way through, claiming he just couldn't handle it. "No sir, it takes *rum* to sing a song like that," he said laughing. Others have found it difficult, too. *"Oh Jesus boy," Charles Sibley of Argyle, Maine, said back in 1957, "you've asked me for a hard one there"; and while he sang it for me, it was obviously an effort. The combination of a long set of words and a tune with a wide range gave singers trouble, and Wilmot solved it in 1963 by putting a new tune to it. He'd sung the ballad to the old tune for some forty years, *"but it's an awful hard air, so I went to work and shifted this air, and I can sing it an awful lot better, because it's a terrible long song." The air he chose was one he had heard Frank and Ray Estey use at the Miramichi Folksong Festival several times for their singing of "The Maid of Sweet Gartine":[10]

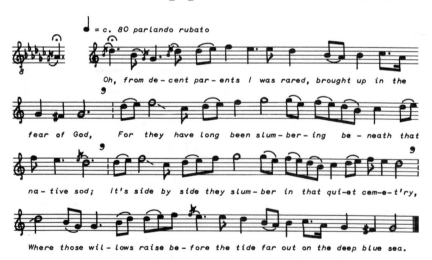

Oh, from de-cent par-ents I was rared, brought up in the

fear of God, For they have long been slum-ber-ing be-neath that

na-tive sod; It's side by side they slum-ber in that qui-et cem-e-t'ry,

Where those wil-lows raise be-fore the tide far out on the deep blue sea.

What Wilmot did is what many singers have done with other songs over the years, either for the same reason (to make a song easier to sing) or for any one of several other reasons. The point is, they knew exactly what they were doing. Conscious change of this sort is one way of accounting for the fact that the same song can be found sung to completely different airs—not just variants of the same air—even within a limited area;[11] and it may be the *best* way of accounting for that occasional "sport" in a basically stable tune-text tradition, which is the situation with "Benjamin Deane." The remarkable thing is not that such change takes place, but that given a tradition in which tunes and texts were so easily interchangeable it didn't happen more often. It is simply one more example of the basic conservativeness of oral tradition—and of the boldness of innovation.

Can this boldness account for the only other tune I have found to "Benjamin Deane"? There is, of course, no way of telling that now, but it is interesting that the two variants I have of it were collected from cousins, Billy Price of McNamee (Priceville) and Chester Price of Blackville, New Brunswick. Here is Chester's singing of it:[12]

The correspondence between the two men's versions is made even closer by their being the only two versions of the ballad with any pretensions to completeness that leave out stanza 19, the one in which Ben's wife finally leaves him. That omission makes it appear more as though the murder took place in Ben's own home, where he found his wife with another man. Two versions are not enough to allow me to make a claim that a local version of the ballad was being formed along the Southwest Miramichi, but I can modestly say that a plot change and a special tune do point in that direction.

"Benjamin Deane" has always been a very personal ballad for me. It was the first Joe Scott ballad I ever heard of, the first I collected, the first I ever explored the background for, and the first I ever published an article on.[13] But there's more than that. Right from the beginning, from that first time Billy Bell went over it for me, the picture Joe created of Ben looking at his dead wife has been with me. There's a real tenderness in those lines, and they made me wonder: what did he feel as the anger passed and the deed was past undoing? And what were his feelings for this woman he'd killed "as the years rolled swiftly by" and the end came on? For the first, I knew there was no answer. But for the second?

That second question was on my mind that afternoon in Berlin after I found the newspaper story, but it wasn't what got me going. I'm not sure what did start me off—perhaps a sense of wanting to complete Ben's story—but I decided I ought to try to find Ben's grave. I knew he'd been buried in the city cemetery, but since the office was closed, I also knew I might have to walk through the whole cemetery. However, I'd been lucky so far that day, and my luck might just continue. It did. Before I had gone three rows I found the Deane family plot. In the forward right-hand corner, overgrown and badly canted, was a low headstone: BENJAMIN F. DEANE / 1854–1924. Next to it was another: LIZZIE / wife of B. F. Deane. The grass had grown high around them, and the brown benevolent lichens were doing their work, I noticed. Assuming I could have spoken at all, there didn't seem to be much to say. But I think I found what I was looking for. I took a couple of pictures and headed for home.

LIST OF VERSIONS

JS   Original printed slip, as copied from the notebook of Bert Thorne, Jemseg, N.B. 25 sts.

FH   Printed copy prepared by the *Family Herald* and mailed out to people requesting it. A smoothed-out version of NS.1, 25 sts.

NH.1   Cliburn S. Locke, ca. 90, Berlin, N.H., Sept. 9, 1965; NA Ives tape 65.14, sung, 18 sts. Bought a copy from Joe Scott in a lumbercamp up Cupsuptic about 1899. In Aug., 1964, Locke had sent me a typed copy of nineteen stanzas.

NH.2   Fred Lafferty, 80, Gorham, N.H., Sept. 11, 1965; NA Ives tape 65.16, recited, 14 sts. Knew it was by Joe Scott. *"I read it on a barbershop door one day in Berlin. . . . I went by and this song was posted on the door. I was on the police force and I read it over, and the more I thought of it the more I'd like to learn it. So I took and read it a couple of times and then it all come to me."

NH.3   James W. Custeau, Lincoln, N.H., June 16, 1964; in a letter, manuscript, 5½ sts., fragment. Originally from Thetford Mines, P.Q., Custeau learned the song in Berlin from a man named Forrestal.

Me.1   John Brown, ca. 80, Mexico, Me., July 10, 1964; NA Ives tape 64.4, recited, 16 sts. Knew it was by Joe Scott. Learned it in Chipman, N.B., from his older brother, who had learned it in the lumberwoods in Maine. This was before Brown himself came to Maine in 1904. Used to recite it; never knew the tune.

Me.2   Omer McKenna, ca. 80, Rumford, Me., Sept. 28, 1965; NA Ives tape 65.19, sung and recited, 11½ sts. Knew it was by Joe Scott. Learned it on P.E.I. (Waterford) before he came to Maine in 1908 from his brother, who in turn had learned it in the lumberwoods around Rumford. About a year previously, he had dictated a version to his daughter, Mrs. Ralph Gallant, who typed it up— fifteen and a half stanzas, the last four of which were the final stanzas of "Howard Carey." When McKenna sang the song for me, he stopped at the point where he suddenly recognized that he had gotten it mixed up with the other ballad.

Me.3   Charles Sibley, ca. 75, Argyle, Me., Mar. 24, 1957; NA Ives tape 1.11 and ATL 2143.7, sung, 15 sts. (last two recited). Claimed it was by Benjamin Deane himself.

Me.4   Bessie Lary, Dover-Foxcroft, Me., Apr. 15, 1963; manuscript, 25 sts., at the head of which: "Copy by Mrs. Grace Smith, Tarrateen N.S., 1960."

Me.5   Edward MacDonald, Hampden, Me., Apr. 15, 1963; NA Ives tape 62.2, sung, 1 st., fragment. Had known more at one time. Used to hear it sung around his home in Harcourt, N.B., before 1915.

Me.6   William Bell, 75, Brewer, Me., Dec. 13, 1956; NA Ives tape 1.2 and ATL 2137.1, sung and recited, 19 sts. This is the version printed at the beginning of this chapter.

Me.7   Harry Cole, Springfield, Me., "sent in April 9, 1934"; Eckstorm Papers, typescript, 21 sts. Title: "Ben Deem."

Me.8   Ralph Thornton, 88, Topsfield, Me., Dec. 5, 1973; NA 717, sung, 17 sts. For text and tune, see Thornton, *Me and Fannie*, pp. 38–43. Ralph's tune has an ABCA phrase pattern, and the B and C phrases are close to the basic tune for "Howard Carey."

The Songs

NB.1 Harry Keenan, 72, Woodstock, N.B., May 11, 1962; manuscript, 18 sts., with following note at end: "Written by H. J. Keenan at Crabbet Camp on McLean Brook Dec 3rd 1941. Jack Garland was the man she was with when she was shot Garland worked under me on the drive 1926." Keenan sang two stanzas to give me the tune.

NB.2 Fred A. Campbell, 80, Arthurette, N.B., Aug. 13, 1963 (interviewed in Newcastle, N.B.); NA Ives tape 1.54 and ATL 3161.1, sung, 6½ sts., fragment. *"I dassn't go no further. I get it mixed up there. . . . I did know the whole of it one time . . . but it's gone from me and I can't appear to place it." Second version, 6 sts., recited for his daughter July 18, 1965; see NA 80.059–061.

NB.3 Phyllis Woodside, Milltown, N.B., July 5, 1964; manuscript, 15½ sts. Learned from the singing of her maternal grandmother, Mrs. Frank Martin. Scott had worked with Mr. Martin and taught him the songs.

NB.4 Fred Elkinton, St. Stephen, N.B., collected from him by Thomas MacLeod, Baring, Me., who gave it to me June 5, 1957; typescript, 14 sts.

NB.5 Michael J. Noonan, 77, St. Stephen, N.B., June 22, 1964; typescript, 12 sts., fragment. Had worked in northwestern Maine but did not know it was by Joe Scott, nor had he heard of Scott.

NB.6 Billy Price, ca. 75, McNamee (Priceville), N.B., Aug., 1960; collected by James Reginald Wilson, sung and recited, 20 sts. See Wilson, "Ballad Tunes of the Miramichi," pp. 14, 48–50, and Manny and Wilson, *Songs of Miramichi*, pp. 59–63. Did not know it was by Scott.

NB.7 Chester Price, Blackville, N.B., July 11, 1961; NA 1.103 and ATL 3110.2, sung, 18 sts. I was in Blackville talking to Everett Price and his cousin Billy when Chester, who was hitchhiking to Fredericton to the dentist, stopped in, saw my tape recorder, and asked if he could sing a song. After he sang it he left. Did not know it was by Scott. For his tune, see p. 261.

NB.8 Wilmot MacDonald, Glenwood, N.B., June 11, 1957; NA Ives tape 1.24 and ATL 2151.5, sung, 15 sts., recorded at the home of Louise Manny (for a description of this session, see Creighton and Ives, *Eight Folktales from Miramichi as told by Wilmot MacDonald*, pp. 5–6. Second singing: NA Ives tape 1.130 and ATL 3137.1, sung, 15 sts., to his "new" tune; recorded at his home in Glenwood, N.B., July 10, 1963. See pp. 259–260.

NS.1 "A reader," Kennetcook, N.S., Aug. 23, 1951; sent to the *Family Herald*, manuscript, 25 sts., with this note: "W.E.I. of New

Brunswick asked for the song Benjamin Dean. I hope this is the one asked for." See FH above.

NS.2   Mrs. Wentworth Boutilier, Indian Point (Lunenburg Co.), N.S., July, 1951; collected by Helen Creighton, NMC CR–68–622, and published in her *Maritime Folk Songs*, pp. 189–191; 25 sts. On the tape Mrs. Boutilier sings only the first eleven and a half stanzas.

NS.3   Jack Turple, Upper Kennetcook, N.S.; collected by Helen Creighton, 22 sts. I have not seen this version. See notes in Creighton, *Maritime Folk Songs*, p. 191.

NS.4   Dan Cleveland, East River, N.S.; collected by Helen Creighton, manuscript, 17 sts. I have not seen this version. See Creighton, *Maritime Folk Songs*, p. 191.

NS.5   James Curtis (b. 1898), Cape North (Bay St. Lawrence), Cape Breton Island, N.S., 1975; collected by Denis Ryan, MUNFLA 76–345, sung and manuscript, 22 sts. Learned from his uncle Tom Brown, who had worked with Scott in the Maine woods.

PI.1   Grattan McHugh, 60, Tignish, P.E.I., Aug. 25, 1965; NA Ives tape 65.4, sung, 18 sts., with some omissions. Did not know it was by Joe Scott. Learned it locally from Bert Provost when he was about sixteen.

PI.2   Angus Enman, 78, Spring Hill, P.E.I., Aug. 19, 1958; NA Ives tape 1.38 and ATL 2164.3, sung, 18 sts. Knew it was by Joe Scott. For his version see Ives, *Twenty-one Folksongs from Prince Edward Island*, pp. 55–59, 78–79.

NY   Monie Tedford, Waddington, N.Y., Feb. 18, 1967; in a letter, typescript, 15 sts. "I heard it sung and discussed many times in 1913–14 and 15 while in the lumber camps near the Pittston Farm where the North and South Branches of the Penobscot River meet and form the West Branch." Had heard it was by Larry Gorman.

NOTES

1. For more on Berlin at the turn of the century, see chapter 2.
2. G. Malcolm Laws, Jr., *Native American Balladry*, esp. sections E and F, pp. 175–210, and *American Balladry from British Broadsides*, section L, pp. 164–178.
3. William M. Doerflinger, *Shantymen and Shantyboys*, p. 136.
4. For "Peter Emberly," see any of the references in Laws, *Native American Balladry*, C–27, and esp. Louise Manny and James Reginald Wilson, *Songs of Miramichi*, pp. 160–163.
5. Doerflinger, *Shantymen and Shantyboys*, p. 136.

The Songs

6. For typical examples, see such ballads as "The Drawing of the Day" (Laws P–16), "The Iron Door" (Laws M–15), "The Tan-Yard Side" (Laws M–28), "The Gallant Brigantine" (Laws D–25). See also "The Irish Girl" in Phillips Barry, *The Maine Woods Songster*, p. 22. For a Newfoundland songwriter's adaptation of the formulas, see Elizabeth Bristol Greenleaf and Grace Yarrow Mansfield, *Ballads and Sea Songs from Newfoundland*, p. 275, "The Spanish Captain."

7. See, e.g., "The Wexford Lass" (Laws P–35) and "Fair Fanny Moore" (Laws O–38). In neither ballad can the girl's statement that she is not "fit" or "prepared" to die be taken as evidence of real wrongdoing on her part.

8. James Wilson collected a twenty-stanza version from Billy Price of McNamee, N.B. (NB.6). Helen Creighton reports that "Jack Turple, Upper Kennetcook [*Nova Scotia*], has 22 verses." The Nova Scotia version included in her *Maritime Folk Songs*, pp. 189–191, contains all twenty-five stanzas, but on the original tape I can find only that the singer sang the first twelve.

9. NH.1, Me.3, Me.5, Me.6, NB.1, NB.2, NB.8a, NS.2, PI.1, PI.2. For other analogues, see Norman Cazden, *The Abelard Folk Song Book*, pp. ii, 46–47, and Manny and Wilson, *Songs of Miramichi*, p. 108 (and references).

10. See Manny and Wilson, *Songs of Miramichi*, pp. 272–273.

11. For another way, see Edward D. Ives, *Lawrence Doyle*, pp. 64–66.

12. For Billy Price's singing see Manny and Wilson, *Songs of Miramichi*, pp. 59–63, where can also be found some excellent notes on tune analogues.

13. Edward D. Ives, " 'Ben Deane' and Joe Scott: A Ballad and Its Probable Author."

14

"Wreck on the Grand Trunk Railway": The Ballad as Journalism

"It's for you," my wife said, coming in from the kitchen. I looked inquiringly at her as I got up off the couch, but she just shrugged. "Some woman," she said, "asking for Professor Ives."

I was teaching summer school at the time, and I made a bet with myself it was one of my flock, a middle-aged schoolteacher who normally got flummoxed a few days before an exam and would call or come into the office to make sure I understood just how hard all this was for her—all feathered out over nothing, since she always did pretty well. "Hello," I said in my nicest bedside manner.

"Is this the Professor Ives who's writing the book about Joe Scott?"

"That's right," I said. I'd lost my bet, though. That wasn't Mrs. Weatherbee or whatever her name was. Not by a long chalk.

"Well," the voice went on pleasantly, "my father was Jack McGinley from Johnville, New Brunswick, and he and Joe were great friends. They worked in the woods together, and Joe used to come home with him sometimes."

"Do you remember Joe yourself?" I asked.

"No," she said, "but those songs of his were in the family. I've just been visiting my brothers down in Boston, and we've been trying to put some of them together. It's been a long time, but we thought it might be some help to you. Do you have 'The Grand Trunk Wreck'?"

"All I've got is two lines of it," I said.

> "Two tramps was riding on the train
> That never will tramp again.

Or something like that. Do you know the whole of it?"

267

"Well, not the whole of it," she said. "That was a long one. But my brother Bert remembered quite a bit, and I added a few lines, too. Now, I'll tell you what," she went on. "I'm coming to Bangor tomorrow on the four o'clock bus, the bus that gets in at four. I'm meeting my sister there and we're driving up to Johnville for the annual picnic. You meet me at the station, and I'll give you the words I've got to the song and maybe some others. O.K.?"

I agreed, and we hung up. Only then did it occur to me that I didn't even know her name.

It didn't matter. Two people with a Joe Scott song in mind must be distinctive, because we recognized each other immediately. Her name was Alice Flynn, and I offered to buy her and her sister a drink (which they declined) or a cup of coffee (which they accepted). She gave me a small sheaf of papers with the words to some songs, and said it was too bad she couldn't write music. When I said I had a tape recorder out in the car and why didn't she just come on out and sing them over, they both laughed, but she agreed to do it.

It had been a strange venture from the start, and it was made no less strange by the coincidence that Mrs. Coffey, the sister, had parked right next to my car out in the lot behind the Bangor House. I set the recorder up on the hood of her car, and Mrs. Flynn went over the tunes. Then we shook hands all around, and the two ladies drove off to Johnville. As they turned the corner, Mrs. Flynn looked back, laughed and waved good-bye. I waved back. Of such is the kingdom of folklore.

Here is the tune she sang to "The Grand Trunk Wreck," and the words as she and her brothers had written them out (the bracketed lines in stanzas 7 and 9 Mrs. Flynn remembered and sent me some weeks later):

THE GRAND TRUNK WRECK

1. You bold sons of free-dom, Your at-ten-tion I com-mand, And you I will not long de-tain; Of what I'm going to write, It

"Wreck on the Grand Trunk Railway"

hap-pened in this state, Here in this Pine Tree State of Maine.

[1]   You bold sons of freedom,
Your attention I command,
And you I will not long detain;
Of what I'm going to write,
It happened in this state,
Here in this Pine Tree State of Maine.

[2]   On the 18th of February, 1892,
In the northern part of this state,
An accident occurred
Which perhaps you all have heard,
So sad and so shocking to relate.

[3]   'Twas early in the morning,
The hour being one,
To the day and the date I have referred,
Between Bethel Station
And the station of Locke's Mills
Where this dreadful accident occurred.

[4]   Two double-headed freight trains
Were running east and west,
They were running at full speed when they meet,
With a clash and a clang
That made the echoes ring
And the woodlands and the distant hills repeat.

[5]   Some explosives in the wreck
It's loudly they do crack
And for hours continue to burn,
And the booming from afar
Sounds like a battle's roar
That peals out among the distant gloom.

"Some verses lost here. We can't remember the names of the rest of the crew."

[6]   . . . . was the engineer
And others whose names I cannot name,
And C. W. Oliver,
A brakeman so I hear
Were the victims that this monster Death did claim.

[7]   [The flames they soared so high
They nearly reached the sky,
And lighted up the lofty mountain tops.]
And from its fiery bed
Shoots the blue flame from the red
That marks the spot where their dead bodies lie.

[8]   Two tramps were on the train
That will never tramp again,
They were riding on the cars so merrily.
But they now speed on a train
That's not run by mortal man
But speeds along for all eternity.

[9]   [The folks from far and near
They all gathered there,]
Some came a willing hand to lend.
Some more the sight to see
And some to bear away
The remains of a loved one or a friend.

[10]   Now my story has been told,
The ashes they grow cold,
The wreckage is removed from the rails;
And the people all depart,
Each with a broken heart,
And each to tell a sad and mournful tale.

"Last verse, but we don't know all of it—"

[11]   We all drink more or less
From life's bitter flowing glass
For it is a beverage prepared for all.

There is no doubt that Joe Scott was the author of this song. The McGinley clan was all agreed on that, for one thing, and Roy Lohnes had told me about it, too. When J. A. Polley wrote Robert W. Gordon about "Guy Reed," he added that "Scott wrote a song in 1903 called the Grand Trunk wreck it was about a freight train wreck between So Paris and Bethel Me several tramps were killed in the wreck."[1] But the clincher came when Daisy Severy found and let me have her copy of Joe's original printed slip, which I reproduce here:

WRECK ON THE GRAND TRUNK RAILWAY.

[1]   Ye brave sons of freedom
Your attention I would call,
   And you I will not long detain;
For of what I am going to write
It happened in this State,
   Here in the Pine Tree State of Maine.

[2]   On the eighteenth of January,
Early Friday morn,
   In the northern part of this State
An accident occurred,
That perhaps you have all heard,
   So sad and so shocking to relate.

[3]   It was on the Grand Trunk Railway,
The hour being one
   On the day and date that I have referred;
Between Bethel station
And the station of Lockes Mills,
   That this dreadful accident occurred.

[4]   Two double-header freight trains
Running east and west,
   Were running at full speed when they met
With a crash and a clang,
That makes the echo ring
   In the woodlands that the distant hills [*repeat*].

[5]   The very earth did shake,
As if by an earthquake,
   That dreadful sound the very air it thrills
That echoes and re-echoes
Through the lofty mountain tops,
   Then dies away among the distant hills.

[6]   Those heavy engines with a shriek,
Amid a sheet of flame
   Like lightning they upward quickly bound,
And to one another cling
Like frightened living things,
   Then with a dreadful crash fall to the ground.

[7]   Those freight cars are jammed together
In a frightful mass,
    Catch fire e'er the dawn of day,
And the flames reach up so high
That they seem to reach the sky
    That disperses the gloom far away.

[8]   Some explosives in the wreck
It's loudly do they crack,
    And for hours continue to boom,
And their booming from afar
Sounds like a battle roar
    That is peeling out upon the morning's gloom.

[9]   The grey dawn appears,
And the daylight draweth near,
    And soon appears the golden orb of day,
That shines upon a scene
That some will e'er retain
    In memory till they pass away.

[10]   Those burning ruins doth conceal
Some people who were killed,
    Or who by the cruel flames did die,
And from their fiery bed
Shoots a blue flame in the red,
    That marks the spot where those dead bodies lie.

[11]   Fathers' cheeks grew pale;
While children weep and wail,
    Wives and mothers wring their hands and cry;
They sadly mourn for those
That so silent do repose,
    So peacefully in death's embrace do lie.

[12]   They came from far and near
By thousands so I hear,
    Some came their willing aid to lend,
And some the sight to see,
And some to bear away
    The remains of a loved one or friend.

[13]   And now I will relate
The names of those whom fate
    Had destined that death should overthrow,

The e'er the morning sun
In the east had rose again,
   To home and friends on earth had bid adieu.

[14]   Peter Thompson, an engineer
Upon the west bound train,
   Clarence Tibbetts, a fireman of same,
And C. W. Oliver,
A brakeman so I hear,
   Are the victims that monster Death did claim.

[15]   Two tramps were on the train
Who will never tramp again,
   They were riding on the trucks so merrily,
But now they speed on a train
That's not run by mortal man,
   That rolls along through all eternity.

[16]   The sun its tale has told,
Those embers they grow cold,
   The wreckage is removed from the rail;
The people then depart,
Each with an aching heart,
   And each tell a sad and mournful tale.

[17]   And now in behalf
Of those who are bereft,
   Of loved ones so noble, brave and true,
Weep not for those that's dead,
Rather those who live instead,
   For death is rest and life on earth is woe.

[18]   This world is full of woe,
No matter where you go,
   It visits the rich, the great and small;
And we all drink more or less
From its flowing bitter glass,
   For it is a beverage prepared for all.

                              BY JOE SCOTT.
Price 10 cts.

   The wreck itself was sensational. There had been a number of
collisions along this division of the Grand Trunk over the preceding
weeks, "and some of them," the reporter for the *Bethel News* said,

"were not altogether tame affairs." But the one that occurred at one o'clock in the morning on Friday, January 18, 1901, made them all seem piffling. Eastbound was the fourth section of regular freight number 92, heavy laden and powered by two locomotives. It had just passed through Bethel and was going at full throttle (about thirty miles an hour) to gain momentum for the upgrade west of Walker's Mills. Westbound was regular freight number 85, another double-header, traveling flat out at about the same speed, having just come down the Walker's Mills grade. They met about two miles east of Bethel, "and in an instant," said the *Bethel News*, "four engines and thirteen loaded cars lay in one frightful mass, extending a distance of not more than ten rods along the track, but piled some forty feet high" (see fig. 8).[2] The *Bangor Daily Commercial* had a story on it that very evening. "One of the trains," it said, "had a large quantity of explosives on board and as the cars took fire just after the collision there were numerous explosions during the early morning and forenoon and nothing could be done to clear away the wreckage. At nine o'clock the cars were still burning and explosives were scattering the embers in all directions."

The wrecking crew set to work under fantastic difficulties, and the curious arrived with their Kodaks. "People flocked from all sections to view the scene," said the *Bethel News*, "all of whom looked upon a sight that they will always remember. All who had cameras took them along but smoke from the consuming mass made it difficult to get a good view." The wrecking crew persevered, but it took them seventeen perilous hours to clear the right of way. "It was not until 6 p.m.," said the *Bethel News*, "that a tunnel of sufficient width was cut through the mass to allow trains to pass, and when the afternoon express passed through at that hour, the burning wreck towered up for several feet on either side." Nothing is said about it, but I hazard the passengers on the express saw something they wouldn't forget, with or without cameras.

Miraculously, all of the crew of eastbound 92 leaped to safety in time, and so did the crew of the head engine on westbound 85, but the men on the rear engine didn't make it. Engineer Peter Thompson was taken from the wreck alive but died a few minutes later. Nothing was ever found of fireman Clarence Tibbetts and brakeman W. C. Oliver except a few charred bones. The Bangor *Commercial* reported "two unknown tramps" as victims, and

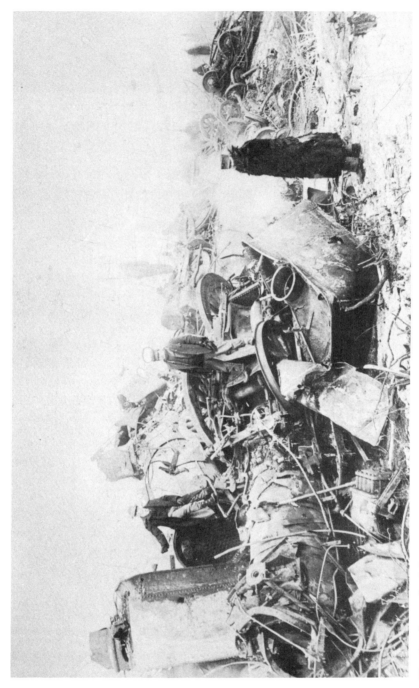

Fig. 8. Aftermath of the Grand Trunk wreck of January 18, 1901. (Courtesy of Guy Swan, Bryant Pond, Maine. NA photo 362.)

275

amplified the report the next day: "The two supposed victims who were seen a few minutes before the accident riding on a bumper between two loaded cars were tramps. The cars were smashed to kindling wood and afterwards destroyed by fire, and it is supposed the tramps met a fate similar to that of Oliver and Tibbetts."[3] Neither the *Bethel News* nor the railroad commissioners' report[4] acknowledges their existence or, more properly, its sudden termination.

Was Joe Scott one of those who flocked to view the wreck? He could have been, but I doubt that he would have made a twenty-mile trip in midwinter to gather material for his ballad. There is nothing in it he couldn't have gotten from newspaper accounts or from talking to someone who had been there. It is much more likely that what he did was to make up his ballad and then hustle over to the scene of the accident to sell it. How quickly he could make up a ballad I don't know, but I doubt that he made it over by the next day.

Disaster balladry was very much a tradition in America, and while railroad disaster songs never developed the rather clear set of patterns, themes, and clichés we find in ballads on sea disasters, such patterns did exist. There was the tendency, for example, to write about passenger train wrecks in which many people lost their lives, and it was the habit to focus on some individual act of heroism or on one pathetic scene, as in "The Hartford Wreck":

> There is one we ne'er forget
> It was little Joe McGret
> Who was with his father on that fatal train
> And though wounded by the fall
> When he heard his father's call
> To free him from the wreck he tried in vain.
>
> "It's no use, my boy," said he,
> "There's no help for you or me."
> Just then, the flames around them curled
> Little Joe began to cry
> When his father said "goodbye
> We meet again but in another world."[5]

Several ballads made a hero of the engineer who stayed with his engine to the end, as in the well-known "Casey Jones" (Laws G–1) or

"The Wreck of Old 97" (Laws G–2), or they build sympathy for the engineer of "old Number Nine" (Laws G–26), who was going to be married the next day and had just bid his sweetheart good-bye. That is consistent with Malcom Laws's statement that "the ballad with a single victim or hero has a much better chance of popularity than one in which many are killed. Mass tragedies," he continues, "can be looked upon with some detachment, but the death of an individual whose character has been delineated is far more moving and meaningful."[6] It can also help explain the failure of "Wreck on the Grand Trunk Railway" to become firmly established in northeastern oral tradition. No matter how much Joe insists on the horror with such phrases as "dreadful accident," "the very earth did shake," "sheet of flame," and "frightful mass," he never really involves us in it. The song remains a piece of sensational journalism and never rises above that.

The parallel of "The Miramichi Fire" immediately comes to mind. Although that ballad, too, was sensational journalism and certainly does not concentrate on a single figure, it won a place for itself in northeastern tradition. Yet it is an odd kind of place, representing what I have called elsewhere "an oral tradition somewhat awed by a subliterary one."[7] As Louise Manny said, "Probably no Miramichi song was written down as often when it was first composed, and probably none has appeared in print as many times."[8] Newspapers printed and reprinted the song, and most people who sang traditional songs had a clipping or even a handwritten copy around somewhere, but very few people could sing more than a few stanzas from memory. It was a song well known *about* but not well *known,* and in a lesser way that describes very well the position "Wreck on the Grand Trunk Railway" held. People remembered there was such a song, some might recall a line or two, but only the McGinley clan was able to put together what amounted to a fragmentary version. Even the one printed slip survived only by chance.

Still, it cannot be denied that while their traditions are very similar in quality, "The Miramichi Fire" persisted while "Wreck on the Grand Trunk Railway" did not. That is understandable. "The Miramichi Fire" told of an episode that was a traumatic experience for a whole countryside. Thousands of square miles of timber went up, hundreds of homes were burned, and about two hundred people lost their lives. Practically everyone who lives in Miramichi and most of those who come from there but now live elsewhere have that great fire as part of their family tradition. On the other hand, the train wreck Joe wrote about was, for all its being sensational, an isolated incident. A dull pedestrian ballad on the Miramichi fire— even one a lot duller and more pedestrian than the one we have— might have survived simply because it was about what it was about. A ballad on the Grand Trunk wreck would have had to survive on its own intrinsic merits, not because it told of a memorable event, but because it was a memorable ballad. Obviously, Joe Scott's opus did not pass the test.

But we are on the verge of a usual mistake. I doubt that Joe was creating for posterity in "Wreck on the Grand Trunk Railway" any more than he was with his other ballads, and very possibly he had posterity in mind a whole lot less. The ballad is such a piece of hackwork I cannot believe he didn't put it together as fast as possible to sell while the news and the wreckage were still hot. In this respect it reminds me very much of "Wilfred White and John Murphy," a ballad he would compose that coming fall (see chap. 16). It tells its story in journalistic form, summarizing and then going into detail; it names the names; and it ends with a nod in the direction of piety or a moral. It is not hard to imagine Joe Scott arriving at the scene of the accident while the wreckage was still being cleared away and the ink had hardly soaked into his paper; we can be sure that he was at least into the lumbercamps with his song hard on the heels of the news. It may have sold very well, in which case it would have been a great success from Joe's point of view. But it never stood a chance in oral tradition.

When Mrs. Flynn first showed me the manuscript copy she had with her that August afternoon in Bangor, my immediate reaction as I looked at that first stanza was "Fuller and Warren." That's not particularly to my credit, since I've collected this love-murder ballad a couple of times,[9] and the parallel is obvious. Here is "Fuller and Warren":

> Ye sons of Columbia,
> your attention I do crave
> While a sorrowful ditty I will tell
> Which happened of late
> in the Indiana state
> Of a hero that none could excel.

And "Wreck on the Grand Trunk Railway":

> You bold sons of freedom
> Your attention I command,
> And you I will not long detain;
> Of what I'm going to write,
> It happened in this state,
> Here in the pine tree state of Maine.

Therefore I was not at all surprised to find that Mrs. Flynn's tune was a set of the same air that Mrs. Lidelle Robbins of Hudson, Maine, used when she sang a fragment of "Fuller and Warren" for me back in 1957. On the other hand, I was very surprised when I began searching the literature and found that none of the other versions of "Fuller and Warren" had this same tune, though some resembled it in a phrase or so. Yet there need be no question that Joe was using "Fuller and Warren" in making his song on the Grand Trunk wreck, and the version he knew almost certainly had this tune.

The really fascinating question is, Why did Joe Scott use this unlikely parallel, a ballad about a man who was hanged for murdering the cad who stole his truelove's affections, as the model for his song on the Grand Trunk wreck? The safest thing would be to assume it was mere chance and therefore does not need an explanation; but if we are willing simply to admit that "mere chance" in such matters could well be aided by, if not a function of, circumstances, there is an interesting possibility. We should at least take a look.

To begin with, the relationship between the two ballads is not close. In constructing his ballad Joe used the "Fuller and Warren" tune and its stanza form, and emphasized the parallel by using similar phrasing in the first stanza. That's about all, though; from there on, the two songs bear no relationship to each other. It doesn't look like a parallel one would have sought out or considered very carefully. My hunch is that at the time of the Grand Trunk wreck, "Fuller and Warren" was somewhere near the front of Joe's mind. It was right there handy, and he was in a hurry.

Why would "Fuller and Warren" have been on his mind? Remember that the wreck occurred on January 18, 1901, and on January 10 Joe had had a deputy sheriff serve papers on Emma for divorce on grounds of adultery, extreme cruelty, and abusive treatment. In other words, at the time of the accident, marriage and its problems were much on his mind. What would be more natural than for Joe, a man with a head full of songs anyway, to be thinking of the one song that has more to say about marriage than any other ballad in American tradition:

> Of all the ancient history
> that I can understand,
> Which we're bound by the scripture to believe,
> Bad women are essentially
> the downfall of man,
> As Adam was beguiled by Eve.
>
> So, young men, beware,
> be cautious and be wise
> Of such women when you're courting for wives.
> Look in Genesis, and Judges,
> and in Samuel, Kings, and Job,
> And the truth of the doctrine you'll find.
>
> For marriage is a lottery
> and few gain the prize
> That's both pleasing to the heart and to the eye.
> So those who never marry
> may well be called wise.
> So, gentlemen, excuse me; goodbye.

"Fuller and Warren," then, was not so much appropriate to the subject at hand as it was to the poet's state of mind at the moment; but something must have triggered his decision to use it. Having speculated this far, I'll venture a step further and suggest that the "happened in this state" phrase gave Joe his start, but from there he was on his own. The only other parallel is the rather heavy-handed moralizing to be found at the end of both songs. It is perfectly traditional, of course; but while vastations on womankind are moderately apropos in the case of "Fuller and Warren," the same cannot be said about Joe's gloomy philosophizing:

> This world is full of woe,
> No matter where you go,
>   It visits the rich, the great and small;
> And we all drink more or less
> From its flowing bitter glass,
>   For it is a beverage prepared for all.

"Wreck on the Grand Trunk Railway"

Not that there is anything particularly cheerful about a train wreck in which five men died, but the woe is overdone. It makes better sense to see it in the context of Joe's unhappy life at the time rather than in the context of the song.

Finally, it is worth pointing out that a passage characterizing women as evil and marriage as a lottery is replaced by one that speaks of life as full of woe and a bitter glass that all must drink. If that is a coincidence, it is at least a coincidence with Freudian overtones. Bad art may be good biography.

LIST OF VERSIONS

JS   Original printed slip, obtained from Daisy Severy, 83, Gray, Me., July 21, 1966. 18 sts.

NB   Alice Flynn, Allegany, N.Y., as put together by her and her brothers remembering how their father, Jack McGinley, of Johnville, N.B., used to sing it. Given to me, Bangor, Me., Aug. 1, 1964; manuscript, 10½ sts. For tune see NA Ives tape 64.7.

NOTES

1. Polley to Gordon, Mar. 2, 1925, Gordon Manuscripts 928.
2. *Bethel News*, Jan. 23, 1901.
3. *Bangor Daily Commercial*, Jan. 19, 1901.
4. For a full report, see *Forty-third Annual Report of the Railroad Commissioners of the State of Maine, 1901*, pp. 186–191.
5. Helen Hartness Flanders et al., *The New Green Mountain Songster*, pp. 157–158. Laws listed this ballad as of "doubtful currency in tradition" (dG–36), but it has since been collected in Vermont by Margaret MacArthur, and I have collected a version of it here in Maine (NA Ives tape 1.12 and ATL 2143.10). For other ballads on train wrecks, see Laws G–1, 2, 3, 4, 5, 26, 30, and dG–36, 37, 38, 41, 51. For an excellent consideration of the whole railroad tradition, see Norm Cohen's article " 'Casey Jones': At the Crossroads of Two Ballad Traditions" and his forthcoming book on the railroad in American folksong (Urbana: University of Illinois Press).
6. G. Malcolm Laws, Jr., *Native American Balladry*, p. 24.
7. Edward D. Ives, *Twenty-one Folksongs from Prince Edward Island*, p. 33.
8. Louise Manny and James Reginald Wilson, *Songs of Miramichi*, p. 148.
9. Mrs. Lidelle W. Robbins, Hudson, Me., Feb. 28, 1957, NA Ives tape 1.6 and ATL 2140.7); James Cameron, Bloomfield Ridge, N.B., July 21, 1961, NA Ives tape 1.111 and ATL 3118.5. This ballad is listed by Laws as F–16. The version quoted here is from H. M. Belden, *Ballads and Songs Collected by the Missouri Folk-Lore Society*, pp. 305–306; I have rearranged the lines to make the comparison with Joe's song more obvious.

15

"The Norway Bum": A Smile and a Tear

"This isn't the most-approved field work method," I said. "I come booming into town, see a few people who have written me, follow up some leads they give me, and then go booming off home again after a few days. Actually, it's more of a raid than a systematic collecting method, but when you're looking for something as specific as I am, it works pretty well, and besides," I added in self-defense, "compared to some collector-raiders I know, I'm just thorough as hell. How much further out this road does this guy live now?"

"That's his place up there on the left," Reggie said, pointing to a small, quite new house. We pulled into the drive.

Reggie Porter had been born here in Tignish, Prince Edward Island, but he was now going to college in Montreal, where he had become very interested in folklore. He had written me from Montreal earlier in the year (1965) about a folklife project he was interested in setting up in Tignish, and at the end of my answering letter I had said I would be up in Tignish toward the end of the summer and why not get together then. He was agreeable, adding that he knew several people I ought to see. Now we were on our way to see one of them: Frank Buote (pronounced "Bee-YOT").

Buote was home, a vigorous dark-haired man of about sixty, but he was getting ready to move to Montreal, and the house was what one might expect under the circumstances, a confusion of trunks and packing cases. We all sat down on a selection of upturned crates, and Reggie told Frank what I was after. "And one of the songs he's interested in," he concluded, "is 'The Norway Bum,' and I remembered hearing you sing it once or twice, so here we are."

282

"Yes," said Frank, "I used to sing that one, all right, but I don't know, it's been so long now."

"Well," I asked, "could I get you to try it anyhow?"

He thought for a minute. "Sure," he said. "Why not? I guess I still know it."

I set up the tape recorder, and he started in. Reggie had said Frank had a strong voice, and he was right. It completely filled that little house. He went along in grand style until he came to the fifth stanza, where he faltered and then quit. "Nope," he said, disgustedly, "I can't think of it. That's all I know of it." We talked for a few minutes and had a cup of coffee. Frank was obviously disappointed with himself. "But wait," he said. "If you want to get that song, I'll tell you who *does* know it, and that's Emile Arsenault."

I looked over at Reggie. "Do you think we could get *him* to sing it for me?" I asked.

Reggie and Frank looked at each other consideringly. "Hard to say," said Reggie, "but he just might at that. I think it's worth a try anyhow, so let's go. Want to come, Frank?"

Frank did, and we headed off in my car.

Following Reggie's directions, we soon arrived at a big weathered farmhouse set well back from the road out in a district of Tignish called Ascension. "There's his sister coming now," Frank said, as a generous gray-haired woman of about sixty came to the kitchen door. "Hello, Clotilda." They talked for a few minutes, and then Frank asked for Emile and explained our mission.

She thought for a minute. "He's lying down," she said. "Went into his room about an hour ago. I don't know what he'd say. And you know he's almost seventy now and he hasn't been too smart these last few days, kind of tired all the time." There was a long pause in which she seemed to be weighing the fact that her brother was asleep against the fact that it was too bad to turn away callers. "Well," she said at last, "it won't hurt to ask. Come on in, and I'll get him up."

We all went into the kitchen, a big dark room with the feel of afternoon about it. Clotilda went through a door behind the stove, and we could hear her talking with her brother. In a few minutes she came out, smiling dubiously, and sat down by the stove. Then Emile came in.

He was a short man, a little stooped, his hair and mustache still brown, and everything about him from his shuffling, slippered walk to his tousled hair showed a man who had just come out of a deep sleep. He grunted hello to Frank, looked blankly at me, then nodded at Reggie. He sat down near the window on the far side of the room.

Frank mentioned about old songs and asked specifically about "The Norway Bum." Emile took no notice. He hadn't been feeling well, he said; couldn't sleep nights and then tired all day. Frank commiserated, and asked again about songs. Emile shook his head. "No," he said gruffly, looking at me and then at the floor, "damn it all, I'm not singing no songs today. My singing days are over and that's that, so you might just as well forget it! I'm not singing no songs for anyone!"

It sounded pretty final to me. I didn't see much hope in the uncomfortable silence that followed, and the only thing to do seemed to be to make an awkward good-bye and be on our way. I was just about to do that (I hardly blamed Emile his annoyance, anyhow), when Reggie started talking to him in French. He explained about the old songs and how not many people remembered them anymore and that was too bad. Emile nodded. This man (meaning me), Reggie continued, was a professor from Maine and he wanted to preserve these songs and make a record of them with his machine so they would not be forgotten. Emile nodded again, his whole aspect softening a little. Frank chimed in too, telling about how he'd forgotten the words to "The Norway Bum" but remembered that he (Emile) knew it, so here we were. Emile continued nodding thoughtfully, looking around at us. "Oué," he said. Then it was quiet again.

"I used to be a pretty good singer," he said after a bit. "I knew a hell of a lot of songs." Then he looked at me. "What was that song you wanted?" he said.

" 'The Norway Bum,' " I said.

"Well," said Emile, "you better go get your machine."

I went out to the car and brought in the big Roberts I had. We set it up, I made my usual announcement on the tape, and told Emile to go ahead.

He cleared his throat. *"It's a hard song to sing," he said. "I have no wind to—jumping old Judas! Well—." He cleared his throat again and sang.

284

"The Norway Bum"

THE NORWAY BUM

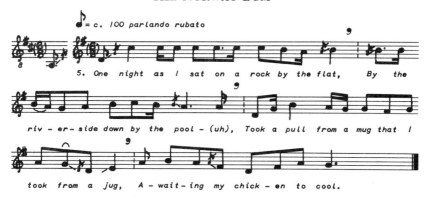

♪ = c. 100 parlando rubato

5. One night as I sat on a rock by the flat, By the

riv - er-side down by the pool - (uh), Took a pull from a mug that I

took from a jug, A - wait-ing my chick - en to cool.

[1]   You may think by my dress I would rob a bird's nest
      Or do anything that is bad;
      I'm sure if you do you will not make a miss,
      You will hit the nail fair on the head.

[2]   You may think by my togs they are all I have got,
      If you do you will sure make a miss;
      In this dirty old sack I just threw from my back,
      I've another far nicer than this.

[3]   Although I'm a rake and a dirty old fake,
      I'm used to the world and its ways;
      Although I'm a bum and addicted to rum,
      I'm a man that has seen better days.

Emile paused for a minute. *"Now what do I say next?" he said.
Then he remembered:

[4]   Give me one glass of rye, for I am so dry,
      'Twould help a poor fellow along;
      I will dance you a reel, an old-fashioned reel,
      I'll sing you an old-fashioned song.

[5]   One night as I sat on a rock by the flat,
      By the riverside down by the pool,
      Took a pull from a mug that I took from a jug,
      Awaiting my chicken to cool.

[6]   After eating my fill with a hearty good will
      And watching the sparks in their flight,

285

A vision rose before my blurrèd eyes
All in the dark shadows of night.

[7]   I saw my dear home by the ocean's white foam,
Way down by those valleys and hills;
The foresty wild that I roamed when a child,
Way down by the rippling rills.

[8]   The church bells they rang and the birds sweetly sang,
In the meadow and down in the dell;
I listened with joy as I did when a boy
To the chimes of the old village bells.

[9]   How I once was a lad to make mother's heart glad,
I was once what they called fair of face;
But I loved a fair lass far beneath my own class
To my father and mother's disgrace.

[10]   My father in his anger drove me from his door,
My mother in grief pined away;
Her cries of despair still ring in my ears,
They will ring on for many a day.

[11]   But my story's not told, nor it's not told for gold,
We were married and settled in life;
Three years passed away like a bright summer day,
How dearly I loved my young wife.

[12]   One night while away a patient to see,
My ears caught a terrible sound;
'Twas the firebell borne on the late evening breeze,
Old Norway was fast burning down.

[13]   I rushed to my home though the terrified town
To find my own buildings on fire;
I stood there aghast for there, there alas,
All peace and happiness expired.

[14]   I saw my dear wife in a window so high,
Who with accent so terrible and wild,
"Oh my God," she would cry, "Oh my God in the sky,
Save me and my dear little child."

[15]   But the flames did hold high between child, wife, and I,
Oh merciful God, what a sight!

With her child in her arms she fell back in the flames,
'Twas the last time I saw her that night.

[16] So it's now for my part with a sad broken heart
To drown sorrow I plunged into rum;
Now my days they are past, and my joys they are cast,
And now I am only a bum.

I was impressed. Emile's voice was no longer strong or sure, but it fit the song and the room very well. *"How in hell would you remember all that?" said Frank with admiration.

Emile seemed pleased. *"I learned that song forty years ago or more," he said. He couldn't remember who he learned it from, but he knew he didn't bring that one home from the woods. *"I learned that in this part of the country," he said.

"Would you like to hear that back?" I asked. He said he would, so we heard it all again. Later Emile sang a couple more songs. Then we stepped outside, I took a few pictures, and we shook hands goodbye. "I'm glad you came," Emile said to me. "Come again and maybe I'll remember some more." Clotilda was smiling broadly on all of us.

When I heard Emile's singing of "The Norway Bum" I thought it was the longest I had ever collected, but it wasn't. Jim Brown of South Branch, New Brunswick, had twice sung me his version, which was two stanzas longer (NB.4), and Gertrude Toothaker's version (Me.5) was at least as long, and so was the version Stanley MacDonald had sung at the Miramichi Folksong Festival in 1959 (NB.6). In addition, five of the manuscript versions I had were as long or longer, and, as it turns out, Joe Scott's original version was eighteen stanzas to Emile's sixteen. Emile's version is interesting for reasons other than its length, and we'll get back to it in due time; but first let's take a look at the ballad the way Joe conceived it.

What follows is taken from Joe's original slip, copies of which I have from both Daisy Severy and Bert Thorne. The slip is identical in every way with a version printed over Joe's name in the *Rumford Falls Times* for April 13, 1901, which probably means that Joe had his printing work done at the *Times* office and that he had this particular song printed up for sale on or before that date. Here it is, then, exactly as it was printed.

THE NORWAY BUM.

[1]   Don't think by my dress I would rob a hen's nest,
          Or do anything that is bad,
      If you think that I would I will tell you the truth,
          You would strike the nail fair on the head.

[2]   Don't think by these togs they are all that I have,
          If you think so you would make a miss,
      In that dirty sack I just took from my back
          Is another one far worse than this.

[3]   For a small glass of rye when I am so dry
          Just to help a poor fellow along,
      I would turn you a wheel, dance an old-fashioned reel,
          Or I'd sing you a bit of a song.

[4]   I know I'm a rake, a poor worthless fake,
          And I know, too, this world and its ways;
      Altho' I'm a bum and addicted to rum,
          I'm a man who has seen better days.

[5]   Last night as I sat on a rock by the flat,
          By my fireside down by a pool,
      Took a pull from a jug I had stole from a mug,
          Waiting for my chicken to cool.

[6]   After eating my fill with hearty good will,
          Sat watching the sparks in their flight,
      Before my bleared eyes a vision did rise
          From the gloomy dark shadows of night.

[7]   Oh I saw my old home by the ocean's white foam,
          Once more saw its valleys and hills,
      And the green forest wild where I played when a child
          'Neath its shades by the rippling rills.

[8]   Saw its meadows and flowers, saw its green shady bowers,
          Saw children at play on the lawn,
      And in play did hear those voices so dear
          Unto me in the days that are gone.

[9]   Oh I saw by the door the old folks once more,
          And around them the sunbeams did play,
      It was only a scene, oh a vision I mean
          That gradually faded away.

[10] But I'll tell you the rest of those I loved best,
    Perhaps you might pity my case,
  Fell in love with a lass beneath my own class,
    And did my fond parents disgrace.

[11] My father in anger turned me from his door,
    While my mother's tears they did pour,
  Her cry of despair still rings in my ear,
    Will ring on I fear for evermore.

[12] The same tale is told, love don't sell for gold,
    I married and settled in life;
  Three years passed away like a long summer day,
    How dearly I loved my fair wife.

[13] One night when away, a patient to see,
    My ears caught the dismal sound
  Of fire bells borne on the evening breeze,
    For Norway was fast burning down;

[14] As I pushed along through the terrified throng,
    I saw my own dwelling on fire,
  E'er I reached my door all joys I gave o'er,
    All love, hope and peace did expire.

[15] From a window on high, I heard my wife cry
    In accents so strangely and wild,
  "Oh God upon high, Oh God," she did cry,
    "Save me and my little child!"

[16] The flames as they whirl catch her clustering curls,
    Oh God, what a terrible sight!
  With her babe in her arms fell back in the flames
    Then I saw no more on that night.

[17] Next morning the sun rose o'er a sad scene,
    There were numbers with shelterless heads,
  Some who were there wrung their hands in despair,
    There were others lamenting the dead.

[18] I for my part, with sad broken heart,
    To drown sorrow plunged into rum,
  My die it is cast, all bright days are past,
    And now I'm only a bum.

                   BY JOE SCOTT.

I don't think there needs to be any question about Joe Scott's authorship of this piece. Not only do we have printed copies with his name on them; it is also very generally ascribed to him, especially by people who knew him. It may happen that someone will turn up evidence that it is a Tin Pan Alley production that he pirated or that simply accrued to him in the Northeast, but I doubt it. It's Joe's work, all right, but it differs from everything of his we have looked at, because so far as we can tell, it is fiction.

Norway, Maine, had two great fires, one in September of 1851, and another on May 9, 1894; neither of them occasioned any loss of life. Both were reported in town histories written by men who would in no way have let such a sensational item escape notice.[1] The 1894 fire is the one usually referred to as the "Great Fire." According to Charles Whitman, it "destroyed the C. B. Cummings & Sons box factory and paste shop plant, the Opera House, Congregational Church, about 80 dwelling houses and other structures"; but with the exception of "about 120 shade trees" there were no deaths. "Rev. B. S. Rideout while fighting fire, fell and dislocated his shoulder," according to the *Norway Advertiser Democrat*. "Elbridge Walker," the story continued, "fell from a ladder and was hurt but not dangerously. It was fortunate that there were no more serious accidents."[2] No mention of any mother and child being burned to death, let alone the wife and child of a local doctor. Neither does the story fit the career of any of the Norway medical men mentioned by either of the town's historians, nor have I ever come across anyone who could tell me that he knew of a character who could have been the original for the Norway Bum. Lucy Morse of Norway, who was around at the time of the fire and had known of Joe Scott and his song, simply spoke of "The Norway Bum" as "a made up song." She added (correctly) that "the fire was in the daytime, started about noon time at the Cummings mill."[3]

That should dispose of the "facts." Still, it would be a little presumptuous to speak of this ballad as "pure fiction" merely because we cannot find a clear relationship to some event of historical record. It may have been pure fiction, something Joe invented out of whole cloth, or it may have been a story he had been told about some local character, some woods tramp, some alcoholic drifter from camp to camp and town to town. They were as common in Maine as they were anywhere else; let such a figure become "established" to any extent in an area, and there would frequently be a story, or even a cluster of stories, explaining how he had once "seen better days" and how he "got this way." All that was needed in the present circumstance would have been one bum briefly seen and a friend at Joe's elbow (*"See that old rummy? You wouldn't believe he'd once been a doctor, now, would you? Well, he was. Drink's what did it, but hell, I guess he had reason enough. Seems he was . . ."*). Joe probably knew about the Norway fire; that gave him his title and his setting. From there on, it was "The Face on the Barroom Floor" and a hundred other similar works all over again. That's speculation, of course, but we are left with this choice: either Joe made the story up himself, in which case he followed a pretty standard pattern in nineteenth-century sentimental song; or he was working with a story someone had told him, in which case the story appealed to him because it followed that pattern. It comes to about the same thing; the pattern was what mattered.

"Hobo poesy is never concerned with love," says George Milburn in *The Hobo's Hornbook,* "and the sentimental tramp ballad, known to the barroom and the vaudeville stage, is not heard in the jungles."[4] His contempt is honed to a finer edge a little further along. "Many so-called bum songs," he says, "written for phonograph recording and vaudeville, have precisely the same relation to hobo balladry that 'Ole Man River' has to genuine Negro folk-songs."[5] Milburn's scorn is understandable; he was interested in the esoteric "occupational" songs of the hobo, and the "sentimental tramp ballad" was essentially exoteric, a nontramp's view of tramps for a nontramp audience. Yet such songs were very popular in the late nineteenth century, and even tramps were well acquainted with them and sang them, both straight and in parody—and they were splendidly open to parody because they were so stereotyped.

"Down in Lehigh Valley," which Milburn speaks of as "the logical grandparent of all sentimental hobo ballads," illustrates the type perfectly. It begins in the present as a confessional monologue:

> Let me sit down a minute, stranger.
> A stone got in my shoe—
> Now don't commence your cussin'.
> I ain't done nothing to you.
>
> Yes, I'm a tramp—what of it?
> Some says we ain't no good,
> But tramps has to live I reckon,
> Tho' folks don't think we should.

Then comes the flashback, the explanation of his present state of wretchedness. First in very general terms:

> Once I was young and handsome,
> Had plenty of cash and clothes,
> But that was before I tippled
> And gin colored up my nose.

Then follows the specific story. He was a happily married blacksmith "in Lehigh Valley":

> Me and my wife and Nellie;
> Nellie was just sixteen,
> And she was the prettiest creature
> The Valley had ever seen.

Enters now the villain, a "city stranger" who pays court to Nellie:

> Well, it's the same old story;
> Common enough, you'll say:
> He was a smooth-tongued devil,
> And he got her to run away.

He ruins her and leaves her "without a wedding ring," whereupon they bring her home, where she soon dies "with a raging fever." The mother soon follows:

> Frantic with grief and trouble,
> Her mother began to sink.
> Dead—in less than a fortnight—
> That's when I took to drink.

Wife and child are gone now. But he is a man with a mission:

> Give me a drink, bartender,
> And I'll be on my way.
> I'll tramp till I find that scoundrel,
> If it takes till judgment day.[6]

Milburn follows this with five other ballads of the type, from the straight "May I Sleep in Your Barn Tonight, Mister" to wild burlesques like "The Boss Tramp," in which the erring daughter gets the following welcome on her return:

> I took her to my aching heart,
> I smashed her in the smeller,

> Then I drug the floor with her,
> And throwed her in the cellar.

The existence of parodies only shows the popularity of the pattern, and we can see that same pattern—present wretchedness, past blessedness, domestic tragedy, drink, and back to the present—in such sterling pieces as "The Face on the Barroom Floor," "The Picture That Was Drawn upon the Floor," "Toledo Slim," and even "The Volunteer Organist," though the pattern is less explicit in this last selection than in the others.[7] The same basic idea appears across the sex line in songs of the nineties like "She Is More to Be Pitied than Censured" and "She May Have Seen Better Days."[8] We could go on, but the point has been made: in writing "The Norway Bum," Joe Scott made use of a stereotype common in nineteenth-century sentimental song, the story of the tramp who had seen better days.

But that's not all he had to draw on. There was also the "shabby genteel" tradition. The Englishman Harry Clifton's song by that title came out and was popular back as far as the 1860s,[9] but it seems to have been less well known than "A Gentleman Still," which was often referred to by singers as "Shabby Genteel." It is not a story-song so much as a character study, showing the narrator to be, though penniless, an upstanding moral man:

> Don't think by my dress that I've come here to beg,
> Though the sharp pangs of hunger I feel,
> The cup of misfortune I've drained to the dregs,
> But I'm proud though I'm shabby-genteel.[10]

Joe's direct use of the first line and the same general metrical pattern make it pretty clear that he had this song somewhere in his mind as he wrote "The Norway Bum."

The opening-line-and-general-stanza-form technique is a common parodist's device, and it frequently means that the same tune is used also to reinforce the parallel. The only problem here is that none of the tunes I have seen for "Shabby Genteel" resembles the one Joe used for his song; nor do they resemble each other much. Of course, it is possible that Joe had heard "Shabby Genteel" sung to that tune, but I don't think it is likely. A better case could be made for the nineties ballad "She May Have Seen Better Days," in which the stanza form, rhyme scheme, and even the general attitude toward the unfortunate are close to "The Norway Bum":

While strolling along with the city's vast throng,
  On a night that was bitterly cold,
I noticed a crowd who were laughing aloud
  At something they chanced to behold.
I stopped for to see what the object could be,
  And there, on a doorstep, lay
A woman in tears, from the crowd's angry jeers,
  And then I heard somebody say:[11]

Then follows a chorus made up of the title line and some amplification. But again the tune, though structurally similar, is entirely different.

Where, then, did Joe get his tune? I think I can answer that, but before I do we had better establish exactly what the tune to "The Norway Bum" is. To begin with, it is always a set of the same tune, and (with one lonely exception)[12] I have never heard any other song sung to that tune in Maine or the Maritimes. Nor have I had anyone in the area tell me, "That's the tune to such-and-such," though I have asked about it over and over. No question about it, it *is* the "Norway Bum" tune, and Long Joe Doucette's singing of it is a good one:

This is what I have called elsewhere a double tune,[13] a tune with eight rather than the standard four phrases. In the present instance, the phrase pattern is ABAC/DEAC, the mode is major, the range a seventh, and the meter a basic 6/8. Of the twelve tunes I have collected, three (NB.6, PI.3, PI.4) fit this formula exactly, while the other nine use only half the tune, which is the common fate of double tunes in oral tradition.[14] Even more obviously here than was the case with "The Plain Golden Band," we see Joe's original conception of an eight-line stanza split by subsequent singers into two four-line stanzas. But there can be no doubt that Joe composed his piece with the longer form in mind, and once again we see him turning for his material not to folk but to popular tradition.

It is one of the problems of tune scholarship that in spite of good intentions and considerable effort there is no really systematic way to run down a tune. We are dependent on our having plowed through countless printed collections and having listened to countless singings and recordings over many years. My own experience hadn't helped me with the present tune, and I had tried it on all those people whose memories I have learned to respect—friends like D. K. Wilgus, Joe Hickerson, Norman Cazden, Bill McNeil, to name but a few—all without specific success, although there was complete agreement that the tune was probably popular. Then one evening in the summer of 1967 I found myself in Cooperstown, New York, at a party with a man by the name of Lawrence Older, and we very quickly became old friends. As always happens when two song buffs meet, we began the "Do you know one that goes . . ." game through and over the normal highball hubbub around us, and I soon found that Larry knew a hell of a slug of tunes, so I tried "The Norway Bum" on him. "Yes," he said definitely, and then he hummed the rest of it along with me. "My sister used to sing that," he said, but he couldn't remember anything more. Some months later Larry sent me a tape of his sister, Edith Frances Brown, singing it for me:[15]

295

sat there a - lone, Of youth's hap - py days gone by. I

took from a box where for years it had lain A pack-age both dust - y and

old; 'Twas Nel - ly's love let-ters in si - lence I read As a

fond rel - ic fell from its fold. It was on - ly a fa - ded pic - ture, I'll

cher-ish it till I die; It brings back once more thoughts of

youth's gold-en hour When we're sweet-hearts, Nel - ly and I.

No traditional versions that I have collected have any chromaticism
at all, but that loss of chromaticism is one of the first things to happen
to a popular tune in folk tradition, as Anne and Norm Cohen have so
well pointed out.[16] Obviously, though, this is Joe's tune and almost
certainly his source, especially when we consider that both "Nelly
and I" (if that is its proper title)[17] and "The Norway Bum" are
memory songs—those of an older person sitting alone and recalling
the happy past.

We can sum up this whole business as follows: when Joe decided
to write a song about a bum (probably one he had seen or one
someone had told him about), he had the popular traditions of
tramp, shabby genteel, and memory songs to draw on for tune,
stanza form, story structure, attitudes, and language. The Norway
fire of 1894 would still have been fresh in his mind, too. Using a
memory-song tune, what he wrote was basically a tramp song; but
"The Norway Bum" is so different from any of its sources as to be
almost sui generis. And now we're ready to take a good look at it.

I have been part of the audience when "The Norway Bum" was

sung, and I have sung it myself for audiences large and small. The effect it has is interesting. People laugh at the first stanza, and they may smile a bit at the second, but by the end of the song no one is laughing anymore. I won't say they are moved to tears, but no doubt about it, they have been touched. The song is an artistic success partly because Joe Scott fulfills our expectations (though he fulfills them with a difference) and partly because he thwarts them.

The first stanza (1–2), with its "Don't think by my dress" opening, sets us up for the usual shabby-genteel disclaimer; but rather than claiming he is "too proud to steal," the bum says, "You bet I would." The shock-laughter response to this carries on through the rest of the first stanza with the joke about the "togs" he's wearing not being as bad as the ones in his pack, and even into the second (3–4), where he describes what he'll do for the price of a drink. Having destroyed himself pretty thoroughly by the end of the second stanza, having even made it hard for us to take him seriously at all, the bum comes up with the standard line about how it hasn't always been thus: "I'm a man who has seen better days." Now we are back in the familiar structure of the tramp ballad, and we expect the bum to tell his story to make us pity his case. But that is going to be a tougher job for this self-ridiculing clown-begger-thief than it would be for the essentially dignified "Lehigh Valley" kind of hobo. Joe combines, then, the shabby-genteel (which he twists) with the tramp opening (which he goes well beyond). It is an ambitious start.

In the standard tramp ballad, the hero now simply begins to tell his story in most straightforward fashion. Joe decided not to do it quite that directly. What he did was to turn to the memory-song tradition from which he had taken his tune. Stanza 5 is his transition, giving us the bum sitting by his fire, drinking stolen hooch while cooking a chicken (which so perfectly fits the tramp stereotype that we can assume it is stolen, too). Then, as he sits and watches the sparks from his fire, he has a vision of his old home by the sea and spends three full stanzas (7–9) describing it. Which raises a problem of artistic emphasis.

The main point of the bum's story is that he took to drink out of grief over the death of his wife and child. Why, then, does Joe Scott spend three whole stanzas describing something as irrelevant as the childhood home? Why did he not spend his time describing the wife or how happy the marriage was, matters he dismisses in two lines (st.

12, ll. 3–4)? By literary standards this is not as it should be, perhaps, but as I have said elsewhere, a literary aesthetic is of limited use in discussing traditional song. Again we can speak of an emotional core: the happy past, the days that are no more. The idyllic childhood serves well here; the hero is banished from this Eden for love—not only excusable, but commendable in terms of romantic tradition— whereupon he builds his own Eden: three happy years with a young wife, a child, a home of his own, and a successful medical practice (at least that's what the word "patient" suggests and that is how the song is universally interpreted). Furthermore, he has cut himself off from his parents now. When the catastrophe comes, it is just that much more final and complete: there is nothing left at all. He is as alone as a man can be.

The childhood vision disappears, and now the bum takes up the direct narration of his story, beginning with the establishment of his new happiness. Then comes the terrible picture of the fire, culminating in his collapse upon seeing his wife and child burned to death. It is worth remarking here that as Joe began this narration with a fire, he ends it with one. His final stanza allows for a certain "falling action"—call it a "conclusion" if you like—in which Joe shows us the town the next morning and allows the hero to state that that's when he took to rum. The last two lines bring us back to the present time, ending the song.

"The Norway Bum" went very solidly into northeastern tradition, as the list of versions will show, and the geographic spread was the same as that of Joe's other pieces: northern New Hampshire, Maine, New Brunswick, Nova Scotia, and Prince Edward Island. Two versions (Me. 6 and NB. 4) were copied directly either from Joe's original slip or from the *Rumford Falls Times* print; otherwise the ballad's tradition was entirely oral. The *Boston Globe* version (BSG) had very little if any demonstrable influence, and even the manuscript versions seem to have come from memory or from someone else's singing.

The ballad has kept its shape very well, too. That might have been predicted, of course; since it is a tightly constructed narrative there wasn't much room for stanzas to get out of order. On the other hand, transpositions did occur, and the results are interesting, especially when we notice that they almost always occur in the first five stanzas. Ernest McCarthy (NB. 6), for example, begins this way:

"The Norway Bum"

Come listen to me and a story I'll tell
'Bout a man who has seen better days.
Though I'm a bum and addicted to rum
I know of the world and its ways.
I can give you a spiel, dance an old-fashioned reel
Or sing you a bit of a song.

Last night as I sat. . . .

Several versions, among them Emile Arsenault's, reverse stanzas 3 and 4, which makes no difference at all in the story. Once we get beyond these introductory stanzas (1–4), the ballad is extremely stable. Most of the changes we do find are caused by the omission of this or that stanza, but even omissions are unusual, and I can find no pattern to describe (let alone explain) those that do occur.

If transpositions and omissions are rare, is there any evidence that anything has been added in the course of tradition? Yes, and this is what makes Emile Arsenault's version so interesting. In his version, Joe's original stanzas 8 and 9, two of the three stanzas describing the old home, are omitted, and their place is taken by the following:

The church bells they rang and the birds sweetly sang,
In the meadow and down in the dell;
I listened with joy as I did when a boy
To the chimes of the old village bells.

This is probably a stanza from another song, a statement I can support partly by the vague but near-certain knowledge that I have seen or heard it somewhere and partly by the fact that I have seen a request in the *Family Herald* for a song containing the last two lines.[18] It is impossible to say where in the chain of tradition this substitution took place; but that it took place so perfectly is evidence that Joe Scott was doing good work in an idiom that was part of the ambience of northeastern song. The transition to the next section is also neatly handled in Emile's version:

How I once was a lad to make mother's heart glad,
I was once what they called fair of face;
But I loved a fair lass far beneath my own class
To my father and mother's disgrace.

The first two lines may be from an entirely different song, or they may be the original work of some singer, be it Emile or one of his predecessors. At any rate, the whole substitution is a splendid example of the kind of creativity-within-limits one expects to find within a living tradition of song. It does not lead to a new song, but it does lead to the creation of local versions, of oicotypes, if you will, that are very distinctive. Fred Campbell's concluding stanza is another example of the same sort of thing, involving a transposition and what sounds like a substitution (misremembered or reshaped, perhaps) from another song (NB.2):

> I'm only a bum at misfortune
> It's caused by my bright past astray;
> I'm only a bum, addicted to rum,
> I'm a man who has seen better days.

"The Norway Bum" has always been a great favorite of mine, which is irrelevant, perhaps; it also turns out to have been a great favorite among people who knew old songs in the Northeast. A lot of people have remarked to me that it was a song they always liked to hear, even though they themselves did not know it, and I find it especially interesting to see how it gets through to people, quite "sophisticated" people, too, who hear it for the first time. It hits hard, largely, I am sure, because its "smile and a tear" development is so effectively handled. Whatever the reason or reasons, I can vouch for the song's being surefire. I have yet to see it fail.

As a concomitant to its being a song that is well liked, "The Norway Bum" is generally accepted as being factual. It may have been, as Lucy Morse said, "a made up song," but most of the people I asked about it were sure it was true. Edmund Doucette's comments are typical: *"Oh, I really loved it. I *liked* that song. True song, you know. Things like that would happen. She was a poor girl, and he was kind of high, he was a doctor. He married her against his parents because they thought she wasn't good enough for him. But he was leading a really happy married life, but *this* had to happen. Turned out to be a bum in the long run." John Morrison also said it was true, adding the following: *"It is a nice song, a lovely song. It just goes to show how he—well, he went, he fell in love with this lass, as it said there, and his parents didn't approve of it. And they thought that they were so high and mighty. Well, at the last of it he just turned out to be a bum over the head of, actually, that."

There were variant stories, too. *"It's about a Norwegian doctor who came to this country after he lost his wife in a fire," said Ernest

McCarthy of Blackville, New Brunswick, and Alice Flynn wrote the story out for me as it had been known in her family (her father was Jack McGinley of Johnville, New Brunswick): "The Norway Bum is the story of a young doctor that went to Chicago to a meeting of some sort. He registered his wife and baby in a hotel, and when he came back he heard the engines and bells and saw that the hotel was in flames. He saw his wife standing in the window with the baby in her arms, and before he could do anything they fell back in the flames."[19] The last example is especially intriguing because it raises the possibility that Joe may have done some tampering with the "truth." It is certainly not the story the ballad tells, but it seems to suggest that the incident described is where Joe got his "idea." And that in turn can bring us to jesting Pilate's question, "What is truth?" But let us stay for an answer.

Both Doucette and Morrison seem to be praising the song more for its *moral* truth than for its factual truth, more because it is *true to life* and "goes to show" that such things "would happen" than because it tells about something that actually *did* happen. The McGinley family story may be seen as supporting a similar distinction (if it isn't simply a mistaken memory of what the song is about). Folklorists have not really worked this distinction very hard—in our field work we certainly haven't asked the kinds of questions that would allow us to clarify it—but in general I do not think that traditional singers and their audiences were much bothered by it. With this song, as with others, veracity was accepted as prima facie; that these things *would* happen was reinforced by the fact that they actually *did* happen. About the most guarded statement I have been able to elicit from singers in this matter is something like "At least that's what I was told." True was true, and that's all there was to it.

All things considered, "The Norway Bum" may well be Joe Scott's most remarkable song. It is basically a tramp song, but in no other tramp song I know of is the movement from a smile to a tear so clear and emphatic. In no other tramp song do we begin with a comic figure and end with a tragic one. The downfall is pretty complete—no "Lehigh Valley" quest for revenge, just an endless round of cadging drinks, stealing chickens, and playing the fool. Finally, in no other tramp song is the denouement brought about not through someone else's treachery or infidelity, but through romantic love and blind chance. Joe brings it all off, in my opinion, first by allowing the bum to give a believable and wryly realistic self-appraisal, and second, by having him tell his two-stage story in such a leisurely fashion, moving from the beauty of the home by the ocean to the terror of the fire. He brought the popular tramp ballad into folk tradition; had he known how to get "The Norway Bum" into popular tradition (in a somewhat shortened form, perhaps), it could have stood with the best work of songwriters of national reputation.

What brought Joe to write this ballad at all? There is a perfectly obvious explanation available: he saw it as an acceptable (read "traditional") subject that he could work up and sell. That explanation may be all that is needed. I will not insist upon what follows, but I am intrigued by the possibility that in "The Norway Bum" Joe Scott was once again unconsciously symbolizing or dramatizing his own problems. I have already suggested something like that for both "Howard Carey" and "William Sullivan," and of course "Guy Reed" was a pretty direct representation of *every* river-driver's lot. Did Joe identify with the Norway Bum, too? Was the "young wife" Lizzie? Certainly Joe saw his own life go up in flames when she jilted him; *"he just got to be an old bum after that," said Angus Enman. Was the young wife Emma? I am sure that Joe felt he was marrying "beneath his own class"—after all, she *was* "French"—and I am even more sure that the prideful Scotts of Lower Woodstock made it clear to Joe that that was the way *they* saw it when he took his new family home with him in the summer of 1900. That relationship, too, went up in flames, taking with it not one but two children, and Joe went back to being the amiable woods tramp he always had been. Add to these speculations Angus Enman's odd report that when Joe sang this song he'd *"act it right off," as if he were the Norway Bum himself, which shows him assuming identity on one level, anyway.[20]

It's too bad we can't date "The Norway Bum" more precisely. What dates we do have in no way gainsay the interpretation I have suggested. Joe returned from Lower Woodstock in the midsummer of 1900, and the earliest datable version of the song we have is the one published in the *Rumford Falls Times* for April 13, 1901. It was during this nine-month period that his marriage fell apart, too. Admittedly, it is a heavy burden for so few facts to bear, but I am convinced that they bear it well. There really was a Norway Bum: his name was Joe Scott, and it was Lizzie and Emma both who fell back in the flames. But the last man to know these things would have been Joe Scott himself.

"The Norway Bum"

JS.1   Original printed slip. Copies obtained from Daisy Severy, Gray, Me., and Bert Thorne, Jemseg, N.B. 18 sts. (set as 9 double sts.).

JS.2   Version printed in *Rumford Falls Times*, Apr. 13, 1901. Identical in every way with JS.1.

BSG   Version printed in *Boston Sunday Globe*, in the 1930s. Taken from the scrapbook of Irving Ashford, Andersonville, N.B., Oct. 10, 1965. Title: "The Norway Bum"; directly under the title: "Joe Scott"; at the end: "Sent in by L.D.E., Boston, Mass." Clipping read onto tape (see NB.3); NA Ives tape 65.21, 18 sts., set as 9 double sts.

NH   James Custeau, Lincoln, N.H., July 27, 1964; in a letter, manuscript, 17 sts. Learned it about 1914 from a man named Connolly up in Thetford Mines, P.Q. (Custeau's home town), and had also heard his father sing it. *"There was one time that it appeared in the *Boston Sunday Globe Magazine Section*." Wrote this version down from memory to send to me. Did not know it was by Scott and did not know for sure it was a true song, *"but chances are that it was based on something that actually happened."

Me.1   Anna Thurston, Farmington, Conn., from the recitation of her father, Roger Thurston of Andover, Me., Nov., 1957; manuscript, 3 sts., fragment. Knew it was by Scott.

Me.2   Roy Lohnes, Andover, Me., summer, 1958; taken down by dictation by Anna Thurston, typescript, 18 sts., no stanza breaks. Knew it was by Scott.

Me.3   John Brown, 80, Mexico, Me., July 10, 1964; NA Ives tape 64.4, recited, 18 sts. This version almost identical with a longhand version given me by his grandson, James Brown, a student at the University of Maine, which Brown's widow felt he had written down about 1908. Brown said he had first learned the song back home in Chipman, N.B., before he came to Maine in 1904. Learned it from his older brother, Eldon Brown, who had learned it in the Maine woods. Claimed he did not know the tune, and had heard it recited more than sung. Knew it was by Scott. Brown's longhand version is almost certainly taken from the original printed version (JS.1)

Me.4   Gertrude Bradbury, Mexico, Me., as written down by her daughter, Pearl Longley, in a notebook lent to me Sept. 29, 1965; manuscript, 10 sts. Mrs. Bradbury probably learned this around her home in Bridgewater, Me.

Me.5   Gertrude Toothaker, 80, Rangeley, Me., July 29, 1959; NA Ives tape 1.57 and ATL 2180.4, sung, 16 sts. Had known Scott and knew he had written this song.

Me.6 Lucy Morse, ca. 75, Norway, Me., May, 1960; collected by Madelyn Whitley, Lewiston, Me., NA 413.017–019, 18 sts. (9 double sts.). Almost identical with original printed version (JS.1). Knew it was by Scott.

Me.7 Ms. B. Field, Detroit, Me., July 1, 1964; in a letter, manuscript, 17½ sts. Note at end reads: "From an old copy of 50 yrs. ago." In a letter to me, July 22, 1964, she says she believes she learned the song from her brother back in Brockway, N.B., who "used to sing that type songs & I copied it when I was small, probably more for the story it told than for any other reason." Did not know it was by Scott.

NB.1 Alice Flynn, Allegany, N.Y., Aug. 1, 1964; manuscript, 3 sts., fragment. When she gave me the manuscript, she sang the tune for me; see NA Ives tape 64.7. Learned it in her home in Johnville, N.B.

NB.2 Fred A. Campbell, 82, Arthurette, N.B., July 17, 1965; NA 80.056–058, recited, 16 sts. Had known Scott, and bought this song from him once, but the copy had disappeared.

NB.3 Irving Ashford, 68, Andersonville, N.B., Oct. 10, 1965; sang from newspaper clipping, 4 sts. See BSG and NA Ives tape 65.21.

NB.4 James Brown, 76, South Branch, N.B., at the home of Tommy Whelan, Chatham, N.B., Aug. 20, 1959; NA Ives tape 1.63 and ATL 2182.6, sung, 18 sts. Did not know it was by Scott. Second singing July 13, 1963, at his home in South Branch, almost identical; see NA Ives tape 1.142 and ATL 3149.4.

NB.5 Ernest McCarthy, Blackville, N.B., July 17, 1965; collected by Kay Hayes, NA 193, sung, 13½ sts. According to McCarthy, *"It's about a Norwegian doctor who come to this country after he lost his wife in a fire." Did not know it was by Scott.

NB.6 Stanley MacDonald, 59, Black River Bridge, N.B., Aug. 18, 1959, at the Second Miramichi Folksong Festival, Newcastle, N.B.; NA Ives tape 1.70 and ATL 2189.5, sung, 16 sts. First two lines accidentally erased from recording. Did not know the song was by Scott. Says he learned it from James McRae of Black River Bridge, who used to come to Stanley's house to saw wood. That was about 1913.

NS   Charles W. Budge, 76, New Haven (Victoria Co.), Cape Breton Island, N.S., June, 1964; in a letter, manuscript, 16 sts. Did not know it was by Scott. Learned locally from a man who had "in his younger days worked in the lumberwoods in Maine."

PI.1 John Morrison, 53, Charlottetown, P.E.I., Aug. 30, 1965; NA Ives tape 65.8, recited and sung, 11 sts., fragment. Did not know it was by Scott.

PI.2 Mrs. Underhill Coughlin, ca. 65, Alberton (Brooklyn), P.E.I., Aug. 23, 1965; NA Ives tape 65.3, sung, 9 sts., fragment. Did not know it was by Scott. Learned it locally from some other girls when she was quite young.

PI.3 Joseph Doucette, 58, Miminegash, P.E.I., Aug. 17, 1958; NA Ives tape 1.36 and ATL 2162.3, sung, 5½ sts., fragment. Did not know it was by Scott.

PI.4 Edmund Doucette, 69, Miminegash, P.E.I., July 14, 1963; NA Ives tape 1.145 and ATL 3152.2, sung, 10 sts., fragment. Learned it from a girl over around Newcastle, N.B. *"Very old song, I imagine. I have the words here somewheres written down. . . . It must be forty years or over [*since I sang that song*]. . . . I still remember that much. I might remember it all if I was to think it over, you know." Did not know it was by Scott.

PI.5 Frank Buote, 60, Tignish, P.E.I., Aug. 26, 1965; NA Ives tape 65.6, sung, 4 sts., fragment. Did not know it was by Scott. Learned it locally.

PI.6 Emile Arsenault, 68, Tignish, P.E.I., Aug. 26, 1965; NA Ives tape 65.7, sung, 16 sts. This is the version reproduced at the beginning of this chapter. See also pp. 299–300.

NOTES

1. William B. Lapham, *Centennial History of Norway, Oxford County, Maine, 1786–1886;* Charles F. Whitman, *A History of Norway, Maine, from the Earliest Settlements to the Close of the Year 1922.*

2. *Norway Advertiser Democrat,* May 15, 1894. An informative eyewitness description of the fire by Fred E. Smith was published in the *Lewiston Daily Sun,* Jan. 25, 1963. Jayne Lello's thorough search to see if she could discover a historical basis for "The Norway Bum" was unsuccessful; see her report, NA 760.

3. Morse to Ives, Dec. 27, 1965, and corroborated in a later conversation.

4. George Milburn, *The Hobo's Hornbook,* p. xiv.

5. Ibid., p. xv.

6. Ibid., pp. 41–43. The entire "Lehigh Valley" sequence runs from pp. 41 to 58.

7. For "The Face on the Barroom Floor," see ibid., pp. 153–157; for "The Picture That Was Drawn upon the Floor," see Sigmund Spaeth, *Weep Some More, My Lady,* pp. 189–190; for "Toledo Slim," see Milburn, *Hobo's Hornbook,* pp. 192–197; for "The Volunteer Organist," see Vance Randolph, *Ozark Folksongs,* 4, p. 346.

8. For "She Is More to Be Pitied than Censured," see Sigmund Spaeth, *Read 'em and Weep*, pp. 209–210; for "She May Have Seen Better Days," see ibid., pp. 141–142.

9. See Spaeth, *Weep Some More*, pp. 53–55.

10. Randolph, *Ozark Folksongs*, 4, pp. 349–350. See also *Delaney's Song Book No. 47*. Norman Cazden collected a version of it from Aaron Van Der Bogart in New York's Catskill Mountains. Helen Creighton collected a version from Freeman Young, East Peteswick, N.S., in July, 1953 (NMC CR–108B, 1167).

11. Spaeth, *Read 'em and Weep*, p. 141.

12. Ralph Thornton of Topsfield, Me., sang a version of "The Lightning Express" to this tune Dec. 5, 1973 (NA 717, tape 30). About halfway through he slid over to another tune, though.

13. See, e.g., Edward D. Ives, *Lawrence Doyle*, pp. 28–30.

14. Ibid., p. 29. For "The Norway Bum," Me.6, NB.1, NB.3, PI.1, and PI.2 use the first half of the tune; NB.4, NB.5, PI.5, and PI.6 use the second half. See also pp. 219–220.

15. See NA 762 for this rendition. Readers to whom Larry is a stranger may begin to correct this defect by listening to his record, *Lawrence Older of Middle Grove, New York*.

16. Anne Cohen and Norm Cohen, "Tune Evolution as an Indicator of Traditional Music Norms," p. 41.

17. A careful check of Library of Congress and Copyright Office files (looking under several possible titles) has failed to turn up the "original" version of this song.

18. *Family Herald*, Aug. 23, 1944.

19. In a manuscript given to me in Bangor, Me., Aug. 1, 1964.

20. See p. 58.

16

"Wilfred White and John Murphy": One That Didn't Make It

On March 3, 1966, the *Family Herald* published a sort of clean-up request for me on their "Old Favourites" page, asking for a number of songs I had little or no information about. Among them was "White and Murphy," and a few weeks later the paper received a letter from Mrs. R. C. Kibblewhite of Willowdale, Ontario, which they forwarded to me. "I am enclosing a copy of 'Wilfred White and John Murphy' for Professor Ives," Mrs. Kibblewhite said. "I got the words from an old notebook full of songs that my uncle brought back in 1902 after a winter of shantying, in Maine, I believe." The song itself follows:

WILFRED WHITE AND JOHN MURPHY

[1]   Come all you loyal shanty boys, so hardy brave and strong,
I would kindly ask you to draw near and listen to my song,
For it concerns two shanty boys, so noble, true and brave
Who, by an accident of late, met with a watery grave.

[2]   It was on the sixth of October, nineteen hundred and one,
The chilly wind blew from the north, dark clouds concealed the sun,
The snow was falling thick and fast, the winds were howling wild,
That is governed by the unseen hand of the pure and undefiled.

[3]   That morn they left Fred Flint's hotel to climb the winding hills

307

To Carl Wright's camp, twenty-one miles north of Wilson's
    Mills,
With a supply of horses that had lately come that way,
And, by an accident, were drowned in the big Magalloway.

[4]   Win York, the foreman of the camp—that camp they ne'er did
        reach—
He did intend, so I was told, to meet them by the beach,
And at the crossing just above the lower Metalluc Pond,
That takes its rise in Parmachenee Lake, twelve miles be-
        yond.

[5]   Now at the crossing-place the river runs both deep and wide,
The ferry boat you see was lying on the north-[east] side.
When they would reach the south-west shore, there they
        would have to wait
Till Win York brought the boat across, who was twenty min-
        utes late.

[6]   When Win York was about half-way between the camp and
        shore
He met a horse all dripping wet, its breast was stained with
        gore.
He knew then there was something wrong and hastened to the
        shore
And just across the stream he spied, tied to a tree, three more.

[7]   There was no other creature near that he could hear or see.
But where were White and Murphy? Oh, how strange! Where
        can they be?
He called both loud and often but his echo, that was all,
Far off among the mountains, that responded to his call.

[8]   A party soon was organized, a search was soon begun,
That lasted from noon-time until the setting of the sun.
But all in vain for those they fain would find lie side by side
So pale and cold, in death's embrace, beneath the sparkling
        tide.

[9]   And now I will refer to those who came to volunteer
To search and find those missing ones; their names will soon
        appear,
Whose voices rang out on the air to ring the echo bells
In deep ravines and valleys low, on mountains, hills and dells.

"Wilfred White and John Murphy"

[10] Win York, the foreman of their camp, and Maurice Ripley,
Dave Berryman, Walter Buckman and William Kennedy,
And William Norton, Ross McGuire and Audbury Blue,
Those are the men who did complete their loyal searching
crew.

[11] The search next morning was resumed; at twelve o'clock that
day
They found their bodies near the crossing 'neath the stream
midway.
They raised their bodies from the deep and laid them on the
shore
The treacherous waters, with their secrets, rolled on as before.

[12] Then all the party soon drew near, with faces pale and sad,
And there was one among them who was only a lad,
Whose pearly tears like raindrops fell upon the cold, damp
ground,
Whose cries would penetrate the skies for his comrade who
was drowned.

[13] It was supposed that one of the two, who could not swim, had
tried
To swim his horse across the stream unto the north-east side,
But, when about midway, his horse was thrown upon its side;
His friend swam out to save him and both sank beneath the
tide.

[14] They did what little could be done for those who had been
drowned,
They soon prepared their bodies for the cold and silent
ground,
And their remains were taken home by two of their crew
And now they lie at rest beneath the morn and evening dew.

[15] John Murphy lived in Stoneham in the Province of Quebec,
And Wilfred White lived at Mars Hill in the old Pine Tree
State.
These men were both unmarried and just in the prime of life
Who left us for a land we hope, free from all care and strife.

In all honesty, I wish I could say that Joe Scott was not the author
of this song, but there doesn't seem to be the slightest chance that he

wasn't. Not that there is any direct evidence of his authorship, but everyone who knows anything about the song attributes it to him. "Mr. Scott appeared where I was employed," wrote Fred Wiggett of Plymouth, New Hampshire, "at the head of Magalloway River near Parmachenee Lake. . . . There had been a drowning there of two young men. Mr. Scott heard of the accident concerning John Murphy and Alfred [sic] White—and wrote a song about them." Dennis Taylor, Fred Campbell, and Tom Pollock had all known Joe and knew all about the song. It's his work—on that head there need be no question at all.

Nor need there be any question that the song tells about something that happened in country that Joe Scott knew well, the Magalloway River over by the Maine–New Hampshire border. Around the turn of the century, civilization had crept up this river about fourteen miles to Wilsons Mills at the foot of Aziscohos Mountain and just below the falls of the same name that marked the head of any practical navigation. From there on up, the Magalloway was what it is today, a wilderness river known only to hunters, fishermen, woodsmen, and river-drivers.[1] One great change has taken place, though. Aziscohos Dam, built at the falls in 1913, flowed the river back about twelve miles, which means that the entire scene of our ballad—Upper and Lower Metalluc ponds, the Meadows, and Parkertown Crossing—is now under the waters of Aziscohos Lake.

The accident took place on Sunday, October 6, 1901. What happened is clear enough. Lumbering operations were getting started, and men were moving in supplies for the winter's work. This particular operation was being conducted by A. C. Wight of Milan, New Hampshire, somewhere in the country between the Magalloway and the Cupsuptic. Joe's statement that it was twenty-one miles from Wilsons Mills seems excessive; that would put it almost to the Canadian border. But if we take into account the crooks and turns in the road we can get it down more realistically to the east of Parmachenee Lake. More than likely, though, Joe was simply wrong about the distance. My guess is that the camp was in Parkertown (Township 5, Range 3), south of Lincoln Brook on the lower slopes of Deer Mountain. That would be about twelve miles from Wilsons Mills, but if I know anything about what a tote road would be like in that country, I'll bet it *felt* like twenty-one miles! This much we can be sure of, though: Win York was camp foreman, and he had assigned two young men, Wilfred White and John G. Murphy, to bring four horses up from downriver.[2]

Fred Flint ran the Aziscoos House in Wilsons Mills. The men came that far on Saturday; then on Sunday morning they started into the woods. *Stuart's Atlas* shows a woods road leading from Wilsons Mills to Lower Metalluc Pond, a distance of about ten miles.[3] This is probably the road they followed, and they would have reached the southwest bank of the Magalloway about eleven in the morning. They had to get across the river, and the scow was on the other side. But there is little sense in my telling the story myself when we are fortunate enough to have it twice from men who were nearby at the time. Their versions are close, but different enough to justify giving them both.

Fred Campbell was about eighteen at the time and was working at a different camp further up in the woods. He remembers that he had brought horses in over the same road about a week before:

*Well, I'll tell you the story now. . . . They was four of us, no, three of us. We went to start to go into the woods in the fall of the year, and we took six horses. We came to the Magalloway Stream, and it's a very deep deadwater stream, and it ain't very wide—I suppose maybe fifty feet wide. And we had to put them all in a big boat—scow they called it—and take them across the river, and I tell you when we got them six horses in there it was pretty well loaded! But we poled it across and took them out.

Well, the next week this Wilfred White and John Murphy was coming in the same place with four horses. And they was a man supposed to be there and have the boat back to them. I don't know whether we'd left the boat or whether somebody else had brought it over in the meantime. But they come and they waited a while, and they made up their minds that one fella would get on a horse's back and swim it over and get the boat. Well, he did; he got onto the horse's back. I don't know now just which one it was, but I think it was Wilfred White because he had on calked shoes. And out in the middle of the river, why, he upset the horse somehow. (It's an easy job to upset a horse in a river. I know that because I've done it, and the horse, then, he'll try to get on top of you.) Well, he kicked the horse, see, tried to kick it away from him.

And when this other [*i.e., a third*] man that was coming to bring the boat back [*was coming along the path*], he met the horse about a mile from the river, and it was all soaking wet and its breast was all bleeding where [*White*] he'd kicked it, see, with the calked shoes.

Well, [*meantime*] his chum [*i.e., Murphy*] went out to try to save him in the river—couldn't swim, I suppose—and when he did, why they clinched together, and he beat this fella in the face till his face was just as black. His eyes was black when they found them just a few rods below clinched together on the bottom of the river.

Well, that's what happened to them.

Tom Pollock was about ten years older than Fred Campbell and says he was right in Win York's camp that winter:

*And he composed one about Wilfred White and John Murphy. This Murphy was from Stoningham, Quebec, and Wilfred White was from up country. We was up on the Magalloway, and they went out for the horses. . . . And when they came back it was on a Sunday. They started from Fred Flint's to come into the camp. . . . And when they got to the Magalloway there, the scow was over on the opposite side . . . of the river. . . . One fellow says, "Oh, we'll take one horse and swim him across." Well, they didn't understand how to swim a horse. For to swim a horse you got to give a horse his slack rein and catch the wither lock in your hand, for a horse will throw his head up. If you hold a tight rein on a horse you're swimming you'll upset him. . . . This fellow didn't know enough, Murphy, about swimming a horse, or he wouldn't have upset the horse. He'd of swum nice. A horse swims awful low, you know. The water just bubbles across between his shoulders. . . .

So he had a tight rein and he upset the horse, and . . . he got tangled in the harness, and this Wilfred White went out to catch him, to help him . . . bring him ashore, and by cripes! they both got clinched. Clinched together, and you know what happens then! They both drownded right there, see.

So the boss, Win York was our boss, and he went out to meet them, and he found the horse coming. ([*That horse had*] been in there for years up that tote road.) . . . He took him back and tied him to a tree to see where the boys was. And [*he saw*] the other horses was tied on the other side, and the scow was on *this* side, you see. So Win knowed just what had happened. . . .

So he untied the horse, and he come up and brought the horse up. I was going from the camp over to the hovel. Some of the boys was over there taking care of the horses and I was going over. And I see him and he stood and told me what he found. And he was wiping the tears out of his eyes, and he told me, "I'm afraid they're drownded." So by Jesus we went down there and we grappled, and the first one come hard and the next one come easier. They were clinched together.

Joe composed a song about that. . . . Joe was working there the same winter. . . . And the setting of that song, it come in (I didn't know much of it), "He called and called, and all he got was the echoes from the hills far beyond."

Was Joe in Win York's camp at the time Pollock claims? I don't think so. Fred Wiggett's account of Joe "appearing" at the camp suggests that he came in to sell his songs. Had Joe been there, my hunch is he would have told the whole story in the first person—"*our* loyal searching crew," "*we* found their bodies," "*we* did what little could be done"—perhaps even including himself in the searching crew. Then there is line 2 of stanza 4, which states that Win York "did intend, *so I was told*, to meet them by the beach." The italicized clause may be simply a rhetorical "filler," but I doubt that Joe would have used it had he actually been in camp at the time. The whole ballad smacks of what I see as Joe's usual modus operandi anyhow; he'd hear of a calamity via bush telegraph, "get it right" by talking to "eyewitnesses," make his song, and then head into the woods to sell it to the very men who already would have known about it either directly or the same way Joe did.

How about that business of the "searching crew" looking all Sunday afternoon and then again Monday morning? Neither Campbell's nor Pollock's account implies that the search took the better part of two days, nor does the account in the *Berlin Reporter*. On the other hand, the *Rumford Falls Times* (fifty miles downriver and two weeks later) *does* mention it, saying that the "bodies were recovered Monday."[4] That's how it was, I'm sure. Joe almost certainly has it correct, right down to the names of the men (we already know that Aubrey Blue, mentioned as one of the searchers, was a friend of Joe's). He wouldn't have been wrong about such matters, not only because it would have been bad songmaking, but also because it would have been bad business. Too many people would have known that Joe "had it wrong there," and since there would have been no justification for it in the tradition (as there might have been for a "poor old aged father" or even a "lad" whose "pearly tears like raindrops fell"), it would have been recognized as just plain bungling or, worse yet, lying.

Since I have already discussed the structure and language of ballads about death on the river in the chapter on "Guy Reed," there is no need to go into it again here in any detail, but obviously this song fits the pattern. It begins with a come-all-ye stanza (1) that gives us the subject in general terms and is so close to the language of "The Jam on Gerry's Rock" as to be a veritable carbon copy:

> Come all ye loyal shanty boys, wherever you may be,
> I would have you give attention and listen unto me,
> Concerning six brave shanty boys, so loyal, true and brave,
> Who broke the jam on Gerry's Rock and met a watery grave.[5]

The accident itself is covered in stanzas 2 through 7—except it really isn't covered; it simply becomes obvious that something terrible has happened. Joe devotes what amounts to a whole stanza to the weather (2), and then goes on to bring White and Murphy to the crossing place (3). The next two stanzas (4–5) are an attempt to explain to us what the difficulty was: the ferryboat was on the wrong side of the river and the two men would just have to wait. There is some bad geography here: Metalluc Pond did not "take its rise" in Parmachenee Lake, but the matter is so irrelevant it is hard to see why Joe brought it in the first place. In the last two stanzas of this section (6–7) the scene shifts from White and Murphy standing on the south shore to Win York some time later standing on the north shore wondering where the men can be. All in all, it is a rather diffuse section.

The "discovery" takes up six stanzas (8–13), the first three of which have to do with the formation of a searching party (8–10); while lists of proper names are common enough in traditional song, I don't recall ever seeing one used in just this way. In woods tradition, monicker songs are plenty, but usually they name and comment on all the men in a camp, as in "The Camp on McNeil":

> Blakely drives the fiery team,
> He calls them Tim and Clyde;
> He cracks his whip and cries aloud,
> "They are the forest pride."
>
> Next we come to O'Donnell
> With old Dick and the carvel gray,
> And if he's heavy loaded
> It's there he's got to stay.[6]

Ballads commemorating sea disasters often mentioned the names of the victims:

314

They were Captain Farrell and his brother Will, the mate was
   Doherty,
Frank MacAulduff, Alf Matthews, all married men were they,
The cook was Johnny Oliver, supercargo was Doiron;
I have numerated all her crew all in this simple song.[7]

But nowhere else do I recall a list of searchers or anything like it. It is
tempting to suggest that Joe's purpose in including this list was
pecuniary—he could count on selling a few copies each to the men
who were named—but I don't know that that was his reason. It's just
that aesthetically the list seems gratuitous, and it certainly brings
the ballad's movement to a complete stop. Joe liked a leisurely
development, to be sure, and this list can be spoken of as innovative,
but it's a bit much.

The bodies are finally found in stanza 11. Then in the next stanza
we get a scene so suggestive of "The Jam on Gerry's Rock" again that
we can be sure that that ballad was in Scott's mind. Compare them.
First, "The Jam":

They raised him from his watery grave, combed back his coal black
   hair
There was one fair form amongst them whose cries would rend the
   air:
There was one fair form amongst them, a girl from Saginaw town;
Her moans and cries would rend the skies for her true love that was
   drowned.[8]

And now "White and Murphy":

Then all the party soon drew near, with faces pale and sad,
And there was one amongst them who was only a lad,
Whose pearly tears like raindrops fell upon the cold, damp ground,
Whose cries would penetrate the skies for his comrade who was
   drowned.

It's pure circular speculation, but Joe is probably reporting what one
of his sources told him (*"And when they brought Murphy's body up,
little Frisbie—he was cookeein' for us—he started to cry some. I
guess he and Murph had been pretty good friends, and . . ."*). It
would have stuck in Joe's mind because it reminded him of "The Jam
on Gerry's Rock" and was the proper sort of stuff for a song.

The last stanza of this section (13) is really the wrap-up of the
accident section, telling us what the rescuers think happened. It is

an unusual way of working it out, but it is not without precedent of
sorts. "John Roberts" has the following stanza:

> We think he got his fatal blow
> While struggling in the undertow;
> By some huge rock beneath the waves
> Where soon he found him a watery grave.[9]

But in "John Roberts" that stanza comes at the end of the accident
section, not at the end of the discovery section, as Joe has it.

The final two stanzas (14–15) simply tell about the funeral in very
general terms and tell where the two men came from. The ballad
ends in a most traditional manner, with a pious hope.

"White and Murphy" never really caught on, never got into oral
tradition. The only oral version I collected was from old Dennis
Taylor of Green Farm, Maine, who mumbled it over for me a couple
of times one afternoon. Insofar as acceptance into wide oral tradition
is a measure of a song's success, this one can only be called a failure,
and I don't think we have to look too hard to see what the problem
was: the song is virtually unsingable.

To begin with, the language is flat and dull, reaching a dead level
of reportage unequaled in any of Joe's other songs. It reads like the
work of a rank beginner, rather than that of a seasoned songmaker.
That may be a very subjective judgment, but it is interesting that the
few people who recalled a single line or two (Tom Pollock is a good
example) usually recalled the more poetic bits, like the mountains
that "responded to his call." In addition, the story line is very diffuse,
which would make it hard for a singer to put together at first or keep
together later on. Worst of all, some of the verses are so awkward it is
hard to see how they could have been sung coherently to any musical
phrase. They "fit," yes, which is to say they "count out" right, but
that's about all; and if the reader wants a demonstration of what I
mean, let him try to sing "White and Murphy" to any tune, say, to
"The Jam on Gerry's Rock" or to any double-stanza tune in this book.
I recognize, of course, that in such an opinion I run all the ethnocen-
tric risks inherent in any judgment passed on a tradition that is not
one's own, but I submit it on the basis of my twenty years of
collecting these songs, talking with singers about them, and singing
them myself, woods fashion. Let's leave it at that and move to higher
ground.

In suggesting that "White and Murphy" was unsingable, I am only offering an explanation of why the song did not pass into oral tradition; if that was what Joe Scott wanted or expected for it, then it can be called a failure all around. But we should temper that judgment in two ways. First, a number of people remembered that there *was* such a song, which may mean that it was well known at the time but was simply too topical to persist for very long. That's a point I have made elsewhere about other songs,[10] but I think its application in the present instance is limited at best. Second, and this is much more to the point, Joe's production may have been looked on less as something to sing (though it probably was sung some) than as something to keep. The men involved, friends and families of the deceased, and fellow woodsmen and townsmen who knew of the accident, all would have bought copies from Joe (which is certainly one thing he wanted). They probably would have approved of it, partly because Joe "had it right," partly because an obituary ballad was such an acceptable memorial it almost wouldn't have seemed right *not* to buy it, and it certainly wouldn't have seemed right to feel it was anything but "good." Mrs. Kibblewhite remarked in her letter that John Murphy's younger brother was still alive, which suggests that she knew the family, and that may be a good part of the reason her uncle saved the song in the first place. Even more relevant, Jack Keating's mother grew up right next door to the Murphys, and not only did she write the ballad out very carefully in her notebook, but right along with it she pasted Murphy's obituary and funeral notice as they had appeared in a local paper. Finally, Fred Campbell's comments are to the point: *"Now this Wilfred White he lived down here in Tracey Mills out from Woodstock there . . . out Centreville way there. . . . I worked in the woods with this Ed Longstaff. He was from there, out [*toward*] Centreville, and he knew Wilfred White. I never learnt the whole song to sing it, you know, but I was telling him about it. And in the spring when we come out of the woods he come to my place and stopped there, and the wife wrote it off for him."

I can see Ed Longstaff now, reading it over, thanking Mrs. Campbell, folding the sheets up carefully, and putting them in his pocket. Back home he shows it around, and people read it, shaking their heads over the sad death but nodding approval of the song as they hand it back to Ed who puts it—where *did* he put it, now?

317

"That's funny. Why I was only just last week showing it to that McDougall fella who was over here from Bath and said his brother knew this Murphy. Where is it? What did I do with that? Can't find it now, but anyhow, mister, it was a good job. Told all about it."

LIST OF VERSIONS

FH   Mrs. R. C. Kibblewhite, Willowdale, Ont., in answer to a request published in the *Family Herald* early in 1966, and forwarded to me in Nov., 1966, by Sheila Bûcher, then editor of the "Old Favourites" column; typescript, 15 sts.

Me.   Dennis Taylor, ca. 85, Green Farm (Dallas Plantation), Me., Mar. 30, 1959; NA Ives tape 59.1, recited, fragment. Delivered as a kind of rhythmic prose; two separate versions. For further information see chapter 18, on "Norman Mitchell."

NH   From the scrapbook of Gertrude Keating (d. 1958, at 79), Berlin, N.H., and copied out by me, Sept. 10, 1965, at the home of her son, John Keating; manuscript, 15 sts. Mrs. Keating (née McKay) was born in Stoneham, P.Q., and grew up across the street from the Murphy place. Her son is quite sure she wrote the piece down back in Stoneham. Her older brothers used to come down to Berlin to work in the woods, and she may have gotten the song from one of them. On the flyleaf of the scrapbook: "Scraps and Songs / London, Ont., 1908" (she had lived in London when she was first married).

NOTES

1. For an interesting picture of the river more than a hundred years ago, see Marshall M. Tidd, "Up the Magalloway River in 1861."

2. Several of the details in this and the following pages are taken from the account of the accident in the *Berlin Reporter* for Oct. 11, 1901.

3. *Stuart's Atlas of the State of Maine*, 12th ed., p. 70.

4. *Rumford Falls Times*, Oct. 26, 1901.

5. See Laws C–1.

6. As sung by Arthur MacDonald, Black River Bridge, N.B., NA Ives tape 1.103 (ATL 3110.4).

7. "The Schooner *Gracie Parker*," as sung by Mrs. Ben Smith, Alberton, P.E.I., Aug. 27, 1965, NA Ives tape 65.5.

8. Edith Fowke, *Lumbering Songs from the Northern Woods*, p. 96.

9. Edward D. Ives and Sharon Sperl, *Folksongs from Maine*, p. 38.

10. See esp. Edward D. Ives, *Lawrence Doyle*, p. 250–251.

17

Two Little Girls

"Charming Little Girl"

Arthur and Ivan Nisbet of Augusta, Maine, had told me to look up Angus Enman next time I was up on the Island. The year was 1958, and "next time" turned out to be in August. I found the name on the mailbox and pulled off the MacArthur Road into the barnyard. A tall, slight man, very straight, with still-dark curly hair, was just closing the barn door. I hailed him by name; he answered, and I told him who had sent me. "They tell me you spent a lot of time working in the Maine woods," I said.

"Yes," he said ruefully, "and much to my sorrow. I lost the sight of this eye there," he said, pointing. "Wood chip came back and hit me."

It didn't sound like I'd chosen the best possible opening, but when I mentioned Joe Scott's name Angus's face lighted up, and the next thing I knew, I had the tape recorder all set up in the kitchen and we were talking. He told me a lot about Joe that afternoon, and sang several songs. One he thought he couldn't remember. *"Mark Ladner, old Mark used to sing that," he said, "and I just got only the [chorus]. How did that go?

> Charming little girl, so pretty, neat and sweet,
> Her mouth extends from ear to ear, her chin and nose they meet.
> She's just the one to charm you if you her breath could endure,
> Still she is fair and sweet to me, will be for evermore.

And he said—he took her out for a walk, and he said,

> The moon was shining brightly, the grass with dew was wet,
> She had been eating onion, and I think I smell them yet."

319

Angus's housekeeper began to laugh. So did I. And so did Angus.
*"Oh, it was a great little song," he said. "I wish I knew it for you.
And he married that girl. And then he left her, see? . . . He was up in
the woods one time, [*and someone asked,*] 'Why didn't you keep her,
Joe?' 'Oh,' he said, 'I don't know. I didn't like her. She chewed
tobacco, and she could spit in a cat's eye ten yards away!' But ohhh!"
Angus added emphatically, "he was in love with that—the one [*in*]
'The Plain Golden Band,' though. That was a lovely one. . . . It
ruined poor Joe, killed him. He just got to be an old bum after that.
. . . [He got down] or he'd of never married that other old thing."

None of this made much sense to me at the time, except the part
about "The Plain Golden Band," and the song fragment Angus
recited for me didn't sound like anything of Joe Scott's I had heard.
But Angus had known the man, and the tape recorder had done its
job. Years later as I relistened to the interview I realized that Joe
must have been referring to his brief marriage to Emma Lefebvre,
but the reference was made even odder by being the only record I
had of Joe's ever mentioning that matter. Nor has continued research
changed that. With one exception, the silence was complete. Odd
that he'd make a song about it, I thought.

Then in 1964 John Brown of Mexico, Maine, had just worded over
"Benjamin Deane" for me. Was that a true song, I asked him?
*They're all true songs, all of them true, yeah," he said.
*"Then there's one there about Walter Clements," his wife said.
Brown laughed. *"Oh, I don't know," he said. "I don't think he
[*Joe*] made that. That was just made up by someone."

Mrs. Brown said it was kind of a funny one, and I tried to get Mr.
Brown to go over it for me. *"Oh, I wouldn't think of putting that on
there," he said, motioning toward the tape recorder. He told me
later he just felt it had been too foolish, and he was sure that I
wouldn't be interested in that sort of thing, but he finally gave in and
recited it for me, twice:

> My name is Walter Clements, near Rumford I reside,
> There is a darling that lives there I hope to make my bride.
> Her father is a jockey and owns a little place,
> And two fine cows I gave him to gain his daughter's grace.
>
> Charming little maid, so full of love and grace,
> With eyes as large as saucers and a mouth all o'er her face.

She's just the one could charm you, could you but stand her breath,
She is so fair and sweet to me and will be unto death.

She told me that the other night her father old and gray
Called her to his bedside and this to her did say,
"If that scapegrace of yours, dear, don't bring another cow,
For burning up my wood at night, there'll be a dreadful row."

I pressed her to my bosom, I kissed her mouth so wide,
Forgive me, oh forgive me, but that time I nearly died.
The moon was shining brightly, the grass with dew was wet,
She had been eating onions and I think I taste them yet.

Charming little maid, so full of love and grace,
With eyes as large as saucers and a mouth all o'er her face.
She's just the one could charm you could you her breath endure,
She is so fair and sweet to me and will be evermore.

*"That's all I know," Brown said. "That's all I ever heard of it." He really wasn't sure about Joe's authorship of this piece. *"I wouldn't say that he did or he didn't," he said. "I just don't know." Clements was a real person, he added, but the song probably wasn't true. *"They probably just made that up on him" he said. "I don't know. He was quite a joker, you know. He was all the time making jokes on somebody else. I guess maybe someone made it up on him. I don't know. . . . Oh yes, I knew him. He was around here; then he went to Pennsylvania. He died over there."

While it was obvious that I was dealing with the same song that Angus had remembered bits and pieces of, this time it was not presented as Joe talking about some girl, but as a song about a local joker; the only thing that might imply that Joe had had anything to do with it at all is that it came up in the context of a conversation about him and his songs. Had Joe just taken a local song and adapted it to his own circumstance while putting on a performance one time when Angus happened to be present? Or had he made it up and then adapted his *own* work—and if so, which way did he "adapt" it? Or did someone else adapt it to Walter Clements? I had no way of answering any of these questions.

Then the picture changed again in the fall of 1966 when Sheila Bûcher sent me that cache of Joe Scott songs that Bert Thorne had carefully written out and sent in to the *Family Herald* twenty years before. Now I had what I could be pretty sure was a complete text, but it wasn't until I saw Thorne's notebook in 1974 that I could claim to have Joe's original. Here it is the way I found it there:

CHARMING LITTLE GIRL.

———

[1]   I'm Ephraim Brown, a farmer,
      In Plymouth I reside,
   And every night I go to see
      That girl who is my pride.
   Her father is a jockey,
      Who owns a little place
   And two fine cows I gave him
      For to gain his daughter's grace.

CHORUS.

   Charming little girl,
      So pretty, sweet and neat;
   Her mouth it spreads from ear to ear,
      Her nose and chin they meet.
   She's just the one to charm you,
      Could you her breath endure,
   But still she's sweet and fair to me,
      And will be evermore.

[2]   Some people say she's homely,
      But to me she's always fair;
   She's not as bright as some I know,
      But then, what do I care.
   I love her, yes, I love her,
      With all her faults, so there.
   What makes me sad some times
      Is this, she seldom combs her hair.

CHORUS—

[3]   Her character is not as good
      As some girls in this town,
   But still she is quite popular,
      She's known the country round.
   I know that she's inclined to flirt,
      She is a little wild,
   But still I love this charming girl,
      Sweet Annie Jennie Guild.

CHORUS.—

Two Little Girls

[4]   The other night, she told me,
          Her papa, old and gray,
      Called her to his bedside
          And unto her did say,
      "If that scapegrace of yours, my dear,
          Don't give another cow
      For burning up my wood at night
          There'll be a dreadful row."

      CHORUS.—

[5]   I pressed her to my bosom
          And kissed her mouth so wide,
      Forgive me if I say it,
          But that time I nearly died;
      The moon was shining brightly,
          The grass with dew was wet,
      She had been eating onions
          And I think I smell them yet.

                              BY JOE SCOTT.

   Thorne bought his songs from Joe in 1901, which at least gives us a
tentative terminal date for the song's composition. But is it a true
story? I have been unable to establish anything one way or the other.
Plymouth, Maine, is somewhat outside Joe's normal haunts, and so
is Plymouth, New Hampshire; and the name Ephraim Brown is
possible, but almost too good a farmer's name to be believed. Nor
have I been able to track down the girl's name. It could have been
simply a bit of lumbercamp gossip Joe picked up about a guy who'd
paid a man a couple of cows for the favors of his daughter (who, while
not much to look at, was the local bread-line), only to have the father
complain that he'd better bring another cow if he's going to sit up all
those nights with her. In other words, it was local satire, a "good one"
on somebody, but it also seems to have been adaptable to others like
Walter Clements one might want to make fun of. Angus Enman's
story even makes me wonder if Ephraim Brown might really be Joe
Scott and Annie Guild might be Emma Lefebvre. Knowing what I
do of Joe, I don't think that is likely, but since we don't have the local
data necessary for understanding a local song of this sort, almost any
speculation is worth mentioning.

One thing is certain, however. In writing this song Joe was working within the well-established popular tradition of songs about ugly women, a tradition that turned the beautiful/sentimental tradition plumb inside-out. Hughey Dougherty of minstrel-show fame had a parody called "Dear Evelina," which will set the pace very nicely:

> She's thin as a broomstick, she carries no meat.
> She never was known to put soap on her cheek.
> Her hair is like rope and the color of brass—
> But oh, how I love her, this dear little lass![1]

Or there is "Liza Jane":

> Her mouth was like a cellar, her foot was like a ham,
> Her eyes were like an owl's at night, her voice was never calm,
> Her hair was long and curly, she looked just like a crane,
> I bid goodbye to all my love, so goodbye Susan Jane.[2]

The girl in "No More Booze" is in the same league:

> She's the only girl I love,
> With a face like a horse and buggy.[3]

So is Mary Jane, who promised to meet him "as the clock struck seventeen":

> She's my darlin', my daisy,
> She's humpbacked, she's crazy,
>   She's knock-kneed, bow-legged, and lame—
> (*Spoken:* Got the rheumatism!)
> They say her breath is sweet,
> Bud I'd rather smell her feet,
>   She's my freckle-faced, consumptive Mary Jane.[4]

What Joe did in "Charming Little Girl," then, was to combine the folk tradition of local satire or gossip songs with the essentially popular minstrel and music-hall tradition of "ugly beloved" songs. It was obviously adaptable; yet it never really seems to have caught on, though like other satires it may have been very much in demand for a while locally. From our point of view, it can show us another aspect of Joe's talent. He could be funny, plain old slapstick funny. The song is not a great one, but it's pretty good for what it is, and I can imagine its being one his friends often asked for.

"Sacker Shean's Little Girl"

Clyde Dickinson of Lower Woodstock, New Brunswick, was just a boy when Joe Scott returned home those two times in the early 1900s, and while he could remember hearing Joe sing, he couldn't remember any of the songs. In fact, he couldn't even recall the names of any of them with the exception of "Sacker Shean's Little Girl," and he could recall that only because one of Joe's nieces used it for a recitation piece in school. I talked to Dickinson first in 1957, but it wasn't until I went through the complete *Family Herald* files almost ten years later that I ever saw the song itself in the form in which they published it. Then Sheila Bûcher found and sent me the handwritten copy Bert Thorne had sent in. Finally in 1974 I found Joe's original slip in Bert Thorne's notebook:

SACKER SHEAN'S LITTLE GIRL.

[1]   Now I am only Sacker Shean's
      Poor little girl, you know,
   Who was cast upon this cruel world,
      No home, no place to go.
   My father is a drunkard
      And my mother, don't you know,
   Oh she left me in my infancy,
      She died long years ago.

[2]   I never knew my mother dear
      That people say was fair,
   They say she was a lady gay
      With dark and wavy hair.
   But I often think about her
      And last night, near by this town,
   Oh I wonder if she saw me
      As I stood there all alone.

[3]   The night was dark and stormy
      And the winds blew cold and bleak,
   I wonder if she saw me there
      So hungry, cold and weak.
   I saw the bright lights of the town
      Not very far away,

With wearied foot-steps I approached
   Those lights that looked so gay.

[4] When on the bridge, I paused to rest,
    And on it's brink looked o'er
At the tumbling, laughing waters
    Rolling on for ever more.
I wonder if she saw me
    As the briny tears rolled down
My freezing cheeks, then dropped and froze,
    E'er they had reached the ground.

[5] I wandered from the bridge away
    Into the crowded street,
Where people bustle to and fro
    With hurrying, flying feet.
I heard sweet strains of music
    From the ball room bright and gay,
And saw the gay throng, clad
    In costly garments, on their way.

[6] I guess she must have seen me there
    And told to God my case,
A lady that was passing by
    Looking down into my face.
What happened then I do not know,
    When I again could see
I was seated by the fire-side
    Upon this lady's knee.

[7] She kindly gave me food to eat,
    My story I did tell,
I saw a tear roll down her cheek
    I saw it when it fell.
I'm glad I have found a home
    So good bye I must go,
For I'm only Sacker Shean's
    Poor little girl you know.

By JOE SCOTT.

When was this song written? As always, Bert Thorne's version gives us at least a presumptive terminal date of 1901, but that's all we know for sure. Is it possible that Joe's niece learned the song from a copy that had been around since before Joe left for Maine in the eighties? Yes, but it's much more likely that someone got it from him after his return to Lower Woodstock in the early 1900s, which means that "pre-1901" is as good a date as we're going to get.

But if the date is problematic, it is perfectly clear what Joe's models were. The child in distress—cold, starving, penniless, whatever—had been a favorite theme in English and American traditional and popular song for a long time. "A Farmer's Boy," for example, which had had a vigorous life in England as a stall ballad and may go back as far as the eighteenth century, is typical. A young boy, wet and cold, knocks at a farmer's door and asks for work:

> My father's dead and my mother left,
> And with three children small;
> And what is worse for my mother still,
> I'm the oldest of them all.
> But as little as I am I will do what I can
> All for to seek employ.[5]

They take him in, largely at the wife's and the daughter's insistence, and he does well. Ultimately he marries the daughter, and when the farmer dies, the lad inherits the farm. "A Soldier's Poor Little Boy" alters the pattern only slightly. A boy, "quite frozen," knocks at a rich lady's door:

> My mother died when I was young,
> My father went to the war;
> And many a battle so brave he has fought,
> Always covered with wounds and scars.
> Many a mile on his knapsack
> He carried me with joy.
> But now I'm left quite parentless—
> I'm a soldier's poor little boy.[6]

The rich lady, having lost her only son in the war, takes him in. A popular song, "Don't Tease the Old Man," adds an Algerish moral twist by having a ragged newsboy chastise some children teasing an old man who is lost. When the old man says the poor lad must have a fine mother, the boy replies that he is an orphan, whereupon the old man takes him home with him, saying he is "immensely wealthy."[7]

Another group of songs in this tradition is even sadder, because the child does not fare so well. "The Orphan Girl" is probably the classic example. She begs at a rich man's door:

> My father, alas, I never knew,
> And the tears dimmed her eyes so bright,
> My mother sleeps in a new-made grave,
> 'Tis an orphan begs tonight.
>
> It was cold and dark and the snow fell fast,
> But the rich man closed his door,
> With his proud lips curled with scorn he said,
> No home nor bread for the poor.[8]

She freezes to death at his door, but her soul goes to a "home above, / Where there's room and bread for the poor." In another favorite, "Poor Little Joe," the unfortunate one is a newsboy:

> While strolling one night through New York's gay throng,
> I met a poor boy who was singing a song,
> Although he was singing he wanted for bread,
> Although he was smiling, he wished himself dead.
>
> Cold blew the blast, down came the snow,
> He had no place for shelter, no place to go,
> No mother to guide him, in a grave she lay low,
> Cast in the cold streets was poor little Joe.
>
> A carriage came by with a lady inside,
> She looked on poor Joe's face and saw that he cried,
> He followed her carriage, she not even smiled,
> She was fondling and caressing her own darling child.

A policeman finds Joe later that night frozen to death, "eyes turned toward Heaven."[9] The popular song "Little Barefoot" follows the same pattern; the girl dies begging bread for her mother. A preachment is added in the chorus:

> While we beg for those with plenty,
> And for them to us unknown,
> We'll not forget our "little barefoots,"
> They are heathens nearer home.[10]

Sometimes the fate of the child is left unresolved, the pathos itself being the whole point, as in Will Hays's "Nobody's Darling," in which the child, parentless and freezing, is "sitting on poverty's knee":

> Often at night when I kneel, Lifting my sorrowful eyes,
> Asking my mother to smile, Down on her child from the skies,

Then I forget all my grief, Mother and Heaven I see;
There I am somebody's darling—Somebody cares for me![11]

One could go on into other adaptations of the pattern, such as the great 1894 Marks and Stern hit, "The Little Lost Child,"[12] but the point has been adequately made that children in dire distress were very popular song subjects around the turn of the century. The stock of clichés through which these songs were developed was amazingly limited, and in writing "Sacker Shean's Little Girl" Joe Scott doesn't seem to have missed a one. No home, a drunken father, a mother in Heaven, a stormy night, winds cold and bleak, hunger, tears, all contrasted with the bright lights of the town and the gay throng in costly garments. The girl is rescued by a lady, who takes her home, warms her, feeds her, and evidently adopts her after hearing her sad story.

I don't think we need to question what it was Joe set about to do here. He wanted to write a hit. In my personal judgment, "Sacker Shean's Little Girl" is every bit as good a song as many of those we have discussed that did become hits; but since Joe had no idea how to get his song on the market, it never stood a real chance. Why didn't it get better circulation locally? For the other side of the same reason: there were too many well-known songs on the same theme, and Joe's song offered nothing they didn't already supply in abundance. It is either an application of Gresham's Law or its direct opposite, whatever that may be. And that may be as good a place as any to leave it.

Both "Charming Little Girl" and "Sacker Shean's Little Girl" show us Joe Scott trying his hand at different genres of song rather than staying pretty much with one the way Larry Gorman or (though he was less single-minded than Gorman) Lawrence Doyle did. In the next chapter we will see him trying out yet another. As Ned Stewart put it, *"He was a clever dog."

LIST OF VERSIONS

"Charming Little Girl"

JS   Original printed slip, as obtained from the notebook of Bert Thorne, Jemseg, N.B. 5 sts., with chorus.

Me.   John Brown, 81, Mexico, Me., July 10, 1964; NA Ives tape 64.4, recited, 5 sts.

PI   Angus Enman, Spring Hill, P.E.I., Aug. 19, 1958; NA Ives tape 1.39, recited, 1½ sts., fragment.

"Sacker Shean's Little Girl"

JS   Original printed slip, as obtained from the notebook of Bert Thorne, Jemseg, N.B. 7 sts.

FH   *Family Herald*, Nov. 14, 1957; 7 sts. Taken from a manuscript copy of the original sent in by Bert Thorne.

NOTES

1. Douglas Gilbert, *Lost Chords,* p. 113.
2. Vance Randolph, *Ozark Folksongs,* 3, p. 185.
3. Carl Sandburg, *The American Songbag,* p. 209.
4. Ibid., p. 207.
5. H. M. Belden, *Ballads and Songs Collected by the Missouri Folk-Lore Society,* p. 272.
6. Ibid., p. 275.
7. Sigmund Spaeth, *Weep Some More, My Lady,* p. 173.
8. Randolph, *Ozark Folksongs,* 4, p. 195.
9. Ibid., p. 180. I have also collected this in New Brunswick from Spurgeon Allaby of Passekeag (letter, Mar. 27, 1957; NA Ives tape 1.149 and ATL 3156.9).
10. Spaeth, *Weep Some More,* p. 168.
11. Ibid., p. 22. See also Randolph, *Ozark Folksongs,* 4, pp. 188–191.
12. See Sigmund Spaeth, *Read 'em and Weep,* pp. 167–169, and don't miss the wonderful cover picture facing p. 180 and the selections from the slide show facing p. 184.

18

Three Unfortunate Men

"William McGibbeny"

Fred Campbell bought a bunch of songs from Joe Scott one winter up the Magalloway (it would have been right around 1901), and among them was one he called "William McGivney." I had never heard of it, Fred couldn't remember anything about it, and the mice had eaten up the original. No one else I talked to seemed to know or even know of the song, although several people said that the name "sounded familiar." I had just about written it off when it turned up in that batch of manuscript Bert Thorne sent in to the *Family Herald*. Then in 1974, when I finally got access to Bert Thorne's notebook, I found it there as follows (material in parentheses was written in in Thorne's own hand where the original had been obliterated by a fold or tear):

WILLIAM McGIBBENY.

[1]   Within a cheerless cot,
       In a lone and desolate spot,
       Lay a dying man just e're the close of day,
       Who e'er the morning light
       Would disperse the gloom of night
       From this world of woe and care would pass away.
       No loving hand was near
       For to wipe away a tear
       Or the clammy prespiration [*sic*] from his brow,
       And as the wind did wail

Round that cottage old and frail,
These sad words they heard him utter weak and low.

[2]   Will you raise the window please,
Let me feel the scented breeze
And let me once more the setting sun behold
For e'er the glorious sun
Sinks behind those hills again
In death's fond embrace I will be still and cold.
I would watch the sunbeams smile
On the hillside near the stile,
Oh, I fain would hear again the bird's sweet song,
And I fain again would look
On the flowers and the brook,
For I know my time on earth will not be long.

[3]   Those bright sunbeams on the hill
And the babbling brook or rill
And the flowers so fair, the birds that sing with glee
And the balmy breeze of spring,
(oh how sweetly they do ring)
Those fair charming silver bells of memory;
How they call me back once more
To an old familiar shore
Where the myrtle and the ivy thickly grow,
In a pleasant shady spot
Round a humble little cot
Where I was born so many years ago.

[4]   Round the place there's many a change
And the people would seem strange
Who would come to greet me from that humble cot,
For my kindred so dear
They are scattered everywhere
And some sleep where blooms the sweet forget-me-not.
There my dear old mother sleeps
Where the drooping willow weeps,
Where the feathered warblers carol all the day;
Oh, near where the billows roar
As they break upon the shore
In the sunny east so many miles away.

[5]   Now the sun has set at last
In the far off golden west,

Three Unfortunate Men

And the smiling sunbeams fade into twilight,
And the birds they cease to sing,
Hide their heads behind their wings
Just to rest in sleep throughout the hours of night.
On that stand that lamp you see,
Will you light it please for me,
Will you bring to me that satchel resting there,
It contains two pictures fair
Of my wife and child so dear,
Some old letters and a lock of golden hair.

[6]   And my name you soon will see
That it is McGibbeny
On some letters that were written years ago,
They were from my mother dear,
And the lock of golden hair
Once it bedecked my daughter's snow-white brow,
But she sleeps beneath the earth
Near the spot that gave her birth,
In the town of Anson in the state of Maine,
On the Kennebec's green shore
And near where the waters roar,
There her green and grassy mound it may be seen.

[7]   And my other daughter dear
In the future I do fear
From the paths of virtue will be led astray,
For her mother, to her shame,
Turned a woman of ill fame
And left and took my little child away;
When I found that they had gone
Gone and left me all alone,
Deepest grief and sorrow nearly drove me mad,
And my thoughts were night and day
On those loved ones far away
And it's many a time I wished that I was dead.

[8]   It is many and many a night
When the moon and stars shone bright,
Down by the river's flowery bank would roam
And among the dewy flowers
I would weep there many hours
For those absent ones so far away from home.
(oh how my heart did yearn)

333

And with longing seems to burn
For that little fair haired child of mine, he cried,
How 'twould make my heart rejoice
Just to hear my daughter's voice
Saying, "Papa dear, your child is by your side."

[9]   E'er they lay me low to rest
Place those pictures on my breast,
Those old letters and that lock of golden hair,
And let my remains be laid
'Neath the willow's quiet shade
By my mother's side, who calmly slumbers there.
"We will grant you this request,"
Said a man among the guests,
Who were standing by the sufferer's dying bed,
And the dying man's reply was,
"God bless you sir—good-bye."
In a few brief moments later he was dead.

[10]   And then everything was still
But a little whip-poor-will
That awaking from its sleep began to call,
As its notes so loud and clear
Fell upon the watcher's ear,
Intense sadness seemed to hover over all.
"See, the sky is overcast,
And the rain is falling fast,"
Said a man who slowly from the window drew,
"And it's blessed are the dead
That the rain rains on," he said,
And we hope and trust those solemn words are true.

BY JOE SCOTT.

In addition to having a "signed original" and a good solid ascription by Fred Campbell, I would certainly say that "William McGibbeny" sounds like Joe's work. Its tremendously leisurely quality—it is much longer than any other song of its type I know of—and both the quality and the sheer amount of nature imagery it contains are, as we have seen, characteristic of Joe's songs. I have no question whatever about his authorship.

The only trouble is that I have been unable to find out anything about the real William McGibbeny. No one seems to remember him, and there is absolutely no record that I can find, official or otherwise, of the man's existence. The name McGibbeny is unusual enough to be distinctive, and my searches have turned up nothing under that name; but I assume the correct spelling was McGivney, and that's a pretty common name in certain places here in the Northeast, say around Berlin, New Hampshire, and in central New Brunswick (where there's a McGivney Crossing on the railroad halfway between Nashwaak Bridge and Boiestown). According to Berlin city records, a William R. McGivney, aged fifty-five, died in the state hospital in Concord on February 17, 1915, and is buried in the city cemetery;[1] but since both Thorne and Campbell bought their copies of the ballad from Scott in the early 1900s, I am sure that this is not our man. Nor have I been able to track down the daughter's "green and grassy mound" in Anson, Maine. In spite of all this unsuccess, I am just as sure Joe was telling a "true" story as I am that he authored the ballad itself. He is too circumstantial for me to draw any other conclusion. It is unfortunate not to be able to determine just where he was being factual and where he was allowing his facts to be aligned with a well-established song tradition: the death-bed scene.

Like the child-in-distress tradition, the death-bed tradition had a basic pattern that allowed for several common variations, and there is a cluster of stock images through which the theme is developed. The invariable core is the dying person's speech to some listener or listeners whose presence is either directly expressed or at least implied. The well-known "Dying Soldier" is a good example:

> The sun was sinking in the west and fell in ling'ring rays
> Through the branches of a forest where a wounded soldier lay.
> On the banks of the Potomac 'neath the southron, sultry sky,
> Far from his loved New England home, they've laid him down to
> die.
>
> Now a group had gathered round him, comrades with him in the
> fight,
> And a tear fell down each manly cheek as they bade him last good-
> night.
> One kind friend and companion was kneeling by his side,
> Striving to quench his life's blood, but alas, in vain he tried.
>
> His heart filled with deep anguish as he saw 'twas all in vain,
> And upon his loved companion the tears fell down like rain.

Then up spoke the dying soldier, saying, "Harry, weep no more for
  me.
I am crossing the dark river, beyond where all is free.

He goes on to tell his comrades that his sister back home will now be
all alone, since his father and mother are both dead. What is to
become of her?

"Listen, comrades, gather round me, listen to my dying prayer.
Who will shield her with a brother's love and with a father's care?"
Then the soldiers spoke together, like one voice it seemed to fall:
"She shall be to us a sister! We'll protect her, one and all."[2]

He smiles radiantly, and dies at peace, whereupon his comrades
bury him, "with his knapsack for a pillow and his gun upon his
breast." Several other ballads are developed almost identically, like
"The Battle of Mill Springs" (Laws J–6 and J–7), and always in the
background there is the old recitation favorite, Lady Maxwell's
"Bingen on the Rhine":

A soldier of the Legion lay dying in Algiers;
There was lack of woman's nursing, there was dearth of woman's
  tears.[3]

In a second group of death-bed ballads, there is no third-person
introduction and conclusion; the entire ballad is a monologue by the
dying person, but the audience is clearly there, and the last requests
will just as clearly be respected. Sometimes the one dying is a girl, as
in "The Dying Girl's Message":

Raise the window, mother darling,
For no air can harm me now,
Let the breeze blow in upon me,
It will cool my fevered brow.

She has a last message for one who, "though I cannot speak his
name," long ago rejected her for another:

Take this ring from off my finger
Where he placed it long ago,
Give it to him with a blessing
Which in dying I bestow.

Tell him 'tis a token, mother,
Of forgiveness and of peace,

336

>Bid him hush his voice in passing,
>Will this watching never cease?

She sees her Saviour's form, asks her mother for a last kiss, and dies. "The Dying Nun" begins with the exact same stanza. The poor girl asks Sister Martha to hold her:

>Hold my hands, so cold and frozen,
>Once they were so soft and white,
>And this ring that falls down from it,
>Clasped my finger round so tight.
>
>Little ring they thought so worthless
>That they let me keep it there,
>Only a plain golden circlet
>With a lock of Douglas' hair.[4]

The situation is different here, though, from that in the foregoing song, and much is suggested, though little is said. After wondering if mother and father can forgive their "stray lamb" at last, she drifts between two worlds:

>I was thinking of some music
>That I heard long, long ago.
>Oh how sweet the nuns are singing
>In the chapel soft and low.
>
>But a strain of heavenly music
>Breaks the solemn midnight dream,
>And I hear the wild waltz pealing
>As I seem to float with him.
>
>Douglas, Douglas, I am coming,
>Where you are, I too am there,
>Freed at last, I come, my dearest,
>Death gives back your little Clare.[5]

Then, of course, there is "The Little Rosewood Casket":

>In that little rosewood casket
>Setting on a marble stand,
>Is a package of old letters
>Written by a lover's hand.
>
>Bring them to me, oh dear sister,
>And read them o'er to me,

I have often tried to read them
But for tears I could not see.

Bring the locket and the letters,
Place them here upon my heart,
And that little ring he gave me
From my finger never part.[6]

In "The Dying Californian," which may well be the earliest of the
whole genre, a man is dying aboard ship on his way to the goldfields:

Lay up nearer, brother, nearer,
    For my limbs are growing cold,
And thy presence seemeth dearer
    As thy arms around me fold.[7]

He gives his brother messages for mother, wife, children, father, and
sister; hears his Saviour calling; and bids a last farewell. Helen
Creighton collected a different song with the same title from
blacksmith William Ireland of Elgin, New Brunswick, which covers
the same ground in a similar fashion. The man speaks of his loved
one, Mary, and sends her a ring. Then:

Here is a token, she gave it me, from which I cannot part,
Comrades when I am cold and dead place it upon my heart,
It seems as if I could not rest should it be wanting there,
Through the pain of death I could not part with a gift from one so
    dear.[8]

"William McGibbeny" is obviously Joe's attempt to write a real
tear-jerker in the death-bed tradition, and there is no question that
he knew the tradition well. Into the essential framed structure of
"The Dying Soldier" with its third-person opening and close, he has
poured the heavy sentiment of the dying-speech songs we have just
discussed. All the elements are there: close of day, the request to
raise the window, the packet of letters, the lock of hair, the story of
unhappy love, the dying plea. But "William McGibbeny" goes far
beyond any of its models, not only in its length, but also in the
elaborateness of its story. In "The Dying Nun" and "The Dying Girl's
Message," for example, the raising-of-the-window theme takes four
short lines, while in "William McGibbeny" it extends over a stanza
and a half—nearly a stanza and a half of vintage Joe Scott nature
imagery. Notice, too, how the song moves from sunset to storm,

which gives Joe a chance to bring in a proverb, something he loved to do.

We do not know what tune he had in mind, but the stanza form was ambitious. There is an exact parallel in the old Gussie Davis hit of 1896, "If I Could Only Blot Out the Past," another song of death and unhappy love and separation and distant yearning; while it is not in the direct tradition we have been discussing, the application of its tune to a song in that tradition would not have seemed inappropriate, I am sure, either to Joe or to his audience.[9] In sum, "William McGibbeny" shows Joe Scott's thorough acquaintance with and understanding of the whole death-bed tradition, which he extended and elaborated in ways that by now we can see were typically his. It is another beautiful example of Joe's special talent for blending folk and popular traditions in a most inventive way.

Why didn't this song catch on, then? There can be no question of Joe's intentions in this case. That is, with songs like "Wreck on the Grand Trunk Railway" and "Wilfred White and John Murphy," it is possible that Joe was more interested in creating a "keepsake" that would sell, a poem people would buy and put in their scrapbooks, than a "song" they would sing. "William McGibbeny" just isn't that kind of song. Lacking both calamity and sensation, it had no public dimension, and therefore Joe could not have counted on any general interest that would encourage people to buy it. Either "William McGibbeny" was made to be sung, or there was no sense in it at all. In my opinion Joe did a good job with it, too, but its fate has been an oblivion most oblivious. Only two people even recalled it by name, and one of them just happened to keep a print of it. What went wrong?

My first guess is that "William McGibbeny" was just too much. By a simple line-count, it is about three times as long as any other song in the death-bed tradition, and unlike that other excruciatingly long song, "Benjamin Deane," there was no simple way for singers to cut it down to size. Either it had to be sung whole or not at all. And it would have been a very hard song to learn; only a "real singer" would have attempted it, and obviously few if any of them did. Its failure was a failure of excess; in a sense, it can be spoken of as too well made, and in that sense, too good is apt to be worse than not quite good enough.[10]

My second guess is like unto the first. Not only is "William

McGibbeny" long, it is also diffuse. It has no core, no central image or thing that holds our attention. Although the dying man's story is indubitably sad, there is no father's sword to be passed on, no sister at home to be taken care of, no Douglas in the sky. True, there is a packet of letters, *two* pictures, *and* a lock of golden hair, but that's the very point I'm making. They are too many, too much, and their combined emotional weight is less than that of a single rosewood casket.

Joe Scott wrote "William McGibbeny" at about the same time he wrote some of his most successful songs. The internal evidence suggests that the author was a man who was in a position to do what he could do very well indeed. No tyro could have failed in this grand style. "William McGibbeny" is an amazing production, but a case of overreach, of poetic hubris, perhaps, and as such its fate was inevitable.

"The White Cafe"

It was early August, 1963, and the Sixth Miramichi Folksong Festival was in full swing. A bunch of us, a busload and then some, had gone up to Boiestown, about sixty miles upriver, where the parish priest conducted a short ceremony blessing the new stone over Peter Amberly's grave (it's black and shiny and in all ways splendid, though I liked the old white wooden cross with its hand lettering well enough). Now we were back in Newcastle, and I went over to the Beacon Light Motel to see Fred Campbell.

Bob Currie, from Aroostook, New Brunswick, not far from the mouth of the Tobique, had heard me speak or sing (I can't remember just where now, or when), and I'd talked about Joe Scott, asking if anyone knew anything about him. He remembered there was a man up in Arthurette by the name of Fred Campbell who'd known Joe and knew some of his songs, and while he said nothing to me about it at the time, he brought Fred to the festival that year, figuring correctly that I'd be there. Besides, he knew Fred would enjoy the singing and probably even do some himself. Again, he was right. He'd introduced us the night before, and we'd agreed to meet this afternoon after the bus came back.

In the course of the afternoon Fred told me a lot about Joe I'd never known (though it all fit perfectly), sang several of Joe's songs (and sang them well), and discussed several more, like "White and Murphy." It was an exciting time for me, and it was made even better by the fact that Fred was a hell of a nice guy who enjoyed talking about his old friend.

One song Fred mentioned I'd never heard of before, "The Maid with Golden Hair." He was going to sing it at the festival that evening, he'd told me earlier, but I wondered if he'd sing it for me now. He said sure, and without further fuss sailed right into it:

THE MAID WITH GOLDEN HAIR

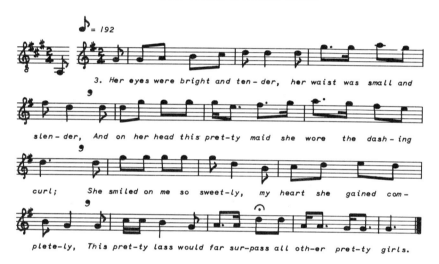

[1]   Kind people pay attention to a few facts I will mention
        Concerning what befell me one day as I did stray;
        It being on a Monday, I had been drunk on Sunday,
        To sober up I took a stroll down to the White Cafe.

[2]   I went inside the cafe, I called for wine and whiskey,
        Seated myself all in a stall to drive dull cares away;
        But as I set there drinking, of my hard luck was thinking,
        A maiden fair with golden hair to me she did appear.

[3]   Her eyes were bright and tender, her waist was small and
            slender,
        And on her head this pretty maid she wore the dashing curl;
        She smiled on me so sweetly, my heart she gained completely,
        This pretty lass would far surpass all other pretty girls.

[4]   I says, "You seem quite cheery. Would you have a drink, my
dearie?"
She said, "Kind sir, I would prefer a glass of lager beer."
The beer she soon did swallow; along with it did follow
Nine cocktails, four mugs of ale, and two of whiskey clear.

[5]   She soon began to chatter—oh, how her tongue did clatter!
She told me many a curious yarn which caused me for to smile.
She was a gay deceiver, I was foolish to believe her;
She beat me bad, she did, by dad, she done me up in style.

[6]   "Where are you from, my fair one? What is your occupation?"
She says, "Kind sir, in Portland here my parents they do
dwell."
But in regard to her occupation I gained no information,
For reasons known to herself alone, the facts could not reveal.

[7]   She said, "Kind sir, please take me to the city of Augusta,
And if you do I'll vow to you I always will prove true."
Oh, she was such a beauty, I thought it was my duty;
I took the bait, now this is straight, pray what else could I do?

[8]   'Twas at the Farmer's Hotel, where some of you are known
well,
Upon my life as man and wife we registered our names;
But before a week was over, I wished she was in Dover,
Or down below, that place you know, amidst the hottest
flames.

[9]   Our honeymoon got stranded, which left me empty-handed,
For what I thought was honey soon turned to hotel hash.
Oh, she skipped out one morning with my grip all filled with
linen
And ninety-two—now this is true—of very hard earned cash.

[10]   We were going home that morning just as the day was dawn-
ing,
I stopped at Gatherin's restaurant; the coach was standing
there.
Whilst I a drink was taking, the coachman he was making
Two horses fly for Togus with that jade with golden hair.

[11]   Now should I chance to meet her, I fear that I would greet her
In such a way that some of you might think were very mean of
me.
But if I do not lick her, my name it is not Decker;
I'll black her eyes, I'll thrash her until she cannot see!

The minute Fred got started on this song I knew that I *had* heard it before, twice, but the singers had called it "The White Cafe." Tom MacLeod of Baring, Maine, was the first; he sang me a fragment of it back in 1957, saying that he'd been told it was by Joe Scott, though he himself had never known the man. I was dubious. It didn't sound like anything else I'd come even at that early date to associate with Joe, but since it didn't matter much at the time, I just filed the information away in the back of my mind. Then in 1961 Phil Walsh of Northwest Bridge, New Brunswick, sang it for me shortly after he sang "Guy Reed," but he simply called it a "State of Maine song." I asked him why. *"Well, different people told me it was," he said, "and it's got the 'city of Augusta,' you know." Phil had never heard of Joe Scott, by the way, and I certainly saw no reason to assign it to Joe when all I had to go on then was MacLeod's secondhand attribution. Now here was Fred Campbell, who not only knew Joe well, but also claimed he'd bought the song from him. *"Did he say this was a true story?" I asked. His answer is worth quoting at some length:

*Yes, because he told me about going into this lumbercamp, and he was selling some songs. And somebody said—you know, he would sing a few songs—somebody said, "Sing 'The Maid with Golden Hair.'" Well, this man, this Decker, was there, and Joe said he was a big husky-looking chap, and he said, "I don't know whether to sing it or not."

So they said, "Go ahead. He won't harm you."

Joe sung the song, and he [*Decker*] said, "Well, that's true." Joe said he was very nice about it. . . .

I've seen this Decker. I wasn't very well acquainted with him, but I've seen him.

Less than a year later, in July of 1964, eighty-year-old John Brown of Mexico, Maine, worded most of "The White Cafe" over for me, and he unhesitatingly ascribed it to Joe. Brown hadn't known him personally, though, but his older brother Eldon had, and back home in Chipman, New Brunswick, Eldon had told him Joe'd written it. *"This fella's name was Decker that it was written about," he added. "Decker was mad about that. . . . He was mad about his name being on it. And that 'by dad' that was in the—was his words, you know." Decker's reaction probably depended a lot on what company he was in and what the circumstances were.

Did Joe write this song? All we have to go on are three attributions, two of them secondhand. The towns involved, Portland and

Augusta, are not ones where Joe seems to have spent time, and yet the places named suggest that the author had some real acquaintance with them both. There *was* a Gaslin's Restaurant and a Farmer's Hotel around the turn of the century, both of them on Water Street in a less-than-splendid section of Augusta and both of them frequented by woods types. I am less sure about a White Cafe in Portland, although the *Maine Register* for 1903 lists a Samuel White as having an eating house at 26 Franklin Street, and the 1904 and 1905 editions give the address as 229 Fore. As far as style goes, I can see nothing that would make me attribute the song to Joe, especially since humor hardly seems to have been his forte. Add all these things up, and it looks like we can make a very good case *against* Scott's being the author of "The White Cafe."

Why, then, do I hesitate in reaching a negative verdict? Largely on the basis of Fred Campbell's attribution—yet even here I must argue against myself for a moment. Fred was not infallible; he was one of those who attributed "John Ladner" to Joe, but he did so with some hesitation, saying he *thought* he had written it. Nor does his anecdote represent Joe as claiming he *wrote* the song, but merely wondering whether or not he should *sing* it in front of Decker. The implication is clear enough, but it is still no more than an implication. It is also possible that Joe pirated the song, saying he wrote it when he didn't. All told, my hesitation is no more than that, a hesitation, a matter of "reasonable doubt." Joe Scott *could* have written it. It would be as ridiculous to deny that as it would be to affirm the opposite. My hunch is that he did write it, but I'm not going to insist on anything beyond that. A possibility and a hunch. Leave it there for now, and probably forever.

"The White Cafe" is the only complete Joe Scott ballad for which I cannot assign a date, either through reference to the event it celebrates or through the existence of one of Bert Thorne's manuscript versions. Since this sort of incident does not find its way into print or public record, we'll never known when the incident occurred or even *if* it occurred (though it probably did in some fashion). The best we can do for assigning a date is to note that both Fred Campbell (NB.1) and John Brown (Me.1) learned their versions in the early 1900s, which means we can be reasonably sure that "The White Cafe" was written right around the turn of the century.

True or not, the story is not a particularly startling one. If it wasn't (and isn't) an everyday occurrence, it was (and is) common enough to be a standard joke. Any man should know better than to let himself get taken this way, but every man sees his own involvement as different, which it is until it isn't—and then the snickers begin. I can see the present instance as a barroom anecdote, a bit of deacon-seat gossip (*"Hey, did you hear about what happened to old Decker? You remember him, that big guy who was on the drive with us last spring? Well, the poor son of a bitch . . ."*) that caught the imagination of someone with a poetical turn of mind. That someone was probably Joe Scott; but whoever it was realized that here was the stuff of song, which is to say it fit a traditional pattern beautifully.

Songs about men who "got took" are legion, and while the details may vary, the basic story does not. The hero meets a beautiful woman, they have an affair of sorts, and then she disappears after cleaning him out, leaving him in a pickle. The introductory stanza or cluster of stanzas is usually a come-all-ye, setting the scene, introducing the cast, and getting the action going. "The Shirt and the Apron" is typical:

You sailors all, come lend an ear, come listen to my song,
A trick of late was played on me, it won't detain you long.
I came from sea the other day, a girl I chanced to meet,
"My friends will be expecting me to a dance on Barrack Street."[11]

And so is "The Crockery Ware":

Oh, a Swansea lass as I hear tell,
A Swansea lass I knew right well;
I asked to her one question bright,
If I could stay with her one night.[12]

These ballads next move to a description of the pleasures of the evening. "Shirt and Apron":

At eight o'clock that evening the drinking did begin,
And when all hands had got their fill the dancing did begin.
Me and my love danced all around unto a merry tune,
When she says, "Dear, we will retire to a chamber all alone."

"The Girl with the Waterfall" does it this way:

'Twas at a picnic party
I met her after that,
I quickly introduced myself,

We had a pleasant chat.
I saw her home, we walked along,
An' said we'd never part,
An' when she asked me to come in
I found she'd won my heart.[13]

"The Crockery Ware" varies this by showing the girl setting the trap:

Oh, this pretty fair maid she give consent;
Straightway up to bed she went.
She placed a chair in the middle of the floor
And onto it piled some crockery ware.

Next comes the fleecing itself. Again, "Shirt and Apron":

The dancing being over, to bed we did repair,
And there I fell fast asleep, the truth I will declare.
My darling with my thirty pounds, gold watch and chain had fled,
And left me here, poor Jack alone, left naked in the bed.

In "The Crockery Ware," the young man makes a beeline for the bed and stumbles into the chair:

Oh, the young girl got up in a terrible fright,
Half splitting her joints with the joke she made.
Oh, she says, "Young man, oh don't you fear,
You gotta pay mother for the crockery ware."

And in "The Girl With The Waterfall," the husband comes in. The fleecing is elaborated in that song by a description of the beating:

Before I'd time to say a word
The fellow at me flew
An' while the maiden held me down
He beat me black an' blue.
When I got up I found I'd lost
My money, watch-chain an' all,
I never since go near a girl
That wears a waterfall.

In "The Crockery Ware":

Oh, the bill was called without any more delay,
It was the same I had to pay:
Five shillings for the durn old chair,
And five pound ten for the crockery ware.

"The Shirt and the Apron" contains several hilarious stanzas describing how poor Jack has to go back to the ship wearing a woman's shirt and apron.

The ending is moderately moral, more accurately morning-after moral, involving a bit of what Uncle Remus called "a spell of the dry grins."

> Come all you young sailor lads, a warning take by me,
> Be sure and choose your company when you go on a spree;
> Be sure keep out of Barrack Street, or else you'll rue the day,
> With a woman's shirt and apron, they'll rig you out for sea.

Or a hint on navigation:

> So come all young men when you go to spark,
> Beware of rambling in the dark;
> Beware of every step you steer,
> And try and keep clear of the crockery ware.

These songs and more were current in folk tradition in the Northeast, and popular songwriters were quick to realize the viability of the pattern, giving us such pieces as "The Dark Girl Dressed in Blue," in which the girl bilks a man by getting him to pass a counterfeit bill, and "The Charming Young Widow I Met on the Train," in which the girl weeps on his shoulder, then asks him to hold her baby for a minute while she steps off the train. The train starts up; he tries unsuccessfully to stop it:

> In this horrid dilemma I sought for the hour—
> But my watch! Ha! where was it? Where, where was my chain?
> My purse too, my ticket, gold pencil-case—all gone,
> Oh that Artful Young Widow I Met on the Train.[14]

The girls in these popular songs were defter and more devious, perhaps, and less direct in their granting of sexual favors than the heroine of "The White Cafe," but the pattern is clearly there in all of them. A man gets taken, and it's all very funny.

The poet of "The White Cafe," then, had heard a story about a woodsman named Decker, saw that it fit a well-established song pattern, and was off and running. I have been unable to discover where he got his tune, which is unfortunate, because it would be nice to know what it was in the original song that caught his imagination and made it seem right to him. All I can say is that it sounds like it came from popular, not folk, tradition, but that line can be pretty fuzzy when we consider the milieu in which this song developed and flourished. The stanza form the tune generated, for example, is one of a group found in both folk and popular tradition, the basic double stanza with a pattern of internal rhymes; to insist on the distinction between the two traditions at this point would be pretty academic. It was a song the poet had heard, and for some reason it clicked.

One of the problems the poet faced was clearly created by his choice of tune: a nastily complex rhyme scheme with internal rhymes in every line and—worse yet—those in the first and third lines had to be feminine. The eighth stanza is a good example:

'Twas at the Farmer's *Hotel*, where some of you are *known well*,
Upon my *life* as man and *wife* we registered our names;
But before a week was *over*, I wished she was in *Dover*,
Or down b*elow*, that place you *know*, amidst the hottest flames.

How careful the rhyming was in the poet's original version we will never know, but the rhyming in Fred Campbell's version is very consistent with the rhyming we find in all other extant versions. Only one adds a rhyme he doesn't have, for example; Osborne McKay (NB.4) gives line 2 in stanza 11 as "in a way that you might say is very mean of me." What we have is probably very close to what the poet wrote, which means that there are a lot of places where he just plain didn't make it at all and other places where he was willing to accept some very approximate and slanting rhymes like "head/maid" and "sir/here."

At the risk of seeming to praise him for his lapses, I should like to point out that his apparent attitude toward rhyme is very much the attitude I have found among traditional singers here in the Northeast: rhyme is an ideal, and it is expected that that ideal will be reasonably well achieved, but it is not insisted upon. A poet will be praised as a good rhymer even when it is obvious to anyone with a literary orientation that the very song for which he is being praised has a generous share of make-do's and even not-at-all's. But in an essentially oral tradition, it appears sufficient for the poet to establish a pattern and then simply reinforce it often enough to keep it clear in the listener's mind. Notice also that the internal rhymes are most consistent at those points where the music calls for a doubled time value in the first and third phrases, a bit less so in the fourth phrases, where only one of the rhymed syllables is doubled, and least consistent in the second phrase, where the line is sung right through and there is no doubling to call attention to the lack of rhyme. In discussing ballads, we have to remind ourselves every once in a while that we are dealing with songs, not poems. To sum up for the moment, the poet of "The White Cafe" set himself a tough metrical task and brought it off reasonably well. That tune must have been important to him.[15]

The structure is clear enough. The first two stanzas set the scene; the hero is hung over and looking for a little hair of the dog. Then the girl enters, and we get a full stanza describing her (3). Now begins a description of their pleasures, which will take us through stanza 8, but it is in two stages: Portland (4–6) and Augusta (7–8). Here the poet departs from the tradition; rather, he goes beyond it, by telegraphing his punch so often and in so many different ways: "she was a gay deceiver," "she beat me bad," "I took the bait," and in other little touches like his being unable to discover her occupation. Most ballads of this type save any "I shoulda known better" for the final stanza or so; our poet has Decker kick himself in the pants in almost every stanza. I do not consider this so much a weakness as a strength. The ballad is no longer just a funny incident but a pretty realistic portrayal of the rueful-humorous self-deprecation a man like Decker might take as his stance if he were to tell the story on himself. In support of that statement I offer my three years in the Marines, at least that many years of dormitory life, and thousands of hours of bar-time, in all of which situations I have heard similar stories and may even have told a few myself.

On the other hand, I will not try to defend the lady's drinking record on grounds of realism. "Nine cocktails, four mugs of ale, and two of whiskey clear" is a considerable load in a short while even for an experienced drinker, but the exaggeration does not seem particularly out of place when the song is sung. Perhaps this is partly because there was a whole tradition of gormandizing songs like "The Irish Jubilee" and "The Tipperary Christening,"[16] and more specifically there was the popular song "I Had but Fifty Cents," which describes how much a girl who said she wasn't hungry ate and drank. Her drinking record:

She said she wasn't thirsty, but this is what she drank:
A whiskey skin, a glass of gin which made me shake with fear,
A ginger pop with rum on top, a schooner then of beer,

A glass of ale, a gin cocktail, her appetite was immense,
She called for more but I fell on the floor; I had but fifty cents.[17]

It may be that that is where the author got his idea, but even if we just take the line within the context of the song—and it almost always gets a laugh—it simply seems like one more way for Decker to say, "I wasn't very sharp, was I?"

The fleecing itself comes in stanzas 9 and 10, when she skips out with everything, including his money and the bedsheets. Togus is about five miles from Augusta, but since it is not on the way to Portland at all, Decker gets the message that he's been had. The final stanza is unique in that no other ballad of this genre has the hero vowing revenge.

I have already said that I *think* Joe Scott wrote this song; but whoever wrote it, it cannot be said to have established itself in northeastern tradition as solidly as some of Joe's other songs. Nevertheless, it was pretty well known, and the question arises as to why songs about men who got taken would be popular in what was predominantly a male tradition. First of all, girls of the type represented in this song were notoriously a part of the woodsman's life, just as they were of the sailor's life. This sort of contretemps was a perpetual possibility, and singing about it may have made it a little more acceptable, hence less devastating, when it actually happened. It is true that people joke and sing about anxiety-causing situations, but I don't think that this song or others like it were satisfying so much because they served as ritual actings-out as because they allowed the participants (the singer and his audience) to feel comfortably superior. "*Decker was a fool,*" runs this logic. "*He admits that. He never should have been such a sucker, and I certainly am much too wordly-wise to get taken in that way.*" Everyman is enough of a realist to know that Decker's story *could* be his own, but Everyman is also enough of a coward to welcome the opportunity for self-congratulation that in his own case this is of course not true. Out of this tension grow songs like "The White Cafe." In Decker's weakness is our strength.

"Norman Mitchell"

They told me that in his prime Dennis Taylor had been one of the strongest men in the state. "I've seen him load a wagon with barrels of flour all by himself," one man said. "Nobody to help him. He'd just hist them barrels, kind of bear-hugged 'em right up. Strong? Jesus yes, I guess he was strong!"

I could well believe it. One look at the sloping shoulders and broad wrists of the old man shuffling across the room toward me was enough to convince me. I had come out to the Green Farm in Coplin Plantation north of Rangeley to see him, because I'd been told he'd known Joe Scott. When I arrived, the Wilbur brothers (who ran the Green Farm) couldn't say for sure that he'd known Joe, but we'd soon enough find out. Omer Wilbur went to get him, and in a few minutes he brought Taylor in to the kitchen.

As I said, he was a big man, stooped now by eighty-eight years of hard work, with a wild head of curly dark hair and a tremendous drooping mustache. He looked puzzled by the whole scene, but when he looked at me he smiled into his mustache, then looked shyly away. He sat down in a chair facing me and waited, hands folded in quiet expectation. "You knew Joe Scott?" I yelled at him (he was quite deaf).

"Yes," he said, "I knew Joe Scott." I began to question him, and soon I went out to get my tape recorder. It turned out that he remembered Joe best from the last sad years around Rangeley as little by little he went insane. *"His eyes went insane," he told me. "No, he wasn't blind, but you know, an insane man, his eyes changes. He looks wild."

I asked if he remembered any of Joe's songs. *"Well," he said, "I don't know as I could recall the whole—any of them, the whole of them. There's 'The Plain Golden Band.'" At my request he went over what he knew of it, chanting it as a kind of rhythmic oration that was neither prose nor poetry but something in between. Then he went over "White and Murphy" for me in the same way. Did he know any more, I asked?

*"Ohhh, gosh," he said, "I don't know. There's one where that girl was brought up in Patten, Maine. 'Course nobody wants that probably."

*"Well, I do," I said quickly. "Would you go over it for me?"

*"Well, what I can remember of it, but I couldn't remember the whole of it."

*"That's enough for me," I assured him. He chuckled, and began. Since it was brand new to me I asked him to repeat it about fifteen

minutes later. The two versions were almost identical, but since the second is a little clearer, that is the one I reproduce here:

*I were born in Patten, Maine—(no, I ain't got the first of that right). I were reared in Portland, Maine, by honest and respectable parents until the age of eighteen. It was there I met my dear; 'twas a girl with dark and wavy hair. If I'd herded to a friend's advice I might have led a different life. "Beware of that girl with those dark dreamy eyes. She is false as she is fair. Those florid lips will not the truth reveal. Beneath those winsome smiles the snake lieth concealed [*chuckle*]."

It's well do I remember the day that Pearl and I were wed. 'Twas in the early month of June when the flowers were in bloom, and the feather warblings sang merrily everywhere. I thought if I but used her well, to me she would prove true. But to no avail; like women of her kind she grew bolder day by day [till oth' men const'ly about the house creating jealousy]. But she's always well supplied with every lie my honor and my name to disgrace.

I leased the [wes subrewer] farm just for a temporary home. It was there the wild fawns loved to skip and play, and the robin redbreast sang merrily everywhere.

When one day there came the bearer of a note, and as I broke its seal, from within its folds fell a photograph of my naked wife. Half crazed with desperation, I sank down upon a rock its contents to scan. And briefly thus the note it ran: "I bring to you the proof and shame of the treachery of your wife."

Oh, with such [disquall] advice I could not face my friends. Then to the town some sitronine and laudanum did purchase. My wife and I walked through the dale. The fairness of her face; likewise her hair it did entwine.

And with one awful shriek he fell dead at her feet. Then down upon her knees most humble-ly, but all her pleading and promises could not the dead restore.

We walked through the dales and paused beside a freshly moulded mound. And with a mocking laugh, "Behold," says she.

*"That's as far as I go," said Taylor with a laugh, without giving any indication how much more there might have been. I was puzzled by the name. Sometimes it sounded like "Patten," sometimes like "Portland," though more often a little of both; but when I asked him if the song was about anyone he knew, he was enigmatically emphatic. *"No, no, no," he said, "in Pa'tlan, Maine. I don't know anyone down there." I think he thought it was Portland, but I had assumed it was Patten, and as I relisten to the tape I hear my attempts to make it

that. It's a good example of bad interviewing technique, but it turns out I was right.

Less than a month later, I received a wonderful long letter from Roy Kaulback of New Germany, Nova Scotia, with whom I had had some previous correspondence about his "old friend Joe Scott" and to whom I had recently sent a reprint of my article on Joe that had just appeared in the *Journal of American Folklore*.[18] This letter was four pages of enthusiastic commentary that supported not only things I had said in the article, but also things I had learned since writing it, and one of those things was Dennis Taylor's "song":

> The next fall [*Kaulback said*] Joe and I met again in a lumbercamp working for two contractors, Joe and John Wilbur, up the Cupsuptic River. . . . Joe and I again got to sleeping together. During the winter he told me many of his anecdotes up until then, also singing many of his songs for the entertainment of the crew. He did not need very much coaxing as he loved to sing, and again I must repeat he was an excellent singer. He loved to sing as he called it his latest song at that time called "Norman Mitchell," about a man who poisoned himself because of his wife, which happened up around "Patten, Maine." He also was a wonderful story teller. That spring was the last I ever saw of Joe Scott, as I came east.

Coming as it did right on the heels of my visit with Dennis Taylor, that was exciting news. I spent an afternoon reviewing my notes to see if anyone had said anything about this song to me before that time, and sure enough, I found that William Bryant of Summerside, Prince Edward Island, had mentioned to me the previous summer that he had heard Joe Scott sing only once, when he sang a song he'd made about a man who poisoned himself.

That was all I knew for the next five years, though. Then in the fall of 1965 I went up to Patten to see what I could find. Caleb Scribner, artist and retired game warden, took me down to see Frank Peavey in his barbershop back of the hotel, and the three of us had been talking about old days in the woods when I got the conversation around to Norman Mitchell. Yes, they both remembered the affair and how Norman committed suicide because he believed his wife had been stepping out on him, but neither man knew anything about a song. Next morning I went to the town clerk's office to check for the death record, which told me that on March 14, 1909, Norman

Mitchell, hotel proprietor, married, age twenty-eight, had died of "accidental poisoning." During the rest of that day I was to talk with seven or eight people who remembered the incident, and there was certainly a consensus: her name was Pearl, and she was a "smart" woman, very attractive and fond of men. "A hell of a pretty woman," one man said. "I used to dance with her." She'd married Norman, and they had been running a halfway house about thirty miles back into the woods from Patten. It was a place where the men used to stop for the night on their way in and out from the camps, and as time went on, Norman became increasingly convinced that his wife was being unfaithful to him. One evening he went out to the hovel and drank laudanum. They found his body a few hours later.

The most dramatic story I got was from eighty-three-year-old Lester Webster. The rain was coming down so hard when I arrived at his place that I did not bring the tape recorder in with me, and once inside I got talking so well and so enjoyably with Webster as I dried out by the big wood-range that I couldn't bring myself to go back out to the car and get it. Therefore I reproduce what he said from careful notes I made just after I left:

I was working out at Hemlock Pond that winter [*said Webster*], about ten miles further down the road from the Mitchell place. The night it happened I remember the phone was ringing and ringing, but it wasn't for us, so we just let it ring. Finally, though, we got curious, and the other guy there with me went over and listened in. "My God," he said to me, "Norman Mitchell's taken poison and killed himself!" Me and him took turns listening on the phone all evening. It was an awful business, let me tell you. And I remember that just about a week before that I'd been out to town and stopped at Mitchell's on my way back in, and Norman had been pretty upset and started to tell me all about it, but he never got very far because some people had come in. "Sometime, Lester, I'll tell you the rest of the story," he said. So I knew he was upset, but I never in the world thought he'd kill himself over it.

No one in Patten had ever heard anything about a song. That came as a surprise to everyone, although several people, Lester Webster among them, remembered that Joe Scott had been around at just about that time and might even have stayed at Mitchell's some in the normal course of things.

Since the event seemed newsworthy, I checked carefully in all the daily and weekly papers that would have covered this area. I found nothing at all, but that's understandable. Patten was a small town, and the people involved were townspeople, not transient woodsmen. If there was gossip, it was kept local, being no business of the outside world's. Even the death itself, as we have seen, was recorded as "accidental poisoning," not suicide. The papers couldn't print what they never heard. Besides, there was other news available that week. "MADMAN AT LARGE ON TEASLE TOWNSHIP / Bad Rum Makes Maniac of John Hamilton Who Runs Amuck with Axe . . . TRAGEDY IN BUCKSPORT / Raymond Heath Slashes Wife's Throat with Razor and Ends Own Life Same Way . . . YOUNG MOTHER CUT GIRL BABY'S THROAT / Pitiful Tragedy in Bangor Tuesday Evening," went the headlines. There was also a story of how forty Italians with drawn knives attacked a sheriff in the act of confiscating liquor and made off with four kegs of beer, not to mention an account of Representative Fred Thurlow's scheme for getting rid of all the wildcats in Washington County. Next to all this, a young man, his world collapsing, who in an agony of love and jealousy kills himself by drinking poison in a horse hovel thirty miles north of Patten, itself a hundred miles north of Bangor, was not exactly hot copy.

"Norman Mitchell" is Joe Scott's work, all right. Not only do we have reliable attributions and some evidence that Joe was around Patten at the time of the incident, but the style is right, too, with its flowers blooming, "feather warblings," fawns playing, and redbreasts singing; and of course, the snake that "lieth concealed" seems right out of "Howard Carey." The Joe Scott of it all comes through even in as mangled a version as the one we have.

For his last ballad, or rather, for the last ballad of his we have, Joe returned to the come-all-ye confessional pattern he had used so successfully in "Benjamin Deane" and "Howard Carey" ten or more years earlier. The theme of the young man or woman who commits suicide for love is certainly traditional,[19] whereas the same cannot be said for Howard Carey's depression suicide, as we have seen. At first glance, Norman Mitchell's story might appear to have had more going for it as a possible ballad plot than Howard Carrick's did. Here, after all, was a fine and trusting young husband driven to suicide by the discovery of his beautiful wife's inconstancy. Yet the ballad Joe made out of this likely material bombed and bombed badly, while "Howard Carey" was one of his greatest successes.

355

The Songs

I think we can account for "Norman Mitchell" 's failure in two ways, the first intrinsic, the second extrinsic to the ballad itself. Unfortunately, though, any judgment of its intrinsic worth involves an element of unfairness. It is not altogether copacetic, that is, to criticize Joe's original work on the basis of what Dennis Taylor happened to remember of it. However, it is all the basis we have, and poor as it is, it shows the difficulty that Joe was unable to resolve. As with "Howard Carey," he had the problem of a confessional ballad about a suicide, which meant that in order to complete his story he had to shift his point of view from first to third person; but as I pointed out in the discussion of the earlier ballad, that is not a problem in itself. A ballad is not necessarily a poor ballad *because* it shifts person; but the shift can be handled well or it can be handled awkwardly. In "Howard Carey," after Howard has told us what it is he is going to do and has said his good-byes, the direct action reaches a conclusion, and the shift to an outside narrator seems the most natural thing in the world, his words forming a coda to Howard's. In another way of looking at it, Howard's own account takes us up to the hanging, and the outside narrator picks the story up after it is over, while the hanging itself takes place offstage. In "Norman Mitchell," the suicide takes place very much *on* stage, and we are forced to view it from both within and without in bewilderingly quick succession. It may be, of course, that in his original Joe handled this more deftly, but I have my doubts. Worse yet, he followed this sudden lurch from first to third person with still another, this time from third-person singular to first-person plural—"*We* walked through the dales"—and this shift involved a time jump from the immediate present to some time after the burial. In sum, then, "Norman Mitchell" failed because it was a clumsy piece of work.

The extrinsic reason for its failure is not so elegant, perhaps, but it is no less significant. It was a matter of marketing. Evidently Joe never tried to sell the ballad around Patten, where it might have been expected to sell some on the basis of its being about something of local current interest. Possibly he recognized that in a rather close community like Patten his efforts would not be appreciated, but I think it is more likely that he left that area before he had completed the ballad. In fact, he was probably there only for the winter of 1908–9, returning to Rangeley that spring, and we know that Roy Kaulback heard him sing "his latest song" around Cupsuptic in the

356

winter of 1909–10. But around Rangeley, Joe could not have counted on its having any journalistic appeal at all. If it was going to catch on, it would have to catch on because it was a good ballad, and that is just what it wasn't.

As a final point, "Norman Mitchell" came along at least eight years after any of Joe's other ballads. It is tempting to suggest that he was no longer at the height of his powers as a songmaker, but that's a heavy weight to place on the back of Dennis Taylor's fragment. It is more likely that he was no longer the active salesman he had been around the turn of the century, when men remember him carrying his little satchel of ballads from camp to camp. But while I am willing to raise these possibilities, I am not ready to insist on them. The fact is simple: "Norman Mitchell" never made it. And for all practical purposes, it represents the end of the line for Joe Scott.

LIST OF VERSIONS

"William McGibbeny"

JS   Original printed slip, as obtained from the notebook of Bert Thorne, Jemseg, N.B. 10 sts.

"The White Cafe"

Me.1   John Brown, 80, Mexico, Me., July 10, 1964; NA Ives tape 64.4, recited, 9½ sts., fragment. Learned the song from his brother, Eldon Brown, Chipman, N.B. Knew it was by Scott.

Me.2   Thomas MacLeod, ca. 80, Baring, Me., Jan. 29, 1957; in a letter, typescript, 4½ sts., fragment. On June 5, 1957, MacLeod sang and recited three and a half stanzas; see NA Ives tape 57.12. Knew it was by Scott.

NB.1   Fred A. Campbell, 80, Arthurette, N.B. (interviewed in Newcastle, N.B.), Aug. 13, 1963; NA Ives tape 1.153 and ATL 3160.2, sung, 11 sts. Knew it was by Scott. For a recitation of it, see NA 80.052–055, collected by his daughter, Kathleen Campbell, July 17, 1965.

NB.2   Michael Noonan, 77, St. Stephen, N.B., Aug. 18, 1964; NA Ives tape 64.7, recited, 1½ sts., fragment.

NB.3   Philip Walsh, Northwest Bridge, N.B., July 22, 1961; NA Ives tape 1.96 and ATL 3103.4, sung, 8½ sts. Did not know it was by Scott. Spoke of it as "a State of Maine song." I asked him why: *"Well, different people told me it was . . . and it's got the 'city of Augusta' [in it]."

NB.4   Osborne W. McKay, Newcastle, N.B., June 23, 1964; in a letter, manuscript, 10 sts. "I know the words of that song, having learned it in the lumber woods in 1924 up on the N.W. Miramichi River."

"Norman Mitchell"

Me.   Dennis Taylor, 88, Green Farm (Coplin Plantation), Me., Mar. 30, 1959; NA Ives tape 59.1, recited, fragment.

NOTES

1. My thanks to Miss Dumas of the city clerk's office, Berlin, N.H., for her discovery of this record.
2. William M. Doerflinger, *Shantymen and Shantyboys*, pp. 274–275. This is Laws A–14, "The Dying Ranger"; the more common title for it in the Northeast is "The Dying Soldier."
3. I have also collected this as a song from Ernest Lord, Wells, Me., Aug. 24, 1966, NA Ives tape 66.8.
4. Vance Randolph, *Ozark Folksongs*, 4, p. 169. I have collected this song in Maine, too.
5. Ibid., pp. 167–168.
6. Ibid., p. 271.
7. Elizabeth Bristol Greenleaf and Grace Yarrow Mansfield, *Ballads and Sea Songs from Newfoundland*, pp. 359–360. Kittredge's note, p. 360, dates the original as 1850.
8. Helen Creighton, *Folksongs from Southern New Brunswick*, p. 130.
9. See Sigmund Spaeth, *Weep Some More, My Lady*, pp. 39–40. The same stanza form, or half of it, rather, appears in "The Hartford Wreck," for which see Helen Hartness Flanders et al., *The New Green Mountain Songster*, pp. 154–159, and above, p. 276.
10. For a parallel situation, see Edward D. Ives, *Lawrence Doyle*, p. 42.
11. Laws K–42. See Helen Creighton, *Songs and Ballads from Nova Scotia*, p. 226.
12. Sung by Linus Christopher, Tignish, P.E.I., Aug. 26, 1965, NA Ives tape 65.6. See also Kenneth Peacock, *Songs of the Newfoundland Outports*, 1, pp. 257–258.
13. Laws H–26. The quotation is from Randolph, *Ozark Folksongs*, 3, p. 112.
14. Douglas Gilbert, *Lost Chords*, p. 50. See also Spaeth, *Weep Some More*, pp. 146–147; Randolph, *Ozark Folksongs*, 3, pp. 112–114. For "The Dark Girl Dressed in Blue," see Sigmund Spaeth, *Read 'em and Weep*, pp. 86–88.
15. For further comments on rhyming, see Edward D. Ives, *Larry Gorman*, pp. 154–159, and *Lawrence Doyle, passim*. For other examples of stanzas similar to that of "The White Cafe," see George Milburn, *The Hobo's Hornbook*, p. 37; Spaeth, *Weep Some More*, pp. 79–80, 166.
16. For "The Irish Jubilee" see Spaeth, *Weep Some More*, pp. 225–228. For "The Tipperary Christening," see Manus O'Conor, *Irish Com-All-Ye's*, pp. 15–16. Both songs were traditional in the Northeast.

17. Gilbert, *Lost Chords,* p. 121.

18. Edward D. Ives, " 'Ben Deane' and Joe Scott: A Ballad and Its Probable Author."

19. See, e.g., "Willie Down by the Pond" (Laws G–19), "Minnie Quay" (Laws G–20), "The Silver Dagger" (Laws G–21), "William and Dinah" (Laws M–31), "The Butcher Boy" (Laws P–24).

19

Bits, Pieces, Apocrypha

A chapter like this is always a problem and a disappointment, a problem because it contains a lot of miscellaneous material that seems to point in a dozen different directions, and a disappointment because most of that material is inconclusive. Yet there is no way to avoid this final *omnium gatherum* of oddments; to omit the material would mean that the work was incomplete, and the inclusion of some stray fragment might be all that is needed to jog someone's memory enough to call forth the whole piece later on. Let's get on with it, then.

Alice Flynn gave me a fragment that she had from her brother, Bert McGinley of Malden, Massachusetts, that was part of the family tradition from "back home" in Johnville, New Brunswick. They called it "The Kind Old Province":

[1] I left the kind old province
In the merry month of June
The fiddleheads in blossom
And the buckwheat in full bloom
The old folks they did cry and weep
The day I went away
I went up to Fort Fairfield
To help old Kinney hay.

[2] When I arrived in Patten Maine
I struck the Good Exchange
The proprietor was a big fat man
And Pomroy was his name
Where are you from? The landlord cried
His voice was meek and low

I'm from the dear old province
Where the fiddleheads do grow.

[3] I'm also from your sunny land
The landlord he did cry
As the tears rolled down his big fat cheeks
And heavily he did sigh
I'm also from your sunny land
His voice was meek and low
I'm from the kind old province
Where the fiddleheads do grow.[1]

That's all we have. The area is right, the attribution is from a reliable source, and all we can say about it is, "Could be."

Roy Lohnes of Andover, Maine, mentioned a song he'd heard, but he could recall only two lines:

"Put up your weapon, Jack,
Your angry passion curb."

He couldn't remember what it was about, who was shooting whom or why—just those two lines and that they were from a song Joe Scott had written. Then one day about a year later I was in Rangeley talking to Wallace Ham. He didn't remember much about Joe, but when I asked about a song where a guy shot his wife, he did recall "something about that"; then, when I asked for it by the name of "Benjamin Deane," he said no, the one he'd heard was about a Jack Green. A woman who grew up in Rangeley remembered that there was a girl she went to school with whose father's name was Jack Green, and that the other students used to taunt her with the song. The story line as she recalled it was that Green shot his wife when he came home and found her in the lap of another man (who turned out to be her brother).[2] Apparently there *was* a song about a Jack Green, and it is perfectly possible that Joe Scott wrote it.

Vance Oakes came up with one, remarking that Gert Toothaker (née Ross) had taught him several songs way back years ago. *" 'Course I've forgotten them," he told me, "but I remember 'the iron horse,' and there was 'old Gilman for our boss.' . . . It just barely comes to me. But I know it was going into the woods. . . . I don't remember what they called it, but . . . somebody got killed by the log train and it was all in the song, but I can't remember the words of it." No one else I ever asked about it could add anything to what Vance said.

361

The Songs

Fred Campbell remembered a bit of a song that he said he had bought from Joe. It was a real nice one, too, he said:

> Rest, gentle Rose, in death's calm repose,
> Rest while the wind makes the wild willows wave;
> Wild roses bloom o'er her early tomb,
> She sleeps in the flowery vale.

That sounds like Joe, all right, though it also sounds like any one of a number of late-nineteenth-century songs, such as "Lily Dale":

> Oh, Lily, sweet Lily, dear Lily Dale!
> Now the wild rose blossoms o'er her little green grave
> 'Neath the trees in the flowery vale.[3]

But since Joe could work that métier as well as the best from Tin Pan Alley, we are no further along than we were.

The same could be said for the fragment Daisy Severy remembered of a song she said she used to have in Joe's own handwriting, "Since Poor Mother's Dead and Gone":

> I was young and I remember
> 'Twas the day that Mother died;
> I sat watching, weeping near her,
> When they called me to her side.
> Saying, "I will not see the morning,
> Angels now do bid me come."
> Pray to God we'll meet in Heaven,
> To that place where Mother's gone.[4]

Joe could have written that, but then so could a hundred or so pop songwriters. Perhaps that's the most important thing we can say about it: Joe *could* have written it.

Eddie McSheffrey told me Joe had made up a song about George Gee, who was hanged for shooting his cousin "around the time of the Spanish-American War." Joe wrote that, Eddie said, but he never wanted that song published. True enough, George Gee of Canaan Settlement (near Holmesville, New Brunswick) was hanged for the murder of Milly Gee on July 22, 1904, and while the whole sordid business was covered in detail in the Woodstock papers (including a gruesome minute-by-minute description of the hanging), no ballad on the subject has been forthcoming. A short homiletic piece, "George Gee's Farewell," written by "a neighbor" *did* appear in the

Carleton Sentinel for September 9, 1904, but it is clearly not by Scott. On the other hand, when Benny Swim was hanged in 1922 for the murder of Harvey Trenholm and Olive Swim, there *was* a ballad on that:

> Today I'm lying in my cell
> Up in the Woodstock jail
> Thinking of the deed I've done
> With no-one to go my bail,
> My age is twenty-two, boys,
> And that you all know well
> Brought up by honest parents,
> The truth to you I'll tell.[5]

The note at the end of my copy gives the author as "Harold Chase, next cell." It couldn't have been Joe anyhow, since the murder came four years after his death. The point is that in Carleton County these two murders tend to get confused, and while it is hard to imagine Eddie McSheffrey confusing them, it is possible. But Joe might well have been in Carleton County at the time of the Gee murder.

Another elusive piece was mentioned by William Bryant of Summerside, Prince Edward Island, who recalled that Joe had made up a song about Billy Powers, who started out in a canoe one night to cross Mooselookmeguntic Lake and never returned. He didn't remember the song itself, and no one else did either, but when I asked Sid Harden of Rangeley about Joe Scott one day, he said, "Oh yes, he wrote songs, and he drowned trying to cross the lake one night in a canoe and got swamped." When I said that Joe had died in Augusta, Harden said, "Wait now, I'm mixing him up with that other fellow. What was his name? Billy something or other." He knew nothing of any song about this, but it is interesting that he should confuse Powers and Scott in his mind.

As always when I have been searching out the songs of some particular poet, I have found a considerable apocrypha. Herby Rice, for example, claimed Joe Scott wrote "Jack Haggerty" (Laws C–25), and Lanson Wilbur and his sons were sure he'd written "The Jam on Gerry's Rock" (Laws C–1). *"They were really true songs," Lanson said, "that was the best part of it. Now there at Jerry's Rock—my father was right on that rock. 'Twas down in the Androscoggin, but I can't find that rock down there. Someone said they blowed it out."

363

Of course, any of these classics may well have been songs Joe had sung, and some of the audience simply assumed he had written them. Fred Lafferty's example is to the point here. He had been in camp with Joe one winter, and there was some dissatisfaction with the cook. *"He set there one night and made one about that cook," Fred said. "It was kind of vulgar, but he got an uproar out of it." The only stanza he could remember was the following:

> There was a dirty old cook, from Bangor came he,
> Was the dirtiest old devil you ever did see;
> Cold beans and raw dough he would give us to eat
> And about twice a week a big feed of horsemeat.[6]

All Joe had done was to sing a standard woods song in an appropriate situation.

The same pattern—songs being attributed to him because he had sung them—probably explains Joe's being credited with such popular hits as "After the Ball" and "The Blue Velvet Band," although the similarity of the latter title to that of Joe's best-known song almost certainly aided the confusion. Zelpha Nile of Rangeley was sure he had also written *"the one about the engineer. . . . His boy was sick," she went on, "and he told his wife if the baby is alive show the light as green, and if he was dead to show the light as red. 'And thank God when I passed by the light was green.'" That, of course, is "The Engineer's Child," a popular end-of-the-century sentimental song, but it was Joe's meat altogether, and I'd be very surprised to know that he *hadn't* sung it.[7]

That is probably the explanation for John Dignan's attribution, too. Joe had come into a camp he worked at up in Wentworth Location around 1901, and he bought several songs from him, among them one he called "The Light of a Full Red Moon":

> Twas first a ripple and then a puff
> Was filling our old brown sail.

Perhaps those were the first verses. The song went on to say they came upon a floating object which proved to be a wreck which had been on the sea for a long time as it spoke of the . . . skeleton skipper. As you will see I don't remember the words of the song.[8]

That is a pretty good description of "The Wreck of the *Glenaloon*," and while that song turns up in only one published collection I can find, it is a song I have often heard spoken of here in the Northeast. I have collected two other versions of it, one from Tom Cleghorn of Harvey Station, New Brunswick, who also thought it was by Joe Scott. It is possible that Joe wrote it, but all I can say is that I consider it very unlikely. The style is not quite right, and the subject is a bit out of his normal line, but then. . . .[9]

Frequently I have asked whether or not Joe ever "songed" people the way Larry Gorman used to do. That is, did he ever make up satirical or invective verses about people he worked for or with? Most of the time the answer has been no or, perhaps more typically, "not to my knowledge." George Storer said he never knew of Joe making up any comical songs while he was around Rumford or Rangeley, but if we accept both "The White Cafe" and "Charming Little Girl" as his (and I do), we know he could be both funny and satirical. That's not what Storer was thinking about, though; he was thinking about the little verse or song made up specifically to embarrass or to get a laugh at someone's expense, the sort of thing Larry Gorman did to perfection. My feeling is that that was not Joe's long suit, but there is occasional mention of such products. Martin Harkins of Houlton recalled a piece Joe made up one night out there. *"A fellow by the name of Shoggy Niles asked him to make up a song about him," Harkins said. "He held up his hand—I was right there—and he started in:

> Shoggy Niles it is my name,
> I live in Houlton, Maine;
> For lying and stealing there's few can excel—

and it went right along that way." Evidently Shoggy was none too happy about the song.

Which brings me to a slight digression: to what extent might Joe have made up songs for people on request? The only other report I have of his doing this kind of commission work came from Fred Noad, who had known Joe around Rangeley, and who claimed that a lot of men disliked him for this practice:

He would [*Noad wrote*] for a consideration, write a song in commemoration of some event in which they had participated, and in the event that their name was mentioned, such individuals would increase the ante. I do know for a fact that many of my friends around the Rangeley and Oquossoc region used to kid George Fanjoy with the charge that he paid to have Scott write a song for him with his name in it, but I never heard the song, and when I questioned anyone about it they said that Fan didn't pay enough and consequently never got the song.[10]

There's the story, and it sounds reasonable enough, but it's just odd that no one but Noad had ever mentioned it to me. The business about getting people's names into a song, though, should be kept in mind in regard to a piece like "White and Murphy." It is perfectly possible that Joe did enrich himself from time to time in this manner, but we should remember that even Larry Gorman never seems to have written for hire and did not respond very well to requests for songs, usually turning the point of the song back on the person who requested it.[11] And then there was a man by the name of Shoggy Niles. . . .

The clearest example of Joe Scott "songing" someone came from Fred Campbell. *"They used to play poker," he told me, "and Joe was in the game one day or something, and some fella, he was a little Nova Scotia man [*was in the game, too*]. Now I can't remember just how [*but*] he made up a little string of verses about it, about this little fella. Oh, it told how he cheated in the game, and then [*Joe*] he said, 'He's the poker shark from hell.' And that's all I can remember of it. They was quite a little string of it. 'Twas good, you know, too. The fella cheated. Joe quit the game, got up. He must have got a pot or something out of Joe, and then Joe made this little poem up." But that is absolutely the only example I have of Joe using a song to even a score, although the practice was entirely traditional.

Larry Gorman was famous for his impromptu "graces," many of which represented less what actually did happen than what Larry later said happened, and several of the graces themselves were ones he simply appropriated from tradition.[12] It was inevitable that the most widespread of these graces would get told about Joe. Harlan Curtis of Rangeley was the first of several people to mention it to me. He remembers a friend of his saying that one day he and Scott were haying for someone near Bangor, and they'd been getting fed mush and milk three times a day. One night some company came to the house, and real food was placed on the table. At the meal the farmer's wife asked Joe to say grace, thinking that since he was always quoting poetry he must be very religious. Joe said,

> Lord be praised I am amazed
> To see things oriended

With cake and tea and such a-glee
When porridge was intended.

After that they never got mush and milk from the farmer again. Joe didn't make that verse up any more than Larry Gorman did, and the whole incident probably never took place. But it is perfectly possible that Joe, like Larry, told that "good one" on himself.

On the other hand, Dan Hoyt's story must have happened just about the way he tells it. He saw Joe over on the Boundary Line one night, *"and they asked him to give a toast, and he says,

This world has stood a good long time
And I believe it's good for ages,
But who'd ever have thought J. W. Scott
Would stand up to the bar and drink his hard-earned wages."

Did Joe ever write any obscene or "dirty" songs? It wouldn't surprise me to know that he did, and at least two people remembered fragments of such songs they claimed were his. One woman (she prefers to remain anonymous) says her father remembered that Joe made up several dirty songs while he was working around the Bank Farm up in from Bridgewater, but she could recall only a few lines from one called "Big Abbie Jane":

Down in old Lincoln on Saturday night
The sky it was cloudless, the moon it shone bright;
I tell you, boys, it would have put you in pain
If you'd seen me hook onto big young Abbie Jane.
I took Abbie down, and how she did roar,
Saying, "Pull out your beef augur, my cunt you have tore."

And Fred Noad sent the following to me via Bob Pike:

I hired with Sammy Golden and to the K.P. was sent
And with a bunch of Pollocks up the Allagash I went.
When we arrived in Patten, it was there we stopped for chuck.
I searched around that little town trying to find a f- k [sic].
At last I met a maiden whom I had known before.
I gave to her a dollar bill—I hadn't any more—
She took me up into her room where I made her cough and sweat
And the injection that I gave her boys she never will forget![13]

And that is the end of the line—really the end of the line. Joe Scott probably wrote dozens of songs in his lifetime, but they're gone now

The Songs

forever. A few more will turn up, perhaps, and some one or two of those supposed to be his will possibly turn out not to be. But we've covered his entire extant repertoire now, and it's time to move on to other things.

NOTES

1. Alice Flynn, Allegany, N.Y., manuscript given to me in Bangor, Me., Aug. 1, 1964. For a fragment of the tune, see NA Ives tape 64.7.
2. Carrie A. Walker Reed, Dover, Del., to Ives, Apr. 10, 1972.
3. Sigmund Spaeth, *Weep Some More, My Lady,* p. 28.
4. NA Ives tape 66.7.
5. From a handwritten copy in the scrapbook of Mrs. Arthur Acker, Moores Mills, N.B., June 6, 1957. For much of the information on the Gee murder, I am indebted to Monica Morrison of Woodstock, N.B.
6. Interview, Nov. 11, 1965, NA Ives tape 65.16. For other versions of this song, see Helen Creighton, *Songs and Ballads from Nova Scotia,* pp. 265–266; Roland Palmer Gray, *Songs and Ballads of the Maine Lumberjacks,* pp. 60–62; William M. Doerflinger, *Shantymen and Shantyboys,* p. 217; Louise Manny and James Reginald Wilson, *Songs of Miramichi,* pp. 66–67.
7. For the text of the original, see Spaeth, *Weep Some More,* pp. 140–141.
8. Dignan to Ives, May 30, 1959.
9. See W. Roy Mackenzie, *Ballads and Sea Songs from Nova Scotia* pp. 387–388. For Cleghorn's version see NA Ives tape 64.6. For a P.E.I. version, see NA Ives tape 69.3.
10. Noad to Ives, Aug. 22, 1964.
11. See Edward D. Ives, *Larry Gorman,* pp. 42, 87.
12. For a full discussion of this genre, see ibid., pp. 143–147.
13. In a letter to Robert E. Pike, July 4, 1964, forwarded to me. Pike also included the lines in his book, *Tall Trees, Tough Men,* pp. 154–155.

Part
III
The Tradition

20

Lumbercamp Singing:
Up from the Valley of the Dry Bones

General Problems

In everything that has been said up to now about Joe Scott's songs and songmaking, there has been the tacit assumption that there *was* something we could call a lumbercamp singing tradition. That is to say, we have assumed that singing—and of course listening to singing—played some part in woodsmen's lives here in the North-east. That assumption is perfectly correct, but it is also dry bone. What part *did* singing play in the lives of these men? Where did it take place? At what times and under what circumstances? What did it sound like? Who sang? Who listened? What was the repertoire? Finally, that the bones may come together, what was the relationship of "woods tradition" to other traditions? So far as such things can be, we have called up both the man and his works. Let us now lay sinews and bring flesh upon the tradition. But that is no more than a manner of speaking—one cannot flesh a ghost.

That Joe Scott's ballads went into tradition and spread over a large area of the Northeast is easily said, partly because it is obviously true—I've collected better than two hundred versions of them from two states and the three Maritime Provinces—and partly because a phrase like "went into tradition" has the comfortable sound of meaning something. Students of folksong have been talking about "the tradition" and how songs either "entered" it, were "altered" by it, or perhaps "rejected" by it for so long and with such confidence that we have come to think of it as something that's really there, when of course it is nothing but a convenient abstraction. Reification is nothing new, and a full-scale discussion of how we have reified

371

"tradition" would in fact be nothing more than a battle report from one front of the great "culture war" ("Does culture exist? Come, come, I mean *really?*"). Others have written well on this subject, and without minimizing its importance in the least, I will skirt it by adopting Melville Herskovits's compromise as my starting point. That is, if we are careful never to forget that tradition is a concept having no independent reality, we can frequently learn things by *assuming* that reality for the time being.[1] In short, we may flesh out our ghost, just so long as we deny his existence.

In order for "song tradition" to assume even a fictive reality, we need to have observed carefully an abundance of specific examples of the sort of thing we're talking about, and that is exactly what we do not now and cannot ever hope to have. The old lumbercamps are a thing of the past. At the time, no trained field workers were present to take down the kind of data we now know we need; and now that we have some idea what to look for, there's no place left to look. Fortunately, though, the situation isn't quite so bad as all that. We do have some data, but in dealing with it there are four closely related methodological problems we must keep in mind.

First, it is true we have thousands of songs recorded as they were sung by men who used to work in the lumbercamps. However, these recordings were made not along the deacon seat, but years later in front parlors and farmhouse kitchens—and the junketing folklorists who made them were not always careful (or able) to distinguish between men who had really been lumbercamp singers and men who simply remembered the songs and were willing to sing them. Even so, taking that distinction (or lack of it) into account, and making whatever allowances might be required for the oddness of the situation (a stranger with a recording machine!) and the dirty tricks time plays on lungs and tracheae, I think we can safely assume that what we hear in these recordings is very close to what we would have heard years ago in the lumbercamps. That is, we have good data on singing *style*, and, if we make further allowances for the fact that collectors were variously (but rather predictably) selective in what they did or did not record, we have pretty good data on repertoire.

That brings us to the second problem. If we want to learn what part singing played in lumbercamp life, who sang, who listened, when and where singing took place, how men learned songs, and so on, we don't even have the simulacrum of direct data we do for style

372

and repertoire. In other words, there is nothing to "observe" any more. We are completely dependent on what we are *told* by those who were there, and the hell of it is that for something so recent, so close to us in both time and space, it is amazing how little of even this secondary data we have. This is largely due to the brand of salvage archeology we folklorists have carried on. We wanted to "get" the songs before they were "gone," and in our diligent haste we ignored the matrix from which they grew, in which they flourished, and without which they shriveled and died. I say no new thing here; in fact, it is a cliché of contemporary folksong scholarship. Yet for all its being a cliché, and for all its being (like many clichés) basically correct, some of us have from time to time miraculously asked the right questions. But that raises the third problem.

Most of our secondary data on singing has been obtained during collecting sessions from men who enjoyed singing and for whom it was important. In the breaks between songs, we collectors have sometimes asked, "Where'ja learn that one?" or "Was there much singing in the camps, Mr. McDonough?" and we've gotten wonderful answers. Such testimony may be extremely valuable, giving us details no one else would be likely to remember; but it may also suffer from foreshortening and other perspective distortions. To correct this, we should check enthusiast testimony against that of all kinds of woodsmen, some of whom liked singing, some of whom were indifferent to it, some of whom got out of the room. Fortunately, we have some such testimony, and I have made use of it wherever possible.[2]

The fourth problem is the tendency to hypergeneralize. It is seldom intentional, and more often than not we slip into it out of a desperation born of the bewildering variousness of human behavior or whatever else it may be we tell ourselves we are "observing." So much depended, for example, on who happened to be or not be in a particular camp, or on the predilections and personality of whoever was in charge. Certainly there was variation over time, not only in the sense that what was done in 1890 might not be the same as what was done in 1920 (our data covers that time span and sometimes a bit more), but also in the sense that in any particular camp what went on one week might be different from what happened the next. There may have been regional differences, too, say between Maine and New Brunswick camps or between the Penobscot and the Androscoggin. We will comment on these regional and temporal variations where we can, but even taking them into account leaves us with men who claim there'd be singing and dancing every night and men who claim they never heard any singing in the woods at all.

Where? When? What? Who?

Mindful of all these problems, we can now attempt to describe singing and the part it played in the day-to-day life of the lumber-camp and river-drive, and we can begin with the very obvious fact that it was simply one form of entertainment or pastime. It was not something used to time the blows of the axes or to keep men moving together while they were rolling or lifting logs on the drives or on the yards or landings. In this way the lumberman's life contrasts rather sharply with what we read about the sailor's life, where the shanties were worksongs and were very distinct from the songs men sang for pleasure in the forecastle off watch.[3] There were no worksongs in the woods at all, in the strictest sense of the term. Once in a great while one finds a report of men singing while at work. *"Out in the woods in the daytime when men are working," John Colbath said, "you might be walking along and you'd hear a man singing at the top of his voice; even when he was doing his work." But it is clear from the context both that Colbath was emphasizing how the Irish were great singers—"always at it"—and that it was a bit odd. Even here, it is more than likely that the singing was done to pass the time, not to time the work—a swamper or a road-monkey on a not-too-demanding task, or a teamster with a load of logs on the way to the landing:

> Crack, snap, goes my whip, and I whistle and I sing,
> I set upon my timber load as happy as a king.[4]

The only specific reference I have ever heard to anything like worksong proper is from a woman who remembers hearing men singing while they were winding on the head-works warping a boom of logs down a lake, a task just about identical in form and tedium to manning the capstan aboard ship.[5] But I have also had men specifically deny that they ever sang while they were doing that job. In spite of these few exceptions, there is no need to labor the point: singing was an off-hours or leisure-time activity for woodsmen.

We should also keep in mind that singing was just one of the many things woodsmen might do to amuse themselves in their off hours. A man might have things of his own to do, like whittling or reading, or he might spend some time simply shooting the breeze or yarning with friends. Card games, from cribbage to "forty-fives," were popular, too. Even when it came to more formal entertainments—by formal I mean those where one or more people performed while others watched—singing was by no means the only métier. There was step-dancing, harmonica or fiddle playing, storytelling, recitations, and I've even heard several times of a man putting on a puppet show for his friends! The point is obvious, to be sure, but like so many obvious points it has to be remade from time to time. Song was just one of a whole range of entertainments woodsmen might enjoy in their leisure time.

Conspicuously absent from that range of entertainments were fighting and drinking. Woodsmen were notoriously heavy drinkers, and when they hit town in the spring there were notable binges galore, but up in the woods there was very little alcohol. Occasionally someone got hold of a bottle or would steal some of the cook's vanilla extract, but that's about all. The bosses saw to that, knowing that the presence of any large amounts of liquor in a camp would be sheer murder. Old John Sharpe of Argyle, Maine, recalled what his father had told him, though:

*When he first started in the woods . . . they bought a barrel of rum and set it in the dingle, out where they keep the meat and stuff. Cover over it, and a pint dipper [*there. And the boss would say*] "Now, any time youse fellas wants a drink, need it, you take it and put your dipper back. The first man that gets drunk loses his job. He can't work no more." And there was twenty men to take his place, so he didn't dare lose his job. . . . So that's the way they kept the peace in a lot of their camps.

But by John's time (around 1900) liquor was strictly forbidden. That and a rather general prohibition against gambling probably helped keep fighting to a minimum, but inevitably fights would occur. John Sharpe recalled how they were handled in his time: *"Once in a while one would pick one, but the boss most always stalled them up with that. He'd grab 'em and part 'em and charge 'em ten dollars apiece, and they didn't fight long. . . . The boss was generally about as good a man as there was there, and he looked after it. And if he

couldn't stop 'em anyway, 'All right, boys, if you want to pay for it, go to her. Take a month's pay out of you.' And by God they cooled off."
What could happen when that discipline broke down can be seen from an occasional newspaper article describing the resultant carnage when entire crews went after each other not only with fists but with axes and peaveys as well.[6]

Very well, then, where was leisure time spent, and when did it come? Men spent most of their nonworking time in the "men's part," sometimes called the bunkroom or barroom, and while this has already been described,[7] we should keep in mind the picture of a none-too-large room, pole-floored and roughhewn, dimly lit by kerosene lanterns and probably overheated by the big ram-down woodstoves, and filled with anywhere from a dozen to seventy-five or eighty men who have put in a hard day's work in the outdoors. That would be home for four months. Some camps were near enough civilization that men could get out occasional weekends; in others they might get out at Christmas or New Year's; but it was not at all uncommon for men to be in the woods from October right through until March. It was a lonely life.

There would be some contact with the world outside, of course. Sometimes, if there were a series of camps along a tote road, men would visit from one to the other, and there would always be the walking boss or others on business coming up from the depot camp. Hunters would pass through, and sometimes a photographer would come in on a Sunday and get everyone outside for a picture; then he'd come back and sell copies to the crew. *"A minister'd come in there about once in the winter or something and try to convert some fellows," said Harry Dyer, "and sometimes there'd be a jewelry salesman that'd come in with a box or suitcase or something with a lot of watches and rings and stuff to sell to the fellows and so on." Joe Scott himself, as we know, used to travel from camp to camp selling his songs. All of these were exceptions, though. For the most part, through the whole of the long and bitter winter, the men in the lumbercamp were an isolated community. Six days a week they went to work by lantern light in the morning, worked in small crews quite isolated from each other all day, and then—*"when it was a pretty hard job to tell a spruce from a yellow birch," as Ned Stewart said—they'd take up their lanterns again and return to camp.

Supper would be over as quickly as the cook could clear the men out of the cookroom—no lingering over coffee (or, more likely, tea) and absolutely no conversation. Lumbercamp food may have been plain ("beans and brown bread for breakfast, brown bread and beans for dinner, and a mixture of the two for supper"),[8] but it was plentiful and generally appreciated. However, there was to be no nonsense about its consumption. Shut up and eat; then get your hide out and over to the men's part where you belong. That was the rule, which meant that by six or six-thirty the men were back along the deacon seat, and lights didn't go out until nine o'clock. Every evening, then, there would be a good two hours of free time.

On the whole, nothing much was apt to happen in terms of organized activity on week nights, because there were usually a number of odds-and-ends chores to be taken care of. *"Of course in a woods camp like that the evenings aren't long," said John Colbath. "You know, men working hard and they don't get in until after dark. By the time they get their supper and get their clothes taken care of—'course working in the woods in the snow your clothes get wet and they have to be hung up around the stove to dry out. And they have tools, now," he continued. "Like the choppers, they have to grind their axes and the sawyers have to have their saws filed, and by the time they get those necessary things taken care of, the end of the evening's pretty well gone." Then there were always the animals to be looked after. *"After supper we'd go out and take care of the horses for the night," said Guy Kirschner, an old teamster. "Give them some more water if they wanted it and like that, before we went to bed." There was leisure time in the evenings, but the men seem to have tended to their own affairs, patching pants, mending mittens, taking care of tools, whittling out a new axe-handle or perhaps a gum book,[9] reading a magazine, or just sitting around talking. Psychologically, they were looking to the next day's work— and to getting a little rest after this one.

The weekday evening was work-oriented, then, but sometimes something would get going. One man might challenge another to a leg wrestle or a game of "lazy-stick," or a man might take out his mouth organ. *"You'd hear them mouth organs going back in the shadows in them bunks there in the evenings," said Ben Cole evocatively, and that might inspire another man to dance. But it was occasional, more individual than group, and it would occur at *"an odd time," as Wilmot MacDonald said, "just according to how hard you were working. Maybe Wednesday night, maybe when you was hauling off or something like that, you know, having a pretty good time, everything like that. And maybe some fella starts to sing." Card games, of course, were apt to get started at any time. "Forty-fives" was a favorite, and so was poker (if the foreman or walking boss would allow it), but card players were more apt to move across the dingle into the cookroom where they could use the tables. The point is that while singing or other forms of entertainment could and frequently did take place during the week, it was, as Wilmot said, "an odd time," not the regular or expected thing.

How about Sundays? Once again, nothing special. Sunday, the traditional day of rest, was in spirit an extended weekday evening. Men could sleep in as long as they had a mind to, and they'd generally spend the rest of the day at personal tasks or just plain loafing. It was the usual day for gathering fir boughs for freshening up one's "mattress," and some men have told me this was the day they'd go out to look for spruce gum. Sunday would be the day for visiting other camps, if that was possible, and once in a great while a minister might arrive to conduct services. Suffice it to say that Sunday was Sunday, as it has always been Sunday.

Saturday night was the big one. If anything special in the entertainment line was going to take place, that's when it was apt to be. That should come as no more of a surprise than that Sunday was Sunday. In our culture Saturday night has always been the night to howl. The work week is over, and Sunday is a day of rest. Men in the lumbercamps were simply continuing a pattern they had been following all their lives. Saturday night was special, and symbolic of that specialness was the fact that the lights were left burning after nine o'clock, some say until midnight, others claiming they'd be left on as long as anyone wanted them on. Ernest Lord of Wells, Maine, gave a good description of how it all went in the central and eastern New Brunswick camps he used to work in:

*There wasn't too much time on the average evening, because it was late when we got in. By the time our clothes were dried out and we had our supper and so forth, it was almost time to go to bed. They'd hang around for a little while. Maybe one or two would sing [or] would be called on to contribute something, whether it was to dance or to play the harmonica or to sing a song or tell a story or whatever it might be.

But on Saturday night they'd whoop it up until pretty late. That was the big singing night, because the lights stayed on until very late Saturday night. That was the boss' order. The lights were to be out at nine o'clock other nights, right on the button. There was no fooling around about it. But on Saturday night they'd let it go on and on, and he'd let the boys more or less relax and enjoy themselves. So Saturday night was the night that most of the singing was done, although there was some during the week. . . .

Somebody would pipe up, "We haven't heard from Jim Brown over here. Come on, Jim, give us something." And they didn't care what it was, whatever he had that he could render to add to the entertainment, why, he did it. Some cases they couldn't even sing, but they knew the words of some song, and they'd go over them as though they were singing, but there was no tune, no lilt or anything to it at all. And some of them would say, "Well, I can't sing, but I'll step dance if Bill over here will play the harmonica." And that's the way it would go.

There is no agreement as to just how organized and extensive the entertainment was, and I think we can assume that this varied tremendously from camp to camp. There are those who claim that, all told, Saturday night was just longer than other nights and nothing special happened at all. Wilmot MacDonald gave a good description of one situation that might not work out well:

*There was some camps you was in where there wasn't too much. Maybe the four of us, say, go in together from our own country here. Maybe we'll go in there and oh, maybe there's a whole lot of French. Not too much going on in that camp. . . . Talking and blathering away; there'd be hardly any fun at all. Whatever fun you was going to have, maybe, it's between the four fellas that we went with. . . . You take on Saturday night, you know, it was kind of a big night, because you didn't have to work Sunday. . . . Some French fellas they'd have a mouth organ or something like that . . . and might be a couple of step dancers and there'd be a fella telling an odd story. But not too much in that camp. Well then, there'd be other camps you'd go in, you'd have the greatest crowd in the world.

But most of the time language wasn't the problem that made for fun or no fun; it was simply the chemistry of the group who happened to be there. *"We used to generally have a pretty good crew and they were always jolly and made life enjoyable in the woods at that time," Sam Jagoe of Newcastle, New Brunswick, told me, but it didn't always work out like that.

Some men remember that singing would take place right along with other activities. John O'Connor, who worked in Miramichi lumbercamps in the late teens and early twenties, recalled it that way: *"No, they wouldn't all be listening," he said, "because the camp would be a big place. There'd be a fella singing here, and those that would be interested—there might be four or five or half a dozen around him—they'd be listening." A good deal may have depended on the size of the camp, of course. That would make sense, but there's not much data to support a conclusion either way.

Sometimes Saturday-night entertainment would be highly organized and would involve the entire crowd. Angus Enman of Spring Hill, Prince Edward Island, was especially eloquent in this regard. He had worked for years over in the Androscoggin watershed in Maine and New Hampshire, and when I asked him about singing in the camps he replied,

*Oh great! Ohhh great! Well, you know, it wasn't what it is now, singing. Most singers now gotta have a guitar, but then there was no music at all. Saturday night, you see, when you'd come into the camp after supper you had to tell a story or sing a song or dance. If you didn't, they'd ding you; they'd put the dried codfish to you. . . . They had these old dried codfish, and if you wouldn't sing or dance or do something . . . they'd take the dried codfish and two or three would throw you down and whale you with it. . . . Hit you! Hard! Yeah. You take one of them old Cape Bretoners, great big old Scotchmen; or them Dutchmen, one of them big buggers from River Herbert, Nova Scotia. . . . If you couldn't sing, you could tell a good story [or] perhaps you could dance. There'd be a fella have a fiddle there, see, and give a tune. Old David [Dyment (a neighbor)] used to dance, and he was a pretty good singer, old David, and he could step-dance pretty good. Oh yes, somebody he'd go round: "Now boy, come on. Do what you're going to do."

It is interesting to compare Enman's testimony with that of Bill McBride, a Michigan lumberjack, who told Herbert Halpert that on Saturday night a man would have to "sing a song, tell a story, dance a jig—or up he went—he'd have to go up in a blanket."[10]

Up to this point we have talked only about what went on in the woods camps. How about on the river-drives? Was there any singing there? Not much, is the usual report, because there simply wasn't time; but then there seem to have been plenty of exceptions. Old John Jamieson of Bathurst, New Brunswick, remembered drives in both Maine and Miramichi. *"At night, after supper, lying back in bed, they'd sing," he said. "River-driving, we'd be in the tents. . . . They'd shovel the snow away and put big fires there to melt the ground a little, and build their camp there. Had a big fire at your feet. You'd lie there with your feet to the fire. . . . At night those old fellas would sing the songs."

*"Had a shed tent," said John Sharpe, remembering his days along the Penobscot, "and they was all setting in there waiting for their clothes to dry off a little to spend the evening. And somebody would lay back and sing. Some of them old fellas had some great songs, by God." Linwood Brown of Vanceboro, Maine, recalled being on a pulpwood drive on the Saint Croix River:

> We would drive all day and have supper, after supper there would be a big fire on the river shore, and all the crew would gather around it. Usually the singers would sit handy the fire in a comfortable position with their back against a tree or whatever. As soon as all were seated someone would suggest a singer to sing a certain song that he knew very well. Of course it didn't take too much persuasion of the singer to get him started. These songs were sung without music in a kind of high key and somewhat of a chant common to this type of singing. This would last perhaps an hour and one half, then all hands would "turn in." And the performance would happen again the next night and so on all the way down the river.[11]

That was in the late thirties, which is very late for anything like this, but Brown added that the singers themselves were older men who used to be on the long-log drives. Finally, time and again throughout this book there are notes of men who learned a particular song on this-or-that drive. Obviously, there was occasion for singing on the drive, and there were drivers who sang. And drivers who listened.

How much singing there was seems also to have been a function of both time and place. Both Wilmot and Sam were describing Miramichi lumbercamps as they remember them mainly during the time between the two world wars, especially the twenties and thirties. Most accounts I have of lumbercamp singing in Maine come from the years preceding World War I. "This may be the time to say that singing in the camps in general was before my time," Walter Creegan wrote me, "and I went into the woods in December of 1917. . . . In all those years I only heard *one man* sing, and that was Bob Turner, who sang THE COOK AND THE TEAMSTER for me at the farm the company ran at Seboomook."[12] Creegan put in forty years working for the Great Northern Paper Company, the colossus of the Penobscot watershed, and his word carries authority. Singing seems to have held on a little longer in the Androscoggin area and in the smaller camps throughout Washington and parts of Aroostook counties, but most descriptions of singing in Maine camps come from around the turn of the century—almost never later than 1920. Interestingly, the practice seems to have continued in New Brunswick camps for another good twenty years.

What did lumbercamp singing sound like? The most obvious suggestion one can make here is to refer the reader to the cassette recording I have prepared to complement this book, or to offer a discography of representative lumbercamp singers from the Northeast and say, "It sounded like that."[13] But there are a number of aspects of style that such recordings cannot give us, because they were not made *in situ*, but only years after the fact. Besides, that is really ducking the question, even for those aspects of the style that turn up on the recordings; for while most of the stylistic traits are common to all Anglo-American traditional singing, woods singing *was* special. And the difference is not simply a scholarly construct; both singers and their audiences have used phrases like "woods singing" or "woods singer" often enough to make it clear that they, too, felt there was a real distinction to be made. We ought at least to try to see if we can make it.

First of all, it was a solo tradition: one man singing while others listened in silence. Occasionally the listeners might join in on the chorus or refrain if there was one, but the general practice was for a man to sing even these parts solo. Once in a great while there'd be two men who would sing "in tandem," like Frank and Ray Estey of Sevogle, New Brunswick, but the effect was that of two men singing solo at the same time, mostly together but often one beginning a line or phrase a little ahead of the other, with no attempt at harmony. Ernest Lord had an interesting comment: *"[Men would sing]* mostly solo, excepting the French people, the French-Canadians. They used to sing in unison. The whole gang would sing the same song." (*"But the English speakers?"*) "Very seldom. Most of them had their favorites and they clung to them. And if they were going to sing, if they felt it was really their turn to sing, they sang something they liked and probably it was something that the other ones didn't know at all."

The singer's part was to sing, then, and the audience's part was to listen. It might be, as John O'Connor pointed out, that in a big camp not everyone would be part of the audience; but those who were part of the audience were quiet and attentive, and it seems to have been pretty generally accepted that when someone was singing there wasn't to be a lot of noise in the room. No one, for example, would "board the grindstone" while a man was singing. I asked Bill Cramp if there wasn't apt to be a lot of noise over which a man would have to sing: *"Oh, never a sound at all," he said. "Just as though there wasn't a stirring person in that camp. . . . Just the man that was singing. . . . It was always so in every camp ever I was in. No matter how much fun and conversation there was, the minute a man started to sing a song that was it right there. Everybody kept still, listening to that song."

Coaxing seems to have been an important part of the singer-audience interplay. That is, certain men may have wanted to sing, and they may even have known full well that others wanted to hear them, but they not only waited to be asked, they frequently insisted on being coaxed. The basic pose was one of a man singing under protest (*"Hell, I can't sing," "My throat's awful hoarse tonight,"* that sort of thing), a pose that made it incumbent on his audience to listen attentively once a man had agreed to sing, thus serving as both reminder and reinforcement of the expected singer-audience relationship. Often, the better singer a man was, the harder it was to get him singing. *"I was in camp one time," Tom MacLeod told me, "and half the winter went by and all of a sudden we heard a fellow humming. And I said to somebody, 'There's a fellow that can sing.' Well, I got after him. No, he couldn't sing, he couldn't sing. Well, he was a darn good singer!" Bill Cramp remembers that Joe Scott was a hard man to get to sing. *"You know that nine times out of ten that's the case," he added. "A man that's a real damn good singer you can't *get* him to sing, and a man that can just sing, that's all, he'll sing any time you want him to." On the other end, though, it has often been pointed out to me that once a man *did* get started, he wouldn't want to stop.[14]

Not only was the singing solo, it was also entirely unaccompanied. I spoke earlier of musical instruments that were apt to turn up in camp, but they were almost always used to accompany dancing or, occasionally, played for their own sake. The only reports I have heard of accompanied singing come from the 1920s and thirties, when there seems to have been an occasional guitar and an even more occasional banjo, certainly a direct result of the burgeoning country-music tradition. The late E. C. Beck found Michigan lumberjacks accompanying themselves on guitars, mandolins, and even hammered dulcimers, but that is an aspect of midwestern tradition that must have come from the South. It certainly didn't come from the Northeast. [15]

The traits I have discussed can hardly be called distinctive. They could be used to describe general northeastern singing tradition and, for that matter, Anglo-American singing tradition as a whole. The same can be said for such traits as the *declamando* endings (though this is *not* found in the South), the use of head- (as opposed to chest-) voice, and the "undramatic" delivery (that is, not using such things as dynamics or change in tempo to underscore or "explain" content). Why, then, was woods singing thought of as different?

I believe there are two reasons. First, while woods singing certainly shared all its traits with general Anglo-American tradition, it had its special emphases. It tended to be a "harder" kind of singing, with men putting tremendous pressure on their voices, and that meant also that it tended to be loud. Frequently I have heard men praised for "singing high," too, which would be another consequence of "hard" singing. Joe Scott has been described to me as a singer who could "just get it up there so nice and high." That does not mean falsetto singing or any such thing; it just means pushing toward the upper limits of one's voice. Nick Underhill, a favorite performer at the Miramichi festival, made a revealing comment to me one day:

*When I was going into the festival in 1958, you know, I never was on a stage [*before*], and Mr. Weatherspoon down here—he's from Scotland and he's a wonderful singer, high-class singer, you know, and he's a great friend of mine and we used to talk—and he said, "Now Nick, when you go up on that stage, just go easy. Don't sing high. Just take your time and go along." . . . Well, it was very good advice, but Sandy, when I got out on the stage I couldn't do it. I just couldn't do it, because my style is way up. [*I was*] used to singing in the camps and I just couldn't get away from it.

Actually, Nick did *not* sing at a level much above his speaking voice, but he valued going way up and holding a note for a long time, a common enough practice that he carried to the extreme.

Nick's singing also exhibits another common feature of woods style: the tendency to sing slowly, often almost to the point of losing the meter and sometimes even beyond that. I find it difficult to decide at times whether a man is singing a true parlando rubato or singing very slowly, and the difference is probably academic anyhow. The pace *is* slower than that generally found, which leads to frequent pauses, the taking of breath in odd places, and so forth. It also makes possible the use of considerable ornamentation, but my own experience has been that in general this ornamentation is limited to simple appoggiaturas, slides to and away from accented notes, and an occasional trill or mordent. I would not, that is, describe it as a *heavily* ornamented style, a term that I would certainly use in describing some Irish and Gaelic singing that I have heard, or Acadian style in French Canada. Rather, I would say that it tended that way modestly.[16]

This tendency is our final clue, perhaps, because what is called woods singing style resembles nothing so much as it does Irish singing style. Nor am I the first to point out that similarity, since both Edith Fowke and James Reginald Wilson have discussed it, particularly in regard to the spoken or *declamando* ending.[17] That makes demographic sense, too, since there is no question but that the Irish, both first and second generation—and especially those from the Maritimes—made up the bulk of the lumberwoods labor force in the late nineteenth and early twentieth centuries. In my opinion, this can also help explain Acadian singing style, as well as other heavily Celtic elements in French-Canadian folklore.[18] It comes to this: woods singing style, with its hard, loud, head-voice quality, its slower tempos, its tendencies toward ornamentation and parlando rubato rhythms, and its use of the *declamando* ending is clearly an extension of at least one kind of Irish traditional singing style. To put it another way, it represents the strongest and best Irish singing to be found in the basically British (English and Lowland Scots) traditions of the United States (the Canadian situation is a little more complex, as we shall see).

It should not be assumed that this was the only kind of singing one would hear in a lumbercamp. Tom MacLeod made this point for me one evening:

*What singing I done was probably a little bit more modern. I had a little more of the—I used to sing that "Klondyke Vale" quite a lot . . . and that "Pictures from Life's Other Side" there. Some of those old fellows, you know, they got a great—that was quite touching, anyhow. They'd get me to sing that. One night there was four or five of them. I had been singing [*a lot*] and I told him, I says, "Let the other boys [*sing*]," I says. "You're getting singing enough. You don't want to hear me howling tonight." The old fellow said, "By gorry, Tom," he said, "you can sing better than those fellows can." Well, probably I'd practiced a little bit more than they had, because I used to be around church choirs when I was a youngster. There was a song there this [*other*] fellow [*would sing*]. He would sing it so darn loud!

I have heard other men sing minstrel and vaudeville songs in styles entirely appropriate to the repertoire, such as "The Preacher and the Bear" done with elaborate gestures and flamboyant "darky preacher" accent. Other styles of singing were both heard and appreciated; but when I hear someone speak of woods singing, I find he usually means singing of the sort I have described.

One reason, then, why woods singing was thought of as different is that in some ways it *was* different. But there is a second reason. The lumbercamp, as we have already seen, continued to offer an occasion when old-time singing could form an important part of the entertainment long after it had ceased to be important at home. Not that there wasn't plenty of singing at home, but new styles and new repertoires were coming in and taking over. There was more singing around the parlor organ, and new songs were becoming increasingly popular. As we have just seen, the new material was welcome in the lumbercamps, but there the old style hung on, which would mean that many people came to associate old-time singing of *any* kind with the lumbercamps.

Much of what I have said about the distinctiveness of woods singing is reinforced by what we know about who did most of the singing. Who, that is, were the singers? First of all, we frequently hear these singers described as "old" or "older." Both John Sharpe and John Jamieson referred to men they heard singing on the drive as "old fellas," for example, but Harry Dyer is probably right when he says that they'd be anywhere from twenty-five or thirty on up. Most of the men I have talked to went into the woods when they were very young; hence "old" more nearly means simply "not young." But as time went along and the singing styles became more various, it would be the older men who would sing the old repertoire in the old way.

More common than references to older men being the best singers are references to men from the Maritimes, who as often as not are spoken of as Irish or sometimes Scotch. Emile Leavitt's comments are to the point:

*There was an awful lot of people that came from the province of New Brunswick and Nova Scotia. You know, English-speaking people, Scotch, Irish. They worked in the Maine woods then, and they had a lot of these songs, you know, ballads. I've heard the, Saturday nights they'd sing all night almost, till twelve o'clock. It was always ballads about somebody's girl or something. . . . About the girl they left behind, you know, all that kind of stuff. These were woodsmen from Nova Scotia and New Brunswick. They were country people, you know, but they had an awful lot of these songs. And Saturday night they always got out and sang them. Some of them lasted a long time; some of them must have been fifteen, twenty verses to them. Long, long songs. The whole story. It was a story by itself.

Joe McCullough of Mineral, New Brunswick, agreed. *"There was more singers from here than there was from over there [*in Maine*]," he told me, adding that he didn't know why that was. Others claim that the Prince Edward Islanders were the greatest singers of them all. But whichever province may be said to have borne the palm away, there is no doubt in my mind that the better singers came from the Maritimes. In my own collecting work—even a cursory check of the list of informants at the back of the book will bear this out—I have found ten good singers from Prince Edward Island and New Brunswick to every one from Maine. Even those from Maine had strong Maritime ties; Ernest Lord of Wells was born and spent his young manhood in New Brunswick, and Billy Bell of Brewer was from the Island—and more an Islander than a Mainer any day. Franz Rickaby claimed that in the lumbercamps of Michigan, Wisconsin, and Minnesota "the hegemony in song belonged to the Irish."[19] We can say the same for Maine lumbercamps, but they were mostly second-generation Irish from New Brunswick, Prince Edward Island, or Nova Scotia farms.

The names of particularly notable singers help bear this provenience out. Joe Tosh of Ellsworth recalled that the two best singers he ever heard were Shorty Campbell and Jimmy Ritchie, and both were from the Provinces. Frank "Bungie" McElroy of Sherman, Maine, told me that Len Gilks was a great singer. "He was a Miramichi man," he said, "and he was an awful man to sing. So was Paddy McLaughlin. He was from over there, too." Of course, Joe Scott himself is a case in point (except that his ancestors were not Irish, but Scottish and English), and so is Jack McGinley of Johnville (as Irish a community as there is in the province of New Brunswick, by the way), who several people have told me was a wonderful singer. His daughter remembered people telling her there was a saying that "Joe Scott writes the songs but Jack McGinley sings them."

The list of singers from the Provinces could be extended, but perhaps it should be balanced some. *"I knew a man that would hear a song and not over twice would know it," said Asa Flagg of Carthage, Maine. "At one time he knew over six hundred songs. . . . His name was Eugene Flagg. . . . He was a second cousin to me. . . . I remember one time he come into the house . . . and he sung till way long into the night and didn't sing a song over twice." And Kenneth Packard of Carrabassett, Maine, told of Patsy Jacques. *"That man, if he would have had training . . . could have been right up there in the class with Perry Como," he said. "It's a shame that someone with a voice like that just couldn't have it developed. He was a real good singer, and of course a man like that they keep him pretty busy most of the time. . . . They'd have him singing two or three times a week."

Then there were the mysterious figures like "Scotty." No one remembered him by any other name or knew where he was from or what became of him, but he could sing. D. L. Coady of Biddeford, Maine, described him:

"Scotty" was a woods cook and had one stiff leg. He was a great singer (I mean he was continually singing) and that means drunk or sober, because he was, when I knew him just as apt to be drunk as he was to be sober. But he was such an amiable old fellow that it was difficult to tell whether he was drunk or sober. . . . He was always around Patten those years [ca. 1910–15] but I don't know for whom he used to work—cooking in the woods—I don't think he ever cooked on the many river drives, and so spring brought him to Patten as soon as the woods operations were over come March. Then he would be around Patten most of the summer.

Francis Peavey ran a restaurant in Patten back then, and he remembers how the boys would always treat Scotty to beers in order to keep him singing. *"It just rolled right out of him," he said. "He told me that he used to sing behind the scenes for Julie Marlie, and laugh for her. She was a wonderful actress—Marlowe, Julia Marlowe. Oh, he could laugh just like a woman." Some people have confused him with Joe Scott, as I did for a while, but there is no question they were different people. Whoever Scotty was, he was one of a kind, obviously. In spite of exceptions, the point is clear that the Province men were generally the best singers in the Maine woods, and their tradition was distinctly Irish.

What was it made a good singer? Although that has been touched in glancing or tangential fashion in the foregoing pages, direct statements are hard to come by. It is more usual for someone simply to say that so-and-so *was* a great singer and leave it at that. Even when pushed for specifics, men are likely to come up with something like "Well, that's sort of hard to say," or "He had a good voice, you know." But in regard to voice quality certain adjectives do recur: "high," "true," and "clear." Wilmot MacDonald, himself the finest traditional singer I have ever heard, clearly found my question difficult, but answered it in this way:

Well, I don't know whether, well, what we used to say, we used to call a man a good singer—a man that we called a good singer, you'd set back and listen to him. But for me (I never was a very good singer), but I've heard men singing, and they could carry that air of that song, never drift one sign off that air. They'd carry that air, that tune of that song right out, just as true. . . . Lookit, Jack Underwood could sing that ["Skibbereen"*] the prettiest that you ever heard in your life. Lookit, dear, he could make you fall right to sleep. And he appeared to have such a good voice, and his voice would never tremble, and he never had a thing in his throat, no frog in his throat.

Charles Sibley of Argyle, Maine, supported this in a backwards fashion when he described Rideau Spencer as a singer: *"Boy Jesus, he could sing!" he said. "He was a nice singer, but the last of his days he was a good deal like me. You get old, your voice gets trembly, and them things," he added, pointing to his cigarettes, "them things don't help any."

Clarity, trueness, and a voice like Joe Scott's that could "get it up there so nice and high"—certainly these were qualities that were valued. But if there is one thing that comes through about good singers, it is that they had good memories. They knew the words, and they had a large repertoires; and, just as important, they could make themselves understood. That's what really made the difference, and I think Bill Cramp put it very well: *"Everybody that could sing, whether he could *sing* or not, if he knew a song and got the words out, that was all it amounted to. They didn't care whether you was a good singer or a poor singer or what you was. It was the song that counted." He added a little more later on: *"Whether he could sing or not, as long as the words were there, that's all they cared about. . . . Oh, of course they enjoyed a good singer the same as anybody else would, but they'd pay just as much attention to a man that couldn't sing as to one that could, as long as he had the words."

What made up the repertoire of these singers? It varied tremendously, to be sure, but all of its variousness centered in the British broadside ballad tradition, which is about what Emile Leavitt meant by songs *"about the girl they left behind" or what is generally meant by "come-all-ye's." Equally as popular were many native American ballads, especially those having to do with war and the sea; but since these ballads represent what is essentially an extension of the British broadside tradition, the distinction is largely academic. "The *Flying Cloud*," "The Wexford Lass," "The Mantle So Green," "India's Burning Sands," "The Last Fierce Charge," "The *Cumberland*'s Crew," "Morrissey and the Black"—these and others like them were the standbys.[20] The so-called Child ballads were, with only a few exceptions, almost nonexistent in woods tradition, a point we will return to in due time.

How about the occupational songs of lumbering and driving? It is almost as easy to underestimate their importance as it is tempting to overemphasize them. Songs like "The Jam on Gerry's Rock" and "Peter Emberly" were always popular and became solid fixtures in local Maritimes tradition, too, as did many others like them. It might be best to say that such songs formed a significant category in woods repertoire, but not a dominant one.

Popular songs, parlor songs, sentimental songs—call them what you will—were well known and much in demand, although published collections just about totally ignore them. "When You and I Were Young, Maggie," "Mother Was a Lady," "Just Plain Folks," "The Black Sheep," "Let Me Call You Sweetheart," and a host of others were very common, as were a whole series of "darky songs" like "Slavery Days" or "The Preacher and the Bear" and stage-Irish pieces like "When Murphy Ran for Mayor" or "McSorley's Twins." Some men specialized in that kind of song. Tom MacLeod spoke about his repertoire as *"probably a little bit more modern," including songs like "The Klondyke Vale" and "Pictures from Life's Other Side," for example, and I remember spending a good part of an afternoon listening to a man sing one turn-of-the-century show tune after another. He claimed he'd go to Boston almost every year after coming out of the woods, and he'd pick up a whole bunch of new songs to have ready for the woods that fall. Popular songs seem to have increased in importance as time went along, but all through the period we are interested in, they were very much in demand in the lumbercamps as elsewhere.

Finally, we come to the oh-so-vexed question of obscene songs. Published collections have ignored them, with the exception of Doerflinger's, which presents the first three stanzas of "The Red Light Saloon" and a song called "Tom Dixon."[21] There's a good deal of opinion on how important this kind of song was to woodsmen. Stewart Holbrook snorted and bellered and pawed the dirt and rolled his eyes a lot when he came to the subject in *Holy Old Mackinaw*, but cutely he gives us only those first three stanzas of "The Red Light Saloon."[22] Gerald Averill, in his good book *Ridge Runner*, spoke of "foul ditties . . . droned out in doubtful melody around the evening fire. Some of these," he continued, "are funny but unprintable, and the favorites are so obscene there is no point in them—no rhyme or anything else to appeal to one's sense of humor, just a mass of filthy words."[23]

On the other hand, while no one has ever denied the *presence* of such songs in woods tradition, plenty of men have suggested that they were not all that important. Spurgeon Allaby of Passekeag, New Brunswick, who had spent many years working in southern New Brunswick camps, offered the following unsolicited opinion one day: *"And there's another thing that you never heard much in the camps, for all they were rough and ready lads, was dirty songs. . . . There's only one crew that I ever worked with that I heard any amount of dirty songs, and that was a [*saw*-] mill crew. And there was a fella there—he was a sailor most of the time—and he worked in there. He didn't know anything else."

Allaby gives us a clue here that turns up time and again in testimony on this subject. *"Some fellas," said Tom MacLeod, "that's all they would sing," and Wilmot MacDonald said much the same thing: *"Well, then, we had another fella, Alec Norrad. . . . He was a scaler. . . . I tell you he was a blackguard singer. . . . All the blackguard songs he'd sing, them dirty songs. . . . Well now, he'd make a dog laugh. He would certainly make a dog laugh! But the songs that he would sing, the blackguard songs. . . . But oh mercy goodness, he was such a good one. And he had a lovely voice." Just as there were men who knew all the latest hit tunes and men like Sam Jagoe who specialized in tragedy or like Tom MacLeod whose songs were *"probably a little bit more modern," there were men who specialized in obscenity. If a fellow was in a singing camp and there happened to be a blackguard singer in the crew, he'd hear blackguard songs that winter. If there were two blackguard singers, he'd be apt to hear a whole lot more. But it is ridiculous to assert that that was all there was. Lots of men enjoyed them; others didn't. Ernest Lord didn't, but he admits they were there. I had asked him if there were many dirty songs sung in the woods:

*Too many. I never memorized them because I frowned on that sort of stuff from the time I was a kid. I've heard so much of it, and I've—. In one case, [now that] you bring it to my memory, there was a father and son on a river-drive, and that was the year we were on the Sou'west Miramichi. And that father-and-son team—the son was fairly young, the same as myself at that time—they would get together very frequently and sing those dirty songs. And it used to shame me. I couldn't quite figure it. . . . But there was always a certain group, certain people who would know those.

Ernest Lord learned many songs in the woods, none of them obscene. That son probably heard lots of old come-all-ye's. Perhaps he didn't learn them the way he learned his father's blackguard songs. So it went.

To sum up this whole matter of repertoire, the simplest way I know to get a good picture of what was sung in the Maine lumber-woods is to read through any of the standard collections of folksongs from the Maritime Provinces of Canada. Some corrections have to be made for range and windage, of course. The pioneer works of Roy Mackenzie and Helen Creighton predictably overemphasize the Child ballads, while Manny and Wilson's *Songs of Miramichi* gives local or indigenous songs more importance than they would have had in the normal repertoire. In none of the collections are popular songs well enough represented, and obscene songs are not included at all. But once we have made the necessary allowances, these collections can give us a very good idea of the core of Maine lumberwoods tradition. Essentially it is what we might have expected men from rural New Brunswick and Prince Edward Island to have been singing in the late nineteenth and early twentieth centuries. It is hard to see which way the influence ran strongest—camp-to-home or home-to-camp—but that's a pretty academic question. What is more important is to see that Maritimes tradition and Maine woods tradition were—with one important qualification—basically one and the same.[24]

The Two Traditions Redefined

Very well, what *is* the "important qualification"? It lies in resolving the apparent contradiction of my saying that lumbercamp tradition was different from local tradition and then saying that the best way to get a good idea of woods tradition is to look at local Maritimes collections. How can they be both different and the same? Were there really *two* traditions? Yes, but the terms "local" and "lumbercamp" are wrong. What we should really be talking about is a "public performance" as opposed to a "domestic" tradition or—a little more adventurously—a "men's" as opposed to a "women's" tradition. Wilmot MacDonald's childhood memory from Glenwood, New Brunswick, is a good place to begin working this out:

[My father was] a beautiful singer. And my father was something like myself; my father had all friends. He never had no one else, only friends. And when that Snowball's Mill was running in Chatham, when we was little lads not over six or seven year old, I seen as high as nine hired horses in my father's yard on Saturday night, pay night. They all come in and each fella would have a bottle of whiskey (whiskey was awful cheap then: one dollar and a quarter a quart). And they'd all land at the old man's, and they'd all set there, and the old man would sing songs. He might take a couple of drinks of liquor, and he set there; maybe he'd sing ten songs. . . . They all come to Will MacDonald's; that's where they come from Chatham. Oh, yes, I guess I could remember some of those Saturday nights!

Notice, first of all, that it is still Saturday night we're talking about, the end of the workweek, with the difference that now there's drinking involved (and outside the lumbercamps that drinking/

singing linkage is very standard for men in this area). Second, the emphasis is still on "singers," in this case Wilmot's father. Third, notice that it is still a *men's* gathering, or at least the men predominate *even though it takes place in a home.* It is Will MacDonald singing for the "fellas," and this pattern is manifest—either expressly or by implication—in much of the testimony I have gathered about singing occasions. There may have been women present; in fact, there usually *were* women present, but when they weren't looking after the children or out in the kitchen preparing a "lunch," they were listening quietly. As a rule they didn't sing in public. We're not talking about a taboo or a prohibition or anything of the sort, and the record shows that at an odd time a woman *would* sing at a Saturday-night or public gathering; but the record is just as clear that it wasn't the usual thing. I asked Wilmot about this. Did his mother ever sing? Yes, he said, she was a beautiful singer, but only around the house:

*Mother would sing any time she got them dishes cleaned up and maybe two or three of the children there and she maybe putting a child to sleep in her old rocking chair. . . . She never sung for [*outsiders*]. Now, anyone come there, you know, she hardly—in fact, I don't believe she sung a song at all. The old man used to entertain them, but I noticed . . . that any time she was singing she was just in the rocking chair singing there to the children and maybe sewing, even spinning at the wheel.

His mother knew a lot of songs, but Wilmot wasn't much interested in them, and while he learned his only Child ballad (Child 4, "Lady Isabel") from her, he never cared much for it (until he discovered that it raised goose-pimples on visiting folklorists).

There is at least one general exception to this rule of male public performance. One can hardly pick up an old newspaper that gave coverage to rural happenings in the Maritimes without finding reference to a "concert" put on by this-or-that society for some community cause. These were formal occasions, with a chairman who opened the evening with "a few well-chosen remarks" and then introduced each performer on the carefully planned program, which would include recitations, instrumental numbers (solos, duets, etc.), and skits ("dialogues") in addition to singing. There seemed to have been no problem about women singing in concerts; in fact, they generally outnumbered the men. But since these events had a definite air of "culture" and "the finer things" about them, both the repertoire and the singing style tended to be more cultivated ("The Last Rose of Summer" sung sweetly and with great expressiveness in the best Jenny Lind manner by someone who at one point in her life had "taken lessons"). Concert singing was obviously perfectly proper for a woman—even praiseworthy—but that is a far cry from singing at Will MacDonald's when the neighbors gathered in of a Saturday night for a "time." No question about it, that was men's work, and the occasional exceptions were no more than that: exceptions.[25]

Women did sing. Some of them, like Wilmot's mother, sang quite a lot, but they would be more likely to do so around the house at chores during the day or in the evening, and only within earshot of the immediate family or at most a near neighbor who might have dropped in. That is why I speak of the "public" or "performance" tradition as essentially a men's tradition. And there are three implications of this split that I would like to suggest at this point.

First, the so-called lumbercamp tradition was largely an extension of the male public-performance tradition found in the Maritimes. As I have said before, the lumbercamp offered an occasion when singing was an accepted entertainment form long after it had ceased to be all that important elsewhere. In addition, the lumbercamp was looked on even by Maritimers as a place where a man would be apt to learn songs, which would then be sung and learned back home. Edmund Doucette made the point well in talking about old times around Miminegash, Prince Edward Island: *"A lot of the boys used to go to New Brunswick in the lumberwoods. We'd always look forward for when some of them would come home; they'd learn some of those new songs. . . . They'd all gather into this house where this fella was . . . and he'd have to sing the song, and that's the way they learned them." Just to show how complete the interchange could be, we can take Jack Rodgerson's experience. He came to the Maine woods from Crapaud, Prince Edward Island, and while he did a lot of singing in the camps, he claimed he learned most of his songs (including some of Joe Scott's) before he left the Island, *"because when those [woodsmen] would come home we [kids] would stand around," he said, "and I think a kid retains."

Second, we have the lovely paradox that the men's tradition of lumbercamp and public performance was involved with the serious business of leisure-time entertainment, while the women's tradition of domestic, in-the-family singing was often work-oriented in that songs were sung to pass the time while one was spinning or sewing or cooking or looking after the children or other such frivolous pursuits. And that is all I think I'm going to say about that.

Third, by the very nature of the tradition within which they moved, and since they were around the house more of the time and for longer than boys were, girls would be more apt to learn and repeat the songs their mothers and grandmothers sang, absorbing them along with their skills in spinning and bread-making, and naturally associating them with these activities that would fill the rest of their lives. Since these songs did not depend upon public approval in any major way, is it possible that the domestic tradition would contain older, more "old-fashioned" songs than would the public tradition? Is that why most of the Child ballads found in the Northeast have been collected from women? It is a subject worthy of a whole lot more study.

A modest warning before we leave this subject of the two traditions: we should not expect anything like a dichotomy or a polarity. I doubt that the distinction was ever consciously maintained, to begin with; it's just the way things worked out. There was a good deal of similarity and sharing. We are not surprised to hear women singing songs they learned from their menfolk, and if I am right that Child ballads are essentially women's songs, we shouldn't be surprised to find men a little scornful of them. (*"Never cared much for that kind of song."* . . . *"My poor old mother used to sing that"*). But songs flowed both ways, and Bill Cramp's story of how he learned his favorite song, "The Old Elm Tree," from his sister not only shows that, but is also a nice example of domestic tradition with which to close this part of the discussion: *"I was going by the house this evening. She was to her supper dishes. The door was open, and I could hear her singing that song. And I thought that was the prettiest tune that I ever heard. I walked right up within a few rods of the kitchen door and set down there and listened to it till she finished that song. I knew if I let her know I was there she wouldn't finish it."

A Digression upon Learning

That brings us to one final matter: how in this tradition did men go about learning songs? This juncture, this synaptic leap between the neurons of two worlds, this incorporation of new material into one's *own* world from the world of another, is one of the crucial moments in all cultural transmission, and in folklore it has not been much studied. It would be presumptuous to discuss the physiology or even the psychology of this transfer, nor will I go into the question of why certain men learn certain repertoires.[26] But what have men had to say about how they learned songs?

First of all, what did "learning" mean in the more general context of Anglo-American song tradition? Very simply it meant getting a song by heart, getting it word for word, getting it "right." It was a tradition of rote memory. In no sense was it a tradition of improvisation, or getting a story or gist that one could then develop through a series of stock phrases and formulas. A man had learned a song when he felt he was able to perform it just the way he had heard it in the first place. That absolute repetition is humanly impossible for any number of reasons is beside the point. That is what was aimed at, and, as nearly as possible, that was what a man did. There was nothing fuzzy-minded about learning a song; you *learned* it, that's all.[27]

The most common way for a man to learn a song was clearly by hearing it sung. But no man has ever told me that he could learn a whole song by hearing it only once. Three times is more like it, although occasionally a man would claim two hearings would do it, while others would say four or five times, especially for a long song. Often this is put in the context of being young, the man claiming that he couldn't learn that easily now, but back then it was different. I asked Sam Jagoe how he learned a song: *"Just by listening to the individual singing it and took an interest in it. And the first thing you'd always try to conquer was the air of it. The words wasn't too hard to pick up. I'd get the air and then I'd add the words to it. . . . [*I'd have to hear it*] probably four or five times. That time, when I was younger, I could remember things quite well, and it didn't take me too long to get the words to one." No one else has ever made the distinction for me between learning words and tune, but that is certainly part of what John O'Connor had "going through his head" after hearing a song once:

*I'd hear a man singing a song tonight, and I'd listen pretty attentively, and I'd like it, you know. Well then, the next day it would be going through my head and I'd be getting different words of it, perhaps two or three lines out of a verse, and I'd be humming it all the time, you see. And I'd say to myself, "Gosh, I must go again and hear that fella." Well, I'd get in touch with him or go to his place, and I'd hear it again. And I'd have the most of it the next, second time. Oh, about the third time [*I'd have it all*].

A song would get in a person's head, enough of it, anyway, to become a kind of nuisance, a half-formed thing demanding completion, and to complete it he'd pester the man he heard sing it. Wilmot Mac-Donald gives an excellent picture of the process:

*Here's a fella, he's good at singing. He's singing a new song, boys, and lookit, you're going to get right over alongside that lad. And maybe there's two of us now. Well, next day out in the woods, eh? Maybe you'd learned a whole verse of that song that night, maybe two verses. But then you get hold of the other fella and he maybe knows a different verse; he wouldn't pick up the same verses you picked up. Well, the first thing maybe you'd know half the song the first night . . . and then we'd get him to sing her again. Oh, yes, if you didn't know it twice, you had to get him to sing, oh, he'd sing her a third time, you know. Then you knew it. You could sing it then. Didn't care whether he ever sung her again or not; *you* were singing her anyway. So that just carried down from one to the other.

And that's just about the way Irvine van Horne of Bloomfield Ridge, New Brunswick, told Jim Wilson he learned Larry Gorman's "Donahue's Spree": *"I learned that in 1927 . . . ," he said. "I learned that from Fred Fairley. I was working with Fred [*in the woods*] swamping main roads, and he used to sing it, and I'd get him to sing it over so I could learn it all, and that's how I come to know it. 'Christ,' he said, 'ain't you ever going to learn that?' "28

Did writing play any part in learning songs? Most men claim they never saw a written or printed copy, nor did they themselves ever write one down; but Nick Underhill admitted he used to write a song down sometimes so he could be sure to "get it right." Spurgeon Allaby said much the same thing. I had mentioned to him that someone had recently sung me a version of a song that was two stanzas longer than the one he'd sung for me:

*People would learn the, I suppose, word of mouth, you know, and they wouldn't get them quite all. I know that's the way it works with me. That "Dying Soldier" that I sung there. I wrote it all out. I got this fella to say it for me, and I wrote it off. And after I finished writing it off I knew it. I didn't have any more studying to do, but I got it all that way, whereas if

I'd've learned it from him singing I probably would never have learned it all, you know. I'd have skipped some of the verses likely.

*"In some of them I'd get them wrote down," said Sam Jagoe, "and then I'd study it off." As a way to learn a song, writing played its part, but it was not a major one.

Nor does print seem to have been a major factor. Men admit to learning songs from newspapers like the *Family Herald,* but more often than not that meant "filling in," getting all the words to a song heard earlier but not learned properly. Even Joe Scott's printed versions seem to have functioned largely in this way. On the other hand, Fred Lafferty, who had been in Berlin, New Hampshire, around the turn of the century, learned "Benjamin Deane" from a printed version. *"I read it on a barbershop door one day," he said. "I went by and this song was posted on the door. I was on the police force and I read it over, and the more I thought of it the more I'd like to learn it. So I took and read it a couple of times and then it all come to me." However, for Lafferty it was a poem, something to be recited, not sung. The best example (and one of the few) I have of someone learning a song from print was given me by Wilmot Mac-Donald. It all happened years after he was out of the woods, but it is still worth quoting. The song in question is "The Chapeau Boys," a woods song from Ontario:

*[*I learned it*] just right out of the *Family Herald.* You have it there [*referring to a clipping in my hand*]. That was in an old trunk down here at Will Cameron's place. God knows how old the paper is. . . . They gave it to me and I got looking at the words of it, you know, and I thought to myself, 'Well now, there's damn good rhyme in that song. I believe I'll try and make an air and I'll sing it.' So I started on one air; it didn't suit. I took an air off another song, and finally got that one and it fitted all right. So I learned it then.[29]

The tune he chose, by the way, was that of "The Threshing Machine," a blackguard song he knew, which also happens to be a set of the original Ontario air, though Wilmot had no way of knowing that.

Essentially, then, the process of learning began when a song caught one's attention for some reason and "got into one's head." Then came the "filling in," the "studying," in which one either got his source to repeat it several times or (less often) worked from a written or printed version. Finally, at some point, he discovered he knew and could sing it. Charles Sibley's account of how songs finally "came to him" is too revealing not to quote at length:

*Songs always come to me in the night. Always. . . . It wasn't no job at all for me to learn a song, but it came to me in the night, the whole of it. I'd have sketches all through, and then I'd forget the tune, and then I'd wake up in the night sometime. I know I was working in the woods for Kennedy one time, and I was trying to think what song that was, but I wanted to learn it awful bad. And I'd get some of it, and then I lost the tune, and then I couldn't get any of it at all without I'd have to hear it sung again. Well, I woke up one night, and that come to me. I got up and I sat right on the deacon seat, oh I guess twelve, one o'clock at night, and I started in humming that. Well, I suppose that as I went along that I kept getting a little louder and a little louder. By and by the old man riz up. "Get into that bunk," he says, "before I kill you." But I didn't. I stayed there and I finished it.

An important point to be made here is that while singing may have taken place only at certain specified times, those who were interested spent a lot of time thinking about it, learning new songs, talking about them, trying them out in private, "getting them together." Singing may not have been the most important thing in lumbercamp life, but for the singers it could amount to an obsession at times.

Finally, if we have in any way laid flesh and sinews upon the bones, we must remember that nothing stands still. The breath goes in and out, the flesh waxes and fails, and even the bones replace themselves, so that what continues is never the same as what was. Julian Bream, the great contemporary lutenist, once remarked that he has been criticized for not playing Dowland's music on a lute made in Dowland's time; "but when Dowland played," he said, "he was playing what for him was a new lute." It is a point well taken here. We talk about the "old songs," and we discuss "the tradition" as if it were something closed, established, final. Yet over and over again in the foregoing pages we have seen men seeking novelty, learning "new" songs, cornering men coming home from the woods "to learn some of the new songs." Wilmot MacDonald remembered how when he came down out of the woods people would ask him, "Did you learn any new songs, Wilmot?" And if he said he had, they'd want him to sit right down and sing them. It is a paradox that

Lumbercamp Singing

in order for there to be continuity there must be constant change. A closed tradition is a dead tradition, and the bones of a ghost are very dry.

NOTES

1. See Melville J. Herskovits, *Man and His Works*, p. 28.
2. The Northeast Archives of Folklore and Oral History, e.g., has many interviews with woodsmen of all kinds, and in most cases the interviewers were instructed *not* to ask about singing until they had more thoroughly explored the whole question of leisure time, when it came, and what filled it.
3. See William M. Doerflinger, *Shantymen and Shantyboys*, p. 103. There is a substantial literature on shantying; Doerflinger's bibliography in the 1972 edition of his book (retitled *Songs of Sailors and Lumbermen*) is very good.
4. As sung by Charles Sibley, Argyle, Me., Mar. 24, 1957, NA 1.10 and ATL 2143.1. For other versions of this well-known song, see Franz Rickaby, *Ballads and Songs of the Shanty-boy*, pp. 69–75, and Edith Fowke, *Lumbering Songs from the Northern Woods*, pp. 34–39, and the references given there.
5. Grace Shaw Tolman to Ives, Mar. 10, 1969. For more on the headworks, see David C. Smith, *A History of Lumbering in Maine 1861–1960*, p. 66 (and the photograph facing p. 288); Fannie Hardy Eckstorm, *The Penobscot Man*, pp. 185–216, and the photograph included in the 1972 edition; Edward D. Ives and David C. Smith, *Fleetwood Pride, 1864–1960: The Autobiography of a Maine Woodsman*, pp. 20–21, and the notes on p. 52.
6. See, e.g., "Men Fought with Axes," *Madison* (Me.) *Bulletin*, Dec. 27, 1900, reprinted in *Northeast Folklore*, 2 (1959), 17–18.
7. See p. 29, and the description in Edward D. Ives, *Larry Gorman*, p. xiii.
8. *Eastern Argus* (Portland, Me.), Dec. 8, 1884, quoted in Smith, *History of Lumbering*, p. 18.
9. A gum book was a little box carved out with a pen-knife in the shape of a book and often elaborately decorated. For some examples see Smith, *History of Lumbering*, facing p. 145.
10. Herbert Halpert, "A Michigan Lumberjack Singer," p. 83.
11. Brown to Sister Saint Jude, Aug. 13, 1962, NA 331.016a.
12. Creegan to Ives, Sept. 23, 1956. For the version of "The Cook and the Teamster" mentioned, see Fannie Hardy Eckstorm and Mary Winslow Smyth, *Minstrelsy of Maine*, p. 108.
13. See, e.g., Folkways FM 4051, *Irish and British Songs from the Ottawa Valley Sung by O. J. Abbott;* FM 4052, *Lumbering Songs from the Ontario Shanties*, edited by Edith Fowke; FM 4053, *Folksongs of the Miramichi*, recorded at the Miramichi Folksong Festival, Newcastle, N.B., edited by Louise Manny.
14. For a similar observation, see Edward D. Ives, *Lawrence Doyle*, p. 230.
15. E. C. Beck, *Songs of the Michigan Lumberjacks*, pp. 3–4.
16. For an excellent example of the highly melismatic Irish style I am referring to, see *Paddy Tunney*, Folk-Legacy FSE–7. For Acadian style, see *Acadie et Québec*, RCA Victor LCP–1020.

401

17. Fowke, *Lumbering Songs*, pp. 7–8; Louise Manny and James Reginald Wilson, *Songs of Miramichi*, pp. 42, 286. See also Wilson's more extensive discussion in his "Ballad Tunes of the Miramichi," pp. 98–107.

18. For a brief discussion of this influence, see Helen Creighton and Edward D. Ives, *Eight Folktales from Miramichi as Told by Wilmot MacDonald*, pp. 8–9 and *passim*. See also Luc Lacourcière, *Le conte populaire français en Amérique du Nord*, p. 9.

19. Rickaby, *Ballads and Songs*, p. xxv.

20. For the most thorough consideration of these two traditions—and we should never forget that the distinction is not a "folk" distinction but a convenient scholarly construct—see G. Malcolm Laws, Jr.'s two syllabi, *Native American Balladry* and *American Balladry from British Broadsides*.

21. Doerflinger, *Shantymen and Shantyboys*, pp. 249–251.

22. Stewart H. Holbrook, *Holy Old Mackinaw*, pp. 134–135.

23. Gerald Averill, *Ridge Runner*, pp. 94–95.

24. See W. Roy Mackenzie, *Ballads and Sea Songs from Nova Scotia;* Helen Creighton, *Songs and Ballads from Nova Scotia, Maritime Folk Songs, Folksongs from Southern New Brunswick,* and (with Doreen Senior) *Traditional Songs from Nova Scotia;* Louise Manny and James Reginald Wilson, *Songs of Miramichi.* Another collection that could be useful in this connection is William M. Doerflinger, *Songs of the Sailor and Lumberman.* Also, for Prince Edward Island, see Edward D. Ives, *Twenty-one Folksongs from Prince Edward Island;* Randall Dibblee and Dorothy Dibblee, *Folksongs from Prince Edward Island* (although for repertoire purposes, this book, like Manny and Wilson, *Songs of Miramichi,* overemphasizes local songs).

25. For more on concerts and concert singing, see Ives, *Lawrence Doyle*, pp. 232–235. For an excellent consideration of the performance roles of men vis-à-vis women, see Gerald L. Pocius, "The First Day That I Thought of It Since I Got Wed."

26. The best study of repertoire I know (and it is a whole lot more than that, too) is Ellen Stekert's "Two Voices of Tradition."

27. For fuller exploration of this subject, see Henry Glassie, " 'Take That Night Train to Selma' "; see also Stekert, "Two Voices," pp. 214–221. For the oral formulaic theory see Albert B. Lord, *The Singer of Tales.* For an enthusiastic and wrongheaded application of this theory to balladry, see James H. Jones, "Commonplace and Memorization in the Oral Tradition of the English and Scottish Popular Ballads" (and Albert Friedman's "Counterstatement").

28. Ives, *Larry Gorman*, p. 72.

29. For more on "The Chapeau Boys," see Fowke, *Lumbering Songs*, pp. 61–64. For Wilmot's singing of it, see NA Ives tape 1.108 (ATL 3115.5).

21

Conclusion

Joe Scott moved through the world. Along the way, certain things caught his attention, and he made songs about them, and then the songs moved through the world, too. Insofar as possible, I followed Joe's progress and tried to show something of the world he knew; then I followed the unique progress of each of his songs; and finally I tried to show something of the world through which they all moved. It almost seems as though that might be enough, especially since conclusions scare me. They have a way of taking over, of assuming an ersatz life of their own, of seeming more important than the details. But the life is in the details; the parts are more than the sum of the whole, always. Beethoven, when asked to explain a sonata he had just played, sat down and played it again.

Yet that's all very well for Beethoven. It is also one thing to be wary of conclusions, even to distrust them, and quite another thing to refuse to draw them at all. In a study of the present sort it would at best be precious, at worst irresponsible. We *are* interested in patterns, in tendencies, in whatever generalities can be drawn from the particulars presented, and no doubt about it, there are some general conclusions to be reached from a survey of the foregoing chapters. As carefully as we can, then, let's get about the business of reaching them.

The Songs

If we begin with the songs themselves, the most obvious and sweeping generality we can make is that they are all narratives. Each tells a

story of sorts, and every one of them is "true," at least in the sense
that they are reports of things that "really happened" or (as is most
likely with "The Norway Bum") that Joe Scott thought had happened. He was not fictionalizing; he was representing. Yet in almost
every case he seems to have been working with secondhand material. All of the people he wrote about were people he could have
known personally, and in fact he probably *did* know them; but, with
the obvious exception of "The Plain Golden Band," I am sure he was
not an eyewitness to the specific events he chronicled. Something
would happen that involved someone he knew; then he'd talk to
people, and, putting together what they told him with what he
already knew, he'd make his ballad. He may have used newspaper
accounts sometimes—I suspect that was his prime source for "Wreck
on the Grand Trunk Railway," for instance—but the ballads show
that he usually had more and different information than he could
have obtained from print alone.

What Joe was working with, then, was talk, what was going
around, what I have called elsewhere barroom or Hell-I-was-right-
there authority—other people's first- and secondhand accounts. He
took the ephemeral news of the day and transmuted it into something else—a song that men could sing and listen to—that was no
longer "news" at all. A song might be *commentary* on the news for
those who knew the principals involved, and it may have drawn
some sustenance from the general acceptance of its extrinsic truth
("*Them songs was all true*"); but for the most part it had to make its
way on its intrinsic worth ("*I always liked that song*") just like any
other work of art.

But obviously not all news got so transmuted, and even within the
range of possible topics his culture would have considered song-
worthy, Joe Scott was selective. Because he was Joe Scott, for
example, and not Larry Gorman, he chose "serious" subjects, as a
rule. The "comical" song, the satire or invective made "just for fun"
or to "torment" someone, was also based on "news" (read "gossip").
That was Gorman's specialty, and while Joe could work this vein (as
we have seen in "Charming Little Girl" and "The White Cafe"), it
was not his usual ore. What caught his attention, then?

Death is by far his most common theme, being present in all but
four of the songs,[1] and it is usually violent death in some form. Only
William McGibbeny can be said to have died peacefully (if unhap-

pily) in bed. The rest died hard. Guy Reed, William Sullivan, White and Murphy, and the crew of the rear engine on Grand Trunk westbound 85 died in industrial accidents, which is to say they died while they were doing their jobs. Howard Carey and Norman Mitchell were suicides, the former a despondent wreck of the roaring life, the latter shattered by false love. Of the two women who die (note that in neither case are they the principals in their songs), Lizzie Deane is murdered by her husband, and the Norway Bum's wife burns to death before his eyes. For Joe Scott, then, as for generations of ballad makers before him, a hard death was good material for song.

Second only to death is love, or, to broaden that a bit, the "man/woman business," and it is never a happy matter. Infidelity is the basic theme—always perpetrated by the woman and always seen from the man's point of view, of course. It leaves the man a brokenhearted life in "The Plain Golden Band" and "William McGibbeny," and it leads him to suicide in "Norman Mitchell" and to murder in "Benjamin Deane." Only in "The Norway Bum" is there no suggestion of infidelity; here the loss of his beloved wife drives the hero to a life of drunken wandering. Love is overwhelmingly important, it would seem, a great joy and perhaps life's chief blessing; but all this is by implication, because Joe's ballads tell of the loss of love, which is a terrible thing. Even when it is treated humorously in "The White Cafe" it is an unpleasant business. Once again, Joe Scott is following the lead of tradition. If death, especially violent death, has been a basic theme for both popular and traditional song in our culture, love has been no less so, and almost every song Joe Scott wrote is a development of a well-known variation of each of these themes: violent death and loss of love.

So much for the raw materials, the facts, the living matter that he worked up. This leads us very naturally to a discussion of the artistic tradition within which Joe had chosen to work. To put it another way, when he wanted to make a song, where did he turn for models? His sources were two: traditional broadside balladry and late-nineteenth-century popular and sentimental song. We'll get on with this matter in a minute. But first a brief digression on facts and filters.

As I have said before, any work of art is a distortion, a reshaping of reality for an aesthetic end. But to what extent does a particular artist *consciously* reshape his material, and to what extent is his *perception* of that material shaped by the traditions of the medium in which he has chosen to work? Wellek and Warren raise this question when they caution us not to forget "that the artist may 'experience' life differently in terms of his art. Actual experiences," they continue, "are seen with a view to their use in literature and come to him already partially shaped by artistic traditions and preconceptions."[2] Better yet, an example from my own experience.

Anyone who has traveled with a camera may have felt this shaping (I know I have). We have seen thousands of photographs and have a pretty clear idea of what is or is not a good picture. First thing we know, we are looking at something not so much in terms of what it is in itself, but in the limited terms of whether or not it will make a good photograph. For example, I used to enjoy vistas (say, the view from the mountain one gets when he pulls his car over into the "scenic turnout"); but after a while I discovered that the pictures I took of such panoramas were usually dull and disappointing, nowhere near as good as that picture of the horse cropping grass by the overgrown fence-post. It wasn't long before I began to lose interest in "scenic turnouts"—wouldn't even stop the car for them—and I'm sure that there were some I didn't even see because in a way they weren't there for me. Meanwhile, I developed a much keener eye for fence-posts and the like. The effects were two: I tended to look at the world around me as a means to an end, not an end in itself; and I frequently was more interested in the photograph than in the thing photographed (*"I can't wait to get home and see how this one turned out"*). Since ultimately I found this limiting, if not a bit poisonous, I quit, and now leave the camera at home. I had become an artist, and I didn't like it.

Joe Scott was an artist, a ballad maker. He would be apt, therefore, to view an event in terms of whether or not it would make a good ballad to begin with. Once he had chosen a subject, how much of what he saw or didn't see was dictated by the frame and filter through which he saw it? We can demonstrate—in fact, we *have* demonstrated—that he frequently departs from the "facts," even from the facts as he must have known them, or rather, that would have been knowable by someone in his particular position. Did he consciously change those facts for artistic reasons, or was this simply the way he saw them? Did he know he was changing facts, or were the changes facts to him?

If we are willing simply to demonstrate the difference between what happened and what a ballad says happened, then there is no problem. If, on the other hand, we are interested in the process, in how the world becomes art through that alembic known as an artist, then we should be concerned with what he does consciously as compared with what is almost reflex for him, what is unconscious. The hell of it is that it is impossible to sort out the changes wrought by these two processes with anything less than a Ouija board and a parapsychological T.A.T. I raise the distinction because it seems to me that it has theoretical importance for the study of the creative process; but in the present study I must be content with something less. And now we can get back to work.

I have said that Joe drew his models from two sources or traditions, broadside balladry and late-nineteenth-century popular and sentimental song, and both kinds of songs were common in his world. Of the two (insofar as they can be easily distinguished, and it isn't always that easy), the broadside ballad was his basic pattern, the chief frame and filter through which he as an artist saw the world. Not only did these ballads furnish him with such basics as tune and stanza form, they also provided him with their rather simplistic morality and its concomitant stock of plot and character stereotypes. All the clichés are there: come-all-ye openings, naming stanzas, the honest parents who reared one tenderly, the idyllic childhood, the mother's good (and not-to-be-followed) advice, the downfall through greed, whiskey, or bad women (or all three), pat eulogies, adieus, moral or consolatory closings—he got them all in somewhere. Three times, for example, we find Joe working with the basic death-in-the-woods pattern (in "Guy Reed," "William Sullivan," and "White and Murphy"). On the other hand, we can see him ranging out to ransack popular and sentimental traditions in songs like "Sacker Shean's Little Girl" and "William McGibbeny." Probably "The Norway Bum" owes more to this than to folk tradition, too, and the same can be said for pieces like "Charming Little Girl" and "The White Cafe." It all comes to this: Joe Scott knew the song conventions available to him thoroughly, and he had internalized them so well that he could use them naturally and easily.

Between the limits prescribed by his view of the facts—and reinforced by his intention to present them accurately—and the limits prescribed by the tradition he had chosen to work in, a poet like Joe Scott had little room for that "originality," that chance to "offer us something new," that most of us today have come to equate with creativity. To be sure, he brought to birth something that had not existed before, something that was known to his contemporaries as a "new song," but all that meant was new words to an old tune. Even these "new words" would so closely resemble and were often so clearly modeled on—if not directly taken from—the words to other ballads that it seems monstrously inappropriate to speak of creativity or "art" at all in regard to ballad tradition. But really all we are displaying is what T. S. Eliot described as our modern tendency to "praise a poet upon those aspects of his work in which he least resembles anyone else." Eliot found this orientation limiting, and suggested that "if we approach a poet without this prejudice we shall often find not only the best, but the most individual parts of his work may be those in which the dead poets, his ancestors, assert their immortality most vigorously."[3] He might lean out from the gold bar of Heaven to sigh a resigned but aristocratic sigh at seeing his words applied to broadside balladry, but that can't be helped.

Other literary critics have spoken to Eliot's point. "Originality," say Wellek and Warren, "is usually misconceived in our time as meaning a mere violation of tradition. . . . Misconceptions of the artistic process underlie much [*critical*] work of this kind, e.g. the many studies of Sir Sidney Lee on Elizabethan sonnets, which prove the thorough conventionality of the form but do not thereby prove, as Sidney Lee supposed, the insincerity and badness of the sonnets. To work within a given tradition and adopt its devices," they conclude, "is perfectly compatible with emotional power and artistic value."[4] If, then, we limit ourselves to looking for Joe Scott's artistry in his skillful adaptation of a rather broad range of traditional elements to new yet equally traditional subjects, we can nonetheless still speak of him not only as a good workman, but also as a creative and original artist.

But let's insist on a difference. Keeping to the narrow perspective of the literary critic, let us demand that Joe be shown to be "original," to have "broken new ground," to have "made a contribution," before we praise his art or speak of him as an artist. Joe Scott more

408

than measures up to this standard. Anglo-American folksong tradition was essentially restrictive and repetitive, hence noninnovative; bold or even not-so-bold experiment was not highly valued. In speaking of local songmaking on Prince Edward Island I said that those who chose to create within this tradition "had small reason and less temptation to develop personal styles that would only work against the acceptance of their work."[5] Yet even here I was able to find individual differences between, say, Lawrence Doyle and Hugh Lauchlan MacDonald, but only by working at very close range with comparatively minor matters of emphasis and detail that were (I am sure) not generally the result of conscious experimentation. Their work was what Henry Glassie has called "safe," consisting as it did of innovations "within a single model" or combinations "of similar models coming from the same source."[6] Larry Gorman's work was pretty safe, too, and while the same could certainly be said of a lot of what Joe Scott did, there are elements in his work that—given the nature of ballad tradition—can only be described as avant-garde.

To begin with, while Joe's basic model may have been the broadside come-all-ye ballad, he brought to it the diction and imagery of popular and sentimental song. At the very least, he seems to have taken his lead from this type of song for the development of his typical—and quite idiosyncratic—pastoral and conventionalized natural description: bubbling sparkling waters, purling streams, dewdrops bright and fair, roses, moonlight, gentle breezes (zephyrs, even), "the cuckoo and the swallow, the sunshine and the rain." Add to this homes by the ocean, vine-covered cottages, feeble mothers old and gray, and the like, and the case is that much stronger. It is not that such material never occurs in come-all-ye's, but as I have said before, the more we look for a parallel to Joe's use of a phrase, the more often we find that parallel in his own work, rather than in other ballads, and the closer it all sounds to what we can find in popular song. Joe was even writing popular songs *for* folk tradition. "Sacker Shean's Little Girl" and "William McGibbeny" are about as straight out of popular tradition as they can be, and while some parallels can be found for "The Norway Bum" in foregoing folk tradition, it owes much more to the sentimental tramp songs.

The blending of aspects of the two traditions may be Joe Scott's "most important" innovation. Without question, though, this abundance of florid diction in the come-all-ye context was recognized by many people as his hallmark. "Joe loved the birds and flowers," they have said to me, or "He was always putting in something about babbling brooks and purling streams, wasn't he?" Of course, these were often post hoc judgments, with the speaker knowing that a ballad was Joe's before he made the pronouncement; but I've heard it often enough to make it worth remarking here.

The sheer abundance of roses and thrushes and old folks in cottage doors—sometimes as much as a quarter to a third of a song will be devoted to that sort of thing—leads us to speak of a second characteristic of Joe's ballads: their extreme leisureliness and the elaborateness with which certain themes are developed. In "The Plain Golden Band," for example, the whole first double stanza is devoted simply to backdrop, and almost a third of the ballad is devoted to the kind of pastoral imagery we have discussed above. In "Howard Carey," more than a third of the ballad is devoted to the mother's advice, whereas no other ballad I know of that contains this theme takes more than a stanza to develop it. In "Guy Reed," he takes five careful stanzas to develop the death scene, and he spends a whole stanza on the foreshadowing ("Not thinking he e'er night would be . . ."), where a single line is more the usual thing. The same leisureliness and elaboration can be seen very clearly in "Benjamin Deane," notably in the opening stanzas, where, for instance, we find the "parents reared me tenderly" motif run out to a full stanza rather than the standard line or half-line. I could go on, but the point is clear enough.

Not all the elaboration was roses, though. Joe Scott was not in the least afraid of everyday details. Sometimes they overburden his work, as in the long recitation of Benjamin Deane's troubles; but frequently they balance very well with the heavy aureate quality we've been talking about, especially when Joe manages to present us with a particularly sharp detail—Howard Carey gazing at the whitewashed walls, Guy Reed pausing for just a moment before he is killed, Benjamin Deane seeing the sun on his dead wife's face, the Norway Bum watching the sparks fly upward. We can sum up this whole section: lush, leisurely, elaborate, but then at times sharp and quotidian. The combination didn't always come off right, but when it did, it was dynamite.

I have already pointed out the variety of models from both folk and popular tradition that Joe at one time or another took a crack at, and since versatility is looked on as virtue in an artist, we can once again find reason to praise him for his ability to handle competently everything from sentimental orphan songs and tramp ballads through humorous ditties to traditional come-all-ye's about murder and death on the job. That's an impressive accomplishment in itself, but since we are now looking for originality, we should not be satisfied with "mere" imitation, no matter how wide-ranging it may be.

Even a quick glance over the preceding chapters will show that he did his best work when he wasn't simply copying. Speaking of "Guy Reed," for example, as a death-on-the-river ballad may be a little more helpful than calling "When Lilacs Last in the Dooryard Bloom'd" a pastoral elegy, but they are statements of the same class. Both can be "demonstrated," but neither tells us much about the affective quality of the works in question. At best they offer a place to begin our explorations. "Guy Reed" develops that model in such a special way that we forget it almost entirely as Joe Scott leisurely balances the beauty of life and the sleep of death on the fulcrum of a crash of logs. "The Norway Bum" can be spoken of as a "tramp ballad," but Joe leaves the model so far behind that his ballad is almost sui generis.

Nor was Joe Scott afraid to move into areas where the tradition offered him little guidance in the form of direct models or where he had to combine disparate models. Where, for example, was the model for "The Plain Golden Band"? For that combination of tenderness and heartbreak Joe brought together elements of the sentimental torch ballad, the memory song, and, who knows, perhaps "The Rose of Tralee." The whole scenario seems to owe more to popular melodrama than to song. "Howard Carey" at first glance appears to be just like any number of other young-man-gone-wrong ballads—until a close look reveals that there isn't another ballad quite like it in either British or American tradition. His inventions were not always successful, of course, if for the moment we use acceptance into oral tradition as the measure of success. In "William Sullivan," he tried unsuccessfully to bring the long farewell-to-mother scene he had used in "Howard Carey" into a straight death-on-the-job ballad, and in "Wreck on the Grand Trunk Railway" his dependence on "Fuller and Warren" got him nowhere at all. The point is that Joe was willing to try the odd combination.

In my opinion, Joe's inventive use of models can best be seen in "Benjamin Deane." The confessional murder ballad is as standard a form as one can find in British-American tradition, and there are plenty of late-nineteenth- and early-twentieth-century examples that follow it closely. As I have said, Joe knew the form—it is simply impossible that he didn't—but since his purpose went well beyond merely telling about the murder, he ignored that formula and created a novelistic ballad closer to "The *Flying Cloud*" than to anything else. Granted that the original twenty-five-stanza version of "Benjamin Deane" is a bit much, but anyone can run to excesses, and Joe Scott is hardly the only author to have his work improved by sensitive editing. T. S. Eliot had Ezra Pound, Thomas Wolfe had Maxwell Perkins, and Joe Scott had a whole succession of singers who knew what they liked and ignored the rest. That "editing," however, is a whole new area, and before we move into it I would like to sum up my discussion of Joe's artistry.

Given his chosen field of expression, he was a master not only in the sense that he could work extremely well *within* the tradition, but also in the sense that he went beyond it, showing considerable originality in his inventive use of models, his combining of popular and folk traditions (especially in his use of the language of sentimental song in balladry), and his leisurely and elaborate style of development. Had the tradition continued in "expected" fashion, we might well have been able to show how Joe altered its direction by virtue of his work becoming part of it and furnishing new models. But since later songwriters turned more to the burgeoning country-music tradition—to Nashville rather than to Rumford Falls—that's got to remain an academic speculation. But that a series of historical accidents about which he knew nothing were to leave him in a cul-de-sac in no way detracts from my final judgment of him: Joe Scott was an artist, and a damned good one.

The Tradition

Once a work of art has been created, it enters the marketplace and takes its lumps. A poet, for example, sends his work out to the magazines (little or otherwise) and journals, or he tries to find a publisher. Once he gets his work before the public, he hopes people will read it. A composer wants to get his music performed before an audience, and a painter hopes his work will be "hung" or "shown" somewhere. Now, this is certainly a tremendous simplification, covering a very wide range of behavior—from the novelist eagerly searching the magic formula that will make his work sell, to the sculptor who conceives his work as being so avant-garde that only "posterity" will appreciate it. But the same ternary pattern turns up in all of them: creation, publication, and acceptance.

We should not consider a ballad maker as essentially different from any other artist in this respect. He makes a ballad, which he then "publishes" in the hope of reaching a certain audience from whom he anticipates a particular response, which is to say he hopes they will accept it in some way. We've spent a lot of time discussing the ballads themselves, and in the preceding chapter we discussed the prospective audience and also what constituted performance. In simplest terms, Joe Scott was creating songs for other woodsmen in the hope that they would sing them; but there's a little more to it than that. We should never forget that Joe Scott *sold* his ballads from camp to camp. He was interested in making money from them, and that raises once again the question of what constituted acceptance. What was a "successful" song?

In *Lawrence Doyle* I wondered whether persistence in tradition might not be looked on as an accident from the point of view of both the author's intentions and the community's expectations, especially in the case of topical songs or local satire.[7] It would be a mistake, that is, to measure the success or excellence of such songs by their continuity in time, in terms of how many people happen to remember them fifty years later. Such songs are created not for posterity but for the moment, and what we really need to know is how well they were received *at the time and by the audience for whom they were created.* Now of course, persistence in tradition is one measure of how popular a song was in its time, but we should also be very much alive to *reports* of songs, to statements that "Joe Scott made up a song on that, and it was a good one." On this basis, for example, we would have to temper any negative judgment on "William Sullivan," "Wreck on the Grand Trunk Railway," or "White and Murphy," none of which has lasted well in oral tradition, but all of which have been *reported* to me over and over.

There is still another reason, perhaps even more important, for tempering any such judgment, and the latter two songs are my cases in point. We can take it for granted that they were made to be sold (but then I take that for granted with all of Joe's songs). It may even be that Joe considered them potboilers, that they were made up to cash in on immediate situations. I have suggested as much in the chapters on those specific songs, and I have further suggested that Joe may not have looked on them primarily as songs to be sung but rather as printed words to be kept, to be handed around, to be taken home and pasted in scrapbooks. It is not only that people paid him their dimes; they also "approved," and the songs met expectations all around.

It is well to keep these caveats in mind when discussing local songs and songmaking, and certainly that is one of the things this whole book is about. But some of Joe Scott's ballads went far beyond the local scene to become part of general northeastern tradition, so much a part of it that when I asked a man from back of Johnville, New Brunswick, if he knew any old songs he said, "You mean songs like 'Benjamin Deane' and 'Howard Carey' and 'The Plain Golden Band'?" He did not, by the way, recognize the name Joe Scott, nor did he have any acquaintance with the principals involved in the songs. To him the songs were simply typical come-all-ye's. No one, not even Larry Gorman, ever made a stronger impression on or got more songs into the general tradition of Maine and the Maritimes than Joe Scott did, and some very interesting things happened to them in that tradition. We have discussed each ballad individually; it remains for us to take what overview we can.

I have spoken of Joe's ballads as being in *northeastern* tradition, and even a quick checking of the lists of versions will support this: New Hampshire, Maine, New Brunswick, Nova Scotia, and Prince Edward Island. Even the exceptions bear out the pattern. B. H. Rix and Jack Scott, both writing from British Columbia, learned their versions of "The Plain Golden Band" in Maine or New Hampshire, and Monie Tedford, who now lives in Waddington, New York, learned his version of "Benjamin Deane" in Maine. Alice Flynn (née McGinley) from Allegany, New York, and her brothers, now living outside Boston, were only putting together the songs they remembered from their youth in Johnville, New Brunswick. None of Joe's songs has gone into more general tradition, but all of them moved quite freely within this area, which, while it is a part of northern lumberwoods tradition, is still distinctly a subregion.

Conclusion

There is a perfectly good historical explanation for this region-within-a-region. Since before the Civil War, Maine woodsmen had been lured west by better wages, and the panic of 1873 only intensified this exodus, extending it into the late eighties. The vacuum in the Maine woods was filled by thousands upon thousands of Provincemen who would work hard for the wages offered (far better than they could hope for at home), and they kept coming right up into the early years of this century, to work not only in the woods but also in the new and booming paper mills.[8] Some of these Provincemen also went west, of course, along with the Maine men, and while some of these western travelers stayed, many returned after a year or two. What it comes to is this: up into the 1880s there were a lot of woodsmen back and forth between the Midwest, Maine, and the Maritimes, and as a result (since they obviously carried songs with them) we find earlier woods songs like "The Jam on Gerry's Rock," "The Little Brown Bulls," and "Canaday-I-O" about equally well known in the Midwest and the Northeast. Perhaps the best example is "The Banks of the Little Eau Pleine" (Laws C–2). Its author, W. N. Allen, was born of Irish parents in Saint Stephen, New Brunswick, in 1843, but his family soon moved to the Midwest, and Allen spent most of his life as a timber cruiser in Michigan and Wisconsin. He composed "The Banks of the Little Eau Pleine" in the 1870s. In 1957, I collected a splendid version of the ballad from Charlie Gorman at his home on Prince Edward Island; Charlie had learned it around the turn of the century somewhere near Sherman Mills, Maine, giving us the whole back-and-forth in one neat package: New Brunswick, Wisconsin, Maine, Prince Edward Island![9]

But "The Banks of the Little Eau Pleine" is a transitional work that shows the beginnings of the end. Composed, as its author said, "somewhere in the seventies" in Wisconsin, it is much better known in the Midwest than in the Northeast, though it has been found in both places. There was less movement to and from the Midwest as the seventies wore on. As a result we find that "James Whalen" (Laws C–7), presumably composed in 1878, is quite well known in the Midwest but found only in scattered versions in the Northeast, and while "Harry Bale" (Laws C–13), composed in Michigan in 1879, has been found as far east as Pennsylvania and as far west as Arkansas, the only person I have ever found in the Northeast who could sing it was Sam Jagoe of Newcastle, New Brunswick, and he learned

415

a lot of his songs on "harvest excursions" in Saskatchewan.[10] Conversely, "Peter Emberly," composed near Boiestown, New Brunswick, in 1881, is one of the best-known woods ballads in the Northeast, but it has, as Edith Fowke says, "rarely wandered inland."[11] All we really have is E. C. Beck's word that lumbermen in Michigan and Wisconsin are "not unfamiliar" with it,[12] and an oral report by MacEdward Leach that he had found it in a single version in West Virginia.

It is too bad we do not have datable songs from the later eighties to make this almost-too-neat case still neater, but the point is made that as the movement of northeastern lumbermen back and forth to the Midwest operations slowed down, so did the exchange of songs, until by the late nineties both had almost ceased entirely; and it was in the late nineties and early 1900s that Joe Scott's ballads went into circulation. Thus, while they were in plenty of time to move freely in the Northeast, they were a minimum of twenty years too late to get carried to the Midwest—done in by economics and demography.

Let us now look at the distribution of Joe's ballads *within* this area I have defined as the Northeast—but first a warning. In drawing any conclusions, distributional or otherwise, from such a statistically small sample, we should be very careful and very hedgy. There is just too high a possibility for error through coincidence and the happenstances of field collecting. One singer in a town leads to another and yet another, for example, while it just works out that no one ever even tried to collect material in another town fifty miles away. Nor have I or anyone else that I know of deliberately set up control or spot-check field trips to remedy this situation. For such sins I beat my breast, but there is a certain insincerity in my contrition. Statistically my sample may be small, but for a folklore study of a limited area it is huge. On the one hand that may be a sad commentary on the state of one kind of folklore study; on the other it means that I can have a certain rough confidence in my statistics because their base is broader and more solid than that of any other study in the game. My figures will be rough, my pontifications probabilistic, my King's-X in full view. But on the whole I've got it about right, I'm sure. And now, at last, let us take a look. . . .

I have said that Scott's ballads moved freely in the Northeast, but that is not quite true; their movements within this area were controlled by the same economics and concomitant demography that confined the songs to the Northeast to begin with, and they demonstrate almost perfectly my contention in the preceding chapter that lumberwoods tradition is simply an extension of the public-performance tradition of the rural Maritime Provinces. First of all, a little simple arithmetic (comparing the number of versions found to overall population) shows the tradition to have been twice as strong in New Brunswick as it was in Maine and almost five times as strong in Prince Edward Island. Second, a quarter to a third of the versions I have collected in Maine and New Hampshire were from Maritimers like Jack Rodgerson, Billy Bell, and John Brown, and practically all of them learned the ballads before they left home. Third, most versions collected in Maine and New Hampshire came from areas with strong Maritimes ambience. About a fifth came from along the New Brunswick border (Allagash, Westfield, Bridgewater, Monticello, Houlton, Island Falls, Topsfield, and Baring, for example), and about half were collected in or near cities that were lumbering depots that later became pulp- and paper-mill towns (Bangor-Brewer, Rumford-Mexico, and Berlin, New Hampshire). Fourth and finally, almost without exception the best versions—the most complete and best performed—were collected from New Brunswickers or Prince Edward Islanders, whether they were on their home ground or in the United States. Whatever subjective tinge there may be to that judgment could not seriously affect its accuracy; the ratio is in the neighborhood of ten to one.

Such figures make it more obvious than ever that this singing tradition was mainly in the capable hands of Maritimers, and I don't think it is necessary to labor the point that the singers were mainly from the farms, or at any rate from nonurban areas. In New Brunswick, southeastern Charlotte County around Saint Stephen, the middle Saint John valley from Bristol to the Tobique, and the Miramichi valley account for better than two-thirds of that province's versions; and western Prince County ("West Prince") on Prince Edward Island contributed about the same proportion of *that* province's versions. All of these are rural areas, strongly Irish and Scottish, and all furnished more than their share of young men who came to Maine to work in the woods. Again, no real surprises.

There are a few minor surprises when we consider certain clear lacunae in the distributional map, but they are only first-glance surprises. Perhaps the biggest is that of all of Joe's ballads, only a

417

single version of one, "The Plain Golden Band," has turned up in Newfoundland tradition, although the bulk of northern or lumber-woods repertoire is represented there in fine shape, the singing style is identical, and singing has maintained its importance there better than anywhere else in Canada. Some specifically Maritimes songs like "Peter Emberly" and "Young Millman" have found their way there, but their very rarity—combined with the similar rarity of local Newfoundland songs in the Maritimes—is our clue.[13] There were some Newfoundlanders in the Maine and New Brunswick lumber-woods in the early twentieth century, but they weren't all that strong an element, and those who did come tended to stay or move further on. They did not, that is, share the "into the woods and home again" pattern we have found so commonly with Maritimers. Newfound-land tradition and Maritimes tradition come from the same seed sown on similar soils, but their development has been ecotypic, and I suggest that the same concept could and should be applied to closer looks at the Adirondacks, the Catskills, Pennsylvania, Ontario, and the Midwest. If Newfoundland furnishes our biggest surprise, it is not a very surprising surprise.

Nor should we be very surprised to discover that Joe's ballads do not turn up in southwestern Maine or southern New Hampshire. I once claimed that a line drawn from Mount Washington to Calais would neatly separate Maine's two cultural watersheds: to the south, New England; to the north, the Maritimes.[14] That line has stood up very well, but never better than in the present study. Joe's work does not turn up along the coast, for example, nor would I expect it to turn up in that essentially New England area. Even the exceptions turn out not to be exceptions. I collected "Guy Reed," "The Plain Golden Band," and "Howard Carey" from Edward Gavel in Sanford, Maine, way down in the southwest corner of the state, but it turned out Gavel had come originally from eastern Maine and had spent many years working in the woods and on the drives along the Mattawam-keag in particular, but also all over eastern and northern Maine and New Brunswick as well. Then there was Ernest Lord of Wells, Maine, a coastal town only a few miles from Sanford. Though he knew none of Scott's work, he did have a fine repertoire of songs that matched very nicely with standard woods repertoire. Sure enough, it turned out he was originally from central New Brunswick and had come to Wells only later in life. Finally, Helen Hartness Flanders collected songs in the early thirties from Orlon Merrill of Charles-town, New Hampshire, many of them standard woods-repertoire pieces, among them "Guy Reed." Like Lord, Merrill had only recently come to the southland, having grown up in central Maine and spent much time in the lumberwoods in both Maine and north-ern New Hampshire.

Although they are south of my line, the Union and Machias river valleys deserve some special consideration, since they continued to be active lumbering areas into the twentieth century and had had their share of Maritimes woodsmen. Larry Gorman, for example, had worked for almost twenty years along the Union River, and his songs refer to other "P.I.'s" who were there, too.[15] But by the turn of the century, operations in these areas were pretty well able to staff themselves locally, and the "P.I.'s and Miramichi-I's" bypassed them for the larger centers created by the burgeoning paper industry— Bangor and Rumford, for example. It is more difficult to explain why Joe's ballads have not been found much along the Kennebec or around Millinocket, since both were important in the paper industry and both saw plenty of Maritimers in and out. I won't attempt any explanation beyond suggesting that further collection in these areas would probably have settled everything.

A final footnote. I have been stressing the importance of the Maritimes and Maritimers in all I have said, and that is as it should be. Joe Scott himself was a New Brunswicker, and the New Brunswickers and Prince Edward Islanders and Nova Scotians were unquestionably the best singers. Those who love the Maritimes can be proud of that. But it all began in Maine. Joe Scott's ballads were written here and first sung here, and it was from Maine camps that they spread. Those who love inland Maine can be proud of that. And I, an outlander who loves them both, am doubly proud.

Here, then, we can leave the matter of the distribution of Joe Scott's ballads with a feeling of some satisfaction. Not only does this distribution fit the economic and demographic facts in general, explaining why the Northeast is an area-within-an-area, it also fits these facts in considerable detail, explaining the presence or ab-sence of his ballads in specific locations within the Northeast. In a way, a very real way, the whole development can be seen as a last flourishing of a fine old tradition of songs and singing brought about by the special turn-of-the-century demands of the unpoetic pulp and paper industry, a final risorgimento along the deacon seat under the flickering kerosene lamps or around the drivers' fire, doomed like a candle in the multimedia dawn's early light.

So much for distribution pure and simple. Now we can ask what has happened to Joe's ballads in their more than seventy years of wandering, albeit deterministic wandering, in the Northeast. We have had something to say about these matters in the chapters on the individual ballads. Can we generalize beyond that about the changes oral tradition has worked on Joe's original productions? Yes, we can—but having set up my straw men I must once again be indulged the academic pleasure of knocking them apart.

First, there is no such thing as oral tradition. It doesn't exist any more than culture does. Songs don't wander, and something that isn't there can't work changes. We settled all this in the preceding chapter, but it is worth reminding ourselves from time to time that oral tradition is only a concept, a manner of speaking. Second, we also need to be re-reminded that in describing this manner-of-speaking, change is accident, not essence. The essence is continuity. Most singers want to sing a song "right," which means the way they learned it originally; and it is only the rare innovator—in an act almost tantamount to the making of a new ballad—who purposes change. Yet no two versions of a ballad are ever the same, and the variations we find from version to version do exhibit some patterns. To deny that would be as silly as to deny ourselves the *concept* of oral tradition simply because it *is* a concept. We will use the concept, and we will talk about changes, but my repeated monitions can, I hope, at least keep us on terra firma and down out of the circumambient gas.[16]

By all odds, the first question should be why some ballads went into oral tradition while others did not, because obviously only five of Joe's ballads really caught on: "The Plain Golden Band," "Howard Carey," "Guy Reed," "Benjamin Deane," and "The Norway Bum" (although we can add "The White Cafe" to that list, if we want to). It begs the question to say that these are his finest ballads, but that's about the best I can do for a supergenerality on this intriguing subject. I ran into the same problem with Lawrence Doyle's songs, and my solution (or nonsolution) in the present instance will be the same: it will be left at the level of the individual song.[17]

One of the first things I learned as an undergraduate about

folksongs (read "ballads") was that they were authorless or at least anonymous, the author counting for nothing. That was standard fare among both the professors and the textbook anthologists of my day (class of 1948), as it had been standard fare in the graduate schools of *their* day, and it is interesting to see how frequently the concept of anonymity turns up as a ballad touchstone even today. There's a good deal of sense in this; as a matter of demonstrable empirical fact, probably at least 90 percent of all ballads in Anglo-American tradition *are* anonymous, and any touchstone that will work nine times out of ten is far from silly. The silliness enters in when we make the next step, insisting on our ignorance—the fact that we don't know who the authors were—as an essential principle, a matter of basic definition. Joe Scott's ballads are a perfect case in point. Conservatively, well over half of my informants had no idea who made up the songs they sang, and that figure is considerably higher for those who learned the ballad at one remove or more from Joe himself. As one man told me, "If we liked a song, we didn't care much who wrote it." Given another generation or two (and no nosy folklorists around to stir things up), I am sure that the fact of Joe's authorship would have been completely forgotten, though I see no reason to believe that his ballads would not have continued to be sung. One of the effects of oral tradition on Joe's ballads, then, has been the creation of their anonymity, and certainly the same can be said for the multitudinous 90 percent of Anglo-American ballads as well.

Earlier in this chapter I played for a moment with the idea of casting tradition (conceived as a succession of singers) in the role of an editor improving on the original work. One of the most obvious kinds of editing we can see the tradition working on Joe's originals is simple shortening. This is most dramatic, of course, in "Benjamin Deane," where something drastic had to be done in order to bring that ballad within the limits of what was considered singable, and even then it was known as a long song. However, both "Howard Carey" and "Guy Reed" show definite shortening, and while it is less obvious in "The Plain Golden Band" and "The Norway Bum," it is still noticeable in many versions. Almost always the shortening took place in those parts of the ballad where Joe had been the most leisurely: the detailing of Ben Deane's financial troubles, the mother's advice in "Howard Carey," and the "aftermath" section of "Guy Reed," for example. But perhaps the most perfect example we have of this sort of pruning in action is Roy Lohnes's account of how he learned "William Sullivan." It is worth repeating here. "I don't know all of it," he told me. "I never wanted to learn all of it. You know how Joe was, and how he was always putting in about the bubbling brooks and the flowers and stuff? Well, the whole first third of this song was like that, so I just never bothered to learn that part." Considering what I have already said about Joe's special style, it would seem that the tradition had only limited tolerance for novelty.

Beyond the general shortening, the tradition of Joe Scott's ballads is a museum of just about every kind of variation one can imagine, from simple changes on the word and phrase level to stanza inversions, fusions, shifts in tune, right on up to story changes. The latter, however, are very slight shifts. We have Joe Pagett's version of "The Plain Golden Band," which merely omits Lizzie's confession, and two Miramichi versions of "Benjamin Deane" (NB.6, NB.7), which (by leaving out the stanza in which Ben's wife leaves him) make it appear that Ben surprises her at home with another man. If these can't really be called changes in story, they are at least shifts in emphasis.

But the changes are not the important thing. If Menelaus could understand that and hold tight through flood, fire, and raging beast, we should be able to do as much under less Protean circumstances. Joe's ballads have *not* changed appreciably in tradition, and what changes they do exhibit are superficial and minor. That point is crucial, and it leads me to two further observations.

The first is a bit of a dead horse, since I do not believe any serious ballad scholar today really accepts the essentially Darwinian view that it is through this process of oral tradition with its summation of small changes that an individual creation becomes a true folk ballad. Yet it crops up often enough to make it worth our while taking a lick at it. Gordon Hall Gerould stated it this way back in 1932: "The processes by which both words and melodies keep continually changing, yet only very slowly become transformed into something quite unrecognizable as the same, present without doubt the central problem in connection with popular poetry and music."[18] He quotes both Cecil Sharp and Phillips Barry in support of this view, though Barry's most concise statement of his own position shows him closer to De Vries than to Darwin, I believe.[19] There is nothing in my work, however, that encourages me to elevate *process* to such primacy. It would be ridiculous to claim that individuals in the chain of tradition won't make their influence felt, and it is quite clear that occasionally such a change will be extensive enough to make the line between "creation" and "re-creation" pretty tenuous. But the individual poet, not the process of oral transmission, is the primary alembic. Through him the world and the tradition are transmuted to form the ballad—familiar, yet forever new. Whatever Joe Scott's ballads may have become, it is Joe who gave them their whatness, their identity. And that essence, that continuity, is far more to be emphasized than any amount of change.

It has always seemed a mistake to me to confuse the creativity of the original composer/author with the creativity involved in the continued performance of his work. Or rather, it seems a mistake to set "folk" tradition apart from other artistic traditions as being one in which the two kinds of creativity are the same or of equal importance—or even one in which the former is less important than the latter. A composer creates a work, and performers adapt it to their and their audience's needs and expectations. Handel's *Music for the Royal Fireworks* played on the instruments for which it was originally written sounds "odd" to a contemporary audience used to hearing it played on modern instruments. Heifetz certainly has had an effect on J. S. Bach's compositions for solo violin that can be paralleled with the effect a respected traditional singer might have in his locale on J. W. Scott's compositions for solo voice. And while the analogy is not exact, it seems to me that Segovia's transcriptions of Bach for the guitar have something in common with Wilmot Mac-Donald's adapting a new tune to "Benjamin Deane," in that both are consciously creative acts that significantly alter an original (perhaps the Kingston Trio's singing of "Tom Dooley" is a closer analogy, but then . . .). There is no denying the difference—that in the one we have an "original" to "go back to," while in the other we do not—but that happenstance (and that is what it is) should not obscure the basic identity. In both cases we have two kinds of creativity: the one creates a "new" work, something that was not there at all before; the other operates on something already there.

The second observation is not a dead horse. We think of oral tradition as normative and leveling, as rejecting idiosyncrasy and deviation, as being essentially very conservative. Yet Joe Scott's major ballads were full of innovation, and they were accepted and absorbed into that tradition pretty much as he had conceived them. Roy Lohnes may have ignored some of the birds-and-flowers stanzas of "William Sullivan," and singers somewhere along the line may have pruned back the excessive detail in "Benjamin Deane," but that does not alter the fact that the basic structures, proportions, and language of Joe's ballads have been extremely well preserved through time and space. Which means that for all its basic conservatism, folk tradition accepted innovation, and it is through such acceptance that the tradition itself changes and develops. As Homer Barnett said, "All cultural changes are initiated by individuals."[20] It is one of the central simplicities of his splendid book, and Joe Scott's work can be taken as a beautiful illustration of it.

The Man

What part did Joe Scott's songmaking play in his life? In an earlier chapter I said that Joe was unique in his area both for his songmaking and for his song-peddling. That is true, but only in a limited sense. First of all, it is obvious that others were making up ballads in the Northeast at about this same time. We have "John Ladner," made up around 1900 over on the Kennebec. Back in New Brunswick, "The Moncton Tragedy" was made up about a murder that took place in 1896, and "Peter Emberly" was composed in 1881. Over in Bear River, Nova Scotia, there were at least two ballads made up on the murder of Annie Kempton by Peter Wheeler in 1896, while out on Prince Edward Island the Millman-Tuplin murder of 1887 inspired four different ballads, and Lawrence Doyle wrote one on the Callaghan murder that took place there in 1885. The come-all-ye muse was still alive, and she inspired others besides Joe Scott.[21] However, she was less active than her sister, the comic or satiric muse. John Szwed is quite right when he calls satire and sarcasm "the central tradition of Northeastern songmaking,"[22] and examples of the art are so plentiful as almost to defy annotation.[23] Nor are we at a loss for the names of people who made songs, many of whom had local reputations for their skill ("*Anything happen, he'd make a song about it*"). The Maine lumberwoods were full of poets and songmakers of all stripes and intensities, but that is subject of yet another study.[24]

Even Joe's song-peddling was nothing new. In Maine, for example, we know that Larry Gorman used to sell printed versions of his songs not only from his home, but along Exchange Street in Bangor as well, where he had well-known competition from John J. Friend and occasionally from John Young of Old Town.[25] Evidently, though, neither Friend nor Young thought of their work as songs to be sung; rather, they were poems to be read, and even a lot of Larry Gorman's later stuff was more "poem" than "song." But all three of them sold their work in printed form for ten cents a copy, and so did John Mitchell and Sherman Doody from Aroostook County.[26] Finally, as "The Norway Bum" and "Guy Reed" appeared in the *Rumford Falls Times*, so did a lot of other local poetry; much was obituary verse (one Lee L. Abbott being the most prolific writer in this genre), but some of it was sentimental ("The Bugle Boy in Blue" and "Twilight Thoughts" by Annie E. Cutting of Andover), and there was an occasional humorous or satirical piece as well.

In the face of all this, how can I say Joe Scott was "unique," even "in a sense"? All of the parts were already there; what Joe did was put them together in a special way and under special circumstances. Just at the time of the risorgimento, Joe Scott, a crack woodsman and driver who was already known as a fine singer, began traveling from camp to camp selling his songs. Any camp he went into he had friends in. He was well known and extremely well liked, and he'd sing and sell his songs, almost all of which were about events and people his audience would have been familiar with. Add to this the very obvious fact that the products he was selling were top-of-the-line, and the uniqueness claim can stand. There was no one else quite like him.

All the reports I have of Joe's song-peddling come from right around the turn of the century, and if we look at the dates we can assign to his ballads, an interesting parallel emerges. If we assume that the ballads appeared soon after the events they chronicled—and in the present instance I make it with no hesitation—then six of Joe's ballads were written within a five-year period: Howard Carrick died on May 5, Guy Reed on September 9, and William Sullivan on October 20, 1897; Benjamin Deane shot his wife on May 4, 1898; the wreck on the Grand Trunk took place on January 17, 1901, and Wilfred White and John Murphy drowned in the Magalloway on October 13 of that year. This in itself is a moderately arresting statistic; if we add to it other data—less "hard," but reasonably reliable—it becomes positively startling. "The Norway Bum" first appeared in print in the *Rumford Falls Times* for April 13, 1901, which date is a *terminus ad quem*, and since "Guy Reed" had been so published a couple of weeks previously, there is a strong presumption that "The Norway Bum" falls within our five-year period, too. Further, we have Bert Thorne's testimony that he "roomed with Joe Scott at Simon Oakes' Boarding House in the year 1901 at Rangeley, Maine and bought several of his songs from him."[27] Among the songs he bought: "Charming Little Girl," "Sacker Shean's Little Girl," and "William McGibbeny." Finally, although "The Plain Golden Band" is based on an event that occurred in 1894, I have argued that it probably wasn't written until some time later than that, possibly as late as 1898. Acknowledging as I must the temptation to base my facts upon my conclusions, and recognizing as I do the evidential swoop from irrefutable vital statistics to psychological second-guessing, it still appears extremely likely that all but one of Joe Scott's extant ballads were written between 1897 and 1901.

What are we to make of this apparently sudden outburst? It is remarkable, no matter how we look at it; but taken along with other aspects of Joe's life it makes a kind of sense. He was a restless dreamer, a layer of great plans, and a fast starter, but he never stayed with any one thing very long. He was not content back on the farm; there was *"something he was reaching for," as old Emma Merrithew told me, and then one day he was gone. Over in Maine, he became a first-rate woodsman and river-driver, but even in this life—a life that seemed made to order for the footloose and restless—he was generally known as a wanderer, a woods tramp. His brief marriage seems also to have followed the pattern. Later on, when he went back to farming, he threw himself into it by clearing a whole lot of new land and building a big chicken-house; then he left before he ever planted a crop or bought a chicken, and he left for another wonderful scheme: selling sewing machines along the upper Saint John River! Back around Rangeley he tried to interest people in going up to Canada with him and opening some sporting camps; then he went to northern Quebec alone, started a homestead, and was back in Rangeley in about two years.

Seen in this context, Joe stayed with his songmaking and song-peddling longer than with anything else he ever did, and since "Norman Mitchell" came along as late as 1909, there is good reason to believe that he never abandoned it entirely. Through all those years song had an important place in Joe Scott's life, but around the turn of the century he was a Poet like nothing else. He was "the celebrated Joe Scott," turning stuff out like billyho and marketing his product with great energy and imagination.

But there is a second context in which we should see his songmaking. All his life Joe was an entertainer, a performer. It is as constant a theme as we can find throughout his whole biography—Joe putting on a show and making everyone laugh. He loved an audience and could hold one well. *"One time we was to a dance," said Daisy Severy, "and out in the hallway some fellows was singing. They was pretty well lit up, you know, the way they are at these old country dances sometimes. I heard Joe singing [and] I says, 'My Lord!' I went out and he had an audience all around the hall there." Clyde Dickinson remembered Beecher Dow telling him how he and Joe were down and out in Bangor one time. They were sitting in the park, wondering when they'd eat again and where they'd sleep that night, when Joe suddenly got up and went into a butcher shop across the street, where he cadged a sheet of brown paper and a pencil. Half an hour later he had written a new song, and the two friends headed for a nearby tavern, where Joe sang it and put on a general entertainment while Beecher passed the hat. They got enough money together not only for food and lodging, but for several drinks besides.

Many people have remarked what a hit Joe would have been today. *"Supposing that there'd been anything like television," said Mrs. Merrithew. "Joe would have been a good hand. He could've made everybody laugh." David Severy put it a little differently, but the emphasis was the same. *"We always thought," he told me, "that if Joe Scott was living today he'd make a fortune. He's got these hillbillies beat a mile. That's a fact!"

Actually, there is a lot in Joe's career that should remind us of well-known (and some not-so-well-known) southern country-music men. Like Joe, they were often wandering performers and entertainers, and, like Joe, many of them made up their own songs, which they promoted by singing them in public and selling printed copies. But unlike Joe, many of them made the transition to recordings. Blind Richard D. Burnett of Monticello, Kentucky, traveled all over the Southeast in the 1910s and 1920s singing and playing guitar and banjo. Then about 1913 he published six of his own songs in a little booklet that he sold as he went along. He made the switch to recordings in the twenties. His comments are worth repeating here:

Yeah, I sold 6000 o' them books at ten cents apiece. But along toward the last, when I went to making these records, I just quit the other. Oh, I sold the supply o' books I had on hand, but after I'd made the records, I'd sell the records instead. It was better to sell the records—people could listen to the record and the songbooks just had the words in 'em. Oh, I was the first man around here that sold records. . . . Oh, I sold hundreds o' them in this county. And you know, everybody around, they'd come for miles and miles to get them records.[28]

Burnett was typical of many country performers, and it became and remained part of the country-music pattern that the performer sold records and made up some of his own songs. It would have been a perfect set-up for Joe; but as I suggested earlier, he came about twenty years too soon, and he was in the wrong part of the country to be part of that boom.

From this perspective, it does not seem particularly surprising that Joe Scott the singer and songmaker became over the years Joe Scott the magician, the clairvoyant, the worker of wonders, because all the time it was really Joe Scott the showman we were watching. It may be—and this has to be speculation—that his songs weren't bringing him enough of whatever it was he needed from his audience of fellow woodsmen. It wasn't money; Joe probably made more in any one year from his songs than he ever made from his magic in his entire life. Rather, it was regard, prestige, notoriety; call it what we will, it was that insistence on being not just Joe Scott, but *the* Joe Scott, the *celebrated* Joe Scott. Perhaps if he had made it bigger as a singer/songwriter, or if he had been born twenty years later in the South, he wouldn't have needed the magic at all—but to play that game is to let contingencies tease us out of thought. Without abandoning song, he turned to magic for reinforcement, and evidently it served.

Seeing Joe's songmaking in these two contexts—the fast-starting nonfinisher and the showman—can help us understand both its intensity and its concentration in a relatively brief time-span. But why did he choose songmaking to begin with, and why did he start so suddenly just about when he did? If the past few pages have been heavily speculative, what follows will be even more so; but there are some intriguing possible answers, and we should consider them.

Let us return for a moment to a consideration of Joe the showman. I have said that he evidently needed and thrived on repute, but I suspect he had discovered something else about the limelight: it was a very safe place to hide. Almost as common as statements about Joe the performer, always full of fun and jokes, are statements about his reserve. This "keeping his distance" was no new thing; it went back to his young manhood in Lower Woodstock, which is as far as we can go. Joe Scott evidently never allowed himself to get close to anyone, and the "happy-go-lucky showman" drew people to him and kept them at arm's length all at once.

It was a rather neat strategy, and apparently he kept that nice balance for twenty-five years. Then he let one person through, and she betrayed him. A jilting, a break-up, is a terrible thing under any circumstances, but it just about killed Joe. It's a wonder he survived it at all, but he did. He came back, but it didn't happen all at once. It took time. The initial shock, the awful sense of loss and emptiness, the unwillingness and inability to accept what had happened, the anger, the self-pity, the despair—Joe had to work his way through all of this agony just like any other man. My reading of his character tells me that for a while he probably made good use of those two standard anodynes available to the spurned lover: boozing and whoring. *"It ruined poor Joe, killed him," said Angus Enman. "He just got to be an old bum after that." And it was probably during this period that he contracted the syphilis that ultimately did in fact kill him. That's conjecture, of course, but whatever happened, he had a tough time of it. It would not be surprising if it took him two or three years to put things back together again in any form, but one thing we can be sure of. He had been wounded once, and while the wound never healed, he rebuilt his defenses so that no one would ever really touch it, nor would he ever be hurt again. On the military analogy of the best defense being a strong offense, the incipient showman became a celebrity. Again, a neat strategy, and from all we can tell, it seems to have worked reasonably well.

At just about the time, then, that I see Joe Scott as coming to terms with his grief, he went into high gear on his peddling and performing. It sounds like a variation on what we might call the actor's—even the Pagliacci—syndrome. I am always ready to shudder, a stylish academic shudder, at such trite or pat formulations when I read them in popular-press "fan" pieces; but even a cliché can be correct, and I am convinced it is perfectly correct in Joe's case. That is, there *was* a causal connection between his having been hurt and his becoming "the celebrated Joe Scott." Now the next question almost asks itself: was there also a causal connection between the trauma and his songs? Again, I fear the cliché, but again, I am convinced it can be applied.

"Out of my great sorrow, I make little songs," said Heine, and Yeats, though with a slightly different emphasis, is not far from that in speaking of Keats:

> His art is happy, but who knows his mind?
> I see a schoolboy when I think of him,
> With face and nose pressed to a sweet-shop window,
> For certainly he sank into his grave
> His senses and his heart unsatisfied,
> And made—being poor, ailing and ignorant,
> Shut out from all the luxury of the world,
> The coarse-bred son of a livery-stable keeper—
> Luxuriant song.[29]

That suffering and sorrow are the soil from which art grows is one of the most firmly established and generally accepted ideas in Western culture, and while it is less in style now than it has been, it keeps turning up. As a general explanation of the genesis of art, it is, like all such sweeping formulations, highly suspect; but certainly no one will deny its applicability in specific circumstances. "The Plain Golden Band," for example, is a little song that grew directly out of Joe Scott's great sorrow, though actually that's not the problem we're concerned with. What we are interested in is the possible relationship between a particular sorrow, a specific loss, and a subsequent intense period of creativity. To put it another way, were the songs part of Joe's strategy (conscious or unconscious) for working out his salvation?

I could easily stop short here, being neither psychologist nor psychoanalyst, though that would be an academic cop-out. While to speak of proof would be to let enthusiasm outrun circumspection, I will confess to a strong presumption. Michael Owen Jones, in his study of Charley, an Appalachian chairmaker, states that presumption very well. "But of one thing I am now certain," he says, "that the process of grieving over a loss, resulting in the nostalgia for the past and the withdrawal from others, expressed in Charley's chairs by old-timey traits and a sense of enclosure is related to the creative process. . . ." He goes on: "There is no question but that bereavement affects the works of an individual already making and doing things expressive of himself. . . . More interesting is the way in which grief can precipitate the process of personal expression, resulting in the production of a few objects, stories, or songs during a brief period of time, or, more rarely, causing recurrent expressive activity from that moment on."[30] Since Jones was working with a man who was still alive, he could marshall a great deal of evidence in support of his interpretation; at the same time, he admitted that that interpretation was certainly speculative. Having much less to go on, I more than accept his caution as my own; at the same time, I must admit that what he says applies intriguingly well to Joe Scott.

To begin with, the dates are right; but that reasoning gets a bit circular, explaining that the songs came when they did because that was when they came. However, if we look at the content of the songs, if we think about them as a kind of projective screen, we can see things that might well be expressive of Joe's mental state at the time. In a general way, loss of love and violent death are certainly appropriate; but notice how often that more general and less overt theme that I call the Eden motif emerges. Home and childhood are portrayed with nostalgic tenderness:

> Those bright sunbeams on the hill
> And the babbling brook or rill
> And the flowers so fair, the birds that sing with glee
> And the balmy breeze of spring,
> (oh how sweetly they do ring)
> Those fair charming silver bells of memory;
> How they call me back once more
> To an old familiar shore
> Where the myrtle and the ivy thickly grow,
> In a pleasant shady spot
> Round a humble little cot
> Where I was born so many years ago.

So it is in "William McGibbeny," and we can find the same thing in "Howard Carey," "William Sullivan," "The Norway Bum," and (to a lesser extent) "Benjamin Deane." Nowhere else is Joe Scott so lavish with his roses, dewdrops, singing birds, and bubbling brooks as when he lets his heroes tell of their homes or, as in "The Plain Golden Band," of "the days that are gone." It was a beautiful place, full of joy and love and light, a true Eden, but the hero has fallen from it. Sometimes that fall is his own doing, as in "Howard Carey" or "Benjamin Deane," sometimes not, as in "The Norway Bum"; whatever the case, Eden is gone, irrevocably gone, and the hero can only look back—"so sad, so fresh, the days that are no more."

Not irrevocably gone, though; not really. There is a way back through death and the grave:

> The bonny banks of Bash, all robed in leafy green,
> Where winding hills and valleys low and rippling rills are seen;
> Where mountain streams flow gaily on through winding hills and dells,
> There stands a pleasant cottage where an aged couple dwells.
>
> That pleasant cottage was once the home of William Sullivan,
> Whose earthly cares is over now, his work on earth is done;
> He sleeps beside his brothers where bright flowers gently grow,
> Where the birds of spring their notes they sing in the valleys far below.[31]

Even so "White and Murphy":

> And their remains were taken home by two of their crew
> And now they lie at rest beneath the morn and evening dew.

After his flower-filled funeral, Guy Reed "sleeps beside his kindred / Near the spot that gave him birth." In fact, the whole "aftermath" section of that song is filled with some of Joe's most poignant nature imagery:

> The robin and the swallow,
>   The sunshine and the rain,
> The cuckoo and the sparrow
>   With the spring will come again
> The blackbird and the thrushes
>   From foreign lands will soar,
> But loved ones that in death doeth sleep,
>   Will come again no more.

It could be objected here that these things are *contrasted* with death, not made a part of it. Agreed, but the affective quality of the whole passage—the last five stanzas, for that matter—is one of peaceful sleep amid great natural beauty.

Finally, and at the risk of chasing a good idea clean across the county line, there is the recurrent figure of the mother. She is there at the beginning, she is the one set out from, and it is at her side that one sleeps at the end. "Howard Carey" is of course the prime example, but we find touches of it in both "Guy Reed" and "William Sullivan" (is it a coincidence that those three songs are, if my timetable is correct, the earliest we have and that they came within a six-month period?), and in William McGibbeny's final request:

> And let my remains be laid
> 'Neath the willow's quiet shade
> By my mother's side, who calmly slumbers there.

It comes to this, then: in his songs, around the figure of some man who died or had been mortally wounded in body or spirit, images of home, childhood, beauty, death, sleep, and mother glow like a nimbus. They express his aching nostalgia for Eden, the world as it was before his Fall, while at the same time they offer the hope of his regaining it in the grave. If we carry the abstraction one step further, in Freudian terms we have the womb, in Jungian, perhaps the archetypal Primordial Mother. Under any circumstances, it is a compelling cluster of associations. Not all the elements are present in any one song; yet when one occurs it carries with it connotations of the others. In other words, when Joe Scott brings the sparkling waters, the thrushes, the roses, and the willows into his songs—and we know how important such imagery was to him—he is home again, at rest, and it doesn't hurt any more.

Atque Vale

And so I come to the end of a quest that began in a booth of the old Northern Hotel barroom where Herby Rice first told me over cold beer of a man named Joe Scott, who always wanted to write a book. The Northern's gone now, along with the rest of lower Exchange Street, so that Herby's old ghost would have a hard time to slake its thirst among friends and familiar surroundings in Bangor today. For eighteen years I have followed Joe Scott and his songs wherever the search has led me, and I have loved every minute of it. And now it's over.

Not that there haven't been bad moments. I hope that no one devotes as much of his life to a work as I have to this one without wondering from time to time if it's worth it, if it's really "important" enough to merit (and perhaps this is the ultimate and most touching arrogance of all) *our* attention, considering the brevity of the one-way trip we're all ticketed for. There have been few guidelines and even fewer established standards to sustain me here. I came to Joe from the study of Literature and History and Music, as a lover of William Butler Yeats and Peter Abelard and John Dowland, and the conscience created by such elitist study and love has been a nag. To appease this conscience, Joe and his songs may have occasionally borne the burden of my condescension, as I have borne the condescension of my literary friends who from time to time (with tight smiles) said my work was (dear God!) "interesting." I came to Folklore, and found there some support for my conviction of the general worth of the materials I was dealing with, but no real precedents for the kind of intensive study I had in mind. The models were in literary study, and there I was back again. A couple of very good and kindred souls assured me I was a "pioneer," which was nice of them; but who wants to be a pioneer in country that turns out to be swamp and puckerbrush, while up on the ridges "Homer and Whitman roared in the pines"?

If I was an irresolute and somewhat schizoid pioneer, I was also a recent convert to Cultural Anthropology, and in the wisdom of my new religion it might be expected that I would withdraw not to the ridges but to the top of the mountain, where I could see it all in terms of orthodox Cultural Relativism. No doubt about it, that *is* my perspective. No song, no performance, no act of creation can be properly understood apart from the culture or subculture in which it is found and of which it is a part; nor should any "work of art" be looked on as a thing in itself apart from the continuum of creation-consumption. I accept these precepts, but I must confess that while the air at the top of the mountain is clear, it is also thin. Which is to say I have not been entirely comfortable in my new religion, feeling something like an old Two-Seed-in-the-Spirit Predestinarian Baptist who's recently converted to Bahai. In no way do I deny the Higher

434

Truth of cultural relativism; it is only that a literary Sabbatarian like myself breathes easier on the lower slopes.

Where, then, will I find Salvation? In the aesthetic experience itself—something I have always believed in but find easier to identify than define. Since I distrust the terms in which such a definition would have to be couched almost as much as I accept the reality of the experience itself, perhaps an example will suffice.

Back in 1954, I heard Andrés Segovia play the Handel *Sarabande with Variations* in New York's Town Hall. Along with several hundred others I watched a man in complete control of—and entirely at peace with—his instrument, and as he filled the room with the gorgeous contrapuntal simplicity of that music we listened in perfect silence. Then it happened. Of course, I can speak only for myself, but it was as if we were all transformed. We were drawn up *into* the music, and for the moment that was all there was. It was Wallace Stevens's singer by the sea:

> It was her voice that made
> The sky acutest at its vanishing.
> She measured to the hour its solitude.
> She was the single artificer of the world
> In which she sang. And when she sang, the sea,
> Whatever self it had, became the self
> That was her song, for she was the maker. Then we,
> As we beheld her striding there alone,
> Knew that there never was a world for her
> Except the one she sang, and, singing, made.[32]

Not only was the experience real then, it is still real, and years afterward I can contemplate it and draw sustenance from it. In fact, the recollection may be more significant than the original experience, for all I know.

I have a head full of such experiences, and many of them have occurred in kitchens or front farmhouse parlors: Wilmot MacDonald singing "The Doors of Ivory" one night, and no sound in the house besides; Jim Brown and his son Tom, as we were having a final drink round the kitchen table, singing "The *Cedar Grove*" together ("You start it, Pop, and I'll come along"); Joe Walsh singing "Fogan MacAleer" in the middle of a hayfield on a clear September afternoon; Bill Cramp sitting on his bed singing "The Old Elm Tree" as he learned it from his sister; old Ralph Thornton going over "Benjamin

Deane" for Wayne Bean and me as we sat by the stove and the trucks lumbered through the cold December fog along U.S. 1 outside. I am not talking about "natural context" or "folk esthetic" or anything of that sort at all. I am talking about what have been for me moments of great integrity, moments when I have been transformed, moments like that moment in Town Hall. They need no apology, existing as they do in a place beyond understanding, where no tight smile or condescension can touch them. Through this needle's eye, even a middle-aged literary Sabbatarian can enter Heaven.

And there, far from the enormous assaults of the universe, after the ultimate unjudgment of death, I will find Joe Scott and William Yeats drinking beer together in quiet and understanding. That will be good, and I'll hunt up Herby Rice, and we'll go join them.

NOTES

1. The exceptions are "The Plain Golden Band," "Charming Little Girl," "The White Cafe," and "Sacker Shean's Little Girl."
2. René Wellek and Austin Warren, *Theory of Literature*, p. 78.
3. T. S. Eliot, "Tradition and the Individual Talent," in *Selected Essays 1917–1932*, p. 4.
4. Wellek and Warren, *Theory of Literature*, p. 259.
5. Edward D. Ives, *Lawrence Doyle*, p. 248.
6. Henry Glassie, " 'Take That Night Train to Selma,' " p. 35.
7. Ives, *Lawrence Doyle*, p. 251.
8. See David C. Smith, *A History of Lumbering in Maine 1861–1960*, pp. 19–21.
9. For further material on this song and its author, see Franz Rickaby, *Ballads and Songs of the Shanty-Boy*, pp. xxiv–xxxviii, 196–198. For Charlie Gorman's version, see Edward D. Ives, *Twenty-one Folksongs from Prince Edward Island*, pp. 48–52, 78.
10. Laws C–13. See also Louise Manny and James Reginald Wilson, *Songs of Miramichi*, pp. 261–262; Edith Fowke, *Lumbering Songs from the Northern Woods*, pp. 117–120.
11. Fowke, *Lumbering Songs*, p. 129.
12. E. C. Beck, *Songs of the Michigan Lumberjacks*, p. 32.
13. For "Peter Emberly," see Elizabeth Bristol Greenleaf and Grace Yarrow Mansfield, *Ballads and Sea Songs from Newfoundland*, p. 334; for "Young Millman," see Kenneth Peacock, *Songs of the Newfoundland Outports*, 2, pp. 643–644. Both of these works contain a wealth of local Newfoundland material as well.
14. See *Maine: A Guide Down East*, p. 90.
15. Edward D. Ives, *Larry Gorman*, pp. 79–100.

Conclusion

16. For more on change vis-à-vis stability, see Glassie, " 'Take That Night Train,' " pp. 30–33.

17. Ives, *Lawrence Doyle*, p. 250.

18. Gordon Hall Gerould, *The Ballad of Tradition*, p. 165. The chapter entitled "The Nature of Ballad Variation," pp. 163–188, is an important statement of this concept.

19. Phillips Barry, "Communal Re-creation," p. 5. For Sharp's view see *English Folk Song: Some Conclusions*, pp. 16–31.

20. H. G. Barnett, *Innovation: The Basis of Cultural Change*, p. 39.

21. For "John Ladner," see Ives, *Twenty-one Folksongs*, pp. 13–17, 80; for "The Moncton Tragedy," see Manny and Wilson, *Songs of Miramichi*, pp. 152–155; for "Peter Emberly," see Laws C–27; for ballads on Peter Wheeler, see Helen Creighton, *Folksongs from Southern New Brunswick*, pp. 191–193, and W. Roy Mackenzie, *Ballads and Sea Songs from Nova Scotia*, pp. 365–366; for the Millman-Tuplin and Callaghan songs, see Ives, *Lawrence Doyle*, pp. 157–174.

22. John F. Szwed, "Paul E. Hall; A Newfoundland Song-Maker and His Community of Song," p. 155.

23. See Ives, *Larry Gorman*, pp. 167–179, or, for a more extended treatment, idem, "The Satirical Song Tradition in Maine and the Maritime Provinces of Canada," pp. 265–383. To these add Henry Glassie et al., *Folksongs and Their Makers;* Manny and Wilson, *Songs of Miramichi, passim;* Edward D. Ives and Sharon Sperl, *Folksongs from Maine*, pp. 15–34; Ives, *Lawrence Doyle;* Fannie Hardy Eckstorm and Mary Winslow Smyth, *Minstrelsy of Maine*, pp. 3–198.

24. Edward D. Ives, "Silver Poets of the Maine Woods."

25. For John Friend, see Roland Palmer Gray, *Songs and Ballads of the Maine Lumberjacks*, pp. xix–xx, 176–191; for John Young, see NA 544 (an excellent compilation by Nola Sinclair).

26. For John Mitchell, see "When the Taters Are All Dug" (wrongly attributed to an E. J. Sullivan) in Gray, *Songs and Ballads*, pp. 173–175, and Edward D. Ives and David C. Smith, *Fleetwood Pride, 1864–1960*, pp. 46–48; for Sherman Doody, see NA 568.042 and NA 144.

27. Letter to the *Family Herald*, Dec. 16, 1946.

28. Charles K. Wolfe, "Man of Constant Sorrow: Richard Burnett's Story, Part 2," p. 8.

29. From "Ego Dominus Tuus," in *The Collected Poems of W. B. Yeats*, p. 159.

30. Michael Owen Jones. *The Hand Made Object and Its Maker*, p. 164.

31. Roy Lohnes, "William Sullivan" (Me.).

32. From "The Idea of Order at Key West," in *The Collected Poems of Wallace Stevens*, pp. 129–130.

Appendix:
Informants and Correspondents

This appendix lists the names of all people who have directly contributed information I have used in writing this book. Those names preceded by an asterisk corresponded with or were interviewed by someone other than myself, and proper credits are given in each instance.

Dates of birth are given whenever I know them; but since often they were determined from the person's stated age, they may be a year or so off one way or the other. Where I feel less sure of the year than that, I have preceded it with "ca."; where the date is simply a reasonable and informed estimate on my part, I have put the date in parentheses.

Dates are given for all interviews and letters received. If the interview was recorded, either by me or by someone else, the relevant archival information is given. Unless indicated otherwise, letters were addressed to me. All my correspondence and manuscript material is on file in the Northeast Archives of Folklore and Oral History.

If the informant knew Joe Scott, I have said so and have given the circumstances briefly. If the informant gave me one or more of Joe's songs, either on tape or in manuscript, I have given credit here (uppercase means a complete or nearly complete version; lowercase means a fragment).

The following abbreviations and catchwords have been used:

AFS — Archive of Folk Song, Music Division, Library of Congress, Washington, D.C.

ATL — Archives of Traditional Music, Indiana University, Bloomington, Indiana

Beaverbrook Collection — The Lord Beaverbrook Collection of New Brunswick Folksong, a collection made by Louise Manny under the sponsorship of Lord

	Beaverbrook. The originals are in the Old Manse Library, Newcastle, New Brunswick; copies have been deposited in the Folksong Archives of the National Museum of Canada, Ottawa, Ontario.
BD	"Benjamin Deane"
BSG	*Boston Sunday Globe*
CLG	"Charming Little Girl"
Eckstorm Papers	The Fannie Hardy Eckstorm Collection, Fogler Library, University of Maine, Orono, Maine. Included in this collection of letters, clippings, notes, and rough drafts are several hundred ballad and song texts collected by Eckstorm, Mary Winslow Smyth, and Phillips Barry.
FH	*The Family Herald*
Flanders Collection	The Helen Hartness Flanders Ballad Collection, the Library, Middlebury College, Middlebury, Vermont
Gordon Manuscripts	The Robert Winslow Gordon Manuscript Collection, Archive of Folk Song, Music Division, Library of Congress, Washington, D.C.
GR	"Guy Reed"
HC	"Howard Carey"
JS	Joe Scott
MacOdrum Collection	"Nova Scotia Ballads," a typescript by O. O. MacOdrum, Dalhousie University Library, Halifax, Nova Scotia
MUNFLA	Memorial University of Newfoundland Folklore and Language Archives, Saint John's, Newfoundland
NA	Northeast Archives of Folklore and Oral History, University of Maine, Orono, Maine
NAI	Ives Collection, Northeast Archives of Folklore and Oral History, University of Maine, Orono, Maine
NB	"The Norway Bum"
NM	"Norman Mitchell"

Appendix

NMC	Folksong Archives, National Museum of Canada, Ottawa, Ontario
PGB	"The Plain Golden Band"
SSLG	"Sacker Shean's Little Girl"
W&M	"Wilfred White and John Murphy"
WC	"The White Cafe"
WGT	"Wreck on the Grand Trunk Railway"
WMcG	"William McGibbeny"
WS	"William Sullivan"

Informants and Correspondents

Acker, Mrs. Arthur W. Moores Mills, N.B.; brought up in Meductic; int. 6/6/57 (not recorded); ltrs. 3/8/57, 4/12/57.

Allaby, J. Spurgeon. Passekeag, N.B.; ca. 1894; had worked in woods in southern N.B. as a young man; ints. 6/7/57 NAI 1.21–23 (ATL 2148–2151), 7/16/63 NAI 1.148–153 (ATL 3155–3159); ltrs. 2/20/57, 3/11/57, 3/27/57, 5/24/57, 11/4/57, 6/29/64, 7/14/64; many songs in manuscript. pgb.

Anderson, Fred. Juniper, N.B.; 1903; JS used to visit his family in Glassville; int. 10/9/65 NAI 65.21. PGB.

*Armstrong, Judson. Sherwood (Lunenburg Co.), N.S.; int. 6/64 by Helen Creighton NMC CR–1–4. HC.

Arsenault, Emile. Tignish, P.E.I.; 1897; int. 8/26/65 NAI 65.7 (AFS 14,801B). hc, NB.

Ashford, Irving. Lawrence Station (Charlotte Co.), N.B.; 1897; used to work in woods and had lived in Boston, where he clipped many songs from *Boston Sunday Globe*; int. 9/10/65 NAI 65.21; ltrs. 9/29/64, 12/4/64. NB.

Ballum, William J. Summerside, P.E.I.; ltr. 5/22/59. PGB.

*Bartlett, John. Scarsdale, N.S.; ltr. to William Doerflinger ca. 1930. pgb.

*Beeler, Clifford. Scarsdale, N.S.; ltr. to R. W. Gordon (Gordon Manuscripts 2710). PGB.

Bell, William. Brewer, Me.; 1882; b. Enmore, P.E.I., and had worked in woods; ints. 12/13/56, 10/10/57, 8/10/58, all on NAI 1.1–4 (ATL 2136–2138), 10/18/58 NAI 1.41 (ATL 2166). BD.

Belyea, Lloyd. Brown's Flat, N.B.; ltrs. 6/20/64, 7/19/64, 10/?/65. HC, PGB.

Appendix

Bergin, William J. Moncton, N.B.; had worked in woods along Miramichi; ltr. 6/21/64. PGB.

*Bernard, Albert, Sr. Howland, Me.; 1912; woodsman; int. fall, 1972, by Jayne Lello NA 716.

Bohan, Charles. Bath, N.B.; 1897; remembered JS around Bath; int. 10/9/65 NAI 65.21; ltr. 8/22/64.

*Boutilier, Mrs. Wentworth. Indian Point, N.S.; int. July, 1951, by Helen Creighton NMC CR–68–622. BD.

Bowness, Mrs. Arthur. Charlottetown, P.E.I.; ltr. 6/22/64. GR.

Bradbury, Gertrude. *See* Longley, Pearl.

*Briggs, William. Howland, Me.; 1893; woodsman; int. fall, 1972, by Lynn Ohlhorst NA 723.

*Brouillet, Eugene. Taschereau, P.Q.; 1883; knew JS when he was homesteading in Quebec; int. spring, 1966, by Lucièn Rioux (q.v.) at my request.

Brown, James. South Branch (Kent Co.), N.B.; 1883; woodsman, frequent singer in Miramichi folksong festivals; ints. 8/20/59 NAI 1.62–64 (ATL 2182–2184), 8/16/61 NAI 1.120–122 (ATL 3127–3129), 7/12–13/63 NAI 1.136–144 (ATL 3143–3151), 8/8/67 NAI 67.2–3 (AFS 14,818), and at several other times (not recorded). HC, PGB, NB.

Brown, John. Mexico, Me.; ca. 1884; b. Chipman, N.B., came to Me. 1904, older brother had known JS; int. 7/10/64 NAI 64.4 (AFS 14,795A); ltrs. 7/6/64, 5/3/65. GR, BD, NB, CLG, WC.

*Brown, Linwood. Vanceboro, Me.; 1923; had worked on drives on St. Croix; int. 1961 by Sister Saint Jude (Martha Poulin) NA 331; several ltrs. to same. See Ives and Sperl, *Folksongs from Maine*, pp. 31–36.

Bryant, Carl. Bayside (St. Andrews), N.B.; 1897; woodsman; int. 8/18/64 NAI 64.7 (AFS 14,796); ltr. 7/4/64. GR.

Bryant, William. Summerside, P.E.I.; (ca. 1890); had worked in woods and on drives with JS in upper Androscoggin area in early 1900s; int. 8/19/58 (not recorded).

Budge, Charles. New Haven (Victoria Co., Cape Breton Island), N.S.; 1888; ltr. 6/?/64. PGB, NB.

Buote, Frank. Tignish, P.E.I.; ca. 1905; int. 8/26/65 NAI 65.6 (AFS 14,801B). nb.

Burgoyne, Ernest. Plaster Rock, N.B.; 1886; remembered JS selling sewing machines along Tobique; int. 8/20/64 NAI 64.8 (AFS 14,797); ltrs. 7/13/64, 8/12/64.

Cameron, Philip. Wellington, P.E.I.; 1897; had worked in woods in Me.; int. 8/28/65 NAI 65.6,8 (AFS 14,801B, 14,802A); ltr. 3/9/65. pgb.

Campbell, Fred A. Arthurette, N.B.; 1883; had worked with JS in upper Androscoggin area in early 1900s; int. 8/13/63 NAI 152–154 (ATL 3159–3161) and on other occasions (not recorded); also int. summer, 1965, by daughter NA 80. HC, GR, PGB, bd, WC.

Campbell, Walter M. Daytona Beach, Fla., and Whitefield, N.H.; worked in woods in St. Croix area; ltr. 12/15/68. pgb.

Carr, Arthur. Boiestown, N.B.; ca. 1880; knew JS in upper Androscoggin area ca. 1900; int. 7/19/61 (not recorded).

*Carr, Mabel. Canterbury, N.B.; ca. 1905; int. 7/18/65 by Ruth Collicott NA 79. pgb.

Casey, Helen Sutton. Rumford, Me.; ca. 1877; knew JS, and her brother Mike Sutton was a close friend of his; int. 7/?/58 (not recorded); ltr. 9/16/57.

Chesser, Charles. Campbellton, N.B.; ltr. 6/10/64. GR.

Cleghorn, Thomas. Harvey Station (York Co.), N.B.; 1879; knew and worked with JS in western Me.; ints. 8/19/64 (not recorded), 8/22/64 NAI 64.6 (AFS 14,795B); ltrs. 7/6/64, 8/5/64, 8/26/64 (from daughter Gladys Byers). HC, PGB.

*Cleveland, Dan. East River, N.S.; int. (n.d.) by Helen Creighton. BD.

Coady, D. L. Biddeford, Me.; (ca. 1880); grew up around Patten, Me.; ltr. 6/23/64.

*Colbath, John. Bangor, Me.; 1899; worked in woods in northern Me. as young man; int. fall, 1972, by Beth Hartman NA 721.

*Cole, Benjamin. Glenburn, Me.; 1902; railroad man, but worked in woods as a youth; int. fall, 1972, by Larry Gallant NA 720.

*Cole, Harry. Springfield, Me.; ltr. 4/9/34 to Fannie Hardy Eckstorm (Eckstorm Papers). BD.

*Colsie, Eldin. Staceyville, Me.; int. 7/15/41 by Helen Hartness Flanders (Flanders Collection). hc.

Corbett, L. P. Pembroke (Hants Co.), N.S.; worked in woods ca. 1900 in northern N.H.; ltr. 6/?/64. hc.

*Corey, Arthur. Westfield, Me.; 1903; int. 9/21/62 by Beatrice Field NA 128. hc.

Costigan, Victoria. Littleton, Mass.; native of Carleton Co., N.B.; ltrs. 6/16/64, 7/8/64. GR.

Coughlin, Mrs. Underhill. Brooklyn (Alberton), P.E.I.; 1896; int. 8/23/65 NAI 65.3 (AFS 14,800B); ltr. 6/15/64. GR, pgb, nb.

Cramp, William. Oakland, Me.; 1881; knew JS, worked in woods many years; ints. 2/4/65 NA 225 (by George Keller), and 3/16/66, 3/22/66, 3/27/66, all on NAI 66.1–5 (AFS 14,810–812). PGB. Some of his songs published in Ives and Sperl, *Folksongs from Maine*.

Curtis, Harlan. Rangeley, Me.; (ca. 1890); worked with JS around Rangeley; int. 3/31/59 (not recorded).

*Curtis, James. Cape North (Bay St. Lawrence, Cape Breton Island), N.S.; (1898); did not know JS himself, but had heard a great deal about him from his uncle Tom Brown and others who had worked with him in Maine, and learned the songs from Tom Brown; int. 1975 by Denis Ryan MUNFLA 76–345. HC, GR, WS, PGB, BD.

Custeau, James. Lincoln, N.H.; (ca. 1900); lived in Berlin, N.H., for many years; int. 9/11/65 NAI 65.16 (AFS 14,805A); ltrs. 6/16/64, 7/27/64, 12/14/65. GR, bd, NB.

*Desmond, Jerry. Island Falls, Me.; int. 7/10–11/40 by Helen Hartness Flanders (Flanders Collection). PGB.

Dickinson, Clyde. Lower Woodstock, N.B.; (ca. 1890); remembered JS on both occasions of his return to Lower Woodstock; ints. 8/30/57, 8/14/59, 8/22/64 (none recorded).

Dignan, John R. Howlan, P.E.I.; 1882; met JS in a lumbercamp in northern N.H., ca. 1900; int. 8/24/65 NAI 65.1 (AFS 14,799); ltrs. 5/30/59, 6/18/64.

Doucette, Edmund. Miminegash, P.E.I.; 1894; fisherman, but had worked in woods in Miramichi as a young man; ints. 6/26/57 NAI 1.30–31 (ATL 2156), 6/30/57 NAI 1.32 (ATL 2157), 8/16–17/58 NAI 1.34–37 (ATL 2160–2162), 7/14/63 NAI 1.144–147 (ATL 3151–3154), and at other times (not recorded); many letters. hc, pgb. See Ives, *Twenty-one Folksongs from Prince Edward Island*, pp. 11–32.

Doucette, Joseph ("Long Joe"). Miminegash, P.E.I.; 1900; track maintenance man for CNR, has fished and worked in woods; ints. 6/30/57 NAI 1.32 (ATL 2157), 8/17/58 NAI 1.36 (ATL 2161–2162). nb. See Ives, *Twenty-one Folksongs from Prince Edward Island*, pp. 33–40.

Doucette, Malvina. Tignish, P.E.I.; (ca. 1905); int. 8/26/65 NAI 65.5 (AFS 14,801A). HC.

Duplessis, George. Eel River Bridge, N.B.; ca. 1898; fisherman, woodsman, frequent performer at Miramichi folksong festivals through 1961; int. 8/14/61 NA 1.118–119 (ATL 3125–3126), and at other times (not recorded). PGB.

*Dyer, Harry. Caribou, Me.; 1896; woodsman; ints. spring, 1970, NA 568, fall, 1970, NA 581 (both by granddaughter, Jeanne Milton).

*Eddy, Herbert. Gloucester Co., N.B.; ltr. 1926 to R. W. Gordon (Gordon Manuscripts 1520). HC.

Edwards, Ethel. Meductic, N.B.; 1875; remembered JS around Meductic; int. 8/30/57 (not recorded).

*Elder, G. W. Sussex, N.B.; int. 1958 by Helen Creighton NMC CR–196–2, 245. hc.

Appendix

*Elkinton, Fred. St. Stephen, N.B.; woodsman; int. 1957 by Tom Mac-Leod (q.v.), who collected one song from him for me. BD.

Enman, Angus. Spring Hill, P.E.I.; 1880; knew JS and worked with him in woods of western Me.; int. 8/19/58 NAI 1.38–40 (ATL 2164–2165); ltr. 3/6/64. gr, BD, clg. See Ives, *Twenty-one Folksongs from Prince Edward Island*, pp. 53–61.

Farquhar, Mrs. John. Newark, N.J.; (ca. 1900); granddaughter of John Oakes, knew JS around Rangeley; ltr. 6/24/64.

Ferris, Wesley. Magalloway Plantation, Me.; (ca. 1880); had worked with JS in upper Androscoggin area; int. 7/31/57 (not recorded).

*Field, Elwell. Westfield, Me.; int. 11/19/62 by Beatrice Field NA 128. PGB.

Field, Mrs. Vernon. Detroit, Me.; 1899; grew up in Brockway, N.B., brother was a woodsman: ltrs. 7/22/64, 8/5/64. NB.

*Finnemore, Charles. Bridgewater, Me.; int. 8/30/42 by Marguerite Olney (Flanders Collection). GR.

*Finnemore, Stanley. Bridgewater, Me.; ca. 1907; railroad worker, son of Charles Finnemore (q.v.); int. spring, 1962, by Doris Stackpole NA 361. gr. See Ives and Sperl, *Folksongs from Maine*, pp. 41–44, 72–76.

*Flagg, Asa. Carthage, Me.; 1898; woodsman; int. fall, 1970, by Rhoda Mitchell NA 575.

Flynn, Alice. Allegany, N.Y.; daughter of Jack McGinley, grew up in Johnville, N.B.; int. 8/1/64 NAI 64.7 (AFS 14,797); manuscript material given me 8/1/64; ltrs. 3/18/65, 7/21/65, 12/16/65. gr, pgb, nb, WGT.

*Frazier, Gordon. Caribou, Me.; 1880; int. 9/19/62 by Lorina Wakem NA 412. pgb.

*Fulton, George. Salmon River, N.B.; (ca. 1899); had worked in woods along Salmon and Gaspereau rivers; int. 10/13/74 by Neil Rosenberg, his tape 74/5, MUNFLA. HC.

*Gardiner, Isaac. Allagash, Me.; int. fall, 1962, by Ronald Jean NA 207. hc.

Gavel, Edward. Sanford, Me.; ca. 1895; worked in woods as a young man; int. 8/25/66 NAI 66.10–11 (AFS 14,815B); ltrs. 6/11/64, 6/21/64, 8/29/66. HC, GR, pgb.

Gibbs, Atwood. Orono, Me.; 1881; knew JS when he worked along Penobscot; int. 8/13/57 and at various other times (not recorded).

*Glode, Peter. Pubnico, N.S.; int. by William Doerflinger (n.d.). PGB.

Gorman, Leo. St. Charles, P.E.I.; 1898; farmer. HC. For further information see Ives, *Lawrence Doyle*, esp. pp. 19, 256.

Gough, James. Lower Woodstock, N.B.; ca. 1875; knew JS from days in

Lower Woodstock, also knew other members of the family; int. 9/1/57 (not recorded); ltrs. 2/26/57, 3/13/57.

*Graham, Glenna. Fredericton, N.B.; (ca. 1920); grandniece of JS; int. 8/1/65 by Ruby Graham NA 165.

Grant, Hall. Rangeley, Me.; ca. 1878; guide and woodsman, knew JS from days around Rangeley and in upper Androscoggin; int. 3/31/59 NAI 59.1 (AFS 14,783).

Gregory, Sedgefield. Rolling Dam (Charlotte Co.), N.B.; 1874; woodsman; int. 8/23/64 NAI 64.9 (AFS 14,798); ltr. 6/20/64. GR.

*Hafford, John. Dickey, Me.; ca. 1892; woodsman; int. 11/19/62 by Ronald Jean NA 207. gr. See Ives and Sperl, *Folksongs from Maine*, pp. 26–28, 63–66.

Ham, Wallace. Rangeley, Me.; knew JS around Rangeley; int. 3/31/59 (not recorded).

*Hamilton, Margaret. River Charlo, N.B.; kept a notebook of songs, some copied out by her daughter, Ethel Hamilton, summer, 1965, NA 194. PGB.

Harden, Sid. Rangeley, Me.; guide; int. 3/31/59 (not recorded).

Harkins, Martin. Houlton, Me.; 1883; knew JS when he was around Houlton; ints. 8/24/64 NAI 64.9 (AFS 14,798), also earlier in month by Alice Flynn (q.v.), who sent me notes on her interview.

Hoy, Thomas. Gorham, N.H.; 1887; worked in woods with JS; int. 9/9/65 NAI 65.14 (AFS 14,804A); ltrs. 6/23/64, 7/8/64.

Hoyt, Dan. Donnelly Settlement (Magundy), N.B.; 1884; knew JS around Houlton and the Boundary Line; int. 10/10/65 NAI 65.21 (AFS 14,808).

*Irish, Alton. Island Falls, Me.; int. 7/10/40 by Helen Hartness Flanders (Flanders Collection). GR.

Jagoe, Samuel. Newcastle, N.B.; 1897; woodsman and river-driver, frequent performer at Miramichi folksong festivals; int. 8/21/59 NAI 1.64–66 (ATL 2183–2185), also recorded at all Miramichi folksong festivals. PGB.

Jamieson, John A. East Bathurst, N.B.; 1872; woodsman, had worked in northern N.H. as a young man, older brother of Peter Jamieson; int. 6/12/57 NAI 1.25–27 (ATL 2152–2154); ltrs. 1/19/57, 5/25/57, 10/6/57, 12/30/57. PGB.

Jamieson, Peter. East Bathurst, N.B.; 1882; woodsman, had worked in northern N.H., where he met JS; ints. 6/12/57, 6/13/57 (not recorded). PGB.

Kaulback, Roy. New Germany (Lunenburg Co.), N.S.; ca. 1882; knew JS, worked with him and boarded with him at Oakes's in Rangeley; ltrs. 12/?/57, 4/28/59.

Appendix

Keating, John. Berlin, N.H.; had his mother's scrapbook with a copy of
W&M in it; int. 9/10/65 (not recorded); ltr. 6/15/64. W&M.

Keenan, Harry. Woodstock, N.B.; 1890; woodsman, native of Johnville;
int. 5/11/62 NAI 1.122–123 (ATL 3129–3130). HC, GR, BD.

Kibblewhite, Annie. Willowdale, Ont.; ltr. 10/14/67 to *Family Herald* and
forwarded to me. W&M.

*Kirschner, Guy. Farmington, Me.; 1880; woodsman; int. fall, 1972, by
Scott MacDonald NA 722.

Knapp, Florence. Mexico, Me.; 1893; used to live in Houghton, remembered JS when he had boarded with her mother; int. 9/13/65 NAI
65.18 (AFS 14,806); ltr. 6/16/64. gr.

Ladd, Gertrude. Byron, Me.; (ca. 1900); recalled details of Guy Reed's
death, told me where he was buried; int. 8/3/57 (not recorded).

Lafferty, Fred. Gorham, N.H.; 1885; worked in woods with JS; int.
9/11/65 NAI 65.16 (AFS 14,805A). BD.

Lary, Bessie. Dover-Foxcroft, Me.; ltr. 6/13/64. PGB, BD.

Learned, Philip T. Andover, Me.; ltrs. 3/13/60, 7/20/64.

*Leavitt, Emile. Old Town, Me.; 1892; woodsman; int. fall, 1972, by
Sarah Burbank NA 718.

Libby, Ansel. Waltham, Mass.; (ca. 1900); had worked in woods as a young
man, husband of Minnie Libby (q.v.); int. 8/22/64 NAI 64.8 (AFS
14,797). pgb.

Libby, Minnie. Waltham, Mass.; remembered JS and was Ensley Scott's
daughter; int. 8/22/64 NAI 64.8 (AFS 14,797).

Locke, Cliburne S. Berlin, N.H.; 1876; native of P.E.I., knew JS and
worked in woods with him; int. 9/9/65 NAI 65.14 (AFS 14,804A); ltrs.
6/12/64, 8/?/64. pgb, BD.

Lohnes, Roy. Andover, Me.; ca. 1890; int. 8/7/58 NAI 1.33–34 (ATL
2158–2160). HC, GR, WS, PGB.

Longley, Pearl. Mexico, Me.; daughter of Gertrude Bradbury, originally
from Centreville, N.B., took down her mother's songs in a notebook;
int. 9/29/65 (not recorded); ltr. 7/11/64; for a copy of her notebook,
see NA 248. HC, GR, PGB, NB.

Lord, Ernest. Wells, Me.; originally from New Maryland, N.B., had
worked in woods as a young man; ints. 8/24–25/66, 9/16/66 NAI
66.8–12 (AFS 14,814–816); ltr. 12/11/65.

Lund, Lewis. Jacksonville, Me.; (ca. 1885); farmer and woodsman; ints.
10/3/59 NAI 1.83–84 (ATL 2202–2203), 10/23/59 NAI 1.87–88 (ATL
2206–2207), 10/19/63 (ATL 3161).

MacArthur, Anna. Lakeville, N.B.; ltr. 6/15/64.

McCarthy, Clarence. Tracy (Sunbury Co.), N.B.; ltrs. 8/5/66, 2/13/67.
GR.

447

Appendix

*McCarthy, Ernest. Blackville, N.B.; int. summer, 1965, by Kay Hayes NA 193. HC, NB.

McCullough, Joe. Mineral (Carleton Co.), N.B.; (ca. 1900); farmer and woodsman; int. 8/21/64 NAI 64.8 (AFS 14,797). hc.

MacDonald, Arthur. Black River Bridge, N.B.; (ca. 1900); frequent performer at Miramichi folksong festivals, brother of Stanley (q.v.); int. 7/13/61 NAI 1.103 (ATL 3110) and in various festival recordings.

MacDonald, Edward. Hampden, Me.; (ca. 1900); knew many songs, grew up around Harcourt, N.B.; ints. 10/2/61, 4/15/62 and at several other times during 1962 NAI 62.2–3 (AFS 14,790B–791). bd.

MacDonald, Stanley. Black River Bridge, N.B.; ca. 1900; farmer, woodsman, frequent performer at Miramichi folksong festivals, older brother of Arthur (q.v.); ints. 7/15/61 NAI 1.103–105 (ATL 3110–3112), 7/25/61 NAI 1.112–113 (ATL 3119–3120), and in various festival recordings. NB.

MacDonald, Wilmot. Glenwood, N.B.; 1903; woodsman, well-driller, stationary fireman, frequent performer in Miramichi folksong festivals; ints. 6/11/57 NAI 1.24 (ATL 2151–2152), 7/18/61 NAI 1.105–108 (ATL 3112–3115), 7/25/61 NAI 1.113–117 (ATL 3120–3124), 7/9–11/63 NAI 1.123–136 (ATL 3130–3143), July, 1971, by Florence Ireland NA 740, 4/17–18/74 NA 817, and on various festival recordings. hc, pgb, BD. See Creighton and Ives, *Eight Folktales from Miramichi*, for further biographical information.

McElroy, Frank ("Bungie"). Sherman, Me.; 1886; woodsman; int. 10/8/65 (not recorded).

McHugh, Grattan. Tignish, P.E.I.; 1905; int. 8/26/65 NAI 65.4 (AFS 14,801A); ltr. 6/13/64 (from Mrs. McHugh). HC, BD.

McIntosh, Joseph. Ellsworth, Me.; (ca. 1872); woodsman; int. 2/23/57 and at various times thereafter (not recorded).

McIntyre, Frank. Andersonville, N.B.; 1890; woodsman, guide, hunter, had met JS in Bangor; int. 8/23/64 (not recorded).

McKay, Osborne W. Newcastle, N.B.; ltr. 7/23/64. WC.

McKenna, Omer. Rumford, Me.; (ca. 1885); from Waterford, P.E.I., worked in woods and mills around Rumford all his life; int. 9/28/65 NAI 65.19 (AFS 14,807A). hc, gr, pgb, bd.

MacLean, Fred. Magundy, N.B.; ca. 1885; woodsman and farmer; int. 7/17/65 NAI 65.1 (AFS 14,799).

MacLeod, Thomas. Baring, Me.; ca. 1877; woodsman; int. 6/5/57 NAI 57.1 (AFS 14,780), and at other times (not recorded); ltrs. 1/20/57, 1/29/57. gr, wc.

*McMahon, Fred. Chatham, N.B.; (ca. 1890); woodsman; int. by Louise Manny (Beaverbrook Collection). HC, GR. See Manny and Wilson, *Songs of Miramichi, passim.*

Appendix

McSheffrey, Eddie. Bath, N.B.; (ca. 1885); had worked with JS; int. 8/20/64 NAI 64.8 (AFS 14,797). hc.

Mercer, Mrs. Joseph. Sussex, N.B.; ltr. 12/?/57. gr.

*Merrill, Orlon. Charlestown, N.H.; grew up in Me., worked in woods for many years; int. 1931 by Helen Hartness Flanders. GR. Many of his songs appear in Flanders et al., *The New Green Mountain Songster.*

Merrithew, Emma. Woodstock, N.B.; 1872; daughter of JS's maternal aunt, lived in Canterbury, spent much time with the Scotts as a young girl; int. 8/21/64 NAI 64.8 (AFS 14,797).

Mills, E. W. Meductic, N.B.; knew Hazen and Ensley Scott, had worked in woods; int. 8/21/64 (not recorded); ltr. 6/10/64.

Monroe, William H. Monroe, N.H.; ca. 1895; int. 9/11/65 NAI 65.16–17 (AFS 14,805); ltrs. 9/3/57, 10/8/57, 10/9/57, 6/13/64. HC, gr.

*Monzelle, Manny. Dalhousie, N.B.; ca. 1905; int. 7/13/65 by Ethel Hamilton NA 194. gr.

Morrison, John. Charlottetown, P.E.I.; 1912; grew up around Freeland and Conway in West Prince Co., P.E.I., where he heard songs in lobster factories, etc.; int. 8/30/65 NAI 65.8,10 (AFS 14,802); ltr. 2/3/65. HC, NB.

*Morrison, Wilbert. Orland, Me.; 1892; int. 1/9/69 by Bonita Freeman-Witthoft. pgb.

Morse, Lucy. Norway, Me.; ca. 1886; JS was a good friend of her husband; int. 7/20/66 (not recorded); ltr. 9/23/66. PGB, NB.

*Mountain, Gordon. Blackville, N.B.; int. 1957 by Hugh U. Crawford. PGB.

Murray, Anna L. Niagara Falls, Ont.; originally from Richardsville (Restigouche Co.), N.B.; ltr. 7/25/64. HC.

Murray, Dan. Magalloway Plantation, Me.; ca. 1873; knew and worked with JS in upper Androscoggin area; int. 7/31/57 (not recorded).

Nicholson, John. Jordan Mountain (Sussex R.R.), N.B.; 1907; int. 10/12/65 NAI 65.23 (AFS 14,809B); ltr. 6/16/64. GR.

Nile, Leland. Rangeley, Me.; (ca. 1880); woodsman, guide, had worked with JS; int. 7/29/59 NAI 1.58–60 (ATL 2180).

Nile, Zelpha. Rangeley, Me.; (ca. 1880); wife of Leland Nile (q.v.), interviewed at same time, knew JS.

Noad, Frederick. Hoodsport, Wash.; (ca. 1880); had worked in Me. woods as a young man; ltr. 7/22/64, also letters to Robert E. Pike, who forwarded relevant contents to me.

Noonan, Michael J. St. Stephen, N.B.; 1887; carpenter and contractor, had worked in woods around Rumford as a young man; int. 8/18/64 NAI 64.7 (AFS 14,796); ltr. 6/22/64. hc, gr, bd, wc.

Appendix

Oakes, Cleon. Detroit, Mich.; 1886; grew up in Rangeley, worked in woods with JS as a young man; ltr. 6/?/64.

Oakes, Ray. Rangeley, Me.; ca. 1892; John Oakes's adopted son, knew JS around Rangeley; int. 10/1/65 (not recorded).

Oakes, Vance. Rangeley, Me.; ca. 1897; JS had worked on his father's farm; int. 9/30/65 NAI 65.20 (AFS 14,807B).

O'Connor, John. Hope River, P.E.I.; ca. 1900; farmer and woodsman; int. 8/31/65 NAI 65.11 (AFS 14,803A); ltrs. 2/5/65, 3/12/65. HC, PGB.

*O'Mar, George H. Oak Hill (St. Stephen), N.B.; interviewed by Phillips Barry, probably in the early 1930s (Eckstorm Papers, pp. 329–330). GR.

*Packard, Kenneth. Carrabassett, Me.; ca. 1910; lumberman; int. fall, 1971, by Jill Allen NA 704.

Pagett, Joseph. Markhamville (Sussex R.R.), N.B.; 1897; farmer and woodsman; int. 10/12/65 NAI 65.22 (AFS 14,809A); ltr. 7/31/64. GR, PGB.

Patterson, Harold. Patten, Me.; (ca. 1890); town clerk, Patten; int. 10/8/65 (not recorded).

*Patterson, Joseph ("Uncle Joe"). Caledonia, N.S.; knew JS and worked with him in woods near Summit, Me., ca. 1905; int. by William Doerflinger. PGB. See Doerflinger, *Shantymen and Shantyboys*, p. 247.

Peavey, Francis. Patten, Me.; (ca. 1886); barber, restaurant keeper; int. 10/7/65 NAI 65.21 (AFS 14,808).

Pentecost, Patrick. Sydney, N.S.; ltr. 7/11/64. HC.

Peverley, Edward D. South Paris, Me.; 1886; retired teacher, grew up in Bryant Pond, Me., saw wreckage of Grand Trunk wreck of 1901; int. 11/2/74 NA 988; ltr. 10/8/74.

*Polley, J. A. Los Angeles, Calif.; knew JS in and around Rumford; ltr. 3/2/25 to R. W. Gordon (Gordon Manuscripts 928).

Pollock, Tom. Harvey (York Co.), N.B.; 1874; knew JS in woods of western Me.; int. 8/23/64 NAI 64.8–9 (AFS 14,797–798); ltr. 6/14/64 (from son Carl). hc.

Porter, Frank. Rangeley, Me.; 1872; guide and woodsman; int. 10/1/65 (not recorded).

Porter, George. Meductic, N.B.; (ca. 1910); father had known JS well; int. 8/22/64 (not recorded); ltr. 6/12/64.

Porter, Herbert. Woodstock, N.B.; ca. 1879; remembered JS from Lower Woodstock days, nephew of Tom Porter, who married JS's sister Carrie; int. 10/22/65 (not recorded).

Price, Chester. Blackville, N.B.; int. 7/11/61 NAI 1.103 (ATL 3110). BD.

Price, William. McNamee, N.B.; (ca. 1885); ints. 7/11/61 NAI 1.101–103

(ATL 3108–3110), also by James R. Wilson NA 851. BD. See Wilson, "Ballad Tunes of the Miramichi," and Manny and Wilson, *Songs of Miramichi.*

*Ramsdell, Lewis. Plymouth, Me.; 1891; woodsman; int. fall, 1969, by Harriett Connors NA 541.

Reed, Carrie A. Dover, Del.; ca. 1919; great-granddaughter of Mrs. John Oakes, grew up around Rangeley; ltrs; 2/29/72, 3/23/72, 4/10/72.

Reed, Joseph, and Mrs. Reed. Roxbury, Me.; Mr. Reed is a nephew of Guy Reed; int. 8/?/68 (not recorded).

Rice, Herbert. Bangor, Me.; knew JS; int. 12/4/56 (not recorded).

*Richards, Belle. Colebrook, N.H.; int. 11/21/41 by Marguerite Olney (Flanders Collection). PGB.

Rioux, Lucièn. Ste. Irène de Laferté, P.Q.; secretary of the municipality of Ste. Irène de Laferté, interviewed Eugene Brouillet (q.v.), Taschereau, at my request; ltrs. 10/23/59, 5/1/66.

*Rix, B. H. Kamloops, B.C.; had worked in woods with JS ca. 1900; ltr. to *Family Herald* (mid-1940s?). PGB.

Robbins, Lidelle Willey. Hudson, Me.; (ca. 1890); ints. 2/8/57 NAI 1.4–5 (ATL 2138–2140), 2/28/57 NAI 1.6–8 (ATL 2140–2141), 5/21/57 NAI 1.17–19 (ATL 2146–2148). PGB.

Rodgerson, Jack. Berlin, N.H.; 1898; woodsman, b. Crapaud, P.E.I.; int. 9/10/65 NAI 65.15 (AFS 14,804B). GR.

Ross, John. Rangeley, Me.; 1890; worked with and knew JS around Rangeley; int. 10/1/65 (not recorded).

Rush, Harold. Monticello, Me.; 1891; farmer, woodsman, knew JS around Bank Farm; int. 8/24/64 NAI 64.9 (AFS 14,798); ltr. 6/17/64.

Rush, James, Sr. Houlton, Me.; 1882; knew JS around Houlton; int. 8/24/64 NAI 64.9 (AFS 14,798). GR.

Scott, Angus. Meductic, N.B.; nephew of JS, son of Ensley; ints. 8/30/57, 8/14/59, 8/22/64, and at other times (none recorded).

Scott, Henry. Rumford, Me.; 1898; knew JS, mother was Emma (Lefebvre) Scott; ints. 7/11/64 NAI 64.5 (AFS 14,795), 9/29/65 (not recorded).

*Scott, Jack A. Salmon Arm, B.C.; worked with JS in woods of western Me., claimed to have written PGB; ltr. to *Family Herald* 11/18/57. PGB.

Scott, James. Mexico, Me.; woodsman, knew JS; int. 9/28/65 NAI 65.18 (AFS 14,806).

Scott, Mrs. Trueman. Honeydale (Charlotte Co.), N.B.; 1906; int. 8/23/64 NAI 64.9 (AFS 14,798); ltr. 6/19/64. HC, GR.

Scribner, Caleb. Patten, Me.; ca. 1885; game warden, artist; ints. 10/7/65 NAI 65.21 (AFS 14,808), 10/8/65 (not recorded); ltr. 6/24/64.

Appendix

Severy, Daisy. Gray, Me.; 1883; knew JS, younger sister of Lizzie Morse, wife of David (q.v.); ints. 7/21/66 NAI 66.6 (AFS 14,812B), 8/24/66 and 9/16/66 NAI 66.7 (AFS 14,813). PGB, NB, WGT.

Severy, David. Gray, Me.; ca. 1881; husband of Daisy (q.v.), had worked in woods and on drives with JS; ints. same as Daisy Severy.

*Sharpe, John, Sr. Argyle, Me.; 1881; woodsman; int. fall, 1970, by Lillian Shirley NA 621.

Shortall, Dan. South Branch (Kent Co.), N.B.; (ca. 1885); farmer, woodsman, close friend of James Brown (q.v.); ints. 8/16/61 NAI 1.120–122 (ATL 3127–3129) *passim*, 7/12/63 NAI 1.140–142 (ATL 3147–3149) *passim*.

Sibley, Charles. Argyle, Me.; (ca. 1885); woodsman, truck driver; ints. 3/24/57 NAI 1.9–12 (ATL 2142–2143), 12/?/58 NAI 1.55–57 (ATL 2178–2180). BD.

Smallwood, Firth. Patten, Me.; knew some details of Norman Mitchell's suicide from his father's telling; int. 10/8/65 (not recorded).

Smith, Mrs. Benjamin. Alberton, P.E.I.; 1881; sang "The Schooner *Gracie Parker*" and gave details of the event; int. 8/27/65 NAI 65.5 (AFS 14,801A).

Smith, Everett C. Yarmouth, Me.; 1890; eyewitness to Grand Trunk wreck of 1901; int. 11/2/74 NA 989; ltr. 10/6/74.

Smith, Wesley. Victoria West, P.E.I.; 1892; knew and worked with JS; ints. 8/19/58 NAI 1.40–41 (ATL 2165–2166), 7/15/63 NAI 1.147–148 (ATL 3154–3155), 8/28/65 NAI 65.9 (AFS 14,802A); ltrs. 9/11/65, 3/4/66, and other dates. HC, GR. For further information see Ives, *Twenty-one Folksongs from Prince Edward Island*, pp. 62–77.

*Sprague, Thomas. Danforth, Me.; (ca. 1900); woodsman, park ranger; int. spring, 1962, by Eva Fifield NA 129.

Stevens, Harry. St. George, N.B.; ltr. 6/27/64. HC.

Stewart, Ned. Rumford Center, Me.; ca. 1888; woodsman, knew JS; int. 7/28/67 NAI 67.1 (AFS 14,817). gr.

*Stillwell, Marjorie. Chipman, N.B.; daughter of Fred Fulton, who was brother of George Fulton (q.v.). HC, PGB.

Storer, George. Rumford, Me.; 1886; railroad man, knew JS; ints. 9/13/65 NAI 65.18 (AFS 14,806), 7/28/67 NAI 67.1–2 (AFS 14,817–818A).

Sullivan, Herbert. Worcester, Mass.; 1870; lived and worked in Berlin 1892–1917; ltrs. 7/3/64, 8/18/64.

Swan, Guy. Bryant Pond, Me.; 1875; woodsman, railroad man, saw Grand Trunk wreck of 1901 the day after; int. 11/1/74 NA 987; ltr. 10/8/74.

*Swett, Grover. Bangor, Me.; ca. 1888; knew JS slightly; ints. fall, 1969, NA 565, and Aug., 1970, NA 738 (both by Florence Ireland).

Appendix

Taylor, Dennis. Green Farm (Coplin Plantation), Me.; 1871; knew JS around Rangeley; int. 3/30/59 NAI 59.1 (AFS 14,783). pgb, w&m, NM.

*Tedford, Hollis. Millinocket, Me.; ltr. 9/30/40 to Helen Hartness Flanders (Flanders Collection). GR.

Tedford, Monie. Waddington, N.Y.; b. Reed Plantation (Aroostook Co.), Me., worked many years in Me. woods; ltrs. 2/9/66, 10/16/66. BD.

Tellington, J. J. ("Jeff"). Berlin, N.H.; 1885; lifelong resident of Berlin; int. 9/10/65 NAI 65.15 (AFS 14,804B).

*Thorne, Berton Estey. Jemseg, N.B.; 1876; woodsman and farmer, knew JS and worked with him in western Me.; ltr. 12/16/46 to *Family Herald* with copies of slips he had purchased from JS. HC, GR, PGB, BD, NB, CLG, SSLG, WMcG.

Thorne, Earl Grey. Jemseg, N.B.; 1912; farmer, backhoe operator, son of Bert Thorne (q.v.), showed me the original slips his father had bought from JS; int. 12/14/74 (not recorded).

*Thornton, Ralph. Topsfield, Me.; 1885; woodsman, jack-of-all-trades; ints. 1971–74 by Wayne Bean NA 717. BD. For his oral autobiography, see Thornton, *Me and Fannie.*

Thurston, Anna. Farmington, Conn.; daughter of Roger Thurston, lumberman, Andover, Me., who knew JS, took down songs from Roy Lohnes (q.v.).

Tolman, Grace Shaw. Rockland, Mass.; remembered lumbering operations from her girlhood in Me.; ltr. 3/10/69.

Toothaker, Gertrude. Rangeley, Me.; ca. 1880; née Gertrude Oakes, knew JS around Rangeley; int. 7/29/59 NAI 1.57 (ATL 2180). GR, NB.

Tosh, Joe. *See* McIntosh, Joseph.

*Tracy, F. L. Brewer, Me.; several letters to Fannie Hardy Eckstorm ca. 1934 (Eckstorm Papers). PGB.

*Turner, Emma. Bucksport, Me.; int. 10/9/41 by Marguerite Olney (Flanders Collection). hc.

*Turple, Jack. Upper Kennetcook, N.S.; int. 7/?/52 by Helen Creighton NMC CR–97–974. HC, GR, BD.

Underhill, Nicholas. Northwest Bridge (Northumberland Co.), N.B.; ca. 1900; woodsman, frequent performer at Miramichi folksong festivals; ints. 7/8/61 and 7/22/61 NAI 1.93–98 (ATL 3100–3105), 7/10/63 NAI 1.127–128 (ATL 3135–3136), at festival performances and at various other times (not recorded).

*Van Horne, Irvine. Bloomfield Ridge, N.B.; woodsman; int. 8/15/63 by James R. Wilson NA 852.

Virgin, Mrs. Wirt. West Peru, Me.; niece of Guy Reed, gave me his photograph; int. 8/3/57 (not recorded).

Vye, Hazel. Meductic, N.B.; daughter of Ensley Scott; ints. 9/1/57, 8/22/64 (not recorded).

Walsh, Joseph. Morell Rear, P.E.I.; 1893; farmer, woodsman; ints. 9/1/65 NAI 65.12–12 (AFS 14,803), 4/1/68 NAI 68.3 (AFS 14,820A), 7/20/70 NAI 70.6–7 (AFS 14,828), and at other times (not recorded); ltr. 7/17/64. HC. For further information see Ives, *Lawrence Doyle*, esp. the prologue.

Walsh, Philip. Northwest Bridge (Northumberland Co.), N.B.; ca. 1908; woodsman, mill worker; ints. 7/22/61 NAI 1.96–98 (ATL 3103–3105), 7/11/63 NAI 1.136 (ATL 3143). HC, GR, WC.

Webster, Lester. Patten, Me.; 1883; had worked with JS around Patten; int. 10/8/65 (not recorded).

Weymouth, Merle P. Ellsworth Falls, Me.; 1893; woodsman, cook; int. 3/16/57 NAI 1.8–9 (ATL 2141–2142); ltrs. 11/20/56, 12/6/56. hc.

Wiggett, Fred C. Plymouth, N.H.; 1873; knew JS; ltr. 11/25/57. gr.

Wilbur, Joe. Farmington Falls, Me.; 1871; lumberman, knew JS; int. 7/29/59, partial transcription available but tape lost.

Wilbur, Lanson. Green Farm (Coplin Plantation), Me.; 1882; knew JS from the Rangeley years; int. 3/30/59 NAI 59.1 (AFS 14,783).

Woodard, Wilfred. St. Stephen, N.B.; 1886; knew JS; int. 8/18/64 NAI 64.7 (AFS 14,796); ltrs. 6/26/64, 7/14/64. hc, pgb.

Woodside, Phyllis. Milltown, N.B.; JS was a friend of her maternal grandparents; ltr. 7/5/64. hc, pgb, BD.

Woodward, Howard T. Berlin, N.H.; worked in real estate, surveying, business; int. Aug., 1957, and at various times thereafter (not recorded); ltr. 8/30/57.

Worcester, Mabel. Hanover, Me.; 1879; grew up near Roxbury, Me.; int. 9/12/65 NAI 65.17 (AFS 14,805B); ltr. 7/7/64. GR.

Bibliography

Abbott, O. J. *Irish and British Songs from the Ottawa Valley Sung by O. J. Abbott.* Edited by Edith Fowke. 12″ LP record. Folkways FM 4051.

Abrahams, Roger, and George Foss. *Anglo-American Folksong Style.* New York: Prentice-Hall, 1968.

Acadie et Québec. 12″ LP record. RCA Victor LCP 1020. Issued by Les Archives de Folklore, Université Laval, Québec; edited by Luc Lacourcière and Roger Matton.

Agee, James, and Walker Evans. *Let Us Now Praise Famous Men.* Boston: Houghton Mifflin Co., 1941.

Averill, Gerald. *Ridge Runner.* Philadelphia: J. B. Lippincott, 1948.

Avery, Myron H. "The Story of the Wassataquoik." *Maine Naturalist,* 9 (Sept., 1929), 83–96.

Bangor Daily Commercial. Bangor, Me., 1872–1946.

Barker, F. C. *Lake and Forest as I Have Known Them.* Boston: Lothrop, Lee and Shepard, 1903.

Barnett, H. G. *Innovation: The Basis of Cultural Change.* New York: McGraw-Hill, 1953.

Barry, Phillips. "Communal Re-creation." *Bulletin of the Folk-Song Society of the Northeast,* No. 5 (1933), pp. 4–6.

———. *The Maine Woods Songster.* Cambridge, Mass.: Powell Printing Co., 1939.

———. "Notes on the Ways of Folk-Singers with Folk-Tunes." *Bulletin of the Folk-Song Society of the Northeast,* No. 12 (1937), pp. 2–6.

———. "The Transmission of Folk-Song." *Journal of American Folklore,* 27 (1914), 67–76.

———, Fannie Hardy Eckstorm, and Mary Winslow Smyth. *British Ballads from Maine.* New Haven: Yale University Press, 1929.

Bibliography

Beck, E. C. *Songs of the Michigan Lumberjacks*. Ann Arbor: University of Michigan Press, 1941.

Belden, H. M. *Ballads and Songs Collected by the Missouri Folk-Lore Society.* University of Missouri Studies, 15. 1940. 2nd ed., Columbia: University of Missouri Press, 1955.

The Berlin Reporter. Berlin, N.H., 1897–.

The Bethel News. Bethel, Me., 1895–1908 (continued thereafter as *Oxford County Citizen*).

Boni, Margaret Bradford. *The Fireside Book of Folk Songs.* New York: Simon and Schuster, 1947.

Boston Sunday Globe. Boston, Mass., 1877–.

Bulletin of the Folk-Song Society of the Northeast. Cambridge, Mäss. Nos. 1–12, 1930–37.

The Carleton Sentinel. Woodstock, N.B., 1837–.

Cazden, Norman. *The Abelard Folk Song Book.* New York: Abelard-Schuman, 1958.

———. "Regional and Occupational Orientations of American Traditional Song." *Journal of American Folklore,* 72 (1959), 310–344.

Coffin, Tristram P. *The British Traditional Ballad in North America.* Rev. ed. American Folklore Society, Bibliographical and Special Series, 7. Philadelphia: American Folklore Society, 1964.

———. "The Traditional Ballad as an Art Form." *Journal of American Folklore,* 70 (1957), 208–214. Reprinted in Coffin, *The British Traditional Ballad in North America* (q.v.), pp. 164–172, and in *The Critics and the Ballad*, edited by MacEdward Leach and Tristram P. Coffin (q.v.), pp. 245–256.

Cohen, Anne, and Norm Cohen. "Tune Evolution as an Indicator of Traditional Music Norms." *Journal of American Folklore,* 86 (1973), 37–47.

Cohen, Norm. " 'Casey Jones': At the Crossroads of Two Ballad Traditions." *Western Folklore,* 32 (1973), 77–103.

Cole, William. *Folk Songs of England, Ireland, Scotland, and Wales.* Garden City, N.Y.: Doubleday, 1961.

Cox, John Harrington. *Traditional Ballads and Folk-Songs Mainly from West Virginia.* American Folklore Society, Bibliographical and Special Series, 15. Philadelphia: American Folklore Society, 1964. Originally published as American Folk-Song Publications, Nos. 3 and 5. New York: National Service Bureau, 1939.

Creighton, Helen. *Folksongs from Southern New Brunswick.* Ottawa: National Museum of Man, 1971.

———. *Maritime Folk Songs.* East Lansing: Michigan State University Press, 1962.

————. *Songs and Ballads from Nova Scotia*. 1932. Reprinted, New York: Dover Publications, 1966.

————, and Edward D. Ives. *Eight Folktales from Miramichi as Told by Wilmot MacDonald*. *Northeast Folklore*, 4. Orono, Me.: Northeast Folklore Society, 1962.

————, and Doreen Senior. *Traditional Songs from Nova Scotia*. Toronto: Ryerson, 1950.

Dean, Michael C. *Flying Cloud and One Hundred and Fifty Other Old Time Songs and Ballads*. Virginia, Minn.: Quickprint, 1922.

Defebaugh, James Elliott. *History of the Lumber Industry of America*. 2 vols. Chicago: American Lumberman, 1906–7.

Delaney's Song Book. Vols. 1–88. New York: William W. Delaney, 1892–1921.

Dibblee, Randall, and Dorothy Dibblee. *Folksongs from Prince Edward Island*. Summerside, P.E.I.: Williams and Crue, 1973.

Doerflinger, William M. *Shantymen and Shantyboys*. New York: Macmillan, 1951. Reprinted, with additional material, as *Songs of the Sailor and Lumberman*. New York: Macmillan, 1972.

Dundes, Alan. *The Morphology of North American Indian Folktales*. Folklore Fellows Communications, No. 195. Helsinki: Suomalainen Tiedeakatemia, 1964.

Eckstorm, Fannie Hardy. *The Penobscot Man*. Bangor: Jordan Printing Co., 1924. Reprinted, with photos and an introduction by Edward D. Ives, Somersworth, N.H.: New Hampshire Press, 1972.

————, and Mary Winslow Smyth. *Minstrelsy of Maine*. Boston and New York: Houghton Mifflin, 1927.

Eliot, T. S. *Selected Essays 1917–1932*. New York: Harcourt, Brace, 1932.

The Family Herald and Weekly Star. Montreal, 1869–.

Flanders, Helen Hartness, Elizabeth Flanders Ballard, George Brown, and Phillips Barry. *The New Green Mountain Songster*. New Haven: Yale University Press, 1939.

Forty-third Annual Report of the Railroad Commissioners of the State of Maine, 1901. Augusta, Me.: Kennebec Journal Printers, 1901.

Fowke, Edith. *Lumbering Songs from the Northern Woods*. American Folklore Society, Memoir Series, No. 55. Austin: University of Texas Press, 1970.

————, ed. *Lumbering Songs from the Ontario Shanties*. 12″ LP record. Folkways FM 4052.

Friedman, Albert. "Counterstatement" [to James H. Jones, "Commonplace and Memorization" (q.v.)]. *Journal of American Folklore*, 74 (1961), 113–115.

Gerould, Gordon Hall. *The Ballad of Tradition*. New York: Oxford University Press, 1932.

Gilbert, Douglas. *Lost Chords*. Garden City, N.Y.: Doubleday, Doran and Co., 1942.

Glassie, Henry. " 'Take That Night Train To Selma': An Excursion to the Outskirts of Scholarship." In Henry Glassie et al., *Folksongs and Their Makers* (q.v.), pp. 1–68.

————, Edward D. Ives, and John F. Szwed. *Folksongs and Their Makers*. Bowling Green, Ohio: Bowling Green University Popular Press, 1970.

Gray, Roland Palmer. *Songs and Ballads of the Maine Lumberjacks*. Cambridge: Harvard University Press, 1924.

Greenleaf, Elizabeth Bristol, and Grace Yarrow Mansfield. *Ballads and Sea Songs from Newfoundland*. Cambridge: Harvard University Press, 1933.

Halfpenny, H. E., and John W. Caldwell. *Atlas of Oxford County, Maine: Drawn from Official Plans and Actual Surveys*. Philadelphia: Caldwell and Halfpenny, 1880.

Halpert, Herbert. "A Michigan Lumberjack Singer." *Hoosier Folklore*, 1 (1942), 81–84.

————. "Truth in Folk-Songs—Some Observations on the Folk-Singer's Attitude." In John Harrington Cox, *Traditional Ballads and Folk Songs* (q.v.), pp. xiii–xx.

————. "Vitality of Tradition and Local Songs." *Journal of the International Folk Music Council*, 3 (1951), 35–40.

Harper, J. Russell. *Historical Directory of New Brunswick Newspapers and Periodicals*. Fredericton: University of New Brunswick, 1961.

Haverhill Evening Gazette. Haverhill, Mass., 1879–.

Herskovits, Melville J. *Man and His Works*. New York: Alfred A. Knopf, 1956.

Hoar, Jay S. *Small-Town Motion Pictures and Other Sketches of Franklin County, Maine*. Farmington, Me.: Knowlton and McLeary, 1969.

Holbrook, Stewart H. *Holy Old Mackinaw: A Natural History of the American Lumberjack*. 1938. Rev. ed., New York: Macmillan, 1956.

Ives, Edward D. " 'Ben Deane' and Joe Scott: A Ballad and Its Probable Author." *Journal of American Folklore*, 72 (1959), 53–66.

————. *Larry Gorman: The Man Who Made the Songs*. Bloomington: Indiana University Press, 1964. Also published as Indiana University Folklore Monograph Series, No. 19. Reprinted, New York: Arno Press, 1977.

————. *Lawrence Doyle: The Farmer-Poet of Prince Edward Island*. Maine Studies, No. 92. Orono, Me.: University Press, 1971.

————. "A Man and His Song: Joe Scott and 'The Plain Golden Band,'" In Henry Glassie et al., *Folksongs and Their Makers* (q.v.), pp. 69–146.

————. "The Satirical Song Tradition in Maine and the Maritime Provinces of Canada." Ph.D dissertation, Indiana University, 1962. University Microfilms, No. 63–242.

————. "Silver Poets of the Maine Woods." Manuscript.

————. *Twenty-one Folksongs from Prince Edward Island. Northeast Folklore*, 5. Orono, Me.: Northeast Folklore Society, 1963.

————, and David C. Smith. *Fleetwood Pride, 1864–1960: The Autobiography of a Maine Woodsman. Northeast Folklore*, 9. Orono, Me.: Northeast Folklore Society, 1967.

————, and Sharon Sperl. *Folksongs from Maine. Northeast Folklore*, 7. Orono, Me.: Northeast Folklore Society, 1965.

Jones, James H. "Commonplace and Memorization in the Oral Tradition of the English and Scottish Popular Ballads." *Journal of American Folklore*, 74 (1961), 97–112.

Jones, Michael Owen. *The Hand Made Object and Its Maker*. Berkeley and Los Angeles: University of California Press, 1975.

Ketchum, Thomas. *A Short History of Carleton County, New Brunswick*. Woodstock, N.B.: Sentinel Publishing Co., 1922.

Lacourcière, Luc. *Le conte populaire français en Amérique du Nord*. Quebec: Université Laval, Les Archives de Folklore, 1959.

Lapham, William H. *Centennial History of Norway, Oxford County, Maine, 1786–1886*. Portland, Me.: B. Thurston & Co., 1886.

————. *History of Rumford, Oxford County, Maine, from Its First Settlement in 1779 to the Present Time*. Augusta: Press of the Maine Farmer, 1890.

Laws, G. Malcolm, Jr. *American Balladry from British Broadsides*. American Folklore Society, Bibliographical and Special Series, 8. Philadelphia: American Folklore Society, 1957.

————. *Native American Balladry*. Rev. ed. American Folklore Society, Bibliographical and Special Series, 1. Philadelphia: American Folklore Society, 1964.

————. Review of *Shantymen and Shantyboys* by William M. Doerflinger. *Journal of American Folklore*, 64 (1951), 436–437.

Leach, MacEdward, and Tristram P. Coffin, eds. *The Critics and the Ballad*. Carbondale: Southern Illinois University Press, 1961.

Leane, John J. *A History of Rumford, Maine, 1774–1972*. Rumford, Me.: Rumford Publishing Co., 1972.

Lewiston Daily Sun. Lewiston, Me., 1893–.

Lord, Albert B. *The Singer of Tales*. Cambridge: Harvard University Press, 1960.

Mackenzie, W. Roy. *Ballads and Sea Songs from Nova Scotia*. Cambridge: Harvard University Press, 1928.

Bibliography

The Madison Bulletin. Madison, Me., 1885–.

Maine: A Guide Down East. 2nd ed. Edited by Dorris A. Isaacson. Prepared for the Maine League of Historical Societies and Museums. Rockland, Me.: Courier Gazette, 1970.

Maine, Bureau of Industrial and Labor Statistics. *Thirteenth Annual Report, 1899:* "The Pulp and Paper Industry," pp. 32–63; "The Lumber Industry," pp. 64–86. *Sixteenth Annual Report, 1902:* "The Development of Rumford Falls," pp. 116–154.

Manny, Louise. *Miramichi Poet: Six Poems by Hedley Parker.* Edited with a memoir by Louise Manny. Saint John: New Brunswick Museum, n.d.

———, ed. *Folksongs of the Miramichi.* 12″ LP record. Folkways FM 4053.

———, and James Reginald Wilson. *Songs of Miramichi.* Fredericton, N.B.: University Press, 1968.

Map of Carleton County, New Brunswick, Compiled from Official Plans and Actual Surveys. Saint John, N.B.: Roe and Colby, 1876.

Milburn, George. *The Hobo's Hornbook.* New York: Ives Washburn, 1930.

Mitchell, Roger E. *George Knox: From Man to Legend. Northeast Folklore*, 11. Orono, Me.: Northeast Folklore Society, 1969.

Moncton Daily Transcript. Moncton, N.B., 1882–.

Northeast Folklore. Orono, Me.: Northeast Folklore Society, 1958–.

Norway Advertiser Democrat. Norway, Me., 1844–.

O'Conor, Manus. *Irish Com-All-Ye's.* New York: L. Lipkind, 1901.

Older, Lawrence. *Lawrence Older of Middle Grove, New York.* 12″ LP record. Folk-Legacy FSA–15.

Peacock, Kenneth. *Songs of the Newfoundland Outports.* 3 vols. Ottawa: National Museum of Man, 1965.

Pike, Robert E. *Tall Trees, Tough Men.* New York: Little, Brown, 1967.

Pocius, Gerald L. "The First Day That I Thought of It Since I Got Wed." *Western Folklore*, 35 (1976), 109–122.

Pond, T. M. "Lumber Camp Singers." *Atlantic Advocate*, Aug., 1974, pp. 22–25.

The Press, Woodstock, N.B., 1879–.

Railroad Map of Maine. Prepared under the direction of, and presented by Joseph B. Peaks, Parker Spofford, Frank Keizer, Railroad Commissioners of Maine. New York and Chicago: George F. Cram, 1907.

Randolph, Vance. *Ozark Folksongs.* 4 vols. Columbia: State Historical Society of Missouri, 1946–50.

Rickaby, Franz. *Ballads and Songs of the Shanty-Boy.* Cambridge: Harvard University Press, 1926.

Bibliography

Rumford Falls Times. Rumford, Me., 1887–.

Sandburg, Carl. *The American Songbag.* New York: Harcourt, Brace, 1927.

Sharp, Cecil. *English Folk-Song: Some Conclusions.* London, 1907.

Smith, David C. *A History of Lumbering in Maine 1861–1960.* Maine Studies, No. 93. Orono, Me.: University Press, 1972.

Spaeth, Sigmund. *Read 'em and Weep: The Songs You Forgot to Remember.* Garden City, N.Y.: Doubleday, Page & Co., 1927.

———. *Weep Some More, My Lady.* New York: Doubleday, Page & Co., 1927.

Springer, John S. *Forest Life and Forest Trees.* New York: Harper & Brothers, 1851.

Stekert, Ellen J. "Two Voices of Tradition." Ph.D. dissertation, University of Pennsylvania, 1965. University Microfilms, No. 66–4654.

Stevens, G. R. *Canadian National Railways.* 2 vols. Toronto: Clarke, Irwin, 1962.

Stevens, Wallace. *The Collected Poems of Wallace Stevens.* New York: Alfred A. Knopf, 1955.

Stuart's Atlas of the State of Maine, Including Statistics and Descriptions of its History, Educational System, Geology, Railroads, Natural Resources, Summer Resorts, and Manufacturing Interests, Compiled from Official Plans and Actual Surveys. 12th ed. South Paris, Me., 1902–3.

Szwed, John F. "Paul E. Hall: A Newfoundland Song-Maker and His Community of Song." In Henry Glassie et al., *Folksongs and Their Makers* (q.v.), pp. 147–169.

Thornton, Ralph. *Me and Fannie: The Oral Autobiography of Ralph Thornton of Topsfield, Maine.* Edited by Wayne Reuel Bean. *Northeast Folklore,* 14. Orono, Me.: Northeast Folklore Society, 1973.

Tidd, Marshall M. "Up the Magalloway River in 1861." Edited by Benton L. Hatch and L. Felix Ranlett. *Appalachia,* 31 (Dec., 1957), 457–471 (part 1); 32 (June, 1958), 45–65 (part 2).

Tunney, Paddy. *Paddy Tunney of Letterkenny, Donegal, Eire.* 12″ LP record. Folk-Legacy FSE–7.

von Sydow, Carl. *Selected Papers on Folklore.* Copenhagen: Rosenkilde and Bagger, 1948.

Wellek, René, and Austin Warren. *Theory of Literature.* 3rd ed. New York: Harcourt, Brace & World, 1956.

White, John I. *Git Along, Little Dogies: Songs and Songmakers of the American West.* Urbana: University of Illinois Press, 1975.

Whitman, Charles F. *A History of Norway, Maine, from the Earliest*

Bibliography

Settlements to the Close of the Year 1922. Norway, Me.: Lewiston Journal Printshop, 1924.

Wilson, Granville P. *Pioneers of the Magalloway from 1820 to 1904*. Old Orchard, Me.: Privately printed, 1918.

Wilson, James Reginald. "Ballad Tunes of the Miramichi." Master's thesis, New York University, 1961.

Wolfe, Charles K. "Man of Constant Sorrow: Richard Burnett's Story, Part 2." *Old Time Music*, No. 10 (Autumn, 1973), pp. 5–9.

Wood, Richard G. *A History of Lumbering in Maine, 1820–1861*. Maine Studies, No. 33. Orono, Me.: University Press, 1935.

The Woodstock Dispatch. Woodstock, N.B., 1894–1918.

Yeats, W. B. *The Collected Poems of W. B. Yeats*. New York: Macmillan, 1959.

Young, John H. *Our Deportment: Or the Manners, Conduct and Dress of the Most Refined Society*. Rev. ed. Cincinnati & St. Louis, 1884.

Index

Index

"The Blue Velvet Band": attrib. to JS, 364

Bohan, Charles*, 75, 442

"The Bonny Earl of Murray" (Child 181), 165

"The Boss Tramp," 292–293

Boston Sunday Globe, 103, 117, 206, 224, 298, 303, 441

Boutilier, Mrs. Wentworth*, 265, 442

Bowness, Mrs. Arthur*, 176, 442

"The Boys of the Island," 27, 227n

Bradbury, Gertrude*, 134, 172, 222, 303, 442, 447

Briggs, William*, 442

"Bright Eyed Little Nell of Narragansett Bay," 160–162, 165, 168, 169, 177n

Brouillet, Eugene*, 87–88, 442, 451

Brown, Edith Frances*, 295–296

Brown, James*, 129, 132, 136, 152, 191, 223, 287, 304, 435, 442, 452

Brown, John*, 172, 263, 303, 320, 321, 329, 343, 344, 417, 442

Brown, Linwood*, 381, 442

Bryant, Carl*, 173, 442

Bryant, William*, 5, 26, 82, 353, 363, 442

Bucher, Sheila, 105n, 318, 321, 325

Budge, Charles W.*, 203, 226, 304, 442

Buote, Frank*, 282–287, 305, 442

Burbank, Sarah: interviewer, 447

Burgoyne, Ernest, Sr.*, 73–75, 442

Burnett, Richard D.: country music performer, 427–428

"The Butcher Boy," 139, 359n

Calhoun, John: poet, 94n

Calhoun, Undertaker (Rumford, Me.), 116, 155, 185

"The Callaghan Murder," 424

Cameron, James*, 281n

Cameron, Philip*, 226, 442

"The Camp on McNeil," 314

Campbell, Mrs. Agnes, 190n

Campbell, Fred*, 36, 50, 64, 75–76, 77, 109, 136, 174, 183, 195, 208, 224, 247, 264, 300, 304, 310, 311–312, 317, 331–348 *passim*, 357, 362, 366, 443

Campbell, Kathleen: collector, 136, 174, 208, 224, 357

Campbell, Walter M.*, 225, 443

"Canaday-I-O," 415

Carleton Sentinel, 48, 94, 363

Carr, Arthur*, 57, 89–90, 118, 247, 443

Carr, Mabel*, 224

Carrick, Howard *et al.: see* "Howard Carey"

Casey, Helen (Sutton)*, 44–45, 110, 443

"Casey Jones," 276

Catskill Mountains, N.Y.: folksong area, 418

Cazden, Norman: collector, 218, 295

"The *Cedar Grove,*" 435

"The Chapeau Boys," 399

"Charles Augustus Anderson," 249, 251

"Charming Little Girl": song by JS, 98, 99, 319–324, 329, 365, 404, 407, 426, 436n

"The Charming Young Widow I Met on the Train," 347

Chesser, Charles*, 175, 443

Child ballads, 212, 390, 394, 396, 435

Chopper: work described, 29–30

Cleghorn, Thomas*, 135, 139, 224, 365, 443

Cleveland, Dan*, 265, 443

Clifton, Harry: songwriter, 293

Coady, D. L.*, 388, 443

Coaxing: as aspect of performance, 106, 282–284, 320, 351, 383

Coffin, Tristram P.: folklorist, 162

Cohen, Anne: folklorist, 296

Cohen, Norm: folklorist, 281n, 296

Colbath, John*, 374, 377, 443

"The Cold Black River Stream," 176n

Cole, Ben*, 377, 443

Cole, Harry*, 263, 443

Collicott, Ruth: collector, 224, 443

Colsie, Eldin*, 135, 443

Communal re-creation, 98, 212, 422–423

Concerts: singing at, 394–395

Connors, Harriett: interviewer, 451

"Conundrum of the Workshop": poem by Rudyard Kipling, 193

"The Cook and the Teamster," 381

Cookee: job description, 30

Corbett, L. P.*, 137, 443

Corey, Arthur*, 135, 443

Costigan, Victoria*, 174, 443

Coughlin, Mrs. Underhill*, 175, 226, 305, 443

Country music: replacing come-all-ye's, 412

Cramp, William*, 210, 217, 221, 383, 390, 396, 435, 443

Crawford, Hugh U.: collector, 223, 449

Creegan, Walter M.: correspondent, 381–382

464

465

Index

Field, Mrs. Vernon*, 304, 445
Fifield, Eva: interviewer, 452
Fighting: in lumbercamps, 375
Finnemore, Charles*, 172, 445
Finnemore, Stanley*, 172, 173, 445
Flagg, Asa*, 388, 445
Flanders Collection, 135, 171, 172, 173, 221, 222, 440–446 passim, 451, 453
Flanders, Helen Hartness: collector, 135, 171, 172, 222, 418, 443, 444, 446, 449, 453
"The Flying Cloud," 249–257 passim, 390, 412
Flynn, Alice*, 76, 136, 174, 224, 268, 278, 281, 301, 304, 360, 414, 445, 446
"Fogan MacAleer," 177n, 435
Folk tradition, 408–409, 412–424
Food in lumbercamps: described, 28, 364, 377
Foster, Stephen C.: composer, 252
Fowke, Edith: folklorist, 105n, 156, 385, 416
Frazier, Gordon*, 222, 445
Freeman-Witthoft, Bonita: folklorist, 223, 449
French-Canadians: singing, 382
Friend, John J.: poet, 425
"Fuller and Warren," 278–279, 280, 411
Fulton, Fred*, 137, 225, 452
Fulton, George*, 137, 445, 452

Gallant, Larry: interviewer, 443
"The Gallant Brigantine," 266n
Gardiner, Isaac*, 135, 445
Gauthier, J. O., 86
Gavel, Edward*, 134, 173, 223, 418, 445
"A Gentleman Still," 293
"George Gee": possible song by JS, 362
"George Gee's Farewell," 362
Gerould, Gordon Hall: scholar, 422
Gibbs, Atwood*, 445
"The Girl I Left Behind," 250
"The Girl with the Waterfall," 345–346
Glassie, Henry: folklorist, 402n, 409
Glode, Peter*, 175, 225, 445
Gordon Manuscripts, 137, 174, 226, 440, 441, 444, 450
Gordon, Robert W.: folklorist, 45, 103, 110, 125, 137, 147, 166, 174, 194, 226, 270, 444, 450
Gorman, Larry: songmaker, xxi, xxii, xxiii, xxiv, 37, 53, 94n, 172, 203, 223, 228, 229,

256, 329, 365, 366, 367, 398, 404, 409, 414, 419, 425
Gorman, Leo*, 131, 137, 445
Gough, James*, 445
Graham, Glenna*, 446
Graham, Ruby: collector, 446
Grant, Hall*, 54–55, 77, 446
Gray, Roland Palmer: collector, 172, 174
Gregory, Sedgefield*, 173, 446
Grieving: as impetus to creativity, 431–433
"Guy Reed": song by JS, 45, 98, 103, 110, 130, 140–177, 183–189 passim, 195, 255, 270, 302, 343, 405, 407–425 passim, 432, 433

Hafford, John*, 173, 446
"The Haggertys and Young Mulvanny," 159, 160, 176n
Halpert, Herbert: folklorist, 227n, 380
Ham, Wallace*, 361, 446
Hamilton, Ethel: collector, 175, 208, 224, 446, 449
Hamilton, Margaret*, 224, 446
Harden, Sid*, 363, 446
Harkins, Martin*, 83, 365, 446
"Harry Bale," 415
"Harry Dunn," 121
"The Hartford Wreck," 276, 358n
Hartman, Beth: interviewer, 443
Hauling off: task described, 30–31
"Have Courage, My Boy, to Say No!" 121
Haverhill Evening Gazette, 117–118, 122
Hayes, Kay: collector, 136, 304, 448
Hays, Will: songwriter, 328
Heine, Heinrich, 430
Herskovits, Melville J.: anthropologist, 372
Hickerson, Joseph C.: folklorist, 177n, 295
Hirdt, George: collector, 137, 193, 226
Historical background: to JS's songs, 38–44, 100, 114–118, 149–156, 184–186, 197–198, 201, 239–247, 273–276, 290, 310–313, 323, 334–335, 353–355; JS's knowledge of facts behind song, 118–119, 155, 163–164, 185, 186–187, 248, 252, 290–291, 301, 313, 404
Hogan, Cora*, 172
Holbrook, Stewart, 391
Houlton, Me.: description, 83, 88n
"Howard Carey": song by JS, xxv, 45, 53, 98, 103, 106–139, 147, 156, 162, 166, 167, 178,

Index

Index

Index

Index

472

Index

A NOTE ON THE RECORDING

A one-hour cassette recording of songs and singers discussed in this book has been prepared. It includes the following selections:

Side 1. 1. "Howard Carey," sung by John O'Connor, August 31, 1965 (PI.4).
 2. "Howard Carey" (portion only), sung by Wesley Smith, August 28, 1965 (PI.5). Tune and text on pp. 107–109.
 3. "Guy Reed," sung by Philip Walsh, July 22, 1961 (NB.16). Tune and text on pp. 141–143.
 4. "The Plain Golden Band," sung by Sam Jagoe, August 21, 1959 (NB.2).
 5. "Benjamin Deane" (portion only), sung and recited by William Bell, December 13, 1956 (Me.6). Tune and text on pp. 229-232.

Side 2. 1. "Benjamin Deane," sung by Chester Price, July 11, 1961 (NB.7). Tune on p. 261.
 2. "Benjamin Deane," sung by Wilmot MacDonald, July 10, 1963 (NB.8). Tune on p. 260.
 3. "The Norway Bum," sung by James Brown, August 20, 1959 (NB.4).
 4. "The White Cafe," sung by Fred A. Campbell, August 13, 1963 (NB.1). Tune and text on pp. 341–342.

The cassette is available separately from the University of Illinois Press (ISBN 0–252–00727–1).